MONEY IN CRISIS

MONEY IN CRISIS
The Federal Reserve, the Economy, and Monetary Reform

Edited by
BARRY N. SIEGEL

Foreword by
LELAND B. YEAGER

Pacific Studies in Public Policy

PACIFIC INSTITUTE FOR PUBLIC POLICY RESEARCH
San Francisco, California

Ballinger Publishing Company
Cambridge, Massachusetts
A Subsidiary of Harper & Row, Publishers, Inc.

International Standard Book Number: 0-88410-962-3 (CL)
                                    0-88410-963-1 (PB)

Library of Congress Catalog Card Number: 84-9230

Printed in the United States of America

Library of Congress Cataloging in Publication Data

Main entry under title:

Money in crisis.

   (Pacific studies in public policy)
   Bibliography: p.
   Includes index.
   1. Board of Governors of the Federal Reserve System (U.S.)—
Addresses, essays, lectures. 2. Monetary policy—United States—
Addresses, essays, lectures. I. Siegel, Barry N. II. Series.
HG2565.M66   1984   332.1'12'0973   84-9230
ISBN 0-88410-962-3
ISBN 0-88410-963-1 (pbk.)

PACIFIC INSTITUTE
FOR PUBLIC POLICY RESEARCH

The Pacific Institute for Public Policy Research is an independent, tax-exempt research and educational organization. The Institute's program is designed to broaden public understanding of the nature and effects of market processes and government policy.

With the bureaucratization and politicization of modern society, scholars, business and civic leaders, the media, policymakers, and the general public have too often been isolated from meaningful solutions to critical public issues. To facilitate a more active and enlightened discussion of such issues, the Pacific Institute sponsors in-depth studies into the nature of and possible solutions to major social, economic, and environmental problems. Undertaken regardless of the sanctity of any particular government program, or the customs, prejudices, or temper of the times, the Institute's studies aim to ensure that alternative approaches to currently problematic policy areas are fully evaluated, the best remedies discovered, and these findings made widely available. The results of this work are published as books and monographs, and form the basis for numerous conference and media programs.

Through this program of research and commentary, the Institute seeks to evaluate the premises and consequences of government policy, and provide the foundations necessary for constructive policy reform.

PACIFIC STUDIES IN PUBLIC POLICY

For further information on the Pacific Institute's program and a catalog of publications, please contact:

PACIFIC INSTITUTE FOR PUBLIC POLICY RESEARCH
177 Post Street
San Francisco, California 94108

CONTENTS

LIST OF FIGURES

LIST OF TABLES

FOREWORD

Money in Crisis should further help convince its readers of the need for monetary reform and acquaint them with several possibilities. The reforms considered do not merely concern policy details, such as the target rate of money-supply growth or the Federal Reserve's open-market tactics. They would change the monetary regime itself. Our "random-walk monetary standard," as Axel Leijonhufvud calls it, would give way to a new monetary constitution.

Leijonhufvud further develops his insights into the pervasive and subtle kinds of damage wrought by inflation, damage that otherwise perceptive economists had long overlooked. (Having Leijonhufvud's "blueback" scheme in print at last is welcome: the ease of shifting to stable money from a steady, fully expected, and fully allowed-for inflation helps underline what a beguiling chimera such an essentially costless inflation is.)

Stuart Wood documents how inflation can falsify calculations, leading to payment of taxes on and dividends out of largely fictitious corporate profits, thus promoting capital consumption, especially as inflation impairs saving in various ways. Furthermore, use of an unstable unit of account in assessing prospective revenues and costs leads to construction of some capital goods that fail to mesh well with existing capital goods and with consumer demands, so that their true serviceability is less than entrepreneurs had expected.

Inflation and its costs, as explained by Leijonhufvud and Wood, illustrate the fragmentation and short-run bias of decisionmaking in government—its failure to take due account of remote and delayed side effects of blithely conferring short-run benefits on the many groups clamoring for them. Accumulating experience argues against unnecessarily having economic decisions made by the political process.

Charles Wainhouse's topic is business fluctuations caused by inappropriate money and credit policy, especially in the United States from 1959 to 1981. He makes a commendable attempt to test the "Austrian" theory of the business cycle, which so often degenerates into little more than a password recited by members of the Austrian school for mutual identification and encouragement. Evidently derived from his doctoral dissertation, his chapter in this book is too condensed to present his data and calculations in detail and to show whether his results support the Austrian theory *in opposition to* the monetarist theory of David Hume, Erick Bollmann, Clark Warburton, Milton Friedman, Karl Brunner, and Allan Meltzer (to mention just a few of the economists who, over the centuries, have furnished abundant argument and evidence).

Murray Rothbard, Jonathan Hughes, and Stephen DeCanio survey monetary institutions, economic policies, and business conditions in the early twentieth century. Rothbard offers observations and conjectures about the characters and motives of the founders of the Federal Reserve System and its leaders in its formative years. Hughes reviews rival interpretations of the depression of the 1930s, apparently preferring a multicausal interpretation himself. He again punctures the myth that the New Deal saved capitalism. "When we view the New Deal as economics, we are appalled. But the same thing is true of modern economic policies. . . . [T]he New Deal did *not* end the depression of the 1930s. The Japanese did." The policy record of the 1930s should restrain hopes for escape from present-day economic stagnation through government action—"unless American politics change remarkably." DeCanio, developing an index of expectations or business confidence, tries to sort out how changes in expectations and in real wage rates affected unemployment. Before mid-1933, most of the unemployment was attributable to worsening expectations; after that, to excessive real wage rates (and, the author hints, to an excessive level of wages *and* prices in relation to the quantity of money). The sluggishness of recovery was largely due to misguided New Deal policies, "the aftereffects of which are still being felt today."

Richard Timberlake examines the Federal Reserve's performance after 1945. He deplores the System's eclecticism and secretiveness. Its quasi-independence of other branches of government is inappropriate. Timberlake mentions possible reforms: steady growth of the monetary base at the rate of 0.01 percent a day or, alternatively, the competitive private issue of money convertible into gold or other commodities or into government base money, whose quantity would be frozen. He cannot predict the details of the monetary system that would emerge under competition, but users would accept only good money whose soundness was assured by convertibility into something of marketable value.

Michael Bordo contemplates a return to the gold standard in the light of historical experience. In comparison with managed money after World War II, the gold standard before World War I provided greater price-level stability over the long run but less short-run stability in prices and output. Prospects of gold production and of the demand for gold suggest that a restored gold standard would ultimately entail deflation. Bordo reminds his readers of Irving Fisher's proposal for a "compensated dollar," one whose gold content would be periodically adjusted in the interests of price-level stability.

Robert Weintraub, a leading monetarist researcher until his recent death, devises a role for gold in rules to restrain monetary growth. He would also have the government introduce gold coins with flexible dollar prices. His system would not be a gold standard in any ordinary sense of the term. Incidentally, he suggests a definition or measure of money (narrow money, M1) that he would expect to maintain a dependable relation with nominal income even in the face of continuing institutional change: currency plus all fully checkable accounts in depository institutions.

Alan Reynolds describes five episodes in which a return to the gold standard was quickly followed by economic boom. He suggests that the one event caused the other, but he does not really exclude an alternative interpretation for some of his episodes, namely, that returning to gold became possible only after conditions unfavorable to prosperity—in particular, the postwar deflation necessary to make the targeted gold parity workable—had run their course. Many separate numbers and bits of history lend an air of factuality to Reynolds's case. One assertion in particular seems questionable—that the Bretton Woods system did not break down but was deliberately destroyed. On the contrary, policymakers in the United States and abroad made repeated attempts to defend that inherently flawed system and to repair it after its initial crumbling. These unduly prolonged and ultimately futile attempts, together with the worldwide money-supply expansions that they caused, were followed by a worldwide burst of inflation in 1973–1974.

Lawrence White, who is justly renowned for his historical researches into free banking, particularly as it flourished in Scotland before 1844, here turns to the theoretical aspects of the subject. His analysis is relevant not only to the specific type of private money system that he presumably envisages but also to a wide range of alternative reforms that would deregulate financial activity and leave the issue of money largely or entirely to private enterprise. White clears up some serious confusions about competition in money. He stresses a simple but important distinction: that between pressures toward convergence onto a single unit of account or monetary standard and a supposed natural necessity for monopoly in the issue of money. Competition would *not* entail unlimited expansion and boundless depreciation of money. On the contrary, issuers, both individually and in the aggregate, would be restrained by the necessity and costs of keeping their moneys acceptable. The most likely method of maintaining acceptability would be convertibility—perhaps into gold or some other commodity or composite of commodities, conceivably into government paper currency, whose total stock would have been frozen. Convertibility would entail holding reserves. A banknote-exchange system would probably evolve and further exert healthy discipline on issuers. Although White does not stress the point, he clearly does not envisage money backed by *100-percent* reserves; he does not fall into the error of those reformers who expatiate on the beauties of 100-percent money while ignoring the almost irresistible market forces that would press for circumventing any such requirement.

Robert Hall criticizes the monetarist proposal for steady money growth. One difficulty is the changeability of the very concept and measure of money; past measures were artifacts of government regulation. With a fixed stock or growth rate of money, furthermore, changes in how much of it the public desires to hold can cause trouble: Every time the public wants to hold a little more money, interest rates shoot up and real activity declines. Widely fluctuating interest rates contribute to destabilizing the foreign-exchange markets.

Monetarist policy would not, therefore, achieve the three goals of a stable price level, interest rates exposed to no more than moderate fluctuations, and full financial deregulation. Neither would any type of gold standard; instead, it would invite wide swings in the price level.

Hall has previously offered ingenious proposals for a monetary unit defined by a composite of commodities. Now he shows again that he has several strings to his bow. He explains how the three goals he mentions could be achieved through stabilization of government money. (Possibly he has in mind a difficulty of transition to private money: collapse of the demand for and thus the value of existing government or base money would expropriate its holders unless it were replaced by bona fide government securities, increasing the burden of the government's interest-bearing debt.) Under Hall's new scheme, private issuers would be free to link their moneys to government money, which would be stabilized in purchasing power through Federal Reserve open-market operations. A definite rule would instruct the Federal Reserve to raise the interest rate on Treasury bills whenever the price index rose above its target level of 100 and to cut the bill rate whenever the index sank below 100. (Using the interest rate as a guide to the extent or intensiveness of open-market operations, that is, of the speed of honing in on the price-level target, does seem to be the chief novelty of Hall's proposal.) Obeying the rule would find the appropriate level of interest rates in the long run; the system would work like a thermostat.

Some questions remain. Hall's references to control of the Treasury bill rate through open-market operations seem to imply suitable inverse variations in the quantities of bills and actual money in the hands of the public. Other passages, though, refer to a fixed nominal stock of bills. An increase in their rate of return would strengthen the demand for them and so raise the purchasing power of their total stock and of the dollar in which they were denominated; a cut in the bill rate would lower the real value of the bill stock and of the dollar. It remains for Hall, then, to clarify some details of the mechanism he recommends.

Professor Hayek's paper, like Hall's, is for me one of the most interesting of the entire book. Although the most eminent living member of the Austrian school, Hayek transcends the shibboleths—

ones in favor of gold and against money of stable purchasing power — that seem to beguile many other members of the school. The international gold standard, Hayek recognizes, cannot now be restored in effective form. Restoring it would require a return to beliefs long since destroyed, and trying to restore gold would cause fluctuations in its value wide enough to make the system break down. Money of stable purchasing power now impresses Hayek as the best reform to be hoped for. Governments can best be prevented from abusing their power over money by depriving them of any such power. The specification of money units of defined commodity value and the issue of money can be left, as Hayek has explained before, to competitive private firms.

Hayek now suggests some further details of how competition might work. Convertibility could strengthen the operational meaning of each issuer's undertaking to keep the commodity value of his money unit stable. Instead of merely trying to do so by regulating the volume of his outstanding notes and deposits, the issuer would undertake to redeem his money on demand in whatever amounts of competing moneys would buy, at actual market prices, the bundle of commodities whose value defined his own unit. The issuer would maintain redeemability through suitable adjustment of the scale of his operations, that is, through adjustment of the interest rates charged on loans and paid on deposits and of any spread maintained between his buying and selling prices of other moneys in terms of his own. The courts would come to enforce contracts and debts in terms of the stable units of value that the parties had intended; the collapse of a particular money would not be allowed to effect an unintended redistribution from creditor to debtor.

Hayek says he has thought of so appealing a name for a private money unit that it would probably be worth millions. To keep others from beating him to its actual use, however, he must keep that name secret for the time being. My curiosity is aroused.

Hayek claims great macroeconomic advantages for the system he envisages. "[S]uch a semiautomatic regulation of the supplies of the main kinds of money, assuring the stability of their purchasing powers, would eliminate the causes of the alternation of inflationary booms and periods of depression and unemployment that have plagued societies ever since deliberate attempts at a central control of the quantity of money were made." Hayek does not here spell out the analysis he has in mind, but someone familiar with monetarist theory and evidence should be able to reconstruct it. I think that Hayek's claims are justified.

Hayek recognizes that governments would probably resist displacement of their own moneys. He suggests that the use of credit cards geared to new private units of value may play a greater early role in circumventing this resistance than private issues of currency.

Presumably no one would claim that the monetary reforms described in this book include the one best in all respects, the definitive answer to monetary problems. (I happen tentatively to prefer a scheme not described here.) Though any of several might work better than our existing monetary system, the proposed reforms are presumably offered as aids to diagnosing the faults of our existing system and as sources of ideas that might be extended and recombined in various ways.

Some libertarians are inclined to take what I consider a mistaken line. They deplore the "constructivism" of devising alternative systems and comparing their operating properties; they insist instead that we "let the market decide." Our existing system, however, is far from the product of beneficent spontaneous evolution. It has been shaped by numerous piecemeal government interventions. Most of those interventions, considered one by one, may have seemed plausible at the time; but their cumulative result is the absurd system we now endure. Shifting to a new system of a more private or market-oriented character—or even just clearing the way for spontaneous evolution, if that is what one wishes—will necessarily require dismantling the government's current domination over money. The particular way this dismantling is done is bound to influence what type of new system emerges. The government's major role in the economy—in taxing, spending, expressing values, and accounting—is bound to influence how readily some new system catches on. The government cannot avoid, then, exerting at least a nudge on the course of monetary evolution.

Rather than ignore it, we might better deploy economic and other strands of analysis in openly discussing what sort of new system we would like that unavoidable nudge to favor. The present authors deserve congratulations on contributing so well to this discussion.

Leland B. Yeager
University of Virginia

INTRODUCTION

Barry N. Siegel

The Federal Reserve System, or the Fed, was seventy years old on December 23, 1983. Old age should bring serenity and wisdom, but sadly—for us as well as the Fed—the system finds itself embroiled in controversy and unsure of its mission and procedures. During the last twenty years, it has presided over the worst inflation since the Civil War and contributed to the forces provoking the most serious recessions since the 1930s. At the same time, it has adopted and subsequently abandoned several monetary and credit control procedures. In brief, the Fed has not done its job; it has not brought a steadying influence to an unruly economy. A fair case can even be made that the Federal Reserve System has made things worse—so much so that we may now say there is a crisis in our monetary constitution.

The thirteen papers in this book deal with the nature, causes and effects, and possible solutions to this monetary crisis. The source of the crisis is the misbehavior of government—Congress, the presidency, and the Federal Reserve System. Stagflation—the conjunction of high unemployment, deteriorating productivity, and rising prices—is the legacy of this misbehavior. Among the solutions to these problems is reform of Federal Reserve policies and procedures or, more radically, abandonment of our present monetary constitution and a return to some form of the gold standard, a move to a commodity money standard or even adopting a system of free banking.

No single volume can comprehensively deal with a theme of this magnitude. Nonetheless, it is remarkable how deeply this independent work of thirteen different authors has penetrated into the details of the subject. Leland Yeager's summary and comments on the individual papers in the foreword provide convincing evidence on this point.

My job in this introduction is to provide a perspective or framework for interpreting the efforts of the writers. This is not an easy task; professional opinions on issues of macroeconomic and monetary theory and policy vary widely. Compared to microeconomics, macroeconomics, and monetary theory are at the preparadigm stage. To some extent, this is because actual events have upset predictions based upon macroeconomic theories. In the 1960s and 1970s, for example, fiscalists found that Keynes's *General Theory* was not so general after all. Also, OPEC oil price shocks taught monetarists in the 1970s that business cycles do not always originate in the dance of the dollar. The turbulences of the last twenty years have taught professional economists to be more respectful of the influence of governmental policies and other events on the expectations of business people, investors, and consumers and of how those expectations, in turn, may foil the best laid plans of the authorities. It has also become clear that in constructing theories of economic policy, economists should take due account of the perceptions, motivations, and knowledge of policymakers as well as the political constraints authorities face in their work. Finally, it has become painfully obvious that macroeconomic outcomes are heavily conditioned by labor and product market processes, by implicit and explicit contractual arrangements, by disincentives and incentives generated by the level and structure of taxes and transfer payments, and by distortions in the marketplace caused by countless government regulations.

One reaction to this state of affairs has been a downgrading of fiscal and monetary policies as means of stabilizing the economy. Enthusiasm for an activist fiscal policy in the early and mid-1960s, following the 1964 Kennedy-Johnson tax cut,[1] has been replaced by a widely shared (but certainly not universal) belief among economists

---

1. Walter Heller, President Kennedy's chief economic advisor and architect of the "new economics" wrote in 1966, "We must now take it for granted that government must step in to provide the essential stability at high levels of employment and growth that the market mechanism, left alone, cannot deliver." Walter Heller, *New Dimensions of Political Economy* (New York: Norton, 1966), p. 9.

and policymakers rejecting policy activism—except perhaps during election years. Many now favor measures that, in the words of a strong statement made in the 1980 *Midyear Report* of the Joint Economic Committee of Congress, would confine government actions to tax and other policies that "improve the structure and performance of the economy over the long run." This bipartisan statement, based upon a study of the federal government's response to six recessions after World War II, convinced the committee and its staff that fiscal and monetary policies have been unreliable instruments for "fine tuning" the economy and that in some cases, they actually damaged the economy by overstimulating economic recoveries.

A doctrine that rejects an activist fiscal policy as an effective tool for fine tuning the economy logically follows from the study of the policy record. We should note here, however, that such a doctrine serves the interests of legislators and presidents, who are thereby encouraged to pursue tax and expenditure programs that directly help their constituents and keep them out of hot water during election years. At the same time, this doctrine reduces politicians' incentives to look at the overall budgetary impact of individual measures and to consider the inflationary impact of the resulting deficits on the economy. Moreover, such a policy encourages Congress and the administration to shift responsibility for formulating and implementing stabilization policies to the Federal Reserve System. Legislators and administration officials are in a good position to shift blame to the Fed when fiscal policies keep monetary policy from succeeding.

The game is now well understood. The play of interest-group politics creates ever expanding levels of federal government expenditures unmatched by new taxes. By increasing the demand for loanable funds, the resulting deficits—currently in the $200 billion range—raise real interest rates. The prospect of continued and perhaps expanding deficits keeps long-run inflationary expectations alive and helps maintain high actual rates in the present, even though current inflation may be low. High interest rates hurt housing and other interest-sensitive industries; they also work to keep the dollar strong, spoiling export markets for farmers and other producers, while encouraging imports of automobiles, steel, textiles, electronic equipment, and other products. The resulting low profits, failing firms, and unemployment in the impacted industries and communities create political pressures on politicians who, in turn, put pressure on the Fed to push interest rates down.

This political pressure takes a variety of forms, including "studies" of the advisability of putting the Fed under the Treasury — discussed during the Reagan Administration in 1982 — and, to name a few more recent ideas, congressional proposals to force the Fed to target real interest rates, or to stabilize some price index or the price of gold. These attacks on the independence of the Fed complement the uncertainties that normally exist within the System over the course of policy and weaken the resolve of the twelve-member Federal Open Market Committee — the Fed's major policymaking body — to stick with long-term policy regimes that are designed to stabilize the price level.

The combination of pressure from without and controversy within the System helps create the peculiar policy regime referred to below by Axel Leijonhufvud — the "random walk monetary growth standard." A random walk characterizes the path of a drunkard whose ultimate destination cannot be predicted. A random walk monetary growth standard characterizes a managed money standard run by officials whose actions are so buffeted by contemporary pressures or shifting theories of monetary control that members of the public affected by the actions cannot predict where those actions will take them in the intermediate or long-term future. Citizens — and the officials — will not be able, for example, to establish reasonable expectations about the level of prices five to ten years down the line.

How we have gotten into this mess is clearly a complicated story, one that we can probably only partially understand. Even so, no explanation of our history can be complete without considering at least three basic developments: (1) the unleashing of the spending potential of representative government; (2) the conversion of the Federal Reserve System into an agency charged with economic stabilization; and (3) the acceptance by economists and politicians that central governments have the power, knowledge, and responsibility to maintain full employment, stable prices, and a satisfactory rate of growth in per capita income.

Representative government has always had a potential for raising the rate of inflation through budgetary policies. Legislators stay in office by serving constituents — through keeping tax bills down and offering voters programs that increase spending. The artful legislator is expert at scratching the backs of other legislators in passing his or her favorite bills and in avoiding bills that impact directly and negatively on his constituents and those of his colleagues. Deals between such alliances of legislators lead to bills passing that would not command a majority of the legislature taken by themselves. The effects of this process on the overall economy—inflation, crowding out of private expenditures by those of the government, and loss of jobs in the impacted industries—are difficult for the ordinary voter to discern and then trace back to the actions of individual legislators. Most constituents are probably glad to reelect representatives who bring the bacon home to their own districts, even when they understand that buying the bacon with public funds adds something to their tax bills or the government's deficit. Since taxes are spread over all citizens, recipients of benefits from government programs pay for a very small part of their costs.

The true character of the budget-busting potential of representative government did not become apparent until the 1930s. In 1929, total government outlays by federal, state, and local governments were only about 11 percent of the gross national product (GNP), and the federal government's share was only 2 percent of GNP. With jumps in federal expenditures and transfer payments leading the way, government was spending almost 20 percent of GNP by the mid and late 1930s. Things have never since been the same; government outlays now represent over 35 percent of the nation's income.

This fiscal revolution did not happen by accident. It was a result of increased federal government outlays designed to combat the effects of the Great Depression and, most significantly, of a major shift in theoretical attitudes respecting the proper role of government budgetary policy. Pre-1930s fiscal doctrine was dominated by the balanced-budget doctrine—so much so that Herbert Hoover, in the midst of high unemployment in 1931, was able to propose a tax increase designed to close a federal deficit and (by releasing credit for use in the private sector) to increase employment. Over the years this doctrine became so eroded that in 1962 President Kennedy was able to propose a tax cut in order to balance the budget and again increase employment. The theoretical justification for this doctrine—which also took root in Britain and other western countries—was found in Keynesian fiscal theory. The fiscal revolution went hand in hand with the Keynesian revolution in economic theory.[2] Keynes opposed economic orthodoxy by suggesting that government can

2. For a detailed discussion of the fiscal revolution, see Herbert Stein, *The Fiscal Revolution in America* (Chicago: University of Chicago Press, 1969).

lead a country out of a slump by increasing its spending or cutting taxes.

The Keynesian revolution is now dead, but its legacy of high federal expenditures and large deficits remains. An indication of the change is that, unlike supply-side theorists and supply-side politicians, mainstream Republicans and the leaders of the Democratic Party in Congress now favor an increase in taxes and reductions in expenditure—mainly military—in order to reduce the deficit and—shades of Herbert Hoover—loosen credit for use in the private sector. The pre-1930s balanced budget doctrine appears to have returned. Under present circumstances, however, it is hard to see how anything less than its embodiment in some sort of constitutional provision will enable it to overcome the spending propensities of a representative government dominated by interest-group politics.

The fiscal revolution was aided and abetted by the expansion of the discretionary powers of the Federal Reserve System in the Banking Act of 1935. In his essay in this volume, Richard Timberlake reminds us that in creating the Fed in 1913, Congress did not have in mind an agency that would actively pursue stabilization policies. Its main purpose was to create a system of reserve banks that would provide depositories for member bank reserves, sources of new reserves through discount windows, a national check-clearing system, and a fiscal agent for the federal government. It may be, as Murray Rothbard declares below, that the Fed was in fact the creation of a small and influential group of bankers and their supporters in Congress, whose purpose it was to cartelize the American banking system, the effect of which was to create an engine of inflation.

Indeed, it did not take long for the Fed to inflate the money supply to aid the country's effort during World War I and to discover how to use open-market operations and discount policy in the 1920s to affect the level and use of credit and to support Britain's return to the prewar gold standard. Without an official mandate, the monetary authorities were already conducting an activist monetary policy. Nonetheless, by strengthening the power of the Federal Reserve Board to coordinate the activities of the twelve Federal Reserve Banks, by removing from the Board the secretary of treasury and the comptroller of the currency, by giving the seven members of the Board fourteen-year terms (staggered), by giving legal status to the Federal Open Market Committee and vesting it with the power to conduct all open-market operations in the system, and by permitting the Fed to vary reserve requirements, Congress refashioned the Fed into a powerful independent agency for money and credit control.

In creating a new and more powerful central bank, Congress did not at the same time tell it what to do with its powers or how to carry out the policies it settled upon. The Fed itself was in a quandary, and—as Timberlake points out—it used its powers in the late 1930s and the 1940s primarily to support Treasury financings by "maintaining orderly conditions in the bond markets"—a code phrase for keeping interest rates low. The dangerous inflationary potential of this policy was well understood by the monetary authorities, but it took the inflationary pressures created by the Korean War to force the Treasury to accede to the famous Accord of March 1951, an agreement that gave the Fed a freer hand to conduct anti-inflationary policies. To this day, however, the Fed does not feel itself to be totally free from Treasury concerns. The reserves of the banking system contain many dollars generated by open-market policies designed to stabilize the bond markets in the face of heavy Treasury borrowings.

Released from complete dominance by the Treasury, the Fed has had to find its way to a coherent monetary policy strategy. A well-designed policy strategy is one that links the use of policy instruments to a set of operating and intermediate targets that, in turn, have predictable links with ultimate policy goals. The Employment Act of 1946—and, later, the more ambitious 1978 Humphrey-Hawkins Act—set forth high employment and stable prices as goals for the Fed and other government policymakers. Even so, it was not until the late 1960s that the true dimensions of the policy strategy problem became understood. Before that time, Fed policy was focused upon money market conditions—the degree of ease or tightness in money and credit markets as evidenced by free reserves, short-term interest rates, and other money market indicators. Explicit links between these operating targets, intermediate targets such as the money supply or long-term interest rates, and ultimate policy goals were not factored into policy decisions.

It is still not clear how much Federal Reserve policy is guided by a detailed monetary policy strategy. The Fed did explicitly adopt a system of targeting monetary aggregates in the 1970s, presumably to bring inflation under control; but the strategy was designed to control monetary aggregates with the aid of short-term interest rate targets. The record shows that the Fed hit its interest rate targets more frequently than it hit its monetary targets. The growth rate of the money supply increased, inflation rose, and nominal interest rates soared. Moreover, Fed policies failed to produce an economy free of serious recessions. The October 1979 change in monetary control procedures—when the Fed decided to downgrade interest rates in favor of a policy of improving its record of monetary control by installing a system of reserve targeting—gave the monetary authorities a better record on inflation; unfortunately, the new system also produced wide fluctuations in the growth rate of the money supply. Many economists believe that the uncertainties caused by these fluctuations have helped keep real interest rates high and exacerbated the two recessions that occurred in the 1980–82 period.

In the depth of the second recession, during the latter half of 1982, the Fed abruptly abandoned its monetary targeting system and set in motion a major expansion in the money supply. Its principal stated reason for doing so was that an expected bulge in redemptions of all-savers certificates of deposit were likely to badly distort the M1 monetary target: The M1 money supply—consisting of currency, coin, checking and other transaction accounts—was the principal object of the Fed's reserve control procedures installed in October 1979. In retrospect, however, it is now clear that Fed policymakers were afraid of a further deepening of the already deep recession and of the repercussions of the international debt crisis in Mexico, Argentina, Brazil, and other developing countries. In addition, Fed policymakers were on the receiving end of a great deal of political pressure from Congress and the Treasury; plans were in the air to force the Fed to change its policymaking procedures, bringing it more closely under the supervision of the political authorities. Also contributing to the new policy of expansion was the observation—particularly in late 1982 and during 1983—that a major downshift had occurred in the income velocity of money.

The Fed abruptly abandoned rapid monetary growth in the middle of 1983. M1 grew at a moderate 4 to 5 percent annual rate in the latter part of the year—compared to a 14 percent rate of growth from June 1982 to May 1983. The Fed clearly abandoned steady monetary targeting as a basic element in its policy strategy in 1982 and 1983. In early 1984 it adopted a new M2 target range for the balance of the year. Given its recent behavior, however, it is unclear at this writing (February 1984) whether the Fed can ever be trusted to return to a consistent monetary targeting strategy.

As this brief summary of changing Federal Reserve policy practices indicates, the Fed has never fully embraced any particular policy regime. It has always desired flexibility—freedom to pursue policies that seem right at the moment without being bound by any single set of rules. It has, for example, generally opposed Milton Friedman's long-standing proposal for a constant money growth rate rule. While such a rule would make sense in a world where the demand for money is stable, it could spell disaster in a world where the demand for money shifts about in unexpected ways. In such a situation, the authorities would want the freedom to target interest rates instead of monetary aggregates since interest-rate targets in a world of unpredictable shifts in the demand for money are a superior means of influencing ultimate policy goals.

Monetary growth targets are also under attack because financial deregulation has led to a proliferation of new and near moneys in the form of NOW and Super NOW interest-bearing checking accounts, automatic transfers of savings-to-checking-account systems, money market accounts, and so forth. The line between transactions media and savings media has become badly eroded, and many analysts doubt that the Fed will be able to continue to define the money supply in a way that the resulting aggregate will maintain a predictable relationship to the nominal GNP.

My own interpretation of the situation is that over the years monetary policy has been buffeted about in large measure by shifting fashions in monetary theory. These fashions, in turn, are strongly affected by theories currently held by leading members of the academic community—people like Milton Friedman and James Tobin. Friedman and Tobin represent two extremes of a spectrum of possibilities specified long ago by Knut Wicksell.[3] Wicksell's contribution was to show that the monetary theory appropriate to describing the forces determining the level of prices in a country varies with the nature of its financial system. The quantity theory, for example, works best in a country with a pure outside-money system, in which the money supply is exogenously fixed by the government in the form, say, of paper notes or in which gold or some other commodity with a small elasticity of supply determines the quantity of money.

At the other extreme is Wicksell's "pure credit economy"—a pure inside-money financial system that contains a monopoly bank

3. Knut Wicksell, *Interest and Prices*, trans. R. F. Kahn (London: Macmillan, 1936).

that can issue deposits without worrying about reserve losses as it expands the money supply in the process of lending. Since money in a pure credit economy is an endogenous variable, such a world is clearly not the domain of the quantity theory. Prices are not stabilized by movements that bring the demand for money into equality with the existing stock of money, as they are in the quantity theory world of a pure outside money system. They are stabilized instead with bank policies that bring the market rate of interest into equality with the so-called natural rate of interest—the rate that equates saving with investment or the aggregate demand and supply of goods and services.

The job of a monetary authority in a pure outside-money system—if one can imagine such an authority—is to stabilize the price level by adapting the stock of money to the aggregate demand for money. The authority's job is somewhat complicated by the necessity to forecast money demand; but in theory, a pure outside-money system would contain few money substitutes, in which case shifts in the demand for money would be minimized, and the demand for money function itself would not be highly sensitive to interest rate movements.

In contrast, the job of the monetary authority in a pure credit economy is to pursue stabilization of prices by maintaining equality between the market interest rate and the natural rate of interest. Since the natural rate of interest is not observable, the authority cannot actually use it as a policy target. It must, instead, watch movements in the price level to extract signals for policy moves. Rising prices would signal the need to raise the market rate, and falling prices would indicate a need for a cut in the market rate. Robert Hall has suggested such a scheme—using the Treasury bill rate—in his essay in this book. The major problem with this approach is that it assumes the natural rate is fairly stable. If it is not, the market rate of interest is not much good as a policy tool. The pure credit economy is likely to be characterized by wide fluctuations in the price level.[4]

---

4. In a growing economy, stopping monetary growth with a policy that equates the market and natural rates of interest would lead to a falling price level. To stabilize prices, the monetary authority would have to keep the market rate below the natural rate. As Austrian School economists have shown, however, a market rate that persists below the natural rate misinforms the business sector about the relative profitability of capital investments and leads to malinvestments that provoke serious business fluctuations. See Charles Wainhouse's paper in this volume for a detailed discussion of this theory and an attempt to empirically verify some of its elements.

The world we currently inhabit lies somewhere between a pure outside-money system and a pure credit economy. As financial evolution takes place, it moves further in the direction of the latter. That is what is behind the interminable and inconclusive debates over monetary theory and monetary policy. Monetarists, for example, still think the Fed is capable of using control over the monetary base as an instrument for guiding a meaningful monetary aggregate. Moreover, they do not think that financial innovations have seriously undermined the long-run stability of the demand for money. Neo-Keynesians, not surprisingly, believe that the Fed ought to focus on interest rates as intermediate targets for achieving overall policy goals.

The inability of economists to resolve their theoretical differences has helped bring political considerations to the fore in influencing the direction and conduct of monetary policy. As noted above, the Employment Act of 1946 and the 1978 Humphrey-Hawkins bill put heavy burdens on the monetary authorities to stabilize the price level and keep unemployment to acceptable levels. It should be clear by now that the authorities do not have the knowledge or perhaps even the proper tools to carry out this mandate. Their attempts to do so in the 1970s led to the awful inflation of that period and, in so doing, helped dampen – at least for a time – the large gains in output and productivity experienced in this country and abroad in the early postwar years. Unfortunately, this sad experience does not deter many politicians from wanting to force the Fed into unwise policies. Without widespread agreement on the appropriate monetary theory framework to apply to our problems, economists are not in a good position to fight off this kind of pressure.

Nor, unfortunately, is the Federal Reserve System. Evidence is accumulating that monetary policy is being used to influence election outcomes – or at least in a manner designed not to conflict with the desire of incumbent presidents to stay in office. In brief, there may be something to the idea of a "political business cycle." Considering the complex manner in which monetary policy is made and implemented, one must be very cautious about such an assertion. Nevertheless, the timing of shifts in the growth rate of the money supply are intriguing. As the well-known monetarist David Meiselman has recently shown,[5] in the two years prior to each election

---

5. David I. Meiselman, "The Political Monetary Cycle," *The Wall Street Journal*, 10 January 1984, editorial page.

since 1960, the lagged six-month growth rate of the M1 money supply fell until about twelve to eighteen months before the November
elections and rose in the next six to twelve months before the elections. Except during the Carter presidency, the growth rate fell near
to or soon after each election. Since changes in the inflation rate lag
changes in monetary growth by eighteen to twenty-four months, and
output and employment lag it by six to twelve months, this pattern
of monetary growth would fit in well with a policy that tried to
bring inflation under control before or around the election while at
the same time stimulating the economy. Moreover, it fits well with
the notion that it is in the government's interest to bring inflation
under control soon after the election, hoping that the bad side
effects of such a policy will be gone before the next election.

The political business cycle may well be a major source of the
stop-go monetary policies of recent years. But we need not accept
Meiselman's suspicion that such policies were rigged to reelect incum-
bents in order to agree that these policies have been the source of
much turbulence in the economy, which shows itself in the alternat-
ing ups and downs of inflation, outputs, and employment.

If the business cycle is, indeed, the result of stop-go monetary
policies, we may well ask if the cure to economic instability is to
eliminate the stops and to keep the go, to have the Fed simply adopt
a particular unemployment rate, say 4 percent of the labor force —
the 1983 goal of the Humphrey-Hawkins Act — and unwaveringly
manage the growth rate of the money supply so as to achieve this
goal.

We now have enough experience to know that such a policy is
unsustainable politically and also naive economically. Keeping the
unemployment rate below its frictional and structural levels — the
so-called natural employment rate — would require the Fed to pursue
ever more inflationary policies. The public would undoubtedly soon
catch on to the game and would act in a variety of ways — cost of
living contracts, indexed loans, and so forth — to frustrate the intentions of the authorities. Such a policy could be maintained only by
imposing unpredictable monetary shocks on the economy — in brief,
by restoring a stop-go policy cycle.

Inflationary policies have been enticing to many economists because they believe that the short-run costs of stopping inflation
exceed the costs of continuous inflationary expansion. Underlying
this attitude is the idea that a steady and predictable inflation is

unlikely to badly distort the economy and, ultimately, the distribution of income. While this conjecture may be true, it does not follow that it is possible under our present monetary constitution to produce a steady and predictable inflation. Indeed, inflation has been anything but steady and predictable, so little so that our best economic forecasters consistently underpredict it on the rise and overpredict it on the fall.

An inflationary economy generates a great deal of uncertainty. The higher the rate of inflation, the greater its variability. Higher rates of inflation also appear to raise the variability of relative prices between different industries, and the variability of inflationary expectations between individuals.[6] Inflation, in brief, is not neutral in its impacts on the economy.

The distortive effects of inflationary policies and their costs are explored in this book by Axel Leijonhufvud, Stuart Wood, and Charles E. Wainhouse. Leijonhufvud emphasizes the distortions brought about by conflicting inflationary expectations. Wood tries to measure the size of the loss by focusing on the drop in real value of corporate equity in the United States between 1968 and 1980. Wainhouse presents an interesting attempt to empirically test various aspects of Austrian business-cycle theory, a doctrine that depends heavily on the idea that the business cycle originates in the inflationary policies of central banks.

A Federal Reserve System devoted to price level stability might have produced policies that were far less disruptive for the economy. Undoubtedly, policy errors are due in some measure to inadequate knowledge on the part of the authorities. As emphasized above, however, political considerations also play a big role. Murray Rothbard's essay is one of several in this book that stresses the political factor. Jonathan Hughes—whose essay is primarily concerned with suggesting that the Great Depression was a result of a multiplicity of factors—agrees that Federal Reserve and other government policies exacerbated and prolonged the depression and inhibited the economy's recovery. He does, however, assert that the policies' results should be judged by their political effects, not their economic effects, since politics is largely what motivated them: "Viewed as electoral

---

6. Alex Cukierman, "Relative Price Variability and Inflation: A Survey and Further Results," in *Variability in Employment, Prices, and Money*, Carnegie-Rochester Conference Series on Public Policy, 19 (Autumn 1983).

politics, the New Deal was an extraordinary triumph for the Democratic Party; and that is why political historians have celebrated it. When we view the New Deal as economists, we are appalled. . . . Presumably, when Marriner Eccles took over the Board of Governors in 1934, the Fed produced what the Treasury wanted, at least until World War II.''

Stephen De Canio's essay deals with expectations and business confidence during the Great Depression. He finds that the contraction from 1929 to 1933 was accompanied by a persistent decline in an expectations index he has developed. After Roosevelt's assumption of office in 1933, however, the index rose substantially; high rates of unemployment, however, persisted. De Canio blames misguided New Deal policies for this result. Hughes's caution about interpeting those policies as strictly economic is perhaps relevant to De Canio's point.

Richard Timberlake is also hard on the Fed: he charges it with eclecticism in its conduct of policy and believes the Fed does not follow any particular policy strategy. Eclecticism requires liberal doses of discretionary policy behavior, and Timberlake believes that discretionary behavior is at the bottom of most of the Fed's policy errors. He concludes his essay with a discussion of reforms that would either tie the Fed's hands—a return to the gold standard or a stable growth rule for the monetary base—or that would abolish the Fed and legalize free banking.

Monetary reform is very much on the mind of other authors in this book. Michael Bordo examines United States and British experience under varying forms of the gold standard and concludes that a return to a gold standard would generate long-run price stability, reduce the confusion between absolute and relative price changes that occur under managed money systems, and (if adhered to) greatly limit the role of government in determining the price level and overall performance of the economy. A return to gold, however, would not cure short-run instability of the price level or real output and employment. It would entail high resource costs to maintain the standard and require setting a price of gold that would not subject the international economy to a deflationary trend. The latter problem is technically soluble with periodic adjustments to the dollar price of gold. The major problem, however, is to prevent governments from engaging in the kind of profligate fiscal and monetary policies that led to the breakdown of the last gold standard regime.

Gold is also the center of attention in the papers by the late Robert Weintraub and by Alan Reynolds. Weintraub proposed the readoption of full-bodied gold coins as part of the circulating currency and the imposition of a fractional gold reserve requirement against Federal Reserve notes. The purpose of this innovation would be to restrain the growth of exchange media and provide the Fed with signals—in the form of shifts in the demand for gold coins—when its policies are too expansionary. Weintraub's scheme is designed to use gold to restrain monetary growth; it is not a call for a return to the gold standard of yesteryear. In Reynolds's opinion, however, such a return might not be so bad. He describes five different historical episodes in which a return to gold was followed by a return to prosperity. Clearly, cause and effect is difficult to establish in such a matter. Even so, he believes that these episodes help make a case for linking the dollar to commodities, not simply to stop inflation but also to unleash an economic boom.

Robert Hall retains a role for the Federal Reserve System, but he rejects monetarist solutions that prescribe a constant money growth rate rule. Nonetheless, his proposals for reform are quite radical. He favors complete financial deregulation, but he would retain the Federal Reserve note as the economy's basic legal tender and require that it be defined in terms of a bundle of four commodities whose combined purchasing power had stabilized over the last thirty years. All privately issued monetary instruments would be redeemable in legal tender upon request of the owner. As indicated above, the Fed would try to stabilize a price index by raising treasury bill rates while prices are rising and by lowering them while prices are falling.

Lawrence White is not convinced the monetary authorities can be trusted with any policy rule. Nor does he believe that any rule could be sustained in a complex and evolving economic environment. Allowing changes in the rule would be tantamount to reintroducing discretion in monetary policy, so White favors entirely shutting down the Fed and removing the government from the money business. He proposes to provide money through a free-entry competitive banking system whose notes and deposits would be convertible into specie at a rate decided by the forces of the marketplace. White's essay is devoted in large measure to establishing the theoretical case for such a monetary system and endeavoring to show that it would produce a high quality money supply not subject to overissue.

The book ends with an essay by F. A. Hayek, in which he elaborates further upon his well-known proposal for denationalizing money. Like White, Hayek would permit private money issuers to manufacture their own money; but, unlike White he would not impose a specie-backed monetary system. He would, instead, leave it up to the issuers themselves to define the commodity bundles backing their obligations; presumably, an issuer could promise to redeem his money for the currency sold by other money issuers. The resulting exchange rates between currencies would make it impossible for any single issuer to oversell his currency and thus generate inflation. A key part of Hayek's plan would be to allow the government to stay in the game—to issue its own money. In a competitive monetary system, however, the government itself would be restrained from producing too much money.

That such serious scholars as those represented in this book are entertaining fundamental departures from our current monetary constitution is surely a signal to the public that something is radically wrong with our present financial system. Unfortunately, the present monetary constitution serves the purposes of a large variety of special interest groups within and outside the government. Overhauling the system in some of the ways suggested in this volume may seem an unrealistic dream, but our present monetary system was not built in a day. Any new system will probably not emerge full-blown without a series of minor changes taking place over a long period of time. Such an evolutionary process may provide opportunities for serious analysis, such as exhibited in this book, to influence the course of events.

PART I

MONEY AND THE ECONOMY

Chapter 1

INFLATION AND ECONOMIC PERFORMANCE

Axel Leijonhufvud

THE THEORY OF INFLATION

A *monetary regime* is defined as a system of expectations that governs the behavior of the public and that is sustained by the consistent behavior of the policy-making authorities. The effects of the Great Inflation on American economic performance, in my view, are very largely attributable to a change in regime. The conventional theory of the welfare costs of inflation, in contrast, analyzes the consequences of a rise in the rate of depreciation of real balances within an otherwise unchanged policy regime.[1] In so defining the problem, it misses the boat.

One important class of misallocative effects of inflation—namely, those that are due to the nominal ridigity of taxes, subsidies, and sundry laws and regulations—will be slighted in what follows. I do not slight their importance. They are obviously of major significance.

I am grateful for the comments of Carlos Daniel Heymann, Earlene Craver, and Michael Darby.

1. The standard theory of the welfare costs of inflation is surveyed in Part 4 of R. J. Barro and S. Fisher, "Recent Developments in Monetary Theory," *Journal of Monetary Economics* (April 1976). Barro and Fisher indicate their own dissatisfaction with it: "An urgent order of business remains clarification of the reason for the public's dislike of inflation: if it is merely unanticipated inflation that is objected to, is the public under some illusion, or are economists under some illusion?" (p. 146).

They are avoided here, however, because in that direction lies a bottomless swamp of public finance problems, from which one could not hope to extricate oneself in half a paper. The current inflation poses problems that go to the very core of monetary theory. These problems need to be addressed, have not been addressed, and deserve priority.

The Anticipated Inflation Model

To have a willing audience among economists for a discussion of inflation's effects on economic performance, you must first deal with the following syllogism:

> Inflation is a monetary phenomenon.
> Money is neutral.
> When people adapt to it rationally, inflation becomes neutral.

What is wrong with that?

The anticipated inflation model is a most useful analytical tool. Yet for too many of us, it has been a snare and a delusion. It is a good model that makes bad theory.

To see why this is so, imagine a constant-rate, fully anticipated inflation to which the economy has had time to adjust completely. All existing contracts have been concluded on the presumption, shared by both parties, that the inflation will continue at this pace forever. For concreteness, let the inflation rate be 15 percent. Ignoring the inflation tax on real balances or, alternatively, assuming that competition among banks will keep the real rate of return on money unchanged, suppose that this economy functions in real terms exactly as if the price level were constant. By this assumption (and for present purposes only), the inflation is strictly neutral. We want to contrast two ways of getting from this 15 percent inflation to a constant price level.

The slow and painful way is disinflation. Under the assumed conditions, reducing the rate of growth of the money supply by 15 percent should bring on another Great Depression. Nobody expects the deflationary shock. It violates firm and universally shared expectations and will, therefore, bring about the worst possible contraction of output and employment. It changes the real terms of all outstanding contracts and forces a massive transfer of wealth from debtors to creditors. It is unlikely that all of this wealth could in fact be transferred; widespread bankruptcies are bound to occur and an "implosion" of the financial system similar to that of 1929–33 is probable.

This analysis of disinflation from a firmly anticipated inflation verges on self-contradiction. One poses a hypothetical inflationary process that has minimal social cost because it is fully anticipated; one juxtaposes a mode of ending the inflation that incurs maximal social costs because it is totally unanticipated. Less starkly drawn, this contrast is often painted by economists who want to suggest (1) that inflation is not so bad and (2) that the time to deal with it is never now. But the game is rigged. One should not assume that people who live in a regime where a 15 percent deceleration might happen at any time are going to plan confidently on the continuation of inflation at a constant rate. If they do not so plan, however, the costs of inflation are not necessarily minimal, and the entire matter needs to be reexamined.

The quick and painless way to end an anticipated inflation is a currency reform that I call the "blueback" scheme. Since under the assumed conditions, "greenback" dollars depreciate in real purchasing power by 15 percent per year, one should create a new blueback currency and make it, by law, appreciate relative to greenbacks at 15 percent per year. On the initial date the exchange rate between the two monies is one for one, but from that day onward bluebacks grow constantly in their legal capacity to extinguish debts contracted in greenbacks. One year later, eighty-five blueback cents will pay off a one-dollar greenback debt; two years later, it takes about seventy-one blueback cents; ten years later, nineteen cents.

If the originally held expectation of a constant 15 percent greenback inflation of indefinite duration were indeed rational, then the blueback reform would ensure perfect price-level stability indefinitely. The scheme has two advantages over disinflation. First, employment is entirely unaffected. It is not necessary to suffer through a recession to get back to constant prices;[2] Second, no one is swindled in the process. The real terms of contracts remain to

---

2. In the text above, I ignored the inflation tax on real balances and its allocative effects. In the case where greenback money is being taxed at 15 percent per annum, the blueback scheme introduces a new, nontaxed money that will therefore immediately displace the old currency. Since the demand for real balances will be larger once money is no longer taxed, a larger nominal supply must be provided in order to avoid deflationary pressure on the blueback price level and the associated, probable consequences for employment.

be fulfilled as originally envisaged. Creditors who after ten years received nineteen blue cents instead of one green dollar are getting exactly what they expected to get in real purchasing power.

Both of these advantages of the currency reform over disinflation stem, of course, from the fact that *nothing is really done* about the greenback inflation. The rate of greenback inflation is not reduced at all; it is only made subject to an arithmetical conversion. It is a cheap trick, if you will. But it does not evade the real issue. On the contrary, "really doing something" about the greenback inflation would be an irrational, destructive policy under the conditions assumed. It is assumed that we start from a quite stable *monetary standard*, which happens to have the peculiar property that money depreciates in real purchasing power at 15 percent a year. The public firmly expects this regime to continue. To disinflate is to adopt a policy that is inconsistent with this system of expectations. It would break the prevailing regime and wreak havoc. The blueback scheme, by contrast, merely removes the peculiar property of this otherwise stable regime.

The Random Walk Monetary Standard

The wrong way to get rid of an anticipated inflation is to disinflate. The right way is to convert to bluebacks. Nothing could be simpler, or politically easier, than to cure an inflation that conforms to the assumptions of this model. But it does not follow that the blueback scheme is preferable to disinflation in coping with the Great American Inflation. What follows is only the conclusion that the assumptions of the anticipated inflation model itself evade the real issue.

The model presupposes the government's believable precommitment to future rates of money growth. This precommitment extends into the indefinite future. It binds the authorities to create money at the requisite rate so as to keep the 15 percent inflation rate absolutely steady. Only a firm commitment of this sort could sustain the expectations assumed in the model. Rational agents will not anticipate a rate of inflation that no one is even trying to bring about. This, then, is a system where policymakers have either relinquished or been deprived of all short-run discretionary authority. The system operates, in effect, under a *monetary constitution*, and a very restrictive one at that.

What could be less descriptive of the policy regime that has been allowed to develop in the United States during the last twenty years?

How then should we characterize the current monetary regime of the United States? Our definition of the concept of "monetary regime" had two parts to it: It is (1) a system of expectations governing the behavior of the public and (2) a corresponding set of behavior rules for the policymaking authorities that will sustain these expectations. We choose among possible regimes by choosing behavior rules for the policymaking authorities. In the example above, the public unanimously predicts a particular constant inflation rate and the authorities are rigidly bound to produce it.

In 1984 the monetary authorities of the Unites States—that is, the Administration, the Congress, and the Federal Reserve System—do not obey *any* reasonably well defined set of policy rules that would tend to produce some particular, reasonably predictable path of the price level over the long haul. There is no monetary constitution in effect that limits the short-run options of the authorities for the purpose of providing long-run stability.

In order to have a label for the present regime, I will refer to it as the *random walk monetary standard.* This should be understood as a metaphorical name rather than a technical description of the regime. The metaphor captures some of the relevant properties, but the system is not as neat and tidy a money supply process as a random walk in the technical statistical sense.[3] Under the random walk standard, the policymaking authorities decide one period at a time whether to accelerate, keep constant, or decelerate the rate of money stock growth. Only current economic conditions and immediate political pressures are taken into account in making this decision. It is not constrained by concern with a more distant future. What the rate of growth of the money stock is going to be at future dates will not even be discussed until the last minute—and then it will be chosen on

3. Two points on which the metaphor is technically inaccurate should be mentioned. First, the public will not think of *today's* money stock growth rate as something simply "picked from an urn" with a known statistical distribution. For dates very close in time, information will be available or obtainable at some cost that, although subject to varying interpretations, will make educated guesses about the near-term inflation rate possible. On the other hand, for money growth rates two, five, or ten years into the future, the individual investor can hardly do better than to assume that they will be drawn from an urn. Second, however, there is no theoretical reason to expect stability over time in the coefficients of this random walk. It has shown drift in the past—that is how we wandered into the double digits—and may well drift again in the future.

the basis of what seems, under the exigencies of the moment, most pleasant and convenient to those who happen to be in charge. Short-run discretion is maximized. It is constantly exercised. The result is a monetary regime for the United States that is thoroughly bad, albeit not the worst imaginable.

If we look ahead only one period at a time (whatever length of calendar time this might refer to), the theory of a random walk standard does not seem to introduce anything new. Unanticipated monetary policy will, in familiar fashion, cause rates of output and employment to diverge from "natural" activity levels. But it is not obvious that monetary policy over the next six or twelve months is significantly harder to anticipate today than it was twenty years ago. The public knows the people in office, knows the current economic and political conditions they have to cope with, and knows a little something about what economic theories they tend to be guided by. The educated guesses about what actions the authorities will take that rational people make from such information inputs will differ. But in this respect, things have not changed much.

What is harder to anticipate is the cumulative effect of random walk monetary management over several periods. The 1981 price level may not have looked much more uncertain in 1980 than the 1961 price level looked in 1960. But in 1960, reasonable people thought the 1970 price level could be predicted within reasonable bounds. In 1980, putting a number on the 1990 price level could only be a joke. Under a random walk monetary standard, the uncertainty of future price levels increases rapidly the further one looks into the future. It is especially the long-term commitments of the private sector, therefore, that will be adversely affected by the refusal of the monetary authorities to precommit themselves over the long run.

Over the long run, monetary policy is unpredictable because we do not know what people will be in charge, what conditions they will face, or what economic theories they will believe in. Successive growth rates of the money stock are not the results of coordinated decisions at each separate date; rather, they are the outcomes of the confused and unprincipled interaction of Administration, Congress, and Federal Reserve. The rules of this interaction have been more or less designed to dissipate the responsibility for monetary policy in the way most comfortable for all parties. Each can with reason blame the other two. But note that none of these uncertainties would matter very much if some set of constitutional constraints were in force that would prevent the rapid cumulation of moves in one direction. A useful constitution need not be as restrictive as a Friedman rule. A measure of short-term discretion can be allowed if reversion to some mean is built into the system.

The Rate of Inflation and Its Variability

Our examination of the anticipated inflation model taught us that it takes as much monetary discipline to keep an inflation going at precisely 15 percent as it takes to maintain price stability. (By "discipline" we mean simply the narrowing down of the range of otherwise available discretionary policy options.) Discipline is something you accept for the sake of long-run stability or predictability.[4] Conversely, constitutional constraints are relinquished in order to "buy" more scope for short-term discretionary policy.

These considerations help us explain the relationships between rates of inflation and various measures of the uncertainty associated with it.[5] It is not obvious why highly inflationary environments should be in some significant sense more uncertain. But we do not expect to see inflation rates of 15 percent or 50 percent combined with strict monetary discipline. A polity willing and able to uphold a

4. This, obviously, is as true for democracies as for other types of political systems. Constraints on the short-term discretion of elected authorities are regarded by some people as "antidemocratic"—an argument that reveals a failure to understand why democracies adopt democratic constitutions.

5. In the last few years, quite a literature has accumulated on this topic. See, for example, D. R. Vining and T. C. Elwertowski, "The Relationship Between Relative Prices and the General Price Level," *American Economic Review* (September 1976); B. Klein, "The Demand for Quality-Adjusted Cash Balances Price Uncertainty in the U.S. Demand for Money Function," *Journal of Political Economy* (August 1977); D. Jaffee and E. Kleiman, "The Welfare Implications of Uneven Inflation," in E. Lundberg, ed., *Inflation Theory and Antiinflation Policy* (London: Macmillan, 1977); R. Parks, "Inflation and Relative Price Variability," *Journal of Political Economy* (February 1978); A. Cukierman, "The Relationship Between Relative Prices and the General Price Level: A Suggested Interpretation," *American Economic Review* (June 1979); M. Blejer and L. Leiderman, "On the Real Effects of Inflation and Relative Price Variability: Some Empirical Evidence," *Review of Economics and Statistics* (November 1980); A. Cukierman and P. Wachtel, "Differential Inflationary Expectations and the Variability of the Rate of Inflation: Some Theory and Empirical Evidence," *American Economic Review* (September 1979); Dennis E. Logue and Richard J. Sweeney, "Inflation and Real Growth: Some Empirical Results," *Journal of Money, Credit, and Banking* (November 1981).

monetary constitution, with all the self-denying ordinances necessary to guarantee a constant inflation rate with only moderate errors,
might as well also accord itself the additional benefits of a stable
price level.[6] At the same time, we expect to observe double-digit
inflation as a frequent occurrence or as the normal order of business
in polities that have decided to throw off the shackles of monetary
discipline to enjoy the "kicks" of monetary discretion. Inflation
rates of 50 percent or 100 percent are most likely to occur in countries where the stability of the political constitution is in doubt—and
a monetary constitution cannot be guaranteed where the political
constitution is not. In a sample of low-inflation countries, we expect
to find an "undisciplined" one only by the odd coincidence. In a
sample of high-inflation countries, we do not expect to find any
member proving its willingness and ability to forgo future discretionary options or to guarantee a stable inflation rate.

Rational Expectations under a Random
Walk Standard

In the anticipated inflation model, the state of expectations can be
represented by a single number, namely, the expected rate of inflation. We could replace the constant rate of inflation in that model by
a more complicated anticipated time path. Similarly, we could allow
for some uncertainty owing, for instance, to the technical difficulties of obeying the constitution to the letter. These generalizations
would not introduce anything of significant novelty. To keep in the
spirit of the model, one should, however, stick to the assumption
that the overwhelming majority of agents have the *same* probabilistic
beliefs about future price levels. When this is the case, we will call the
state of expectations "coherent." Incorrect expectations are syste-

---

6. Such a polity would not inflate for taxation purposes. *If* real balances are at all suitable objects for taxation, inflation is *not* the right way to tax them under "constitutional"
circumstances. It is far preferable to raise the same revenue by taxing bank deposits and
instituting a Gesell currency, that is, a dated currency valid, for example, only for a year so
that it has to be exchanged at the central bank at the end of the year at the rate of one old
dollar for eighty-five "updated" cents. This arrangement allows taxation of the money
stock while maintaining a constant price level. It will not disrupt contracts between private
parties, avoids the costs of changing prices and the like and is therefore preferable.

Inflation remains, of course, a matchless tool for taxation (and debt-repudiation) without the consent of the governed. But then we are back, surely, in a setting without effective
constitutional constraints on the authorities.

matically punished by losses and correct expectations rewarded by profits. The tendency is strong, therefore, for individual subjective expectations to converge on the constitutionally dictated, objective time path of prices.

If our present regime were a random walk in money growth rates in the proper statistical sense, agents would also learn its objective properties and thus converge on the same expectations. This would be the case, for instance, if the central bank were required (note the "constitutional" language that unavoidably creeps in!) to have a "drawing," at fixed temporal intervals, from some normal distribution with zero mean of accelerations and decelerations of money growth rates. Today's actual inflation rate would then be everybody's expected inflation rate for all future periods.[7] Similarly, the variance of every agent's forecast of future price levels would blow up exponentially with distance from the present in the same way. But the statistician's "drunkard's walk" requires someone who is very drunk — more so than central bankers normally allow themselves to be during working hours.

The actual process does not obey such rigid statistical laws. It is reasonable for rational observers to hold quite different opinions about what is the likely future time path of the price level. States of expectation are then "incoherent." The variance of an individual agent's forecast will be relatively small for the immediate short period; as in the true random walk process, it will grow exponentially with distance from the present. The distribution over agents of expected one-period inflation rates should show a fairly strong central tendency; the "expected rate of inflation" of current macromodels is perhaps best thought of as the modal current one-period expected rate. But the distribution of expected price levels by agent for dates two, five, or ten years into the future is likely to be widely dispersed. It may even be bimodal, for example.[8] Continued experience with living under a random walk standard, moreover, will not make individual long-term price level forecasts converge. The random walk process will each year reward with profits those who guessed the one-

7. This statement assumes, of course, that everyone expects constant real growth and a constant time trend in velocity and that these expectations also agree.

8. The state of expectations relevant to economic decisions with a two-, five-, or ten-year horizon cannot, then, be summarized as a single number for econometric purposes. Indeed, the state of expectations becomes practically impossible to measure, and one is forced to consider it largely unobservable.

period inflation right; it will chastize with losses those who guessed wrong. But it will not teach either group how to make a more "objective," improved two-year or five-year price level forecast. The profits and losses produced by frequent turnarounds in monetary policy serve no social function of improving collective economic performance.

The Redistributive Implications of Abandoning the Random Walk

At any time, the hangovers of past states of expectation will also be present in the form of outstanding contracts that were concluded at various dates in the past. Inflation expectations are different at different times. Hence we have dollar contracts today, the terms of which are still to be carried out fully, that embody inflation expectations ranging from 0 percent on up into double digits. Many of these contracts, moreover, will owe their existence exclusively to the difference in inflation expectations between creditor and debtor on the date that they were signed. (These, as we will see, are associated with inefficiencies in resource allocation.) Picking an agent at random, we might come up with someone who is in a pension plan presuming zero inflation, has a mortgage embodying a 5 percent inflation premium, presently expects a 10 percent inflation rate over the medium term, but is still paying off a loan embodying a 15 percent expected inflation, and so on.

Why are these hangovers relevant? Past states of mind, one would think, should surely belong in the category of "bygones that are forever bygones." What counts for individual private agents is indeed only the forecasts they make now. But the monetary authorities are obliged to take the legacies of the past into account.

To see why this is so, consider the reasons why bluebacking is not unambiguously preferable to disinflating as a means of bringing down the U.S. inflation rate. A return to monetary stability starts with the decision to accord legitimacy to one particular expectation about the time path of prices. Monetary policy will seek to validate the legitimate expectation and, correspondingly, to disappoint all others. Disinflating all the way back to constant prices means that debtors who expected a continuation of inflation will have to pay much larger real sums to their creditors. At the other extreme, stabilizing the greenback inflation rate at 15 percent, preparatory to bluebacking down to 0 percent, means that all creditors who expected the inflation rate to be brought down from 15 percent will see part of their wealth transferred to their debtors.

Whichever way you go, the redistributive consequences are complex and colossal. Any decision to commit government policy to the realization of some constitutionally generated price path implies a certain pattern of such redistributions. A governmental precommitment to a particular inflation rate—of 0 percent, 15 percent, or any other number—is politically easy to uphold in an economy that already has a long history of monetary stability around the inflation rate in question. When all agents hold the same expectations, the choice of what expectations to validate is not going to be difficult. The other easy case occurs in the wake of hyperinflation. Hyperinflation reduces the real value of outstanding nominal contracts to next to nothing. The new constitutional framework for monetary stability can be written on a clean slate.

A random walk inflation in the low double digits may be the most difficult to escape from and the most tempting to let continue.[9] To announce a constitutional rule is to propose a pattern of redistributions that, although largely unknown to the authorities, can be calculated by those affected. A continuation of random walk monetary mismanagement will, it is true, cause at least as many unanticipated gains and losses. But these unfold one period at a time. There is never a point in time when their entire present value is focused on the present. Therefore, an unanticipated return to monetary stability will be highly controversial. It also carries risks of a recession the magnitude of which cannot, because of the incoherent state of expectations, be accurately predicted. Consequently, it is more convenient not to decide today. This daily refusal to decide today is the basic feature of the random walk monetary standard.

Politicization of Central Banking

The redistributive implications of any move toward monetary stability lead to one additional conclusion. The Federal Reserve cannot be expected to decide what expectations are legitimate and should

9. Fortunately, one of the otherwise undesirable consequences of random walk inflation may prove a saving grace: Contracts will be concluded for shorter terms or with call features or renegotiation options. This will reduce the redistributive problems discussed here.

be validated. It is out of the question that the nonelected members of the Federal Open Market Committee (FOMC) should on their own make and enforce decisions with such vast redistributive consequences. The concept of an independent central bank, staffed by professional bankers and standing apart from politics, necessarily requires political agreement on a monetary constitution in order to be practicable. Professional central bankers could be held responsible for managing a gold exchange standard, a Friedman rule, or a price stability rule, for example. Given a constitution, the independence of a professional central bank is desirable. In the absence of political agreement on a monetary constitution, however, a nonpolitical central bank becomes impossible. A fiat money-producing bank, under those conditions, can only bend with the day-to-day shifts in the political pressures on it. It may be staffed with people of unquestionable courage, integrity, and competence, but they will have no legitimate basis on which to resist these shifting short-term pressures.

It is largely pointless, therefore, to blame the Fed for the erratic course of monetary policy over the last twenty years. The responsibility for monetary stability lies of necessity where the U.S. Constitution puts it—with Congress.

ECONOMIC PERFORMANCE IN INFLATIONARY REGIMES

We now turn from the theory of inflation to an analysis of its effects on economic performance. An anticipated constitutional inflation, we know, has only trivial social costs—on the order of milk subsidies, perhaps, or tariffs on foreign shoes. The costs and consequences of random walk inflation make a lengthy litany, not all of which can be recited here.[10] I will discuss three categories of effects. The first concerns mistakes in resource allocation due to the inability to predict the inflation rate. The second concerns distortions in resource allocation that are the consequences of individually rational adaptations to the random walk regime. The third concerns the social and political consequences of random walk inflation.

10. For more on the subject, see my "Costs and Consequences of Inflation," in G.C. Harcourt, ed., *The Microeconomic Foundations of Macroeconomics* (London: Macmillan, 1977); reprinted in Leijonhufvud, *Information and Coordination* (Oxford: Oxford University Press, 1981).

Expected Forecast Errors: Production and Investment

The dispersion of inflation rate expectations under the random walk monetary standard will lead to inefficiencies in resource allocation that could be avoided in constitutional regimes.[11] Production takes time. Producers commit money today to earn revenues at future dates. For resources to move consistently into their highest valued uses, all agents must be guided by the same relative prices. Agents whose inflation forecasts differ will be guided by inconsistent intertemporal relative values.

The simplest illustration runs as follows. Imagine an industry of numerous identical firms all with the same U-shaped average cost curve. The firms have to buy variable inputs at today's prices to produce output that will be sold at next period's prices. Pick a firm whose expected inflation rate happens to correspond to the inflation premium that the financial market has incorporated into the nominal interest rate. Suppose further that our hand-picked firm chooses to produce at the minimum average cost. At this output, its current marginal cost equals the discounted value of next period's price. Firms that expect more inflation will produce more; those expecting less will produce less. In either case, they incur higher unit costs. The average cost for the industry, consequently, is higher than it should be by an amount that varies positively with the dispersion of inflation expectations.

More generally, today's production decision is a commitment to money expenditures to be made at several dates in the expectation of revenues at (mostly) more distant dates. Again, for resources to move into their socially highest valued uses, all agents should be guided by the same real rate of interest in making their intertemporal allocation decisions. The problem caused by the dispersion over

---

11. Note, however, that it is not always possible to guarantee political agreements on a particular monetary constitution. The Great Deflation under the emerging gold standard during the last third of the nineteenth century, for instance, would have been a fairly painless affair if all individual deflation rate expectations had converged on the deflation rate that the system actually produced. But the development of the international gold standard did not follow some obviously preordained course. The decisions of countries to abandon silver or bimetallism and join the gold standard were not foregone conclusions; the dates of these decisions could not have been predicted very far in advance. In the United States, free coinage of silver—which would have turned the trend of prices around—remained a live political issue until Bryant's final defeat in 1896.

agents of expectations is most easily seen by rewriting the familiar Fisher equation as follows:

$$(\dot{r}^e_i + \dot{p}^e_i) \; = \; i \; = \; (\dot{r}^e_j + \dot{p}^e_j)$$

where subscripts i and j denote individual market participants. Competition will ensure that all transactors face the same nominal rate, i. But for both our agents to use the same real rate in their economic calculations, $\dot{r}^e_i = \dot{r}^e_j$, their inflation expectations would have to be uniform, $\dot{p}^e_i = \dot{p}^e_j$. The dispersion over agents of inflation rate expectations is likely to increase as we consider dates further removed from the present. We conclude, therefore, that long-term investment is particularly likely to be inefficiently allocated.

The volume of investment will also be reduced. The expected return on investment is reduced, and its variance is increased. Both factors will tend to depress the demand price for capital goods and thus the rate of capital accumulation.

Consider a firm representative of the industry in our previous illustration. It will make mistakes in choosing its output rates with some representative frequency. Under the random walk monetary standard, such errors will be more frequent and larger than they would be in a regime providing monetary stability. To the extent that the cost of these inefficiencies is born by the firms themselves and not transferred to customers or suppliers, profits on capital are reduced. So are prospective earnings on new investment. This tendency is reinforced when the tax law treats an increase in nominal earnings as if it represented growth in real profits. It is further reinforced by price controls and other forms of governmental intervention that random walk inflation tends to induce.

Expected Forecast Errors: The Negative Real Rate Riddle

In the financial markets, the most obvious consequence of the random walk regime is the thinning out of the long-term bond markets. Since the dispersion of price levels fans out rapidly the further one looks into the future, lenders and borrowers will be equally reluctant to commit themselves to long-term nominal contracts. Neither side can get a risk premium from the other. Consequently, we expect the volume of such contracts to shrink (and the volume of investments that are normally financed in this way to decrease even further than implied above).

A more interesting problem is posed by the fact that, until recently, nominal rates of interest on short- and medium-term placements did not in general rise sufficiently to compensate for the inflation. Such assets continued to be held year in and year out in large volume at *negative* real rates.

A clue to this problem may be found in the strong incentives to procrastinate created by the random walk regime. Agents will try to postpone commitments beyond the time when they would normally be made in a stable money regime and also to reduce the volume of commitments that are difficult or impossible to postpone until late in the game. This incentive affects not only long-term investments and financial contracts, but relatively short-term ones as well.

As an example, consider from the standpoint of date $t = 0$, an expenditure of funds that will produce sales receipts at some later date—for instance, $t = 3$. If we take as our example of a constitutional regime one that operates on a Friedman rule, the variance of the t_3 price level looks much the same from t_1 as it does from t_0. One would pay only a very modest sum for the privilege of postponing the commitment to reduce the uncertainties stemming from monetary policy. Under the random walk monetary standard, the perceived uncertainty of the t_3 outcome will be very much reduced if it is possible to wait until t_1 before making an irrevocable decision.

Haste makes waste. There will be some social cost in the inefficiencies of trying to live with shorter lead times. But the more interesting aspect of this inducement to procrastinate is the increase in *flexibility preference* that it implies.[12] Short-term money-denominated assets will carry an increased flexibility premium; that is, they will earn a real rate of interest that is lower than normal relative to the yield on long-term placements.

The *real* term structure of interest becomes more of a speculative notion than an empirically operational concept under random walk monetary conditions. The dispersion of expectations (which are

12. For the concept of flexibility preference, see A.G. Hart, "Risk, Uncertainty, and the Unprofitability of Compounding Probabilities," in W. Fellner and B.F. Haley, eds., *Readings in the Theory of Income Distribution* (Philadelphia: Blakistone, 1951); and J. R. Hicks, *The Crisis in Keynesian Economics* (Oxford: Oxford University Press, 1974), Chapter 2.

largely unobservable) makes it unclear how one would deduce a number with a good claim to being *the* real long-term rate of interest. But we have argued that real corporate earnings will be reduced under the random walk standard. This is consistent with the behavior of stock markets. The low real rates of return in prospect on long-term fixed investments should put a ceiling on the long-term real rate of interest that people are willing to pay in order to finance such investments. We conclude, therefore, that the entire real term-structure schedule shifts down. In addition, the increase in flexibility preference will push down short rates relative to long rates. In the random walk regime, consequently, fully foreseen negative real rates can be a steady-state phenomenon. Note that the analysis hinges on the increase in the perceived uncertainty of the price level with distance from the present. The flexibility premium could disappear without any reduction in either the present rate of inflation or in the perceived uncertainty about its immediate future. What it takes is a diminution in the ratio of the variance of long-term price level forecasts to that of short-term forecasts.

Social Selection

The market economy is, among other things, a system for selecting people for fame and fortune—mostly fortune. The system is supposed to award material wealth for hard work, for thrift, for alertness to the wishes of the sovereign consumer, and for inventiveness. Reasonable people may disagree about how "deserved" the distribution of wealth is that emerges in this way. What is indisputable is that monetary instability must change the rules of this natural selection and hence promote a different breed.

Under a random walk monetary regime, being efficient and competitive at the production and distribution of "real" goods and services becomes less important to the outcome of socioeconomic activity. Forecasting inflation and coping with its consequences becomes more important. People will reallocate their effort and ingenuity accordingly.

Survival and prosperity under a competitive regime require the capacity to adapt to changing conditions. Inflation brings a marked change in the relative significance of two broad types of adaptive skills. The product designer who can come up with a marginally improved or more attractive product, the production manager who in a good year can increase the product per man hour by a percent or two, the vice-president of sales who might reduce real distribution costs by some similar amount, are all examples of roles that have become less important to the stable functioning or survival of a corporation. Other functions requiring different talents have increased in importance. The vice-president of finance with a talent for adjusting the balance sheet to minimize the real incidence of an unpredictable inflation is one example. The creative financing artist floats to the top in real estate. But the wise guy who does a good job at second-guessing the monetary authorities some moves ahead is the one who really counts. Smart assessments of the risks generated by the political game in Washington outweigh sound judgments of conventional business risks. Other roles gain in importance also (for reasons that we will come to); among them is the lawyer capable of finding ways to minimize the impact of sudden new governmental interventions and the operator who is quick to spot ways of making a profit (or avoiding a loss) from new subsidy, quota, or price control schemes.

In short, being good at real productive activities — being competitive in the ordinary sense — no longer has the same priority. Playing the inflation right is vital. In the sixties and seventies, this has been the way for ambitious Americans to get rich. But an entire people cannot improve their living standards by playing this game.

The Political Consequences of Inflation

In this inflationary environment, the real outcome of private contractual agreements becomes more uncertain. Unpredictable inflation redistributes wealth indiscriminately, producing results that by generally accepted standards are unjust and unfair. Inflationary redistribution is a peculiar injustice in that the injured party cannot seek redress in the courts. The courts cannot deal with inflationary injustices because what is basically at issue in disputes of this kind is what expectations the parties *ought to have had* in signing the contract. In a system with a monetary constitution, legitimate inflation expectations are defined and monetary policy seeks to validate them. In our old illustrations of an economy with a 15 percent constitutional inflation rate, for instance, the courts would have no problem; a creditor who expected a lower rate (or a debtor who expected a higher rate) would have to bear the consequences. In the absence of such a constitution, however, the courts have no norm that could be applied to restore justice to contracts disrupted by inflation.

Contracting is a means of controlling the future activities of others in order to reduce uncertainty to manageable proportions and to make it possible to pursue a course of action with a reasonable prospect of success. Inflation renders contracting a less effective, less reliable strategy for controlling the real terms on which one can obtain or dispose of resources. When private contract fails, political compact becomes the substitute strategy. It is predictable, therefore, that random walk monetary policy will bring in its wake an upsurge of efforts by all sorts of groups to obtain by public compulsion what private cooperation will not achieve. Legislatures will be swamped by demands to control X's prices, to regulate Y's way of doing business, to tax Z—and to subsidize *me*.

Finally, the consequences of the American inflation do not stop at the nation's boundaries. The inflation must be judged also as a momentous foreign policy fiasco, one of far greater consequence in the long run than the sundry setbacks that have so exercised the public. It is in the long-run interest of the United States that as many countries as possible opt for the Western model of economic development and allow themselves to become integrated in the world economy. The performance of the Soviet-type command economies has been anything but impressive. But the rapid and irregular depreciation of the world's leading key currency and the stagnating growth of the major trading nations have obviously reduced the apparent advantages of the pro-Western course. And the inability of the United States, demonstrated over a decade and a half, to put its own house in order makes it seem very doubtful that the conditions will be restored under which free-market economies will be able to resume healthy growth.

No one would wish to argue that inflation has been the only factor in the disappointing performance of the American economy in recent years. Yet, in my opinion, the last decade and a half of monetary mismanagement constitute a self-imposed disaster for the United States the dimensions of which the economics profession has only begun to realize.

Chapter 2

EMPIRICAL EVIDENCE FOR HAYEK'S THEORY OF ECONOMIC FLUCTUATIONS

Charles E. Wainhouse

In 1931, when Friedrich A. Hayek's *Prices and Production* first appeared in English, the analytical structure represented in that study and in his *Profits, Interest and Investment* "met with a sweeping success that has never been equalled by any strictly theoretical book that failed to make amends for its rigors by including plans and policy recommendations."[1] Hayek's work was swept aside by the Keynesian tide, and when the revival of monetary theory began in the 1960s, Hayek was relegated to footnotes to expositions of theory and policy. Today, Hayek's contributions to monetary theory and the theory of the trade cycle are excluded from the mainstream paradigms. Although the interaction of money and relative prices is the essence of Hayek's monetary theory, it is little more than a troublesome distraction and detail in modern monetarism.

Consider Hayek: "Almost any change in the amount of money, whether it does influence the price level or not, must always influence relative prices. And, as there can be no doubt that it is relative prices which determine the amount and direction of production, almost any change in the amount of money must necessarily also influence production."[2]

1. Joseph Schumpeter, *History of Economic Analysis* (New York: Oxford University Press, 1954), p. 1120.
2. Friedrich A. Hayek, *Prices and Production* (1931; New York: A.M. Kelley, 1967), p. 28.

And Friedman: "Of course, it is one thing to assert that monetary changes are the key to major movements in money income; it is quite a different thing to know in any detail what is the mechanism that links monetary change to economic change; how the influence of the one is transmitted to the other; what sectors of the economy will be affected first; what the time pattern of the impacrs will be, and so on. We have great confidence in the first assertion. We have little confidence in our knowledge of the transmission mechanism, except in such broad and vague terms as to constitute little more than an impressionistic representation rather than an engineering blueprint."[3]

Hayek does not offer "an engineering blueprint," and the absence of such technical documentation from virtually all areas of economic *theory* (with the exception of input-output analysis) suggests that they are inappropriate vehicles for economic analyses. However the prospect of producing a blueprint that details the transmission mechanism is not the issue; an economy is not simply a hydraulic machine susceptible to description by appeal to the laws of Newtonian physics. Hayek's explanation of economic fluctuations relies crucially on the nonneutrality of money, and a cogent demonstration of the nonneutrality of money requires an adequate analysis of the transmission of monetary influences through the economy. By contrast, in mainstream monetary theory, the concept of neutrality has become virtually archaic, with discussions in the literature revolving around the existence and role of contracts (e.g., Barro 1976, 1977; Fischer 1977) and the integrity of the natural rate hypothesis within the context of the Phillips Curve, (e.g., Lucas 1973; Sargent 1973, 1976). The neutrality of money has become a largely unexamined assumption.

Hayek's theory of the business cycle can justifiably be classified as a monetary theory; yet one would be hard pressed to locate Hayek's insights in any of the standard expositions of modern mainstream theory (e.g., Johnson 1967, 1972; Patinkin 1972; Clower 1969; Friedman 1956, 1969). And although Hayek was very much a part of the mainstream of economic theory in the 1920s and 1930s, there is nothing in his work that was embraced when a revival of a monetary tradition began in the 1950s.

As a result, Hayek and the Austrians find themselves in a black hole within the cosmos of economic theory. Their unfortunate sep-

3. Milton Friedman, *The Optimum Quantity of Money and Other Essays* (Chicago: Aldine, 1969), p. 222.

aration from the mainstream revolves crucially around the issues of the neutrality of money and the absence of acceptable empirical testing of "the Austrian theory." In an effort to allow some light to escape from the mass of Austrian theory, we first summarize the Hayekian theory of the trade cycle and present, as a tentative formalization, a set of empirically testable propositions consistent with that theory. We then describe the results of testing these propositions.

THE HAYEKIAN THEORY OF THE
TRADE CYCLE

The history of the neutrality of money concept makes for good theatre. Save for the contributions of Cantillon (1755), Thornton (1802), and Cairnes (1873), among classical economists, and Menger (1871), Mises (1912), and Hayek (1929, 1931), among the Austrians (for whom money is distinctly nonneutral), economics has tended either to ignore the existence and implications of nonneutral money or to address the issue sotto voce. In classical and neoclassical mainstream paradigms, the fortunes of the neutrality issue have been tied to the topicality of monetary policy and to applications of the "strict" quantity theory.[4] (For a detailed discussion of the history of the issue of the neutrality of money in economic theory, see Wainhouse 1982.)

Modern interpretations of neutrality focus on, for example, the classical dichotomy, the differential impact of changes in nominal money balances on the real economy in the long versus the short run, and the Phillips Curve. And although the entire neutrality of money issue deserves more complete treatment than space allows, we will enter center stage holding a script that reads: "Modern economics — nominal aggregates affect nominal magnitudes, not real magnitudes.[5] Austrian economics — nominal aggregates do affect real magnitudes." The dramatis personae of course feature F. A. Hayek.

Hayek, in *Monetary Theory and the Trade Cycle* (1929), identifies as the most important task of monetary theory the explanation of shifts in relative prices that accompany and are caused by changes in money:

4. Schumpeter, *Economic Analysis*, p. 703.
5. Charles E. Wainhouse, *Hayek's Theory of the Trade Cycle: The Evidence From the Time Series* (Ph.D. dissertation, New York University, 1982), ch. 1.

The point of real interest to Trade Cycle theory is the existence of certain deviations in individual price-relations occurring because changes in the volume of money appear at certain individual points; deviations, that is, away from the position which is necessary to maintain the whole system in equilibrium. Every disturbance of the equilibrium of prices leads *necessarily* to shifts in the structure of production, which must therefore be regarded as consequences of monetary change, never as additional separate assumptions. The nature of the changes in the composition of the existing stock of goods, which are affected through such monetary changes, depends, of course, on the point at which the money is injected into the economic system.[6]

This quotation illustrates why there has been a dearth of dialogue between Austrians and orthodox monetary theorists on the issue of the neutrality of money; the difference between the two schools cannot be reduced to a dispute over the order of magnitude of elasticities (as is the case in the monetarist-Keynesian debates of the 1950s and 1960s) but centers instead on methodology. What is for Hayek the engine that generates the dynamics observed in an economy—changes in relative prices—is part of the *ceteris paribus* assumption set of standard neoclassical analysis. In both the Austrian and neoclassical paradigms, changes in relative prices will shift demand and supply curves appearing on the price-quantity graph; for Hayek, monetary influences *necessarily* impinge on the structures of relative prices and output, although there is no similar direct linkage between money and the structure of production in the neoclassical paradigm.

Hayek establishes that his monetary theory of economic fluctuations is consistent with any of the "modern interest theories" and need not be based on any particular one. The key is the monetary causes of deviations of the current from the equilibrium rate of interest.

Within the context of the cycle, the boom contains the seeds of the bust; when the initiating monetary impulse ceases, a crisis must occur. Hayek further contends that it is the nature of the monetary and credit mechanism that accounts for the continuous recurrence of the cycle. He identifies three sources of change with respect to the money supply: changes caused by gold flows, open market operations of the monetary authority, and the deposit-creation function

6. Friedrich A. Hayek, *Monetary Theory and the Trade Cycle* (1929; New York: A.M. Kelley, 1966), pp. 123-24.

of commercial banks. It is the last that is most important. (Curiously, of the myriad explanations offered for U.S. postwar cycles, the behavior of the Federal Reserve Board has probably been the culprit cited most often, especially in the financial press; commercial banks generally finish poorly in the blame sweepstakes.)

With respect to the role of the banks, the criterion Hayek offers to demonstrate whether monetary fluctuations must necessarily occur is whether or not banks are observed to "promptly" adjust the rate of interest to all changes in economic data. This adjustment, tantamount to maintaining equilibrium between the supply of bank credit and the supply of savings, would require banks to change either the price or supply of credit in response to savings flows. If these supplies are independent, or if banks have no interest in maintaining an equilibrium between them, or if it is simply operationally impossible to ensure equilibrium over time, then the necessity of monetary fluctuations will be demonstrated. We regard this as our first testable hypothesis and will apply a variant of the Granger (1980) test to the appropriate series to determine if some causal structure exists between savings and the supply of bank credit.

Hayek treats the credit supply–interest rate–supply of savings problem as self-evidently resolved. Because of competitive pressures, the bank or banks that first encounter an increased demand for credit are unlikely to raise their interest charges for fear of jeopardizing relationships with existing customers; they will satisfy the new credit demands even if it means a temporary reduction in liquidity. A general movement by banks to raise interest rates will occur either when the system is fully loaned-up (given reserve requirements) or the monetary authority raises the discount rate. And indeed, since "the rate of interest demanded by banks is not necessarily always equal to the equilibrium rate, but is, in the short-run, determined by considerations of banking liquidity," cyclical fluctuations are inevitable.[7] Despite Hayek's confidence in the nature of the relationship, we will attempt to verify the statistical independence of savings and credit.

As a process, the cycle initiated by the extension of additional credit to entrepreneurs in excess of the amount that could be supported by actual savings is best illustrated by comparing the path of the economy in this case with the path when there is an autonomous

7. Ibid., pp. 179–80.

increase in savings. When there is a shift in the distribution of consumption and investment in favor of investment as a result of an autonomous increase in savings and a consequent decrease in the interest rate, it tends to be self-perpetuating.

Initially, the interest rate falls below the "margin between the price of means of production and of products" (profit).[8] The increased savings activity will be associated with a decrease in the demand for consumption goods (and a tendency for their prices to fall), and an increase in the demand for investment goods will be accompanied by a rise in their prices. There will be a further depressing effect on consumption goods prices as new output reaches the marketplace until the difference between the two price vectors finally corresponds to the new rate of interest.

In the case of a decline in the rate of interest resulting from the extension of new credit, there will be no adjustment in the price vectors. The increased demand for investment goods will result in a net increase in demand for consumption goods. With this credit expansion, inflation stops, the prices of investment goods stop rising, and the differential between investment and consumption goods prices increases beyond the original level, since the structure of production has been altered in favor of production goods from the onset of the inflation. Forced savings represents a situation where, because of an increase in the quantity of money in the form of an expansion of credit by the banking system, some entrepreneurs get increased command over resources and bid up the prices of certain capital goods, thereby promoting the production of these goods and leaving consumers unable to realize planned consumption. This situation occurs early in the process of the shift of resources to investment sectors.

Hayek emphasizes the monetary causes of cyclical fluctuations in *Monetary Theory and the Trade Cycle*; in *Prices and Production* he focuses on the "successive changes in the real structure of production which constitute those fluctuations."[9] A complete theory of the business cycle will emerge as we consider the latter work.

In *Prices and Production*, Hayek initially considers the case where consumers elect to save and invest an increased proportion of their income. The first impact of this autonomous shift of the savings

8. Ibid., p. 216.
9. Ibid., p. 17.

function is that the demand for producer goods relative to consumer goods increases, and so do their prices. Producer prices, however, do not rise uniformly; the propinquity of the application of the producer good to final consumption becomes an important factor. In the stage of production immediately preceding that in which the consumption good is finished, the impact of the decline in the relative price of consumer goods will be more pronounced than the effect of the increase in invested funds available for producer goods of every kind (an effect that would tend to support the price). Although the price of the output from this stage of production will decline, it will decline less than the prices of final consumer goods. As a consequence, the margin between these two stages will narrow, reducing the prospect of profit relative to earlier stages of production; funds will therefore shift to these earlier stages. As funds shift, the margins between the various stages will tend to narrow, setting in motion a cumulative rise in prices in earlier stages.

The rise of the prices of the product, such as specialty steel, of any given producer's stage of production will provide an incentive for increased output in those industries—such as machine tools and electricity—that provide input to specialty steel. The products of the stages of production that feed steel will rise in price both because of the general rise in the demand for producer goods (as a consequence of the initial autonomous increase in savings) and as a result of the rise in prices in industries like coal mining that in turn supply machine tools and electricity. The rise in prices in basic stages of production (coal mining) will tend to increase the relative profits in machine tools and electricity, reinforcing the incentive to produce the latter. The dynamics of this process will result, via the fall of prices in later consumption stages of production (say, home appliances) and the rise of prices in earlier stages (say, steel, plastics, and so on), in a reduction of price margins throughout the system.

The factors of production that are sufficiently nonspecific will shift to earlier stages of the production process. The shift will proceed in the direction of the equalization of the returns available at all stages. Eventually, this shift in resources in response to the shifts in relative prices and profits will be able to support a lengthened process of production.

Nonspecific capital goods rise in price because of increased investment demand. Use- and stage-specific factors of production dedicated only to later stages of production (those closest to final consumption) will suffer a diminution in the rate of return because of the shift of complementary nonspecific capital resources to earlier stages. Specific capital in relatively earlier stages of production will be subject to rises in price and production.

The reverse of these events would accompany an autonomous increase in the demand for consumer relative to producer goods. This would bring on an increase in the differential between the prices of final consumption goods and the prices of different intermediate products and inputs; prices in later stages would rise relative to prices in earlier stages, nonspecific capital would shift from earlier to later production levels, and specific capital goods in later stages would rise in value. (Of course both analyses are contingent on the nature of elasticities of supply at each stage and in each industry; these in turn depend on the specificity of the inputs.)

With the original scenario, where there is an autonomous increase in savings, the market rates of interest in this process give signals regarding the anticipated directions of relative prices. Since the people who save and the people who invest are generally not the same, the allocation of investment funds occurs in the market for loanable funds. Only at a reduced rate of interest will the funds clear, and the extent to which rates decline will be determined by the amount of loanable funds and the *profit expectations* of entrepreneurs willing to increase production. If those expectations (ultimately about prospective shifts in relative prices) are accurate and are realized, the new rates of interest will correspond to the structure of prices that will eventually prevail.

Underlying Hayek's vision of the function of interest rates are the supply of and demand for loanable funds and business's expectations of profits; rates are not regarded simply as direct costs. Examining the dynamics, we see that rates initially fall with the increase in savings and then are adjusted in the market for loanable funds in accordance with expectations about the structure of relative prices.[10] Empirically, one would expect to discover causality running from innovations in savings to changes in interest rates and the existence of an inverse relationship between savings and rates. (We will examine the time series relationships between the supply of savings and an assortment of market rates of interest below.)

10. Hayek, *Prices and Production*, pp. 83–84.

Hayek builds his analysis of forced savings and the business cycle on the supposition that additional funds are injected into the economy through the vehicle of an expansion in bank credits made available to producers. As in the case of an autonomous increase in savings, rates of interest are initially driven down (below equilibrium levels) to promote the use of the additional funds. (We will leave aside, for the moment, the question of the reason for the availability of the additional credits.) Assuming that we begin from a point where there is no excess demand or supply in the system (equilibrium), borrowed sums can be used to secure producers' resources only by a process where prices of these inputs are bid up and attracted away from the producers who used them prior to the credit expansion. Although the initially lower rates of interest provide a competitive edge to capital-intensive processes, at first it is not obvious how new producers, who are creatures of the lower interest rates, would be in a position to outbid existing firms who operated profitably prior to the reduction in rates. Resources will be released, however, as established firms, in response to the fall in rates, shift expenditures from original factors to intermediate inputs. This movement will be reinforced by the rise in the prices of original factors of production. So there is a transition to more capital intensity in production.

This movement to longer production processes is not preceded by an increase in savings (or a reduction in consumption). Given production lags in the system, consumption would probably continue at pre–credit expansion levels for some time after the shift in production.[11] Eventually, however, output of final consumption goods will be reduced as the resource shift proceeds to higher levels of production. (Implicit in this is the idea that additional output emanating from the new investments does *not* appear in the market quickly enough to forestall the fall in output. This assumption stands on even stronger ground when we consider the likely increases in consumption demand accompanying the increase in income to producers and labor.)

Hayek points out, in the expression of what amounts to a version of the permanent income hypothesis, that the involuntary reduction in consumption (i.e., forced savings) will be resisted; people will attempt to maintain their desired consumption patterns and will allo-

11. Ibid., p. 88.

cate an increased share of income for that purpose. At the same time, entrepreneurs will find themselves with greater resources and expect increased profits, and wage income will be rising as a consequence of the expansion of investment. As the prices of consumer goods rise (because of shortfalls in output), these economic actors will devote some of their increased earnings to maintaining desired levels of consumption. This will exacerbate the initial rise in prices.

These trends will change the relationship between the demand for consumer goods and that for producer goods, in favor of the former. Relative prices will shift accordingly, and in the absence of a further credit expansion, production and investment will shift back toward shorter processes in the direction of satisfying the demand for consumer goods. Initially, it may be possible to support an expansion in both directions, with a continued expansion of domestic credit. But suh a process could not continue indefinitely.[12] With the cessation of the expansion of credit, the increase in expenditures on consumer goods is no longer accompanied by increased demand for producer goods.

But by this point in the process, the relative rise in the prices of consumer goods improves the position of producers of consumer goods in the market for factors of production and enables them to expand output by applying relatively more labor and original factors in proportion to capital in production. Although this increased demand for nonspecific factors of production will tend to increase their prices, the prices of intermediate goods devoted to earlier stages of production will tend to fall relative to costs. This movement in prices will cause "free capital" to move toward the now more profitable final consumption stages, earlier stages will become unprofitable, unemployment will rise, and prices will soften.

Hayek regards as impossible a scenario where, through the vehicle of forced savings and a continuing credit expansion, investment (production) expands and consumption is maintained without a rise in prices. This is because he sees no reason to believe that, given full employment, the increase in the supply of consumer goods will keep pace with the increase in the flow of income going to the markets for those goods. Although a credit expansion will ultimately lead to some increase in the output of consumer goods, this increase will lag significantly (since the period of production has increased) behind

12. Ibid., p. 90.

the increase in demand. Eventually, a general and rapid price inflation will be established.

A general inflation is *not* inevitable once credit is expanded, but the process will arrive at that point if the capital and structure of production established as a consequence of the forced savings are to be maintained without the help of voluntary savings.[13] It is the initial forced savings that promotes an artificial lengthening of production processes; this new structure of production will to some extent be reversed as soon as the cause of the forced savings disappears.

What emerges at this point in our discussion of Hayek's theory is a fairly extensive list of propositions that we regard as candidates for empirical examination. The first among these represents the inevitability of monetary fluctuations:

1. Changes in the supply of savings are independent of changes in the supply of bank credit.

If it is demonstrated that proposition 1 is true, this suggests, within the context of Hayek's scheme, that financial institutions will not be observed promptly adjusting rates of interest to changes in economic data. Underlying this proposition is a vision of the role of banks as intermediaries that partly serve to expedite the movement of funds from savers to investors, while tending to establish a supply-of-credit schedule that lies to the right of the supply-of-savings schedule and independent of the economic determinants that impinge on the supply of savings. (The supply-of-credit schedule should lie to the right of the supply-of-savings schedule, given the existence of a fractional reserve system.)

Given that the supply of credit is largely independent of real economic influences, we are led to the proposition that

2. Changes in the supply of credit lead changes in rates of interest. Furthermore, changes in credit and interest rates are inversely related.

Among the factors that will alter the supply of credit are structural changes in monetary policy (such as shifts in reserve requirements or in the discount rate), open-market operations of the monetary authority (changes in nonborrowed reserves), and changes in bank liquidity inspired by changes in the portfolio behavior of firms or households. These changes in the supply of credit will be distrib-

13. Ibid., p. 151.

uted by changes in interest rates: "Only at a lower rate of interest than formerly prevailing will it be possible to lend these funds, and how far the rate of interest will fall will depend upon the amount of the additional funds and the expectation of profits on the part of the entrepreneurs willing to expand their production."[14]

In Hayek's scheme, these two propositions represent the "causes or the necessity of the Trade Cycle." The existence of credit and the independence of its supply from the supply of savings are the factors that generate the cycle; when the supply of credit expands, rates of interest fall below their equilibria (which is determined by the supply of savings and investment demand), and we should be able to identify a Hayekian trade cycle. Indeed, "one must regard it [credit] rather as the new determining factor whose appearance causes deviations [from equilibrium positions] and whose effects must form our starting-point when deducing all those phenomena which can be observed in cyclical fluctuations. Only when we have succeeded in doing this can we claim to have explained the phenomena described."[15]

Let us suppose that proposition 1 receives no support from the data and that changes in the supply of savings cause changes in the supply of credit. Now, if we can verify the corollary proposition— that financial institutions promptly adjust interest rates to changes in economic data—then the primary route by which monetary influences are transmitted to the real economy is eliminated. If "real" savings alone determine the supply of credit, the potential for the nonneutrality of money reduces to the questions considered by Cantillon and Cairnes: Where, when, and by whom is additional specie or fiat money received in the economy? In this case, we are not quite living in a strict quantity theory world.

If the data admit proposition 1, we can turn to considering the propositions that describe a Hayekian credit-induced cycle. The first descriptive proposition revolves around relative output and credit:

3. Changes in the rate of change of credit lead changes in the output of producer goods.

Hayek indicates that it is not the relationship between changes in credit and changes in the price level that should be the subject of empirical investigation, but rather the relationship between "altera-

14. Ibid., p. 84.
15. Ibid., p. 88.

tions in the rate of increase and decrease" (acceleration) of bank credit and output in credit-sensitive industries.[16] A credit expansion accompanied by lower rates of interest should result in an expansion of investment activities. This is a necessary condition for forced savings to occur.

Accompanying the expansion in investment (for our purposes, expenditures on producers' equipment and structures) and the shift in resources from consumption to investment activities, relative prices would move. In particular:

4. The ratio of producer goods prices to consumer goods prices tends to *rise* after the initiation of a credit expansion.

With the expansion in the supply of credit, demand for investment goods rises relative to that for consumer goods. If we begin from a point of full employment, a first-round effect of the credit expansion will be that the prices of investment and producer goods relative to consumer goods will rise in response to the relatively increased demand for the former goods. This is a manifestation of the forced savings imposed on the economy as a result of the credit expansion.

As producer goods prices rise relative to consumer goods prices, relative prices shift within the hierarchy of producer goods. The closer a product or input is to a final consumer good, the greater the impact of the initial relative decline in the demand for final consumer goods. The price of intermediate products will decline relative to the prices of the producer goods and inputs that are not specifically dedicated to the production of the final consumer good. A subsidiary proposition to proposition 4 is:

5. The prices of producer goods closest to final consumption tend to decline relative to the prices of producer goods further away from the consumer good in the production scheme.

The phenomena described in propositions 4 and 5 will occur in the case of either a credit expansion (and forced savings) or an autonomous increase in savings. In the latter case, the shifts in relative prices and resources tend to be permanent and self-perpetuating. Here, the initial decline in interest rates accompanying the increase in the supply of savings corresponds to a new relationship between the demand for (prices of) current consumer and future investment and producer

16. Ibid., pp. 235–38.

goods; output and prices will adjust to reflect the lower rates of interest. The movement to defer consumption will allow the lengthening of production processes, and the ultimate relative price vectors will correspond to the new vector of interest rates if the expectations of entrepreneurs are accurate.[17] In the case where the process is initiated by a credit expansion and the savings required to support the initial resource and price shifts are forced on the economy, those shifts will tend to be reversed.

A second-round effect of forced savings, and a development that distinguishes forced savings from an autonomous increase in savings, is that prices of consumer goods will begin to rise relative to investment goods, reversing the original broad movement. The appropriate proposition is:

6. The prices of consumer goods rise relative to the prices of producer goods, reversing the initial shift in relative prices.

The false movement of resources toward investment and producer goods and away from consumer goods that accompanies the credit expansion proves to be unsupported by any increase in the supply of savings. Consumers will bid up the prices of consumer goods in an effort to maintain desired consumption patterns, and there will be additional upward pressure from labor and entrepreneurs, who receive more income and resources as a result of the initial expansion in income. Further, it is unlikely, given production lags, that the increase in consumer demand will be relieved by any increase in the output of consumer goods derived from the initial increase in producer goods and investment. So, without a continuing increase in the rate of credit expansion, relative prices will shift in favor of consumer goods.

Concomitant with the reversal in relative prices, resources (including labor) will shift toward consumption sectors. Nonspecific capital, especially raw materials, will move away from distant investment toward consumption sectors, and labor, to the extent it is mobile, will similarly shift.

This movement of factors toward consumption in response to relative price shifts is a manifestation of the Ricardo Effect, where "a rise in the price of the product (or a fall in real wages) will lead to the use of relatively less machinery and other capital and of relatively

17. See Wainhouse, *Hayek's Theory*, pp. 20, 22.

more direct labor in the production of any given quantity of output."[18] (For Hayek, the real wage is the ratio of the nominal wage to the price of the good being produced. This is the relevant real wage for labor demand. The ratio of nominal wages to the prices of goods being consumed is the real wage relevant for labor supply.) The Ricardo Effect occurs in the neighborhood of the peak of the Hayekian cycle, where, as consumption demand rises, the prices of consumer goods and of capital goods specific to the stages of production nearest final output will rise relative to current wages; the result is a decline in the real wage. As real wages fall in the consumer goods industries, there will be a substitution of labor for capital and of less labor-saving capital for more labor-saving capital goods. At this point any increase in the demand for consumer goods will result in a *decrease* in investment. (This is an alternative expression of the Ricardo Effect.)

Ultimately, we should observe a movement of labor toward consumer goods industries, and unemployment rates should increase in capital goods and decrease in consumer goods and services. This leads to the proposition that:

7. Toward the end of a Hayekian trade cycle, unemployment should increase first in producer goods industries and then, with some lag, in consumer goods industries.

The dynamics of the Ricardo Effect are that generalized unemployment begins with unemployment in the producer goods industries. As the incomes of the factors of production (labor and capital) previously employed declines, the demand for output begins to weaken. Consumer demand and prices also begin to weaken. With the Ricardo Effect, as consumer demand falls and is accompanied by a decline in the prices of consumer goods relative to nominal wages, the Hayekian real wage rises. Given the increase in these real wages, at some point in this process it would pay to substitute capital for labor. Thus, there is a tendency, contained within the cyclical process, toward a cyclical recovery as the production of capital goods again becomes profitable.[19] (It should be noted that Hayek accepted the notion of wage stickiness; indeed, he envisioned a scenario where

18. Friedrich A. Hayek, *Profits, Interest and Investment and Other Essays on the Theory of Industrial Fluctuations* (Clifton, N.J.: A.M. Kelley, 1975), p. 10.

19. Gerald P. O'Driscoll, Jr., *Economics as a Coordination Problem: The Contributions of Friedrich A. Hayek* (Kansas City: Sheed, Andrews and McMeel, 1977), pp. 112 ff.

real wages might rise to such an extent that the recovery would begin with no improvement in the distribution and arrangement of capital in the economy.)[20]

Although the Ricardo Effect demonstrates the impact of changes in the demand for consumer goods on investment through changes in relative prices *independent* of the existence of credit markets, its chief significance arises in connection with a credit (or money) economy. Here, the distortion in the equilibrium structure of relative prices determined by real factors, which occurs through the influence of changes in the quantity of credit (money), results in investment in excess of voluntary savings (i.e., forced savings). This malinvestment persists as long as the acceleration in money continues.[21] It is the gradient in relative prices in favor of investment goods that encourages investment in favor of, and in a pattern counter to, what would prevail in equilibrium.

At the denouement of this process, when the increase in investment expenditures ceases, prices of investment goods will fall, whereas prices of consumer goods will continue to rise. As a result, investments made under the expansionary regime will become less profitable than before. And throughout this process, "the controlling factor will thus be that, after the inflow of new money has ceased and, in consequence, smaller funds are available for investment, the prices of consumer goods will continue to rise for some time. The result will be that some of the factors which during the boom will have become committed to producing very capital intensive equipment will become unemployed."[22]

For Hayek, the Ricardo Effect is the mechanism that generates the decline in investment, which in turn ends the inflationary expansion. Shifts in relative prices are the principal engine pulling the economy through the Hayekian cycle; the Ricardo Effect stands as a slogan for propositions 4 through 7.

The shifts in relative prices that generate the Ricardo Effect produce a rise in the rate of profit in consumer goods industries and assure that a higher rate of return can be earned on labor (because of the fall in real wages) than on investment in capital (machinery).

20. Hayek, *Profits, Interest and Investment*, pp. 62–63 et seq.

21. Friedrich A. Hayek, "Three Elucidations of the Ricardo Effect," *Journal of Political Economy* 77 (March–April 1969), p. 169.

22. Ibid., p. 174.

This will cause a tendency to apply more labor with existing capital, and output will be produced with relatively more labor and less capital.[23] So, in the neighborhood of the cycle peak, we should observe:

8. Employment will expand in consumer goods industries as relatively more labor resources are applied both in response to the fall in real wages and in an effort to satisfy consumer demand.

This proposition is a companion to proposition 7; both describe the results of the Ricardo Effect and the state of the economy at the end of an expansionary phase.

As a refinement of the analysis in *Prices and Production*, the emphasis in *Profits, Interest and Investment* is on the role of raw materials as factors (costs) of production. Accompanying the increase in demand for consumer goods (a second-round effect of forced savings) is an increase in demand for raw materials (circulating, non-specific capital) as inputs in the production of consumer goods. To the extent that raw materials are complementary to labor-saving, durable equipment, industries where such capital is concentrated will face a shortage of these complementary factors as they are attracted to later stages of the production of consumer goods in response to shifts in relative prices and profits. During the later stages of the cycle, in the neighborhood of the cycle peak, a scarcity of raw materials occurs, and "raw materials prices rise more than the prices of consumers' goods."[24] We are led to the proposition that

9. Around the cycle peak, inflation in raw materials prices will exceed that in consumer goods prices.

Ultimately, it is the shortage of raw materials (circulating capital) that invalidates the investment in producers' plant and equipment made earlier during the expansion phase of the cycle. The decline in real wages encourages this process, as circulating is substituted for fixed (labor-saving) capital.

The propositions developed here describe the expansionary phase and upper turning point of the business cycle, where "the transition to more capitalistic methods of production takes place during periods of low interest rates [low rates of profit] and bring about the boom,"

---

23. Hayek, *Profits, Interest and Investment*, pp. 13–15.
24. Ibid., p. 29.

and "the transition to less capitalistic methods of production is caused by the high rates of interest [profit] and brings about the depression."[25] ("Rates of interest" is the terminology of *Prices and Production*; "rates of profit" is that of *Profits, Interest and Investment.*) Again, Hayek emphasizes:

> We might get the trade cycle even without changes in the rate of interest. We have seen that if the rate of interest fails to keep investment within the bounds determined by people's willingness to save, a rise in the rate of profit in the industries near consumption will in the end act in a way very similar to that in which the rate of interest is supposed to act, because a rise in the rate of profit beyond a certain point will bring about a decrease in investment just as an increase in the rate of interest might do.[26]

For Hayek, the role of the rate of interest is to ensure that investment and voluntary savings are kept in approximate equilibrium; as a condition of this equilibrium, rates of profit are equalized across industries and are equal to the rate of interest. If the rate of profit changes in the system, investment should change in different industries until profit rates are equalized. But since rates of interest do not immediately respond to changes in economic data (savings and investment), movements in rates of profit will fill the role of interest rates.

This does not mean that interest rates disappear from the analysis. Rather, they "ultimately follow the movements of the rate of profit."[27] And though the rise in profit rates would alone induce a turning point, as a practical matter the rise in the rate of interest will bring this effect about before the rate of profit rises sufficiently. But given this analysis, interest rates lose their value as guides for investment decisions: "If in fact movements of the rate of interest follow at a distance behind the movements of the rate of profit, and if in addition the total amplitude of fluctuations in interest rates is much smaller than the amplitude of fluctuations in the rate of profit, the rate of interest would indeed in many fields cease to be a major consideration in deciding investment policy."[28]

To the extent that we could adequately measure rates of profit, this quotation would stand as an additional testable proposition. It

25. Ibid., p. 39.
26. Ibid., p. 64.
27. Ibid., p. 65.
28. Ibid., p. 67.

represents one of the principal themes of Hayek's theory of the trade cycle: Interest rates often do not convey accurate information regarding the real economy. It is a serious indictment of modern rational expectations theory.

To produce acceptable tests of the causal structure contained in Hayek's theory of the trade cycle requires charting a delicate course between the Scylla of theory without measurement and the Charybdis of measurement without theory, the twin perils of causality testing.[29]

Within the constellation of available tests of causality, Granger's (1969, 1980) notion of causality—to the extent that it requires neither the "true" model (e.g., Basmann 1963) nor controllability (e.g., Strotz and Wold 1960)—seems to offer the best prospects for practical implementation. The concept of causality we will pursue is based on an appeal to generalization, not universality, and thus we will be testing for local rather than global causality within the context of Hayek's imaginative model.

EMPIRICAL TESTS OF THE HAYEKIAN THEORY

Here the results of the empirical tests of propositions 1 through 6 are presented and discussed. The first section concentrates on propositions 1, 2, and 3, relating to the tests for the G^*-causal relationships contained in time series measures of credit, savings, rates of interest, and various measures of the output of producer goods.[30] The second section examines propositions 4, 5, and 6, relating to expected movements in relative prices in the neighborhood of the onset of a domestic credit expansion. Following a discussion of the methodology for identifying the onset of a credit expansion from the relevant time series, seventy-seven relative prices are evaluated with respect to their actual versus expected movements after the onset of a credit expansion.

The data used are monthly series for the period January 1959 through June 1981. Monthly observations provide a wider window

29. See Arnold Zellner, "Causality and Econometrics" (Paper for a joint University of Rochester–Carnegie Mellon University conference, April 1978).

30. Definitions of and tests for G^*-causal relationships are discussed in the chapter Appendix.

than quarterly averages for observing movements of the time series, especially the movements of relative prices in response to a credit expansion. The preservation of information also argues for the use of the highest frequency data; stochastic movements, the lifeblood of time series analysis, can be masked by the smoothing associated with quarterly averages of monthly observations.

The choice of January 1959 as the starting point for the data is dictated by considerations of the availability of the series; the selection of a suitable end point for the analysis period is more problematic. Virtually any choice can be regarded as objectionable. During the 1970s and 1980s, we face a long list of potential distortions of the data. Prominent among these are the Nixon wage and price controls (August 1971–April 1974), the Smithsonian Agreement (1971), the first (1973–74) and second (1979–80) OPEC oil price shocks, the shifts in Federal Reserve operating policy (October 1979 and October 1982), and the Carter credit controls (1980). Clearly these structural shifts and exogenous shocks are an integral part of the economic terrain, but it is not clear that one can or should purify the data (using, e.g., dummy variables) to eliminate the influence of these shocks. One can, however, be mindful of these events when interpreting the empirical results.

As an end point, June 1981 seems sufficiently far from the end of the 1980 National Bureau of Economic Research business cycle (July 1980) and the beginning of the current (1981–83) economic cycle to avoid ending the analysis period in mid-cycle.

With the exception of the interest rates, all the data are seasonally adjusted, either by the issuing agency or by applying the Bureau of the Census's X–11 seasonal adjustment technique. Although the standard seasonal adjustment performed on official statistics—equivalent to a filtering process—can introduce distortion into a series by tending toward an overadjustment of the series,[31] the wide variety of alternative methods for deseasonalizing time series and the issue of the impact of the chosen method on the spectral characteristics of the series argues for the appropriateness of seasonal adjustment to be evaluated case by case.[32] For the purposes of this study, the availability of the data dictates that we operate on seasonally adjusted data

31. A.C. Harvey, *Time Series Models* (New York: Halstead Press, 1981), pp. 176–78. This would be evident from comparisons of the spectra of the unadjusted and the adjusted series.

32. Ibid., p. 81.

while remaining aware of the possible distortions of the results arising from the adjustment process.

With respect to the form of the data, an important issue to be addressed is whether the data should be used in nominal or inflation-
adjusted (real) terms. Although Hayek does not explicitly distinguish
between real and nominal aggregates, guidance about the appropriate
form of the data can be extracted from the context.

Proposition 1 examines the relationship between credit and savings, both considered in nominal terms. At issue here is whether the
banking system, in its capacity as supplier of credit, is seen to respond to changes in "real" economic data (the supply of savings).
Within this context, "real" is not intended to represent deflated,
constant-currency-unit time series data. As used by Hayek, "real"
economic data are rather the realizations of "the rigid reaction-
mechanisms of barter economy" and are associated with the inter-
dependence and absolute determinateness of a closed system of equilibrium.[33] In this, they are the data of a Walrasian general equilibrium system, although natural market forces, which would tend to
equilibrate supply and demand, are seen as susceptible to being dis-
turbed by a credit expansion.[34]

For the relationships examined in proposition 1 (credit–savings)
and proposition 2 (credit–interest rates), the time series used are
measured (current dollar) data. In proposition 3 (credit–output of
producer goods), the output data are Federal Reserve Board industrial production indices, which measure industry output in physical
units (e.g., tons, kilowatt hours, etc.).

$G*$-Causal Relationships[35]

Following the methodology outlined above, propositions 1, 2, and 3
were tested for $G*$-causality—Granger's (1980) predictability-based
test for causality (see the chapter Appendix). Proposition 1 relates
to the inevitability of monetary fluctuations:

33. Hayek, *Monetary Theory*, p. 86.
34. Ibid., p. 87. The conventional real-nominal distinction is designed to purify data of a
price inflation component; for Hayek, "real" has an equilibrium connotation that is absent
from modern usage.
35. Definitions of and tests for $G*$-causal relationships are discussed in the chapter
Appendix.

1. Changes in the supply of savings are independent of changes in the supply of bank credit.

Seven alternative measures of both savings and credit were considered and tested.[36] The supply of savings referred to in proposition 1 is a measure of desired (or real, in the sense discussed above) consumer savings, and the series considered are alternative proxies for this aggregate. These series occupy two broad categories. The National Income Accounts (NIA) definitions are based on the residual given by disposable personal income less personal outlays, whereas the Federal Reserve aggregates are based on savings and time deposits at financial institutions.

The supply of credit to which Hayek refers in expositions of his theory of the trade cycle should be construed as commercial bank credit. The series Commercial and Industrial Loans (CILNS) and Commercial and Industrial Loans and Commercial Paper (CIACP) are based on commercial and industrial loans at commercial banks, whereas the Loans and Investments (LISTR) is a broader aggregate that includes, besides commercial and industrial loans, real estate, agricultural, and lease financing loans at all commercial banks. (All the series were prefiltered for stationarity by taking first differences.)

To test for the independence of savings and credit, the appropriate null hypotheses are:

H_0: Δ Savings does not G^*-cause Δ Credit, and

H_0: Δ Credit does not G^*-cause Δ Savings.

The calculated F-values and results of the F-tests for these hypotheses uniformly support the notion that changes in savings do not G^*-cause changes in credit. The null hypothesis is accepted at both the 1 percent and 5 percent significance levels for all measures of credit and savings tested (twenty-one trials).

With respect to the G^*-causal relationship between changes in credit and changes in savings, the null hypothesis is *accepted* for the personal savings and deposits series. Rejection of H_0 seems to be associated only with the addition of personal consumption expenditures (PCE) on durable goods to the savings series. This result is not

---

36. Charts and tables giving descriptions of the data and detailed results of the empirical tests are available from the author.

unreasonable and likely derives from the extent to which PCE on durable goods are financed. Thus, with this lone exception, proposition 1 receives broad support from the data, and the results of the F-tests confirm that changes in credit are statistically independent of changes in savings.

Given that changes in credit are insulated from changes in personal savings and, as Hayek notes, are motivated principally by monetary policy and considerations of bank liquidity, we next consider the relationship between credit and rates of interest, where the proposition to be examined is:

2. Changes in the supply of credit lead changes in rates of interest. Furthermore, changes in credit and interest rates are inversely related.

The measures of credit here are the same as those evaluated for proposition 1, although the rates of interest used represent the entire term structure and government and private financial instruments. (With respect to the stationarity of the interest rate series, first differences seem to provide a satisfactory filter.)

For purposes of testing the first part of proposition 2, the relevant null hypothesis is given by:

H_0: Δ Credit does not G^*-cause Δ Rate of Interest.

The calculated F-statistics and results of the F-tests provide strong corroborating evidence that changes in credit lead, in a G^*-causal sense, changes in rates of interest. The null hypothesis is rejected at both the 1 percent and 5 percent levels for fifty-five of the fifty-seven cases, (three measures of credit, nineteen interest rates) and at the 5 percent level for the remaining cases. In addition, the causality is evidently unidirectional.

To confirm that the G^*-causality is unidirectional, we test the proposition that changes in rates do not G^*-cause changes in credit. Happily, the F-tests result in acceptance of the null hypothesis in all fifty-seven cases.

To investigate whether changes in credit and interest rates are inversely related—such that when credit expands, rates of interest tend to fall—we evaluate the sign of the coefficient on the credit variable from the impulse response form at lag 1 of the autoregressive, moving average (ARMA) representation of the bivariate state space model.

The impulse response form describes the dynamics of the system in terms of distributed lags and captures the impact of past instruments on the system.[37] The impulse response matrix combines the AR and MA coefficients at corresponding lags. Interpreting the AR coefficients as representing the "structure" of the system and the MA coefficients the effects of shocks on the system, the impulse response form provides a convenient means of observing the impact of variables on the system. The signs on the coefficients from the impulse response matrix are all positive and suggest that the credit series used records the demand for credit rather than the supply. However, to verify that we are operating with measures of demand, we examine the coefficient on the interest rate variable from the impulse response form of the appropriate bivariate model. If this is negative, then we may conclude that the credit series do measure demand; if these coefficients tend to be positive, this may be taken as evidence that we are dealing with a supply relationship.

The majority of the signs (thirty-eight of fifty-seven) are positive, suggesting that as rates rise, credit rises—a supply response. The mixed results regarding the signs from the impulse response matrix suggest that the credit series used in the analysis represent realizations of the interaction of supply *and* demand. There seems to be some evidence that, with respect to the nature of the credit variables, we are dealing with a classical identification problem.

Both propositions 1 and 2 receive significant support from the data, and we next consider the first of the propositions describing a credit-induced trade cycle. Proposition 3 is an assertion of non-neutrality and involves the relationship between output and credit:

3. Changes in the rate of change of credit lead changes in the output of producer goods.

The associated null hypothesis is:

H_0: $\Delta \% \Delta$ Credit does not G^*-cause Δ Output of Producer Goods.

The measures of output of producer goods considered are nondefense new orders for capital goods (1972 dollars) and thirty-nine Federal Reserve Board industrial production indexes (IPI).

Following Hayek, we expect to observe, among the forty measures of the output of producer goods examined, an association between the credit sensitivity of an industry and its causal relationship to

---

37. Masanao Aoki, *Optimal Control and System Theory in Dynamic Economic Analysis* (New York: North-Holland, 1976), pp. 47–48.

accelerations in credit. The expected relationship between accelerations in credit and changes in the output of producers' goods obtains in 102 of the 120 cases examined (85 percent). In only three production categories—nondurable goods, textile, paper and chemicals, and paper and paper products—does the evidence indicate that an acceleration in the measures of credit considered fail to G^*-cause changes in output. While at first glance this suggests that these three industries are not sensitive to credit, we must be mindful of the fact that the range of alternatives to the hypothesis specifically tested is so large that there is an enormous number of explanations other than immunity to credit changes which may be valid.

But, absent further detailed investigation of these cases, it is clear that the weight of the evidence supports proposition 3, that is, unidirectional causality runs from credit to output. (Some evidence of bidirectional causality emerges from our interrogation of the data, nineteen of the twenty-one industries considered display bidirectional causality. A suitable explanation of these results requires a detailed investigation of the credit–output relationship for each industry. This would entail an evaluation of the industry- or firm-specific production process, the organization and structure of the industry, and the relationship of the industry to sources of credit, such as access to the commercial paper market.)

Expected Movements in Relative Prices

Having demonstrated that there is strong evidence from the time series to support Hayek's assertions regarding the monetary causes of cyclical fluctuations, we turn now to consider the dynamics of a Hayekian trade cycle. Here, we will test propositions 4, 5, and 6.

Prior to evaluating the behavior of the data with respect to this set of propositions, we must identify periods of credit expansion. Using the approach discussed in Wainhouse (1982), we identified the credit expansion starting points from the monthly data. Interestingly, of the six points of credit expansion (local credit troughs) identified in Table 2-1, only one— 1970: 6 (A) appears to coincide with an NBER business cycle (peak December 1969, trough November 1970). The remaining points predate NBER business cycle troughs by one and a half to three years.

Table 2-1.   Credit Expansion Starting Points.

Credit Series	Episode	Onset of Expansion
CILNS and CIACP	I	October 1964
	II	June 1968
	III	September 1972
	IV	July 1977
LISTR	A	June 1970
	B	September 1976

Propositions 4, 5, and 6 relate to the movements of relative prices after the initiation of a credit expansion. To trace these important dynamics of relative prices, simple averages of the first differences of each relative price are calculated and plotted. For each episode, six averages are calculated. The first represents the period immediately before the onset of the identified credit expansion, defined as beginning twenty-four months after the preceding episode for cases II, III, IV, and B; for I and A, the first average is based on the entire preceding period starting with the first observation. Within each credit expansion, the five remaining averages of the changes in relative price are calculated, where t is the month corresponding to the onset of the expansion, for the periods $t + 3$, $t + 6$, $t + 12$, $t + 18$, and $t + 24$.

These intervals were arrived at by inspecting the movements in each of the relative prices at and in the neighborhood of the onset of credit expansion. The intervals of three, six, twelve, eighteen, and twenty-four months accommodate most of the observed lags in movement relative to the onset and should allow the dynamics of price shifts to become manifest.

Using this approach, we investigate proposition 4, which relates to the dynamics of the ratio of producer prices to consumer prices:

4. The ratio of producer goods prices to consumer goods prices tends to *rise* after the initiation of a credit expansion.

The measure of consumer goods prices used is the Bureau of Labor Statistics' (BLS) consumer price index (CPI) for all items for urban consumers, seasonally adjusted (1967 = 100). The BLS's producer price indexes (PPI) for a wide range of stages of processing and commodity groupings are used as measures of producer goods.

If the relative price of producer to consumer goods tends to rise after the initiation of a credit expansion, we should see the plotted means rise. (If the average increases, the marginal observations are higher, on average, than the previous average of the observations.) Of the 162 cases examined—6 credit expansion episodes, 27 relative prices—the expected pattern is coincident with, or shows a lag with respect to, the onset of a credit expansion in 110 instances. Of the 52 cases in which the relative price displays no evidence of rising in the neighborhood (up to twenty-four months after the onset) of a credit expansion, 26 occur in cases A and B, with 19 in B. In episode B, only 8 of 27 relative prices (5 with a lag) show the expected pattern, suggesting that this episode may be misidentified as a point of credit expansion.

Proposition 5 relates to movements of relative *producer* prices. This asserts that the closer a product or commodity is to final consumption, the greater the impact of the initial decline in demand for consumption goods. In addition, the prices of those intermediate products will decline relative to the prices of producer goods not specifically dedicated to the production of final consumption goods. Proposition 5, auxiliary to proposition 4, reads:

5. The prices of producer goods closest to final consumption tend to decline relative to the prices of producer goods further away from the consumer good in the production scheme.

Before examining this proposition, we must distinguish between producer goods prices located close to (PPIN) and far from (PPIF) final consumption. Fifty relative prices—PPIN/PPIF—are examined for their movements in the neighborhood of each of the points of credit expansion. Conformity with proposition 5 requires that the prices of producer goods closest to final consumption *decline* relative to the prices of producer goods further away from final consumption. Among the PPIN are those for finished consumer goods, various categories of machinery and equipment, whereas the PPIF includes PPIs for, among other things, crude materials, metals, construction materials, and industrial commodities.

Following the same approach used in the analysis of relative prices in proposition 4, we compute averages of the first differences for each of fifty relative prices within each of the six identified points of credit expansion. Of the 300 cases examined, 213 conform to the behavior predicted by proposition 5, either coinciding with (145) or lagging behind (68) the onset of the credit expansion. Of the 87 cases in which PPIN/PPIF fails to move as expected, 59 occur in episodes A and B. In this case, as with proposition 4, these episodes are problem children. Overall, based on our small sample, the performances of the PPIN/PPIF, classified both by credit expansion and relative price category, provide general support for proposition 5.

The demonstrated confirmation of propositions 4 and 5 is, in Hayek's paradigm, consistent with either a credit expansion (and forced savings) or an autonomous increase in savings. In the latter case, the shifts in relative prices tend to be permanent and self-perpetuating, whereas in the former case, where the savings needed to maintain the first-round price shifts initially are enforced on the economy, those shifts will tend to be reversed.

A second-round effect of the credit expansion process, and a development that distinguishes forced savings from an autonomous increase in savings, is that prices of consumer goods will begin to rise relative to prices of producer goods, reversing the initial movement (described in proposition 4). The appropriate hypothesis is:

6. The prices of consumer goods rise relative to the prices of producers' goods, reversing the initial shift in relative prices.

If proposition 6 is supported by the data, we should observe that the averages of the first differences of the evaluated relative prices assume a parabolic shape. Examining the same set of relative prices used in proposition 4, we find that the expected quadratic curve is evident in 89 of the 162 cases, and of these 89, 14 show a lag with respect to the onset of the credit expansion, whereas 75 seem to be coincident. (As we have observed with respect to propositions 4 and 5, the cases where the relative prices fail to show the expected movement are concentrated in credit expansions A and B.) We conclude that, in general, the data seem to support proposition 6, and there is evidence that there has been a forced savings phenomenon in the United States, associated especially with credit expansion episodes I (October 1964 to 1967) and IV (July 1977 to 1980).

CONCLUSIONS

Given the empirical results presented above, we find substantial evidence in U.S. postwar economic time series that confirms propositions consistent with an Austrian theory of the trade cycle. So far as the six propositions examined are a valid representation and description of an Austrian theory of the trade cycle, they pass one of Hayek's falsification tests: The phenomena they explain do seem to correspond with observed facts.[38] Testing the statistical waters, the Hayekian paradigm seems as though it will float. And these are rough, twentieth-century waters. Hayek emphasizes that "this theory never claimed to do more than account for the upper turning point of the *typical nineteenth-century business cycle.*"[39]

To make further progress in this broad-brush empirical examination of Hayek's theory of the trade cycle requires the identification of *Hayekian* trade cycles and associated turning points. (The expansionary phase of a Hayekian cycle is characterized by the transition to more capitalistic methods of production, whereas the "depression" is brought about by the transition to less capitalistic methods of production.) As a first approximation, one might consider a Hayekian trade cycle as matching credit cycles, but the operation of Hayekian cumulative effects would likely make the assumption of correspondence between credit and trade cycles a heroic one.[40] Alternatively, one might interpret NBER business cycles as representing Hayekian trade cycles, in which case the issue of the lag between identified credit cycles and neighboring NBER cycles would need to be addressed. The location of Hayekian trade cycles, with their emphasis on periods of production, would require a significant research effort.

After identifying Hayekian trade cycles and associated turning points, the balance of the research agenda set out in the first part of this paper could be pursued. The remaining propositions focus on the results of the Ricardo Effect. Specifically, proposition 7 discusses the timing of changes in unemployment rates in producer versus consumer goods sectors in the neighborhood of the Hayekian cycle peak, and proposition 8 deals with movements of labor resources across sectors in response to a decline in Hayekian real wages. Proposition 9 is a statement on the relative rates of inflation in raw materials versus consumer prices in the neighborhood of a cycle peak. (Note that although we have not formally tested this set of propositions, to the extent that movements in real resources are concomitant with

38. See Hayek, *Monetary Theory*, pp. 32–33.

39. Hayek, "Elucidations of the Ricardo Effect," p. 282 (emphasis added).

40. Friedrich A. Hayek, *The Pure Theory of Capital* (Chicago: Midway Reprint, University Press, 1941), pp. 34–35.

changes in relative prices, the results on relative price movements—propositions 4–6—do suggest support for propositions 7–9.)

Finally, incorporating Hayek's insights into a full model of the trade cycle requires that attention be given to the process underlying the formation of expectations, the relationship between equilibria and realizations of plans, and the twin issues of who gets additional money or credit (Cantillon effects) and how it is transmitted through the economy (distribution effects). Accomplishing this, one could then proceed to trace the impact of a credit (monetary) expansion on the specified system and verify the predictions from Hayek's theory. In conducting this research program, one could begin with changes in the demand for consumer relative to producer goods and proceed to examine the effects on the prices of individual goods and rates of interest, or one could begin with changes in rates of interest resulting from the change in the demand for producer goods and derive the associated changes in prices.[41] Our empirical tests and interrogation of the data conducted and reported in this study suggest that the returns on the investment required for this major modeling effort are likely to be large.

The returns on investment in modeling would take the form of new insights into the operation of the economic system, especially the interdependencies among sectors and the impact of what evidently is distinctly nonneutral money and credit on the structure of output. These insights would, in turn, require a different perspective on the applicability of the quantity theory as a guide to monetary policy.

From the perspective of the history of neutrality of money, Hayek's theory stands in the tradition of Cantillon, Thornton, Cairnes, and Wicksell, and our empirical investigation should be considered a success if it delivers the stimulus provided by the indication of new problems and a reminder of old but timeless ones:

> See, I pray you, what money can do.[42]
> —Titus Maecius Plautus (254–184 B.C.), *Stichus*

---

41. Hayek, *Prices and Production*, pp. 74–75.
42. Titus Maecius Plautus, *Stichus* (Cambridge, Mass.: Harvard University Press), act II, scene 2.

APPENDIX
G^*-CAUSAL RELATIONSHIPS: DEFINITIONS AND TESTS

Granger's definition of and tests for causality rely on (1) the stochastic nature of the variables and (2) the direction of the flow of time (i.e., the future cannot cause the past). His definitions of causality, feedback, instantaneous causality, and causality lag assume that only stationary series are involved. (In the case of nonstationary series, the existence and direction of causality can change over time.) The operational notion of causality—given objections regarding (1) the scope of the information set, (2) the optimization criterion, and (3) the linear arrangement of the process—reduces to "linear causality in mean with respect to a specified set D."[43] The criterion for the determination of causality that Granger sets and that has been adopted in the econometrics literature is based entirely on the predictability of a particular series given the absence or presence of some other relevant series.

Granger (1980) modified his earlier (1969) definition of causality, partly in response to the criticisms raised by Zellner (1978), and takes a distinctly time series perspective with respect to the implementation of tests for causality. He appeals to three axioms as the foundation for the definition of causality:

Axiom A. The past and present may cause the future, but the future cannot cause the past.

Axiom B. Ω_n (the "universal" information set) contains no redundant information, so that if some variable Z_n is functionally related to one or more other variables, in a deterministic fashion, then Z_n should be excluded from Ω_n.

Axiom C. All causal relationships remain constant in direction through time.[44]

And, assuming these axioms obtain, Granger offers six definitions of causality. The first three require consideration of the entire distribution of some series X_{n+1}, and the last three revolve around point forecasts using a least-squares criterion. It is this last set that is germane to our discussion:

43. C.W.J. Granger, "Investigating Causal Relations by Econometric Models and Cross-Spectral Methods," *Econometrica* 37, no. 3 (1969): 428.

44. C.W.J. Granger, "Testing for Causality: A Personal Viewpoint," *Journal of Economic Dynamics and Control* 2, no. 4 (November 1980): 330, 335.

Definition 4. Y_n is said *not to cause* X_{n+1} *in mean* with respect to J'_n if: $\delta_{n+1}(J'_{n0}) = E[X_{n+1} \mid J'_n] - E[X_{n+1} \mid J_n]$ is identically zero.

Definition 5. If $\delta_{n+1}(\Omega_n)$ is not zero, then Y_n is said to *cause* X_{n+1} *in mean*.

Definition 6. If $\delta_{n+1}(J'_n)$ is not identically zero, then Y_n is said to be a *prima facie cause in mean* of X_{n+1} with respect to J'_n.[45]

As Granger points out, causality in mean is less stringent than full causality but has the virtue of being operational. (Full Granger causality relies on knowledge of the universal information set and the distribution characteristics of the series under investigation.) Granger reformulated definition 6 to consider the variances of the one-step forecast error. Where $\sigma^2(X \mid J_n)$ is the variance of the one-step forecast error of X_{n+1} given J_n, and $\sigma^2(X \mid J_n, Y)$ is the variance of X_{n+1} given the expanded information set J_n plus Y, then the definition of causality is:

Granger causality: Y is a prima facie cause of X with respect to J_n plus Y if $\sigma^2(X \mid J_n, Y) < \sigma^2(X \mid J_n)$.

Granger further modifies this definition to account for the time series techniques used to generate the forecasts as a linear function of the information set by adding "linear" to "prima facie cause." After introducing one additional axiom to Granger's set, we will adopt this definition of causality as the foundation of our empirical tests of Hayek's theory.

The axiom we wish to consider derives from Feigl's (1953) definition of causation: "The clarified (purified) concept of causation is defined in terms of *predictability according to a law* (or, more adequately, according to a set of laws)."[46] The notion that the criterion of predictability should be tied to a set of laws is what we will add to Granger's definition. Although this requires little more than specifying that the choice of J_n and Y be based on some theory, it is important to the extent that it helps us avoid the problem of measurement without theory. Thus, we propose:

45. Ibid., p. 337.

46. Herbert Feigl, "Notes on Causality," in H. Feigl and M. Brodback, eds., *Readings in the Philosophy of Science* (New York: Appleton-Century-Crofts, 1953), p. 408. As an epistemological note, the purification to which Feigl refers was achieved largely by Galileo and Hume and consisted of the elimination of unconfirmable—metaphysical—connotations of causality, such as the teleological, animistic and rationalistic, or entailment concepts.

Axiom D.   The choice of the information set(s) and time series considered as the conditional environment within which an empirical test of causality is conducted is based on economic theory.

This axiom stands as a caveat regarding an important pitfall of practical applications of empirical tests of causality. Realistically, an entire *set* of conditions represents the cause of an event, and one would hope to be able to isolate this relevant set for use in testing the validity of a proposed causal relationship. Practically, this may be an infeasible task; ultimately, the analyst will select, from what will be a virtually inexhaustible supply, those factors that seem most relevant. In addition, one generally relies on an examination of causality in a bivariate setting because of the well-known difficulty of making an unambiguous statistical determination of the causal structure in a multivariate setting without strict orthogonality among the regressors. Therefore, as a practical matter, axiom D is required for the implementation of tests of causality.

Granger skirts this issue in distinguishing between his definitions of what may be called strong-form causality and weak-form (prima facie) causality (definitions 4–6). Axiom D formally integrates the strategy for selecting among the alternative causes of an event using empirical tests.

Following Feigl, we can consider a still less stringent formulation of causality that appeals to a limit process. This would leave us with the notion of asymptotic causality, where the closer an actual condition—or cause—approximates the conceived condition, the more the actual effect will approximate the stylized effect.[47] This is an attractive notion, and it can be argued that, given a stochastic environment, and the problem of plurality of causes, Granger-causal tests are implicitly asymptotic tests.

Modified by axiom D, Granger's predictability-based test for causality (which we will call G^*-causality), seems to be consistent with the notion of causality used in the philosophy of science,[48] and we propose to investigate the G^*-causal content of Hayek's theory of the trade cycle using time series methods to model the relevant series.

47. Ibid.
48. See Feigl, "Notes on Causality," especially pp. 411–16; and see Adolf Grunbaum, "Causality and the Science of Human Behavior," in Feigl and Brodback, eds., *Readings in the Philosophy of Science*, pp. 766–78.

There remains, however, the issue of addressing the problems associated with implementing tests for G^*-causality using time series analysis.

Among these, the thorniest derives from using univariate and multivariate (bivariate) autoregressive–moving average (ARMA) models as the vehicles for generating forecasts and comparing the summary statistics from these models to derive evidence on G^*-causality. As Granger (1980) emphasizes, the use of proper information sets—that is, sets that include the past and present values of the series to be forecast (say Y_t)—can result in a situation where, if the series Y_t can be perfectly forecast using only its own past, there remains no contribution for the candidate causal variable to make.

The forecast criterion (number of forecast periods) and the use of insample versus postsample periods to evaluate forecast ability are also open issues deserving careful consideration. Unfortunately, although we are acutely aware of these problems, space does not allow an extensive discussion at this time.[49]

Restricting ourselves to an evaluation of G^*-causality over the entire sample space, we propose to test for the effectiveness with respect to incremental predictability of a candidate causal variable by comparing the error variance for the particular "effect" variable when the variable is modeled as a function of itself (i.e., it is conditional on a proper information set)—the univariate ARMA case—with the error variance in the bivariate case. (This reduces to a test of the equality of the covariance matrices.) The test statistic (analysis of variance) we will consider is the correlation ratio:

$$\frac{[R^2\,(y\,|\,x,y)\,-\,R^2\,(y\,|\,y)]\,/(k_2\,-\,k_1)}{[1\,-\,R^2\,(y\,|\,x,y)]\,/(N\,-\,1\,-\,k_2)} \sim F\,[(k_2\,-\,k_1),\,(N\,-\,1\,-\,k_2)]$$

where:

$R^2\,(y\,|\,x,\,y)$ is the square of the multiple correlation calculated from the bivariate model of the "effect" (y) variable given information set (x,y),

$R^2\,(y\,|\,y)$ is the square of the multiple correlation calculated from the univariate model,

k_2 is the number of parameters in the bivariate model,

k_1 is the number of parameters in the univariate model,

and N is the number of observations in the models.

49. For a complete exposition of these issues, see Wainhouse, *Hayek's Theory.*

And we will test the null hypothesis:

H_0 : x is not prima facie G^*-causal with respect to y,

and reject H_0 if:

$$F\,[(k_2 - k_1), (N - 1 - k_2)] > F^*.$$

To identify and estimate the appropriate univariate and bivariate ARMA models as bases for the investigation of the G^*-causal structure contained in Hayek's theory, we first estimate state space models for the variable(s) and then consider the estimates from the equivalent ARMA representation of each state space form. The virtue of first estimating a state space model is that we can take advantage of the Akaike Information Criterion (AIC) in the determination of the order of the model, avoid much of the artistry required by the Box-Jenkins methodology, and still estimate the models parsimoniously.[50]

50. See Wainhouse, *Hayek's Theory*.

Chapter 3

CAPITAL FORMATION IN THE UNITED STATES AND THE QUESTION OF A CAPITAL SHORTAGE

J. Stuart Wood

THE PROBLEM: CAPITAL HAS BEEN DESTROYED

For the past two decades, the United States has been consuming capital on a large scale and at an alarming rate. Living standards, already lower than a decade ago, must continue to fall, and long-term stagnation in the British mold seems ever more likely.

This destruction of capital is revealed by the inflation-adjusted market value of equity of U.S. corporations. The value of equity has declined by almost one-third during the past decade, in terms of constant dollars. Table 3–1 shows that the market value of the common equity of all U.S. corporations fell from $2.8 trillion on December 31, 1968, to $1.7 trillion by December 31, 1980.[1] This loss of value occurred in spite of total private capital formation during the period of $4.4 trillion and business expenditures on new plant and equipment of $2.9 trillion.[2] (Market values of all corporate equity have been adjusted by the author to eliminate changes in the purchasing power of the dollar by using constant-size dollars as of June 1981 to express market value.)

1. Securities and Exchange Commission, *Monthly Statistical Review* (Washington, D.C.: Government Printing Office, monthly). Data adjusted by the author.
2. Board of Governors, Federal Reserve System, *Bulletin* (Washington, D.C.: Federal Reserve, monthly). Data adjusted by the author.

Table 3-1 also shows the net proceeds of new stock sales (gross proceeds of new shares sold minus repurchases by the firms) during the period in constant 1981 dollars. Since 1972, $8.5 billion in net new stock has been sold. In spite of such sales, equity value has been destroyed during the past two decades. Many firms had negative operating cash flows, which are indicative of capital consumption. During the period, cash retentions plus new stock offerings totaled $69 billion.

Not only has one-third of the value of the capital stock been eroded, but the attempted additions to this stock have gone for naught. These additions to the capital stock did not prevent the loss of value: Overall, the new goods did not add to the existing system of capital goods in a profitable way.

The reduction in corporate equity value has occurred in spite of additions to plant and equipment that were about equal in value to all equity in 1968. When these dollars were spent, it must have been expected that the capital projects involved had positive net present values—that each dollar expended was purchasing capital value in

Table 3-1. Market Value of Equity of All U.S. Corporations.

Year[a]	Equity Value ($B)[b]	Net New Stock Sales ($B)[b]
1960	1,288.5	9.7
1962	1,380.7	2.1
1964	2,069.2	4.2
1965	2,304.3	-1.1
1966	2,004.5	3.3
1967	2,454.2	6.2
1968	2,798.5	-2.3
1969	2,323.2	10.4
1970	2,169.3	15.9
1971	2,445.5	30.1
1972	2,734.6	28.2
1973	1,817.0	18.5
1974	1,162.2	7.9
1975	1,413.5	17.5
1976	1,584.7	16.7
1977	1,398.7	4.0
1978	1,356.4	3.6
1979	1,450.6	4.4
1980	1,706.2	9.9

a. As of December 31 of each year.
b. Inflated to June 1981 dollars.

Source: Securities Exchange Commission, Monthly Statistical Review.

excess of one dollar. But things have not worked out that way; these new projects did not prevent the destruction of capital value.

The only data available regarding total asset values are for the firms listed on the New York Stock Exchange, which represents only a portion of all U.S. corporations. As shown in Table 3-2, for these firms the combined values of debt and equity fell from $2.2 trillion in 1972 to $1.9 trillion in 1980.[3]

Stock market prices have declined because consumption of capital has reduced both the total value of output and the profitability of firms. Low profitability is revealed by the reduction in real dividends paid. For example, in 1957 United States Steel paid a dividend of $519 million (in 1981 constant dollars), whereas its dividends in

Table 3-2. **Market Value of Firms Listed on the New York Stock Exchange.**

Year[a]	Stocks ($M)[b]	Bonds ($M)[b]	Total Capital ($M)[b]
1961	1,174,208	316,785	1,490,993
1962	1,035,777	332,716	1,368,493
1963	1,216,917	348,843	1,565,760
1964	1,385,286	373,029	1,758,315
1965	1,543,155	380,055	1,923,210
1966	1,346,751	357,639	1,704,390
1967	1,643,562	339,552	1,983,114
1968	1,802,492	313,478	2,115,970
1969	814,067	248,624	1,062,691
1970	1,484,441	262,706	1,747,147
1971	1,659,197	289,521	1,948,718
1972	1,886,859	277,770	2,164,629
1973	1,469,653	245,691	1,715,344
1974	938,749	469,230	1,407,979
1975	1,152,996	530,806	1,683,802
1976	1,365,631	639,968	2,005,599
1977	1,190,791	716,779	1,907,570
1978	1,142,372	645,508	1,787,880
1979	1,198,809	573,916	1,772,725
1980	1,365,118	557,744	1,922,862
1981	1,242,803[c]	507,770	1,750,573

a. As of December 31 of each year.
b. Measured in constant dollars as of June 1981.
c. As of June 1981.
Source: New York Stock Exchange *Factbook*.

3. New York Stock Exchange, Inc., *Factbook* (New York: New York Stock Exchange, yearly).

Table 3-3.   Gross Fixed-Capital Formation.

Year	GNP per Capita ($)	Capital Formation per Capita ($)	Capital Formation as Percent of GNP
1970	11,031	1,495	13.6
1971	11,311	1,613	14.3
1972	11,940	1,810	15.2
1973	12,489	1,881	15.1
1974	12,070	1,686	14.0
1975	11,765	1,548	13.2
1976	12,468	1,679	13.5
1977	12,979	1,897	14.6
1978	13,466	2,083	15.5
1979	13,343	2,079	15.6

Sources: U.S. Department of Commerce, Bureau of Economic Analysis, *Survey of Current Business* (Washington, D.C.: Government Printing Office, 1981); Organization for Economic Co-operation and Development, *OECD Economic Surveys* (Paris, France, 1981).

Table 3-4.   Capital Formation.

Year	U.S. Business Expenditures on Plant and Equipment ($B)[a]	Total Private Capital Formation from Business and Personal Savings ($B)[a]
1960	109.15	157.23
1961	104.06	180.74
1962	111.74	189.88
1963	120.62	188.76
1964	137.18	223.71
1965	156.25	244.04
1966	177.25	261.51
1967	177.62	275.64
1968	176.41	267.80
1969	186.71	273.30
1970	185.93	292.70
1971	181.64	318.50
1972	191.47	323.00
1973	203.30	394.40
1974	206.47	393.50
1975	189.80	374.10
1976	191.17	372.80
1977	202.87	367.40
1978	213.27	409.50
1979	337.53	428.40
1980	324.73	402.80
1981	320.51	387.50

a. Measured in constant dollars as of June 1981.

Source: Board of Governors, Federal Reserve System, *Bulletin* (Washington, D.C.: Federal Reserve, 1981).

Table 3-5. Net New Formation of Equity Capital (Cash Retained by Firms and New Stock Flotations).

Year	Current-Year Dollars ($B)	Constant Dollars ($B)
1950–59	2.0[a]	6.8[b]
1960–69	1.2	3.5
1970	5.7	13.3
1971	11.4	25.5
1972	10.9	23.6
1973	7.9	16.1
1974	4.1	7.5
1975	9.9	16.7
1976	10.5	16.7
1977	2.7	4.0
1978	2.6	3.6
1979	3.5	4.4
1980	9.0	9.9

a. Average per year; the average for 1970–79 was 16.9.
b. Average per year; the average for 1970–79 was 13.1.

Source: John Carson-Parker, "The Capital Cloud over Smokestack America," *Fortune*, 23 February 1981.

1980 amounted to only $153 million, a reduction of 70 percent. Similarly, General Motors paid dividends of $4.3 billion in 1965 (in 1981 constant dollars), but its dividends in 1980 were only $960 million, a reduction of 78 percent.[4]

A widespread explanation in the business community for this condition is that there is at present a "capital shortage." Observers find that there is an insufficient flow of new savings to buy producer goods and also that the different particular capital goods, machines, buildings, and so on do not complement each other as they should. In other words, some particular capital goods are missing from the system.

Although the flow of new savings in the economy has remained roughly the same percentage of gross national product (GNP) for the past few years, as shown in Table 3-3, that percentage should have increased in order to provide the new machines needed to complement existing ones. Although real-dollar capital expenditures have increased, as shown in Table 3-4, they should have increased even more sharply. Table 3-5 demonstrates that the net new formation of equity capital has not increased over time. Equity capital formation has been quite irregular and has recently been quite low.

4. Data taken from appropriate annual reports and adjusted by the author.

THE EXPLANATION

Inflation Distorts Capital Values

The destruction of capital value has come about because the interrelationships of actual and planned capital goods have been distorted by unanticipated inflation, high interest rates, particular regulatory policies, and confiscatory real tax rates.

Capital goods are valuable only if they can give rise to future cash flows. To do this, they must be used to produce goods that will be demanded in the future. An entrepreneur must correctly forecast future demand for the product and then build a complementary set of capital goods to produce it. The new capital goods must be fitted correctly into the existing network of capital goods in order to work smoothly and avoid increased costs. Distortion of the structure of market interest rates causes poor matching of capital goods, which exaggerates their market value. In the United States during the past fifteen years, such distortion has caused the figures reporting spending on new plant and equipment and those reporting the apparent flow of savings as money capital to overstate the value created.[5]

This distortion of the structure of market interest rates has been caused by the inflation of the quantity of money and credit. Inflation causes general and unpredictable rises in most money prices and unpredictable changes in relative prices, and these distort the relationships of interest rates in different segments of the economy. Further, inflation interacts with tax law to divert funds from capital formation into consumption.

Inflation causes entrepreneurs both to misread the current degree of matching of capital goods with each other and to misjudge the appropriate composition of future consumer and producer goods. This leads to mistakes in emplacing new equipment, and the resulting structure of capital goods is inappropriate to consumer demand. The present value of the future cash flows that this mistakenly chosen and uncoordinated system of capital goods will actually yield is smaller than what is expected. This condition persists so long as the deception continues.

5. Fritz Machlup, "The Consumption of Capital in Austria," *Review of Economic Statistics* 17 (January 15, 1935): 13–19.

Volatile inflation rates cause volatile interest rates, further confusing the capital valuation process. Unanticipated growth of the quantity of money causes an apparent lowering of interest rates, thereby making proposed capital projects seem more profitable than they really are. But the expected increase in prices that follows eventually causes market interest rates to rise. To the extent that inflation is better anticipated, market interest rates are no longer depressed, and the planned completion of these new, more capital-intensive, and longer production processes cannot occur. Firms are thus left with incomplete sets of capital goods ill suited to actual demand conditions.

When a mistake is discovered, the capital involved, which had been intended to supply goods for which the entrepreneur now realizes there will be no demand, falls in value. Such unavoidable but unforeseeable capital depreciation must be replaced out of new savings. Replacement funds previously budgeted by, for example, ordinary depreciation expense can only be used for ordinary, expected wear and tear. Unanticipated losses cannot be budgeted in advance. During an inflation, then, a proportionately larger flow of savings is required to correct entrepreneurial errors in previous capital goods purchases. But savings flows usually shrink during an inflation, exacerbating the problem.

There is therefore a twofold disparity (1) between the amount of new capital funds provided today and the amount that in earlier years was forecast to be available today and (2) in the current composition of existing capital goods. Today's spending plans for capital goods were made years ago on the basis of forecasts. These plans involved particular capital projects undertaken then and planned projects to be undertaken today to complement the projects emplaced then. There is too small a flow of new capital today to complete those plans. As a result, the composition of capital goods existing today is wrong. Projects that had been expected to complement, expand, and replace previously emplaced projects and machines have not been implemented. Hence, today's production structure is distorted. The unavailability of planned-for additions to the capital stock means that firms must make do with machinery not precisely matched with the tasks that it must perform. Costs are accordingly higher, and profits are lower. Capital spending has been for "incorrect" projects, and current flows of new capital funds are too small to complete the planned structures of production.

Inflation Constricts Savings Flows

Today there is a shortage of new savings for capital formation relative to the amount that is needed (and that was previously expected to be forthcoming today) to validate the investments of recent years, which were made when interest rates were kept artificially low by inflation. At that time, investments were made under the assumption that further investments would be made to complement those projects as part of a long-range plan. But today new funds are not forthcoming in sufficient volume or at interest rates as low as were then anticipated to allow the emplacement of the complementary projects. Without these new projects, the previous investments are less efficient and profitable than expected.

The flow of new savings is too small relative to what is needed because of individual responses to inflation. In an attempt to avoid reductions in their real standards of living brought on by inflation-induced declines in real incomes, consumers have spent a larger portion of their disposable incomes on consumption goods than they used to; they are saving less than before. Social Security fools workers into thinking they are already carrying on significant saving, but the funds are actually diverted to the consumption purchases of retirees rather than invested. Progressive personal income taxes divert cash from those with high marginal propensities to save to recipients of transfer programs who have low marginal propensities to save.

Personal saving in the United States has fallen from a rate of about 8 percent of disposable income in the early 1970s to under 6 percent today.[6] Measured in constant 1981 dollars, personal saving out of disposable income fell from $158.7 billion in 1975 to $107.6 billion in 1979, and then to about $100 billion in 1981. This contrasts with *real* increases during the first half of the decade of the 1970s. Combined corporate and personal saving rose from $394.4 billion (measured in 1981 dollars) in 1973 to only $402.8 billion in 1980.[7] In real terms, personal saving declined by one-third over five years, and total saving remained constant.

6. Board of Governors, Federal Reserve System, *Bulletin* 61 (September 1975), Table A55; *Bulletin* 68 (September 1982), Table A53; Organization for Economic Cooperation and Development, *OECD Economic Surveys* (Paris: OECD yearly); Federal Reserve Bank of New York, "The Decline of Personal Saving," *Quarterly Review* 6 (Spring 1981): 25–32.
    7. *Bulletin.*

Moreover, households have greatly expanded their indebtedness to purchase goods recently, again to maintain their accustomed living standards. Stated in 1981 dollars, consumer indebtedness rose from $237.8 billion in 1970, through $277.6 billion in 1975, to $389.0 billion in 1979.[8] Debt allows consumers to participate in the round of increased buying even when their incomes increase more slowly than the prices they pay for goods. They can buy before their incomes increase and repay the loan in shrunken dollars. But repayment of this debt in the future out of smaller after-tax real incomes will further constrain the flow of savings.

Inflation Expands Corporate Taxes and Dividends to Unmanageable Size

Inflation causes corporate profits to be overstated so that, during a rapid inflation, real tax rates rise almost to equal real corporate income, leaving little internally generated wealth available for capital investment. Corporate taxes, computed on the basis of inflation-neglecting historical costs, confiscate capital from firms during periods of inflation. Also, distributions of cash dividends are themselves frequently very large in comparison with real economic income, and this further consumes capital. In addition, inflation and tax policy confiscate part of business capital beyond that lost due to the misallocations considered above.[9]

The ordinary computation of net income is so distorted by inflation that firms suffering economic losses are forced to pay taxes on imaginary earnings. Frequently, corporate income tax rates amount to more than half of economic income adjusted for inflation. Inventory profits and insufficient depreciation charges far overestimate taxable income, causing real income tax rates to exceed statutory limits and confiscate corporate capital. Insufficient cash remains to maintain and improve equipment properly. This consumption of capital leads to a drop in productivity and total output.

The 1980 annual reports reveal for the first time the consumption of corporate capital to pay taxes and dividends because FASB 33 mandated the presentation in financial statements of "current-cost

---

8. Ibid.
9. Richard W. Kopcke, "Potential Growth, Productivity, and Capital Accumulation," Federal Reserve Bank of Boston, *New England Economic Review* (May–June 1980): 22–41.

income"—an attempt to compensate for the distorting effects of inflation.[10]

Income is defined as the maximum consumption during the year that leaves capital no smaller than at the start. Current-cost income is calculated by estimating depreciation expense on the basis of current replacement costs of assets instead of historical costs. The discrepancy between traditional net income and inflation-adjusted net income is largest for those firms that own large amounts of older capital assets. Firms are not retaining sufficient cash to maintain the productivity of the capital equipment they presently have, let alone to finance additions.

Depreciation, the loss of economic serviceableness of equipment, is a true economic cost rightly charged against current income. If cash outlays were made to preserve the equipment in pristine condition, they would be charged against revenues, and no replacement of the equipment would ever be needed. In that circumstance, current income would give a true picture of the economic results of the firm and of its future prospects. But if a firm does not maintain equipment and does not charge sufficient depreciation, it overstates its economic income. The firm will have to raise external capital just to maintain its current output level unchanged. This means that the firm has been consuming capital. Normally, one expects a firm to seek new external capital to pursue expansions or new products, not to continue as before.

Not only does inflation cause capital confiscation through high real tax rates (which it masks), but it also encourages corporations to pay out in dividends still more capital by overestimating economic income. For many companies, the cash flow leaving the firm to pay income taxes and dividends exceeds real pretax income. Only consumption of capital can provide this excess outflow.

For example, Ford Motor Company, which had historical-cost earnings of $9.75 per share in 1979 but an economic income based on replacement costs of $1.78, paid income taxes of $2.75 per share and dividends of $3.90 per share. Ford thus consumed over $235 million in capital through excessive dividend payments. Income taxes in 1979 totaled $330 million, or seven times Ford's real income of

---

10. "Financial Reporting and Changing Prices," Financial Accounting Standards Board Statement no. 33 (September 1979).

$48.6 million, and dividends totaled $468 million, or ten times real income.

In 1980, Ford reported a loss of $1,543.3 million, but the actual economic loss was $2,774.8 million, or $23.07 per share. Yet Ford paid dividends of $2.60 per share.

Polaroid lost $0.85 per share economically in 1979 but paid dividends of $1.00 per share, thereby consuming $55 million in capital, or $1.66 per share.

American Telephone & Telegraph had economic earnings on a replacement-cost basis of $2.3 billion in 1979 but paid out dividends of $3.4 billion, thereby reducing the market value of its equity by $1.1 billion through capital consumption.

General Motors paid $2,724.82 million in taxes out of real pretax income of $4,975.23 million in 1979, and it paid dividends of $1,913.39 million, or 85 percent of after-tax net income of $2,250.41 million. In 1980, after an economic loss of $2,250.41 million, GM still paid dividends of $960.13 million.

In 1979, U.S. Steel paid dividends of $171.6 million out of a loss of $1,157.84 million; in 1980, it paid dividends of $153.45 million out of a loss of $269.33 million. Income taxes in 1980 were 1.5 times the real economic loss.

Exxon paid out 75 percent of real net after-tax income as dividends in 1979 and 84 percent in 1980. Income taxes were 78 percent of real pretax income in 1979 and 63 percent in 1980, giving a total outflow of 94 percent of real pretax income for each year.[11]

As a result of the eroding capital stock, the real rate of return on equity has fallen sharply in recent years. For the thirty firms in the Dow Jones Industrial Average, the real rate of return on book equity (economic income after inflation adjustment, divided by net worth) has fallen from 10 percent in 1967 to 5 percent in 1977. Also during this period, the real income tax rate for these firms rose from 40 percent to 72 percent of economic income, and the ratio of real retained earnings to income tax fell from 0.33 to 0.04. In 1977, the thirty firms' aggregate real dividend pay-out rate was 26 percent, and their real retention rate was 2.6 percent. In 1977, out of real economic income of $39 billion, they paid taxes of $28 billion and distributed about $10 billion as dividends. Only $1 billion was retained for in-

11. Data from corporate annual reports adjusted by author. All dollar figures are measured in constant 1981 dollars.

vestment. During the period, the real rate of return on the *market* value of the common stock did not change, however; it was 5.2 percent in 1967 and 5.4 percent in 1977. This stability indicates that market value adjusted to the changing situation and thus validates the use of market values to estimate the consumption of capital.[12]

Inflation Increases Financial Leverage and Risk

Not only has inflation reduced the rate of capital formation and the flow of investment spending, but it has also caused a shift in the composition of the right-hand side of the corporate balance sheet. Firms have been led to expand the portion of debt relative to equity and the portion of short-term liabilities relative to long-term liabilities.

Corporations are becoming more highly leveraged and less liquid. From 1945 to 1965, nonfinancial corporations added debt and equity in roughly equal amounts. But during the fifteen years from 1965 through 1979, debt increased by $756 billion, whereas equity increased by only $522 billion, in current dollars.[13]

In the last twenty-five years, equity has shrunk from about 67 percent of total capital in 1955 to only 51 percent at the end of 1980. The debt ratio of nonfinancial corporations rose from 34 percent of total assets in 1960 to 46 percent in 1970 and 1975, and then to 50 percent by 1980. This increased risk of corporate equity tends further to decrease its value.[14] High long-term interest rates and depressed stock prices have forced firms to finance capital spending with short-term borrowing in the hope that rates will soon fall. This has reduced their solvency and greatly increased their financial risk, exacerbating the depression of share prices.

Short-term debt increased from 7 percent of total capital to 14 percent, and the balance between short-term and long-term debt has worsened from 1971 to 1980. In 1971, short-term debt was only 28.7 percent of long-term debt, but in 1980, short-term debt

12. John Semmens, "Capital Punishment," *The Freeman* 29 (September 1979): 515–22. Even though this was not published in an academic journal, it is a respectable study properly done and merits serious consideration.

13. John Carson-Parker, "The Capital Cloud Over Smokestack America," *Fortune*, 23 February 1981, pp. 70–76. In constant 1981 dollars, new debt capital amounted to $1,890 billion, whereas new equity capital was $1,300 billion.

14. Ibid.

equaled 40 percent of long-term debt. The issuance of medium-term debt exceeded the issuance of long-term debt for the first time in 1981.[15] This dangerous shrinking of the maturity of the debt structure of corporations will continue unless these trends are reversed. Financial risk increases still further as long-term projects are financed with shorter term funds. The composite interest coverage ratio of firms has fallen from an average of 18.0 over the period 1965–74, through 9.9 in 1975, to 4.9 in 1980.[16]

From 1975 to 1981, the "current ratio" of business firms declined from 1.681 to 1.449.[17] The volume of commercial paper and bankers' acceptances has increased by 50 percent in real terms since 1977, from $97 million to $151 million in 1981, in 1981 dollars.[18]

Interest rates can fall only to the extent that the public reduces its expectations of future inflation. Even then, debt-heavy firms will find that their capital costs have permanently risen in response to the higher financial risk they impose on stockholders and bondholders because of their increased leverage.

The distortion of the funds flows of corporations caused by combined high inflation and tax policy has caused corporations to consume capital value, since the composition of capital goods has been distorted by unanticipated changes in long-term plans.

OUTLOOK

The economic problems of today stem from the Federal Reserve System's expansion of the quantity of money. General price inflation is the result only of governmental expansion of the quantity of money. It is this deliberate inflation of the quantity of money by the federal government that has caused all the capital problems discussed above. Inflation causes malinvestment: The capital goods installed are inappropriate to supply the demands of consumers and to interact efficiently with each other.

Errors in entrepreneurial forecasts of demand and in matching new capital goods with the existing capital-goods structure leads to a pro-

15. Ibid.
16. "Why Companies Are Still Wary," *Business Week*, 5 October 1971, pp. 24–25.
17. *Economic Report of the President* (Washington, D.C.: Government Printing Office, 1981), p. A33.
18. *Bulletin.*

duction structure that is less valuable than what could have been constructed using the funds that were available. If demand is not what was expected, the capital goods are seen to have less value than was thought.

Since the expectations that entrepreneurs form regarding the profitability of alternative production processes depend upon interest rates, the return of interest rates to their appropriate heights following a period of artificial reduction of rates by unanticipated inflation causes such a degradation of value. A "shortage" of capital goods exists relative to what might have been if the funds that were actually spent during the past fifteen years had been spent differently— that is, if entrepreneurs had not been misled by the inflation-induced artificial lowering of interest rates.

There is also a shortage of new savings—relative to what had been forecast: the current flow of new savings is too small to allow completion of many continuing projects, thus dooming these projects to unprofitability.

With the present structure of capital goods ill suited to the spectrum of consumer and producer goods now expected to be demanded in the future, more capital spending is needed to change the capital stock so that it can produce these goods efficiently. Previous investments cannot now be completed, because the additional saving that was previously forecast is not forthcoming. The capital expenditures of recent years are now seen to have been partially wasted on equipment that is not suited to current demand conditions. That waste means that the desired combination of consumer goods cannot easily be produced: Living standards will be lower as a result.

PART II

THE RECORD OF FEDERAL RESERVE POLICY

Chapter 4

THE FEDERAL RESERVE AS A CARTELIZATION DEVICE
The Early Years, 1913–1930

Murray N. Rothbard

To most economists, historians, and lay people, a modern economy without a central bank is simply unthinkable. With that kind of mind-set, the creation of the Federal Reserve System in December 1913 can be attributed to a simple, enlightened acceptance of the need to bring the economy of the United States into the modern world. It is generally held, in addition, that a central bank is necessary to curb the natural instincts of free-market banks to inflate and, as a corollary, to level out economic fluctuations. It has become all too clear in recent years, however, that the Fed has scarcely succeeded in this supposed task. For since the establishment of the Fed, we have suffered the longest and deepest depression in American history, and we have, since World War II, experienced the unique phenomenon of a chronic, accelerating secular inflation. Since instability, inflation, and depressions have been far worse since the inception of the Federal Reserve, many economists have concluded that the Fed has failed in its task and have come up with various suggestions for reform to try to get it on the correct track.

It is possible, however, that the current critics of the Fed have missed the essential point: that the Fed was designed to meet very different goals. In fact, the Fed was largely fashioned by the banks as a cartelizing device. The government interventions of the Progressive era were systemic devices to restrict competition and cartelize industry, strategems that followed on the previous failure of industry to sustain successful voluntary cartels. Just as other industries turned to the government to impose cartelization that could not be maintained on the market, so the banks turned to government to enable them to expand money and credit without being held back by the demands for redemption by competing banks. In short, rather than hold back the banks from their propensity to inflate credit, the new central banks were created to do precisely the opposite. Indeed, the record of the American economy under the Federal Reserve can be considered a rousing success from the point of view of the actual goals of its founders and of those who continue to sustain its power.

A proper overall judgment on the actual role of the Fed was delivered by the vice-chairman and de facto head of the Federal Trade Commission, Edward N. Hurley. The Federal Trade Commission was Woodrow Wilson's other major Progressive reform, following closely on the passage of the Federal Reserve Act. Hurley was president of the Illinois Manufacturers Association at the time of his appointment, and his selection and subsequent performance in his new job were hailed throughout the business community. Addressing the Association of National Advertisers in December 1915, Hurley exulted that "through a period of years the government has been gradually extending its machinery of helpfulness to different classes and groups upon whose prosperity depends in a large degree the prosperity of the country." Then came the revealing statement: The railroads and shippers had the ICC, the farmers had the Agriculture Department, and the bankers had the Federal Reserve Board. Hurley concluded that "to do for general business that which these other agencies do for the groups to which I have referred was the thought behind the creation of the trade commission."[1] What, then, did the Federal Reserve do for the nation's bankers?

THE ORIGINS OF THE FEDERAL RESERVE: THE DISSATISFACTION OF NEW YORK BANKERS

The Federal Reserve did not replace a system of free banking. On the contrary, an approach to free banking existed in the United States

---

1. Gabriel Kolko, *The Triumph of Conservatism: A Reinterpretation of American History* (Glencoe, Ill.: Free Press, 1963), p. 274.

only in the two decades before the Civil War. Under the cover of the wartime emergency, the Republican Party put through changes that had long been proposed by the Republicans' ancestor, the Whig Party. The National Bank Acts of 1863–65 replaced the hard-money free banking of pre–Civil War days with the quasi-centralized regime of the national banking system. By levying a prohibitive federal tax, the national banking system in effect outlawed state bank notes, centralizing the issue of bank notes into the hands of federally chartered national banks. By means of an elaborate set of categories and a structure of fractional reserve requirements, entry into national banking in the big cities was limited to large banks, and bank deposits were encouraged to pyramid on top of a handful of large Wall Street banks. Furthermore, an expansion of any one bank in the pre-Civil War era was severely limited, since the free market would discount the notes of shaky banks, roughly proportionate to the distance of the circulating notes from the home base of the bank.[2] The national banking acts removed that restraint by forcing every national bank to accept the notes and demand deposits of every other national bank at par. Genuine redeemability of notes and deposits was also restrained by the continued legal prohibition of interstate or even intrastate branch banking, which severely hobbled the efficiency of clearing systems where one bank presents the obligations of another for redemption. Redemption was also curtailed by a rigid statutory maximum limit of $3 million per month by which national bank notes could be contracted. Furthermore, although private national bank liabilities were of course not legal tender, the federal government conferred quasi–legal tender status upon them by agreeing to receive all national bank notes and deposits at par in dues or taxes.

The banking system of the United States after 1865 was, therefore, a halfway house between free and central banking. Banking was subsidized, privileged, and quasi-centralized under the aegis of a handful of large Wall Street banks. Even at that, however, the large national banks and their financial colleagues were far from satisfied. There was no governmental central bank to act as the lender of last resort. The banks could inflate more readily and uniformly than before the Civil War, but when they got into trouble and bank-generated booms turned into recessions, they were forced to contract

---

2. In contrast, notes of more solid banks circulated at par, even at great distances.

and deflate to save themselves. As we will see further below, the bankers' drive for fundamental change was generally couched in terms of an attack on the "inelasticity" of the national banking system. Translated into plain English, "inelasticity" meant the inability of the banking system to inflate money and credit, especially during recessions.[3]

The big banks' turn to the idea of a central bank came after the beginning of the twentieth century. The increased dissatisfaction with the status quo was prompted particularly by the rising competition of state banks and private banks outside the direct purview of the national banks of Wall Street. State banks had recovered from their initial shock and, after the 1860s, grew rapidly by pyramiding loans and deposits on top of national bank notes. These state and other nonnational banks provided increasingly stiff competition with Wall Street for the banking resources of the nation. State banks were free of the high legal capital requirements for entry into the national banking business, and banking laws, especially in such important states as Michigan, California, and New York, became more lenient during the 1890s. As a result, the proportion of nonnational bank deposits to national bank notes and deposits, which had been 67 percent in 1873, rose to 101 percent in 1886 and to 145 percent in 1901. To make things worse for cartelization, New York City lost its

---

3. See Milton Friedman and Anna Jacobson Schwartz, *A Monetary History of the United States, 1867-1960* (Princeton: National Bureau of Economic Research, 1963), pp. 168-70. Friedman and Schwartz grant validity to the complaints of inelasticity in at least one sense: that deposits and notes were not easily interconvertible without causing grave problems. If bank clients wished to redeem bank deposits for bank notes, the fractional reserve requirements for deposits but not for notes meant that such simple redemption had a multiple contractionist effect on the supply of money and vice versa, since the exchange of notes for deposits had an expansionist effect. Friedman and Schwartz conclude that this defect justified various centralizing remedies. They fail to point out another alternative: a return to the decentralized banking of pre-Civil War days, which did not suffer from such problems of interconvertibility.

One curiosity of the national banking system is that the notes issued by the national banks were rigidly linked by law to the total holdings of federal government bonds by each bank. This provision, a holdover from various state bank systems imposed by the Whigs before the Civil War, was designed to tie the banks to state deficits and the public debt. See Ron Paul and Lewis Lehrman, *The Case for Gold: A Minority Report of the U.S. Gold Commission* (Washington, D.C.: Cato Institute, 1982), p. 67. The source of "inelasticity," however, could easily have been remedied by abolishing this link without imposing a central bank. Many of the early bank reforms proposed during the 1890s aimed to do just that. See Robert Craig West, *Banking Reform and the Federal Reserve, 1863-1923* (Ithaca, N.Y.: Cornell University Press, 1977), pp. 42ff.

monopoly of designated "central reserve city" status—the base of the nation's banking pyramid—to St. Louis and Chicago in 1887. As a result, the total bank deposits of St. Louis and Chicago, which had been only 16 percent of the combined total of the three major cities in 1880, rose sharply to 33 percent by 1912. Banking in the smaller reserve cities rose even more rapidly in this period: The bank clearings outside of New York, 24 percent of the national total in 1882, rose to 43 percent by 1913.[4]

The major New York banks were understandably perturbed at the rising competition of non–New York and nonnational banks. They were upset, too, by the fact that they had to compete with each other for the deposits of the burgeoning state banks. As one New York banker put it: "We love the country bankers, but they are the masters of the situation. We dance at their music and pay the piper."[5]

The New York national bankers were also particularly perturbed at the mushrooming growth of private trust companies in New York, which were gathering the major share of the new and profitable trust business, when national and most state-chartered banks were prohibited by law from handling trust accounts. At the behest of the national banks, the New York Clearing House, a private organization for the clearing of notes and deposits, tried to impose reserve requirements on trust companies to hobble their competition with banks. In reply, seventeen of them walked out of the Clearing House for a decade. Finally, the House of Morgan formed the banker-owned Bankers' Trust Company in 1903 to compete with the private trust companies.[6]

J. P. Morgan & Co. was the most powerful financial grouping in Wall Street and hence in the country. An investment bank that came to own or control the bulk of the nation's important railroads, the House of Morgan controlled such leading Wall Street national banks as Guaranty Trust Company, the First National Bank of New York, and, before the 1930s, the Chase National Bank. Despite (or perhaps because of) its mammoth size and influence, Morgan was doing poorly in the gales of competition after 1900. In addition to the fac-

---

4. U.S. Department of Commerce, *Historical Statistics of the United States, Colonial Times to 1957* (Washington, D.C.: Government Printing Office, 1960), pp. 626–29.

5. Quoted in Kolko, *Triumph*, p. 141.

6. See Kolko, *Triumph*, p. 141, and Lester V. Chandler, *Benjamin Strong, Central Banker* (Washington, D.C.: Brookings Institution, 1958), pp. 25–26.

tors mentioned above that weakened New York banks, railroads, in which the Morgans had concentrated their forces, began to enter their long secular decline after the turn of the century. Furthermore, virtually all the mergers in the 1898–1902 period that tried to achieve monopoly control and monopoly profits in various industries collapsed with the entry of new firms and suffered major losses. Some of the most egregious failures—including International Harvester, United States Steel, and International Mercantile Marine—were Morgan creations.

J. P. Morgan had long favored corporatism and government cartelization where competition proved inconvenient. After decades of abject failure of Morgan-created railroad cartels, Morgan took the lead in establishing the Interstate Commerce Commission in 1887 to cartelize the railroad industry. Now, after slipping badly in the free market after 1900, Morgan joined other big business interests, such as the Rockefellers and the Belmonts, in calling for the compulsory cartelization of the American economy. This alliance of powerful big business interests, professionals who sought guild privilege, statist ideologues, and technocrats seeking political power and place constituted what is now known as the Progressive era (approximately 1900 to 1918). The Federal Reserve Act was a "progressive" Wilsonian reform that, as Edward Hurley and others pointed out, "did for" the bankers what the other reforms had done for other segments of industry.[7]

THE ROAD TO THE FEDERAL RESERVE

During the McKinley and Roosevelt administrations, treasury secretaries Lyman J. Gage and Leslie M. Shaw respectively tried to oper-

7. The major pressure group calling for "progressive" cartelization was the National Civic Federation (NCF), founded in 1900, an organized coalition of big business and intellectual–technocrat groups as well as a few corporatist labor union leaders. On the importance of the NCF, see James Weinstein, *The Corporate Ideal in the Liberal State, 1900–1918* (Boston: Beacon Press, 1968). See also David W. Eakins, "The Development of Corporate Liberal Policy Research in the United States, 1885–1965" (Ph.D. dissertation, University of Wisconsin, 1966), pp. 53–82.

In the past two decades, a massive literature has developed on the Progressive era from both a cartelizing and a technocratic power-seeking perspective. The best treatments are in Kolko, *Triumph*; Weinstein, *Corporate Ideal*; and James Gilbert, *Designing the Industrial State: The Intellectual Pursuit of Collectivism in America, 1880–1940* (Chicago: Quadrangle Books, 1972). On the railroads and the ICC, see Gabriel Kolko, *Railroads and Regulation, 1877–1916* (Princeton: Princeton University Press, 1965).

ate the Treasury Department as a central bank, pumping in money during recessions by purchasing government bonds on the open market and depositing large funds with favored commercial banks. In 1900, Gage called for the establishment of regional central banks, and Shaw suggested in his last annual report in 1906 that he be given total power to regulate the nation's banks. Their efforts failed, and these failures helped to spur the big bankers to seek a formal central bank.[8]

Neither Gage nor Shaw was an isolated treasury bureaucrat whose power was suddenly going to his head. Before his appointment, Gage was president of the powerful First National Bank of Chicago, one of the major banks in the Rockefeller orbit. He also served as president of the American Bankers' Association. After leaving the Treasury Department, Gage became president of the Rockefeller-controlled U.S. Trust Company, and his hand-picked assistant at the department, Frank A. Vanderlip, left to become a top executive at the Rockefellers' flagship bank, the National City Bank of New York.[9] Gage's appointment as treasury secretary was secured for him by Mark Hanna, close friend, political mastermind, and financial backer of President McKinley. Hanna, a coal magnate and iron manufacturer, was a close business associate as well as an old friend and high school classmate of John D. Rockefeller, Sr.[10]

Leslie Shaw was a small-town Iowa banker who became governor of his state in 1898 and continued as president of the Bank of Denison until the end of his term. He reached his post as governor by being a loyal supporter of the Des Moines Regency, the Republican machine in Iowa, and a close friend of the Regency's leader, the

8. On Gage's and Shaw's proposals and actions in office, see Friedman and Schwartz, *Monetary History*, pp. 148–56; and Kolko, *Triumph*, pp. 149–50.

9. John D. Rockefeller was the largest stockholder of National City Bank; its president until 1904 was James Stillman, two of whose daughters married sons of Rockefeller's brother William. See Carl P. Parrini, *Heir to Empire: United States Economic Diplomacy, 1916–1923* (Pittsburgh: University of Pittsburgh Press, 1969), pp. 55–65.

Much later, the Chase National and National City banks switched roles: The Rockefellers acquired control of the previously Morgan-dominated Chase in 1930, and, later in the 1930s, National City switched from Rockefeller to Morgan control. After World War II, Chase merged with the Bank of Manhattan, previously controlled by the investment banking firm of Kuhn, Loeb & Co., and National City merged with the long-time Morgan-dominated First National. The Rockefeller group and Kuhn, Loeb & Co. were closely allied during this period.

10. On Gage's connections, see Philip H. Burch, Jr., *The Civil War to the New Deal*, vol. 2 of *Elites in American History* (New York: Holmes & Meier, 1981), pp. 137, 185, 390.

powerful and venerable U.S. senator William Boyd Allison. Allison was the one who secured the treasury position for his friend Shaw and in turn was tied closely to Charles E. Perkins, a close Morgan ally, president of the Chicago, Burlington and Quincy Railroad, and kinsman of the Forbes financial group of Boston, long associated with the Morgans.[11]

After the failure of Shaw's interventions, and particularly after the panic of 1907, the big bankers turned in earnest to a drive for the establishment of a central bank in the United States. The movement was launched in January 1906 when Jacob H. Schiff, the head of the powerful investment banking firm of Kuhn, Loeb & Co., urged the New York Chamber of Commerce to advocate fundamental banking reform. Heeding the call, the New York chamber immediately established a special committee to study the problem and propose legislation. The committee was comprised of leaders from commercial and investment banking, including Isidor Straus of R. H. Macy's (a close friend of Schiff's) and Frank A. Vanderlip of the National City Bank. In March, the special committee report, not surprisingly, called for the creation of a strong central bank "similar to the Bank of Germany."

The New York chamber proved reluctant to endorse this far-reaching scheme, but the big bankers had the bit in their teeth. In mid-1906, the American Bankers Association followed suit by naming a commission of inquiry of leading bankers from the major cities of the country, headed by A. Barton Hepburn, chairman of the board of Chase National Bank. The Hepburn commission was more cautious, and its report of November 1906 called for imperative changes in the existing banking system, including a system of regional clearing houses for the issue of bank notes. The notes would be guaranteed by a common pool built up by taxes levied on the notes.[12]

A variant of the Hepburn plan was passed by Congress in May 1908, after the panic of 1907, in the Aldrich-Vreeland Act. Aldrich-Vreeland provided for the issuance of "emergency" currency by groups of bankers clustered in "National Currency Associations." Although this regional cartel scheme was devised as a stopgap mea-

11. On Shaw's connections, see Burch, *Civil War*, pp. 148, 402. On Allison and Perkins, see ibid., pp. 65, 121, 122, 128, 151.
12. See Kolko, *Triumph*, p. 152.

sure, the congressional authorization was to be for seven years, a rather long "temporary" period.[13]

In fact, however, Aldrich-Vreeland provisions were used only once, and that was in 1914, shortly after the launching of the Federal Reserve System. By far the most significant aspect of Aldrich-Vreeland turned out to be its clause setting up a National Monetary Commission to study the American and foreign banking systems and to emerge with a plan of reform. The commission consisted of nine senators and nine representatives and, in standard bureaucratic procedure, the chairman of the commission was Senator Nelson W. Aldrich and the vice-chairman was Representative Edward B. Vreeland.

Representative Vreeland was a banker from the Buffalo area of New York, and little more need be said about him. Far more important was the powerful Senator Nelson W. Aldrich, a Republican from Rhode Island who made millions during his long years of service in the U.S. Senate. One of the prime movers in the creation of the Federal Reserve System, Nelson Aldrich was the father-in-law of John D. Rockefeller, Jr., and may be fairly regarded as Rockefeller's man in the Senate.[14]

From the inception of the National Monetary Commission until the presentation of its Aldrich plan to Congress four years later, Senator Aldrich and the commission were a vitally important nucleus of the drive for a central bank. Particularly influential in the deliberations of the commission were two men who were not official members. Aldrich asked J. P. Morgan to recommend a banking expert, and Morgan happily responded with Henry P. Davison, a Morgan partner; the other unofficial member was George M. Reynolds of Chicago, president of the American Bankers Association.[15]

Aldrich and the National Monetary Commission, however, were by no means the only focus of the movement for a central bank. An-

13. On Aldrich-Vreeland, see Friedman and Schwartz, *Monetary History*, pp. 170–72. On the jockeying for power among various banking and business groups over different provisions of Aldrich-Vreeland, see Kolko, *Triumph*, pp. 156–58.

14. When the Rockefeller forces gained control of the Chase National Bank from the Morgans in 1930, one of their first actions was to oust Morgan man Albert H. Wiggin and replace him with Nelson Aldrich's son Winthrop W. as chairman of the board.

15. See West, *Banking Reform*, p. 70. Investment banking houses were—and still are—partnerships rather than corporations, and Morgan activities in politics as well as industrial mergers were conducted by Morgan partners. Particularly conspicuous Morgan partners in both fields were George W. Perkins, Thomas W. Lamont, Henry P. Davison, Dwight Morrow, and Willard Straight.

other was Paul Moritz Warburg, one of the most vital influences on the creation of the Federal Reserve Systen. Warburg, scion of the great international banking family and the German investment banking firm of M. M. Warburg and Company, of Hamburg, emigrated to the United States in 1902 to become a partner in the influential New York banking house of Kuhn, Loeb & Co.[16] From the moment he came to the United States, Warburg worked tirelessly, in person and in print, to bring the blessings of European central banking to this monetarily backward land. Sensitive to American political objections to the idea of centralization or of Wall Street control, Warburg always insisted disingenuously that his plan was not *really* a central bank. His first printed banking reform essay came in January 1907 in his "A Plan for a Modified Central Bank." The plan called for centralized reserves and a centralized note issue as a key to assuring economic stability. The most elaborate versions of Warburg's reform plan were presented in two speeches in 1910: "A United Reserve Bank of the United States" and "Principles that Must Underlie Monetary Reform in the United States."

Warburg's United Reserve Bank delineated the major features of the future Federal Reserve System. The key to its power was to be its legal monopoly on all note issue in the United States; to obtain such notes, the banks would have to keep their reserves at the Reserve Bank. Reserves would therefore be centralized at long last. Depositors at the Bank would be strictly limited to the member banks and the federal government. The Bank was to be governed by a board selected equally by three groups: the member banks, the stockholders of the Reserve Bank, and the federal government. Not surprisingly, Warburg's plan repeated the essential features of the operation of the German Reichsbank, the central bank in his native Germany.[17]

16. Or at least *partially* emigrated. Warburg spent half of each year in Germany, serving as financial liaison between the two great banks, if not between the two countries themselves. Warburg was related to Jacob H. Schiff by marriage. Schiff was a son-in-law of Solomon Loeb, a co-founder of Kuhn, Loeb & Co., and Warburg, husband of Nina Loeb, was another son-in-law of Solomon's by a second wife. The incestuous circle was completed when Schiff's daughter Frieda married another partner, Warburg's brother Felix, which in a sense made Paul his brother's uncle. See Stephen Birmingham, "*Our Crowd*": *The Great Jewish Families of New York* (New York: Pocket Books, 1977), pp. 21, 209–10, 383, appendix.

17. On Warburg's plan, see West, *Banking Reform*, pp. 54–59. Warburg's plan and essays, as well as his other activities on behalf of central banking in the United States, are collected in his *The Federal Reserve System*, 2 vols. (New York: Macmillan, 1930). See also

The greatest cheerleader for Warburg's plan, and the man who introduced his banking reform essays to Columbia University's Academy of Political Science, was Warburg's kinsman, the Columbia economist Edwin R. A. Seligman, of the investment banking family of J. & W. Seligman and Company.[18]

The top bankers were clear from the beginning that, to assuage widespread fears of centralized and Wall Street control, they would have to avoid the *appearance* of an orthodox central bank on the lines of England or Germany. The chosen course was a spurious "regionalism" and "decentralization," the appearance of a virtually uncoordinated set of regional central banks. The idea was in the air when Victor Morawetz made his famous speech in November 1909 calling for regional banking districts under the ultimate direction of one central control board. Although reserves and note issue would be *pro forma* decentralized in the hands of the regional reserve banks, all would really be centralized and coordinated by the central control board. This specious decentralization was, of course, the scheme eventually adopted in the Federal Reserve System.

Who was Victor Morawetz? He was a distinguished attorney and banker and in particular the counsel and chairman of the executive committee of the Morgan-controlled Atchison, Topeka, and Santa Fe Railroad. In 1908, Morawetz had been, along with J. P. Morgan's personal lawyer, Francis Lynde Stetson, the principal drafter of an unsuccessful Morgan–National Civic Federation bill for a federal incorporation law that would have cartelized and regulated American corporations. Later, Morawetz was to be a top consultant to another "progressive" reform of Woodrow Wilson's, the Federal Trade Commission.[19]

In late 1910, someone in the Aldrich circle, probably Henry P. Davison, got the idea of convening a small group of leading advocates of a central bank in a top secret conclave to draft a bill for a central bank. The clandestine meeting was held in November at a duck-shooting retreat for wealthy members, the Jekyll Island Club on

---

Warburg, "Essays on Banking Reform in the United States," *Proceedings of the Academy of Political Science* 4 (July 1914): pp. 387–612.

18. Professor Seligman's brother Isaac N. was married to Guta Loeb, sister of Paul Warburg's wife Nina. This made Seligman the brother of Warburg's brother-in-law; see Birmingham, *Our Crowd*, appendix.

19. On Morawetz, see West, *Banking Reform*, pp. 59–62; and Kolko, *Triumph*, pp. 134, 183–84, 272.

Jekyll Island, Georgia. The cover story given to the press was that the conferees were going down for a duck-hunting expedition. Extraordinary measures were taken to ensure secrecy, with the conferees traveling down to Georgia under assumed names in a private railroad car chartered by Aldrich. Some reporters got wind of the meeting, but Davison managed to talk them out of any publicity.[20]

The blue-ribbon participants at the week-long Jekyll Island meeting were:

Senator Nelson W. Aldrich, Rockefeller in-law
Henry P. Davison, Morgan partner
Paul M. Warburg, Kuhn, Loeb & Co. partner[21]
Frank A. Vanderlip, vice-president of Rockefeller's National
    City Bank
Charles D. Norton, president of Morgan's First National Bank
    of New York
A. Piatt Andrew, Harvard economist and staff assistant to
    Aldrich on the Monetary Commission.

There is no clearer physical embodiment of the cartelizing coalition of top financial and banking interests that brought the Federal Reserve System into being than the sometimes allied, often clashing Rockefeller–Kuhn, Loeb and Morgan interests, aided by economic technicians.

Using the research of the National Monetary Commission, the Jekyll Island conclave drafted a bill for a central bank. The ideas of this draft, which eventually became the Aldrich Bill, were basically Paul Warburg's, with a decentralized *soupçon* taken from Morawetz. The final writing was contributed by Vanderlip. The main disagreement at the meeting was that Aldrich wanted to hold out for a straightforward central bank on the European model, whereas Warburg and the other bankers, oddly enough more politically astute

20. So shrouded in secrecy did the meeting remain that details did not leak out until the publication of the authorized biography of Aldrich twenty years later. It is not even clear which club member arranged the facilities for the meeting, since none of the participants was a member. The best guess on the identity of the helpful Jekyll Island member is J.P. Morgan. See West, *Banking Reform*, p. 71; see also Nathaniel W. Stephenson, *Nelson W. Aldrich* (New York: Scribner's, 1930).

21. Aldrich was in the audience when Warburg delivered his famous "United Reserve Bank Plan" speech to the Academy of Political Science in 1910. The enthusiastic Aldrich, who had been greatly impressed by German central banking views during the Monetary Commission's trip to Europe the previous year, promptly invited Warburg to attend the upcoming Jekyll Island gathering; see Kolko, *Triumph*, p. 184.

on this issue than the veteran senator, insisted that the reality of central banking be clothed in the palatable garb of decentralization. The Jekyll Island draft was presented by Aldrich to the full National Monetary Commission in January 1911. Slightly revised, it was introduced, together with the commission report, a year later as the Aldrich Bill, which in turn became in all essentials the final Federal Reserve Act passed in December 1913.

In the Aldrich–Jekyll Island plan, the central bank with branches was called the National Reserve Association; the main difference between the draft and the eventual legislation is that in the former the national board of directors was largely chosen by the banks themselves rather than by the president of the United States. This provision was so blatantly cartelist that it was modified for political reasons to have the president name the board. The economist Henry Parker Willis, who played a large role in the enactment of the Federal Reserve System, lamented this alteration: "Political prejudice proved too strong for the establishment of this form of financial self-government or 'integration'."[22]

Aldrich and the Monetary Commission took the unusual step of delaying their report to Congress for twelve months, from January 1911 to January 1912. With the Democratic victory in the congressional elections of 1910, it was necessary to spend a year drumming up support for a central bank among Democrats, bankers, and the lay public. Accordingly, at the beginning of February 1911, twenty-two top bankers from twelve cities met for three days behind closed doors in Atlantic City to consider the Aldrich plan; the conference warmly endorsed the plan. In the private deliberation, James B. Forgan, President of the Rockefeller-dominated First National Bank of Chicago, declared outright that everyone there approved of the Aldrich plan and that, as Kolko puts it, "the real purpose of the conference was to discuss winning the banking community over to government control directed by the bankers for their own ends. . . . It was generally appreciated that the [Aldrich plan] would increase the power of the big national banks to compete with the rapidly growing state banks, help bring the state banks under control, and strengthen the position of the national banks in foreign banking activities."[23]

22. Henry Parker Willis, *The Theory and Practice of Central Banking* (New York: Harper & Bros., 1936), p. 77.

23. Kolko, *Triumph*, p. 186.

In November 1911, Aldrich won support for his plan from the American Bankers Association. In his address to their convention, he declared: "The organization proposed is not a bank, but a cooperative union of all the banks of the country for definite purposes."[24]

The major propaganda organization created for the benefit of the lay public by Aldrich and his colleagues in the spring of 1911 was the National Citizens' League for the Creation of a Sound Banking System. The league grew out of a resolution that Paul Warburg had pushed through a meeting of the National Board of Trade in January 1910, setting aside January 18 of the following year as a "monetary day" devoted to a "Business Men's Monetary Conference." At that January 1911 meeting the conference appointed a committee of seven, headed by Warburg, to organize a businessleaders' monetary reform league. A group of leading Chicago businessmen, headed by John V. Farwell and Harry A. Wheeler, president of the U. S. Chamber of Commerce, established the National Citizens' League, with economist J. Laurence Laughlin of the University of Chicago as operating head.

Warburg and the other New York bankers chose Chicago as the site of the Citizens' League to give the organization a bogus appearance of grass roots populism. In reality, banker control was virtually complete. The stated purpose of the league was to advance the cause of "cooperation, with dominant centralization of all banks by an evolution out of our clearing-house experience"; a decade later, Professor Henry Parker Willis, Laughlin's top assistant at the league as well as former student and long-time disciple, conceded that the Citizens' League had been the propaganda organ of the nation's bankers.[25]

There is no need to go into the minutiae of the splits within the Citizens' League or of the shift by the incoming Democrats in 1913 from the dreaded Republican name of Aldrich to a bill named by their own Representative Carter Glass. Much of this conflict revolved around the desire by Laughlin and the Democrats, and to some ex-

---

24. West, *Banking Reform*, p. 73. The full text of the Aldrich speech is reprinted in Herman E. Krooss and Paul Samuelson, eds., *Documentary History of Banking and Currency in the United States* (New York: Chelsea House, 1969), 3: 1202. See also Kolko, *Triumph*, p. 189.

25. Henry Parker Willis, *The Federal Reserve System* (New York: Ronald Press, 1923), pp. 149–50. At the same time, Willis's account conveniently ignores the dominant operating role that both he and his mentor played in the work of the Citizens' League; see West, *Banking Reform*, p. 82.

tent by Warburg, to shed the name Aldrich for a more palatable one. Nevertheless, there was very little substantive difference between the Glass bill, which became the Federal Reserve Act, and the original Aldrich plan. Friedman and Schwartz are surely correct in insisting on "the near identity" of the two plans.[26] The important point is that whatever the difference on minor technical points, the nation's bankers, and especially the big bankers, were overwhelmingly in favor of a new central bank. As A. Barton Hepburn of the Chase National exulted at the annual meeting of the American Bankers Association in August 1913, in the course of his successful effort to get the bankers to endorse the Glass bill: "The measure recognizes and adopts the principles of a central bank. Indeed, if it works out as the sponsors of the law hope, it will make all incorporated banks together joint owners of a central dominating power."[27] Precisely.

All in all, Professor Kolko sums up the point well:

> The entire banking reform movement, at all crucial stages, was centralized in the hands of a few men who for years were linked, ideologically and personally, with one another. The problem of the origin of the Federal Reserve Act, and the authorship of specific drafts, was later hotly debated by [men] who greatly exaggerated their differences in order that they might each claim responsibility for the guiding lines of the Federal Reserve System. Yet . . . although they may have differed on details they agreed on major policy lines and general theory. The confusion over the precise authorship of the Federal Reserve Act should not obscure the fact that the major function, inspiration, and direction of the measure was to serve the banking community in general, and large bankers specifically.[28]

THE STRUCTURE OF THE FEDERAL RESERVE

The structure of the Federal Reserve System—which was enacted in December 1913 and opened its doors the following November—

26. See Friedman and Schwartz, *Monetary History*, p. 171*n.* For similar judgments, see West, *Banking Reform*, pp. 106–07; Kolko, *Triumph*, p. 222. Two decades after the establishment of the Federal Reserve, Paul Warburg demonstrated in detailed parallel columns the near identity of the Aldrich bill and the Federal Reserve Act; see Paul M. Warburg, *The Federal Reserve System, Its Origins and Growth* (New York: Macmillan, 1930), vol. 1, chaps. 8 and 9. There are many sources for examining the minutiae of the various drafts and bills; good places to start are West, *Banking Reform*, pp. 79–135; and Kolko, *Triumph*, pp. 186–89, 217–47.

27. Quoted in Kolko, *Triumph*, p. 235.

28. Ibid., p. 222.

was at once cartelizing and inflationary.[29] The cartelizing nature of the Fed can be seen in its organization: an intimate partnerhsip between the federal government and the nation's banking community. There are twelve regional and district Federal Reserve Banks, the stock of which is held by the member banks in the district. Each Bank is governed by nine directors, of whom three are chosen directly by the banks in the district; three others are supposed to represent commerce, agriculture, or industry, but they too are chosen by the member banks in the district. That leaves only three directors appointed by the overall Federal Reserve Board in Washington. Furthermore, of the three publicly appointed directors, one—who becomes the chairman of the district Bank—must be a person of tested banking experience: in short, an ex-banker.

Not only are six—arguably seven—of each Bank's directors private bankers, but the chief executive officer of each Bank (originally called the governor and now the president) is appointed by the Bank directors themselves, not by the central Reserve Board (even though the latter must approve the choice). The central board has seven members, two of whom must be former bankers; all are appointed by the president of the United States.

Some critics of the Federal Reserve assert that it is really and simply a private central bank, since it is owned wholly by its member banks and it makes profits from its policies. But this view ignores the fact that virtually all profits made by the Banks are now taxed away by the treasury. The point of the cartel is not to make profits directly as shareholders of each Reserve Bank, but to benefit from the cartelizing and inflationary policies of the entire system.

At the same time, those who maintain that the Federal Reserve System is a wholly government-controlled institution overstate the case. It is true that all members of the Federal Reserve Board are government appointed and that all district Bank officials are instructed to act within the guidelines set by the Board. But every governor (or president) of a Federal Reserve Bank is selected largely by the bankers of the district, and these governors can exert a considerable

29. The terms "inflation" and "inflationary" are used throughout this article according to their original definition—an expansion of the money supply—rather than in the current popular sense of a rise in price. The former meaning is precise and illuminating; the latter is confusing because prices are complex phenomena with various causes, operating from the sides of both demand and supply. It only muddles the issue to call every supply-side price rise (say, due to a coffee blight or an OPEC cartel) "inflationary."

amount of influence on Fed policy.[30] As we will see below, the banker-elected governor of the Federal Reserve Bank of New York seized the reins of power from the Federal Reserve Board from the inception of the system in 1914 until his death fourteen years later.

The Federal Reserve System, like all central banking systems, is inherently inflationary. In the first place, the central bank acts as a lender of last resort, a giant governmentally privileged institution standing ready to bail out banks in trouble. Second, by coordinating bank activities, the central bank can pump in new reserves throughout the system and thereby induce a multiple expansion of bank money and credit. Since the banks can inflate uniformly, individual expanding banks no longer suffer from the constraining redemptions by nonexpanding banks that prevail in a regime of free and decentralized banking. If a bank expands credit on its own, it will soon find that its expanded notes or deposits will be passed on from its own clients to clients of other banks and that in the normal course of business they will be returned to the expanding bank for redemption. Yet the expanding bank will not have the funds to redeem these claims. There is also a third reason, which might not be as evident: Even if legal reserve requirements remain the same, the *centralizing* of reserves into the hands of the Fed by itself permits a considerable inflation of money and credit. In short, if before the establishment of a central bank every bank keeps its own cash reserves, and if afterward most of the cash is deposited in the central bank, the bank can then pyramid its own liabilities on top of its cash, thereby exerting a multiple leverage effect on the previously existing cash. In an illuminating book on the Federal Reserve and the Great Depression, Phillips, McManus, and Nelson summarize this process:

> Thus, if the commercial banks prior to the inauguration of a system of bankers' banking are required to hold an average reserve, say, of 10 percent against deposit liabilities, their deposits may be ten times that reserve, or, they may expand credit roughly on a ten-fold basis. With the reserves of the commercial banks transferred to the Federal Reserve Banks, and with the latter required to maintain a reserve of only 35 percent against the deposit liabilities due to the member banks, credit expansion may, at its utmost, proceed to approximately thirty times the amount of the reserves. Thus is seen that the

---

30. A banker's institution of far less importance is the Federal Advisory Council, composed of bankers selected by the board of directors of their district Bank. The council's recommendations garner considerable publicity, but it has no power within the system.

establishment of a central banking system [in the United States] magnified the former expansive power virtually three-fold.[31]

This statement overlooks the fact that the pre–Federal Reserve banking system was not free and decentralized, and it therefore exaggerates the quantitative inflationary effect of the creation of the Fed. But the basic point is correct.

A fourth inflationary effect of the creation of the Fed is inherent not so much in its structure as in the legal power to change the reserve requirements of the banks. Thus, before the enactment of the Fed, the average minimum reserve requirement for the nation's banks was 21.1 percent. The Federal Reserve Act of 1913 slashed those reserve requirements to an average of 11.6 percent, a reduction of 45 percent. Four years later, in June 1917, reserve requirements were further lowered to an average of 9.8 percent—a cut of 54 percent since 1913. In short, added to whatever multiple inflation of money and credit was permitted by the centralization inherent in the existence of the Fed, a twofold expansion in four years was permitted by the slash in reserve requirements.[32] Furthermore, in an inflationary move that was to become highly significant in the 1920s, the Federal Reserve Act drastically lowered the reserve requirements for time deposits in the banks. Previously, there had been no distinction in the legal reserve requirements between demand and time deposits; both had therefore averaged 21.1 percent. Now, however, the requirement for time deposits was lowered to 5 percent and then to a negligible 3 percent in June 1917.[33]

31. C.A. Phillips, T.F. McManus, and R.W. Nelson, *Banking and the Business Cycle: A Study of the Great Depression in the United States* (New York: Macmillan, 1937), pp. 25–26.

32. The Committee on War Finance of the American Economic Association hailed this development in early 1919: "Recent improvements in our banking system, growing out of the establishment of the Federal Reserve System and its subsequent development, have made our reserve money ... more efficient than it formerly was; in other words, have enabled a dollar in reserve to do more money work than before. This in effect is equivalent to increasing the supply of reserve money." It is indeed, provided that money's "work" is to be as inflationary as possible and "efficiency" means producing as much inflation as rapidly as possible. See "Report of the Committee on War Finance of the American Economic Association," *American Economic Review* 9, Supplement no. 2 (March 1919): 96–97; quoted in Phillips, McManus, and Nelson, *Banking*, p. 24n (see also pp. 21–24).

33. Phillips, McManus, and Nelson, *Banking*, p. 29.

THE PERSONNEL OF THE FEDERAL RESERVE

The people in positions of power in America's new central bank were at least as important as its structure. The bankers, warmly hailing the enactment of the Federal Reserve, waited eagerly to see who would be running the powerful new institution.[34]

Of the seven members of the Federal Reserve Board, two were (by statute at that time) *ex officio*, the secretary of the treasury and the comptroller of the currency. Before assuming their posts in the Wilson administration, these two men had been close business and financial associates. Secretary of the Treasury William Gibbs McAdoo had been a failing businessman in New York City when he was befriended and bailed out by J. P. Morgan and his associates. The Morgans set McAdoo up as president of New York's Hudson & Manhattan Railroad until his appointment in the Wilson Administration. McAdoo spent the rest of his financial and political life securely in the Morgan ambit. When he was president of the Hudson & Manhattan for a decade, McAdoo's fellow officers and board members were virtually all Morgan men. His vice-presidents were Edmund C. Converse, president of the Morgan-run Bankers Trust Company, and Walter G. Oakman, president of Morgan's flagship commercial bank, Guaranty Trust. His fellow directors included Judge Elbert H. Gary, chairman of the board of Morgan's attempted steel monopoly, U.S. Steel, and a director of another failed Morgan monopoly attempt, International Harvester; Frederic B. Jennings, partner in the "Morgan" law firm of Stetson, Jennings, & Russell (whose senior partner, Francis Lynde Stetson, was J.P.'s personal attorney); and John G. McCullough, a director of the Morgan-controlled Atchison, Topeka, & Santa Fe Railroad. Directors of Hudson & Manhattan's parent company, the Hudson Companies, included William C. Lane, a vice-president of Guaranty Trust, and Grant B. Schley, a brother-in-law of one of the country's top Morgan lieutenants, George F. Baker, head of the First National Bank of New York. Shortly after his ap-

---

34. See the reference to the proceedings of the conventions of the Kansas and California bankers associations in May 1914, in Kolko, *Triumph*, pp. 247–328. Senator Aldrich wrote to a friend in February: "Whether the bill will work all right or not depends entirely . . . upon the character and wisdom of the men who will control the various organizations, especially the Federal Reserve Board" (p. 248).

pointment as secretary of the treasury, William McAdoo cemented his political stature by marrying President Wilson's daughter.[35]

The comptroller of the currency was a long-time associate of McAdoo's. A Virginia banker and president of the Richmond Trust & Safe Deposit Company, John Skelton Williams had been a director of McAdoo's Hudson & Manhattan Railroad and president of the Morgan-oriented Seaboard Airline Railway. When McAdoo became secretary of the treasury, he appointed Williams as one of his two assistant secretaries.

One of President Wilson's five appointees to the Federal Reserve Board was another close associate of McAdoo's, Charles S. Hamlin, whom McAdoo had appointed as his other assistant secretary. Hamlin was a Boston attorney who had married into the wealthy Pruyn family of Albany, a family long connected with the Morgan-dominated New York Central Railroad.

Of the other Wilson appointees to the board, one was none other than Paul M. Warburg. Others were Frederic A. Delano, uncle of Franklin D. Roosevelt and president of the Rockefeller-controlled Wabash Railway; William P. G. Harding, president of the First National Bank of Birmingham, Alabama, and son-in-law of Joseph H. Woodward, head of the Woodward Iron Company, which had several prominent Morgan and Rockefeller men on its board; and, finally, Professor Adolph C. Miller, economist at the University of California, Berkeley. Miller had married into the wealthy, Morgan-connected Sprague family of Chicago. His father-in-law, Otho S. A. Sprague, had been a prominent businessman and had served as a director of the Morgan-dominated Pullman Company. Miller's wife's uncle, Albert A. Sprague, was a director of numerous large firms, including the Chicago Telephone Company, a subsidiary of the mighty Morgan-controlled monopoly American Telephone & Telegraph Company.[36]

The Federal Reserve Board thus began its existence with three Morgan men, one person in the Rockefeller ambit, a leader of Kuhn, Loeb & Co. (allied with the Rockefellers), a prominent Alabama banker, and an economist with vague family connections to Morgan

35. See Burch, *Civil War*, pp. 207-9, 214-15, 232-33. On McAdoo, see also John J. Broesamle, *William Gibbs McAdoo: A Passion for Change, 1863-1917* (Port Washington, N.Y.: Kennikat Press, 1973).

36. See Burch, *Civil War*, pp. 214-15, 236-37. Wilson also tried to appoint to the board his old friend Thomas D. Jones, a Chicago lawyer and director of the Morgans' International Harvester Company, but the Senate turned down the appointment.

interests. No board could have better symbolized the alliance of banking and financial interests, aided by a few economists, that had conceived and successfully driven through a radical transformation of the American banking system.

But more important from the inception of the Fed through the 1920s was the man appointed as governor of the Federal Reserve Bank of New York, who swiftly took control of the policies of the system. Benjamin Strong had spent virtually his entire business and personal life in the circle of top aides to J. P. Morgan. Secretary of several trust companies in New York City, Strong lived in the then wealthy suburb of Englewood, New Jersey, where he became close friends of three top Morgan partners: Henry P. Davison, Thomas W. Lamont, and Dwight Morrow. Davison in particular became Strong's mentor and in 1904 offered him the post of secretary of the new Morgan-created Bankers Trust Company. Strong soon married the daughter of the wealthy Edmund C. Converse, then president of Bankers Trust, and succeeded Thomas W. Lamont as vice-president. Not long after, Strong was acting as virtual president of Bankers Trust under the aging Converse, and in January 1914, he officially became president of the company.

Strong had favored central banking reform at least since 1907, and in August 1911 he participated with Nelson Aldrich in a lengthy meeting on the Aldrich plan with Davison, Vanderlip, and a few other leading bankers on Aldrich's yacht. He also spoke before the American Bankers Association on its behalf. When, at the suggestion of his close friend Warburg, Strong was offered the post of governor of the New York Fed, he at first refused, since he wanted a "real central bank . . . run from New York by a board of directors on the ground"—in short, a frankly and openly Wall Street–run cartelized banking system. After a weekend in the country, Davison and Warburg persuaded Strong to change his mind and accept; presumably, he now realized that he could achieve a Wall Street–run cartel on a little less candid basis from his powerful new post at the heart of the nation's money market. Strong became governor of the New York Fed in October 1914.[37]

Strong moved for seizure of commanding power shortly after the organization of the Federal Reserve System. At the organizing con-

37. See Chandler, *Benjamin Strong*, pp. 23–41. On the details of the first organization of the Federal Reserve Bank of New York, see Lawrence E. Clark, *Central Banking Under the Federal Reserve System* (New York: Macmillan, 1935), pp. 64–82.

vention of the system in October 1914, an extra-legal council of governors was formed. At the first meeting of the council in December, Benjamin Strong became chairman not only of the council but also of its operating executive committee. From then on, Strong acted as chairman of the governors and assumed the dominant powers that the statute had envisioned for the Federal Reserve Board. William P. G. Harding, who became governor (now chairman) of the Federal Reserve Board in Washington in 1916, cracked down on the meetings of the council, but Strong continued as the dominant force in the system, a position ensured by his being named the sole agent for the open-market operations of all the Federal Reserve Banks.[38]

Two years after the establishment of the Federal Reserve and a year before the American entry into World War I, Representative Carter Glass, a Democrat from Virginia who had drawn up the final Federal Reserve bill in the House, looked back on his cartelizing handiwork and found it good. He pointed out that his objective was very far from injuring Wall Street financial dominance:

> The proponents of the Federal reserve act had no idea of impairing the rightful prestige of New York as the financial metropolis of this hemisphere. They rather expected to confirm its distinction, and even hoped to assist powerfully in wresting this scepter from London and eventually making New York the financial center of the world. . . . Indeed, momentarily this has come to pass. And we may point to the amazing contrast between New York under the old system in 1907, shaken to its very foundations because of two bank failures, and New York at the present time, under the new system, serenely secure in its domestic banking operations and confidently financing the great enterprises of European nations at war.[39]

However, there was still a problem: the failure of the state-chartered banks to join the Federal Reserve System. All national banks were compelled by law to join the system and to keep their reserves with the Fed, but the eagerness with which they joined is revealed by the fact that virtually no national banks abandoned their national status to seek state charters. State banks were free to join or not, and a bane of the Fed's existence is that virtually none of them did so, preferring the lesser regulation of state law.

---

38. On the Strong seizure of power, see Clark, *Central Banking*, pp. 102–5, 161; Chandler, *Benjamin Strong*, pp. 68–78.

39. Quoted in Kolko, *Triumph*, p. 254. Carter Glass was a small-town Virginia newspaper editor and banker.

In a letter of October 1916, Benjamin Strong lamented the situation, writing: "Frankly, our bankers are more or less an unorganized mob. Until they are educated by experience to the advantages of cooperation through the Reserve System, I believe it is unsafe to rely upon reserves contributed by their voluntary action."[40] In such a vein has every cartelist reacted to the ambitions of individual firms or entrepreneurs to kick over the collective discipline of the cartel. All Fed officials felt the same way, and only political considerations have thus far prevented compulsory membership.

THE FEDERAL RESERVE AND WORLD WAR I

The Federal Reserve System arrived fortuitously for the financing of U.S. entry into World War I, for it is doubtful whether the government would have been politically able to finance the war through taxes, borrowing from the public, or the simple printing of greenbacks. As it was, the Fed was able to engineer the doubling of the money supply from its inception in 1914 until 1919.

World War I also led to a strengthening of the power of the Federal Reserve System and particularly of the dominance of Benjamin Strong and the Federal Reserve Bank. With banking subject to treasury demands for financing the huge deficits, Secretary of the Treasury McAdoo and Benjamin Strong assumed virtual joint control of the Federal Reserve. As Willis wrote, "It was the entry of the United States into the World War that finally cast a decisive vote in favor of a still further degree of high centralization; and that practically guaranteed some measure of fulfillment for the ambitions that had centered around the Federal Reserve Bank of New York."[41]

Strong's new dominance was facilitated by the treasury's making the Federal Reserve its sole fiscal agent. The secretary of the treasury had not done so before the war arrived, instead continuing the Jacksonian policy of depositing and disbursing funds from its own sub-treasury branches (the Independent Treasury System). Under the spur of the war, however, McAdoo fulfilled Strong's long-standing ambition; the Fed was now clothed with full governmental power. Strong had previously written: "We must, if possible, persuade

40. Chandler, *Benjamin Strong*, p. 81; see also Clark, *Central Banking*, pp. 143–48.
41. Willis, *Theory and Practice*, pp. 90–91.

[McAdoo] to permit the Reserve Banks to become the real, active, and effective fiscal agents for the Government. If he does that, our place in the country's banking system will be established for all time."[42] Strong's biographer summarizes how treasury operations during the war accelerated the dominance of the New York Fed:

> The war and the delegation of fiscal agency functions had a special effect on the New York Bank and on Strong's position in the System. Situated in the nation's great central money market, the New York Bank sold and distributed nearly half of all securities offered by the Treasury during the war and collected and disbursed great sums of money. At the country's foreign exchange center and gateway to Europe, it handled most of the Treasury's foreign exchange business, made many financial arrangements for the Treasury with foreign countries, acted as a central depository of funds from the other Reserve Banks as well as the New York district for payment to the representatives of foreign countries or to suppliers of munitions to them, and was the principal purchaser of acceptances. Thus it was only natural that the New York Bank came to enjoy the prestige of being the principal bank of the government, the Treasury came to use it as a channel for communicating with the other Reserve Banks, Strong's counsel was given heavy weight by the Treasury, and both the New York Bank and Strong emerged from the war with greater prestige, both absolutely and relative to the other Reserve Banks and the Board.[43]

Moreover, Strong had long wished to concentrate the country's gold coin and bullion in the hands of the Federal Reserve and outside the control of the public. In that way, cartelization would be intensified, and the inflationary potential of the Fed, which pyramided its own notes and deposits on top of its gold stock, would greatly increase. In 1917, in view of the war, the law was changed to permit the Federal Reserve to issue notes in exchange for gold (previously it could only issue them for commercial notes) and to require all legal bank reserves to be kept as deposits at the Fed rather than in cash. Furthermore, relaxed federal regulations on state banks in 1917 finally induced a considerable number of state banks to join the system, intensifying the concentration of reserves and of gold still further. Finally, from September 1917 to June 1919, the United States went implicitly, though not formally, off the gold standard—at least for foreigners. Foreign exchange operations were controlled and gold exports prohibited. As a result of all these measures, gold was

42. Chandler, *Benjamin Strong*, p. 105.
43. Ibid., p. 107.

virtually nationalized and successfully concentrated at the Fed. At the end of 1916, the gold reserves of the Reserve Banks were only $720 million, or 28 percent of the country's monetary gold stock. Two years later, gold reserves at the Fed were up to $2.1 billion, or no less than 74 percent of the nation's gold.

INTERNATIONALIZING THE CARTEL

The fortunes of the House of Morgan had been declining since the turn of the century, and so the Morgans saw a glorious opportunity open to them upon the outbreak of the war in Europe. The Morgans had close and long-time financial connections with England. In particular, Edward Grenfell (later Lord St. Just), senior partner of Morgan Grenfell & Co., the London branch of J. P. Morgan & Co., was also a long-time director of the Bank of England. Grenfell had long been the main informal link between the Bank of England and the New York financial community, and the relationship was formalized when the Morgan Bank became the fiscal agent of the Bank of England.[44] Led by partner Henry P. Davison at the end of 1914, the Morgans got themselves named virtually sole purchasing agent in the United States for British and French war goods. To pay for this immense export of arms and other matériel, the British and French were obliged to float immense loans in the United States, and the House of Morgan became the sole underwriter for these Allied bonds in the United States. Not only did Morgan find these monopolies highly profitable, but it prospered relative to its great rival Kuhn, Loeb & Co.—which, being German and connected with German banking and finance, was excluded from Allied war operations. As the Morgans and the bond market geared up to finance massive munitions and other exports to the Allies, Davison's old friend and colleague Benjamin Strong stood ready to inflate money and credit to finance these foreign loans.[45] The Wilson administration and the Federal Reserve Board were prepared to do likewise.[46]

44. Sir Henry Clay, *Lord Norman* (London: Macmillan, 1957), p. 87; Parrini, *Heir to Empire*, pp. 55–56.

45. On the interconnections among the Morgans, the Allies, foreign loans, and the Federal Reserve, see Charles Callan Tansill, *America Goes to War* (Boston: Little, Brown, 1938), pp. 32–134.

46. With the exception of the two pro-German members of the Federal Reserve Board. Warburg and Miller, both of German descent, who fought unsuccessfully against bank financing of munitions exports to the Allies. See ibid., pp. 105–8.

Benjamin Strong had scarcely been appointed when he began planning for an international cartel, a regime of "international cooperation" between the leading central banks of the world. In practice, such high-sounding terms could mean only cooperation for world monetary expansion. The classical gold standard, which basically prevailed before World War I, placed a firm restraint on the propensity of national central banks to inflate: The expansion of one country's currency would raise nominal income and prices in that country, cause a deficit in its balance of payments and an outflow of gold, thereby causing a check on inflation and perhaps a compulsion on the central bank to deflate back to its previous position. International central bank "cooperation" (or cartelization) then and now means the establishment of formal and informal mechanisms to prevent pressures for redemption and contraction on an inflating nation's currency. If this were *not* the meaning, there would be no need for international cooperation or indeed for central banking at all, since all any individual bank need do to keep itself afloat is to keep its rate of inflating to a minimum.

In the latter part of 1915, Benjamin Strong worked on international central bank collaboration, and in February 1916, he sailed to Europe to launch the first step: the establishment of the banks of England and France as foreign agents or correspondents for the New York Fed. Strong had long admired the central banking record of the Bank of England, and close collaboration with that leading central bank was to be the keystone of the new regime of inter-central bank cartelization. In England in March, Strong worked out an agreement of close collaboration between the New York Fed and the Bank of England, with both banks maintaining an account with each other and the Bank of England purchasing sterling bills on account for the New York Bank. In his usual high-handed manner, Strong expressed his determination to go ahead with the agreement even if the other Reserve Banks objected or failed to go along. Finally, after some backing and filling, the Federal Reserve Board endorsed the scheme as well as the initiating of a similar agreement with the Bank of France.[47]

Strong made his agreement with the governor of the Bank of England, Lord Cunliffe, but his most fateful meeting in England was with the then assistant to the deputy governor, Montagu Norman. This meeting proved the beginning of the momentous Strong-

47. Chandler, *Benjamin Strong*, pp. 93–98.

Norman collaboration that highlighted the international financial world of the 1920s.

Montagu Collet Norman was born to banking on both sides of his family. His father was a partner in the British banking house of Martin & Co. and was related to the great banking family of Barings. His uncle was indeed a partner of Baring Bros. Norman's mother was the daughter of Mark W. Collet, a partner in the international banking firm of Brown Shipley & Co. Brown Shipley was the London branch of the great Wall Street banking firm of Brown Brothers. Grandfather Mark Collet, furthermore, had been governor of the Bank of England in the 1880s.

At the age of twenty-one, young Norman began his working life at the family bank of Martin & Co., and then at Brown Shipley. In 1895, he went to work at the New York office of Brown Brothers, where he stayed for three years, returning to London to become a partner of Brown Shipley in 1900.

Strong and Norman became close friends as well as collaborators almost immediately, writing a steady stream of correspondence, personal and financial, and visiting each other at length every year from 1919 until Strong's death in 1928. They spent long vacations together, sometimes at Bar Harbor or Saratoga but more often in southern France.

BRITAIN AND THE GOLD EXCHANGE STANDARD

Britain, the major gold standard country before World War I, ended the war facing a set of grave, interlocking financial and economic problems, most of its own making. Along with the other warring nations, Britain had inflated sharply to finance the war effort. Each country except the United States (which had de facto suspended gold exports) had therefore been obliged to go off the gold standard. At the end of World War I, Britain determined that its own and the world's economic health required a return to the gold standard. And, in a fateful decision, it also determined—with surprisingly little discussion—that the pound sterling would have to be reestablished at the traditional prewar par of approximately $4.86.[48] Because of

---

48. On the portentous consequences of the British decision to return to gold at $4.86, see Lionel Robbins, *The Great Depression* (New York: Macmillan, 1934), pp. 77–87.

the greater inflation in Britain than in the United States, the free-market exchange rate of the two currencies was far lower than $4.86. The British government, with the help of J. P. Morgan & Co., succeeded in artificially pegging the pound at $4.76 from early 1916 until March 1919. Finally, the British let the pound float, and it quickly plummeted, reaching a low of $3.21 in February 1920.[49]

Britain's curious insistence on returning to the gold standard at a par overvalued by some 34 percent meant that the British had to face a massive price deflation. It was particularly important for Britain—dependent as it always has been on exports to purchase large quantities of imports—to keep its export prices competitive, and for that, deflation would be necessary. Although difficult at all times, deflation did not present major problems before World War I, since prices and wage rates were flexible downward. But during the war, a massive system of high-benefit unemployment insurance and a strong network of trade unions had developed in Britain, making deflation impossible without the repeal of welfare state measures and the rolling back of trade union power. Britain was not willing to take such heroic measures; in fact it wished to continue permanently the pleasant system of cheap credit and inflation that it had pursued during the war. Yet it continued to insist on an unrealistic $4.86 par in order to regain London's prewar prestige as the world's financial center.

Britain, in short, insisted on resting its postwar foreign monetary policy on a pair of inconsistent but fiercely held axioms: (1) a return to gold at the overvalued prewar par and (2) a refusal to permit the deflation needed to make axiom 1 at all viable. In fact, it insisted on continuing an inflationary policy. Britain's entire international financial policy during the 1920s was an attempt to square the circle, to maintain these two inconsistent axioms.

How could it do so? First, Britain would have to force or cajole other countries either to inflate themselves, so that Britain would not lose gold to them, or to return to a peculiar new form of gold standard, which would retain the prestige of gold without the content. Thus, Britain, operating particularly through the Financial Committee of the League of Nations (an organization that it controlled),

49. See Clay, *Lord Norman*, p. 135; Chandler, *Benjamin Strong*, p. 293; and especially Benjamin M. Anderson, *Economics and the Public Welfare: Financial and Economic History of the United States, 1914-1946*, 2d ed. (Indianapolis: Liberty Press, 1979), pp. 63-64.

induced or forced the vanquished or small victor states of postwar Europe (1) to return to gold at overvalued pars, thereby crippling *their* exports and subsidizing British imports; (2) to acquire their own central banks, so that they too could inflate in collaboration with the Bank of England, to discourage exports or gold from flowing from Britain; and (3), and perhaps most important, to return not to a classical gold standard but to a new form of "gold exchange standard." In a genuine gold standard, each currency is backed by gold, and gold flows in or out of the country. In the new form, each European country was expected to keep its reserves not in gold, but in pounds sterling, which would be backed by gold. Then, when Britain inflated, instead of losing gold to other countries, the sterling balances would pile up in London and themselves be used as a base on which to pyramid European currencies.

Britain was further protected from its inflationary policies in the 1920s by pledging to redeem pounds not in gold coin, as before the war, but only in large-denomination gold bullion. This ensured that gold could not circulate within the country and that gold would only be redeemed by large-scale international holders.

Having manipulated most of the European countries into ceasing to become a threat to its inflationary policies, Britain was still faced with the problem of the United States. The danger was that a non-inflating, hard-money, genuinely gold standard country such as the United States would soon drain inflating Britain of its gold and thereby wreck the new jerry-built international monetary system. Britain, therefore, had to persuade the United States to inflate *pari passu* with Great Britain; in particular, U.S. price levels could be no lower than Britain's and its interest rates no higher, so that gold funds would not be attracted out of London and into the United States. To persuade the United States to inflate—ostensibly in order to help Britain return to the gold standard—then became the premier task of Montagu Norman.[50]

50. See Murray N. Rothbard, "The New Deal and the International Monetary System," in Leonard P. Liggio and James J. Martin, eds., *Watershed of Empire: Essays on New Deal Foreign Policy* (Colorado Springs: Ralph Myles, 1976), pp. 20–27. See also Murray N. Rothbard, *America's Great Depression*, 4th ed. (New York: Richardson & Snyder, 1983), pp. 131–32; Chandler, *Benjamin Strong*, pp. 293–94; William Beveridge, *Unemployment, a Problem of Industry* (London: Macmillan, 1930), ch. 16; and Frederic Benham, *British Monetary Policy* (London: P. S. King, 1932).

Later in the 1920s, Emile Moreau, governor of the Bank of France and a caustic hard-money critic of Britain's international financial policy, recorded in his diary that England had established

a basis for putting Europe under a virtual financial domination. The Financial Committee [of the League of Nations] at Geneva has been the instrument of that policy. The method consists of forcing every country in monetary difficulty to subject itself to the Committee at Geneva, which the British control. The remedies prescribed always involve the installation in the central bank of a foreign supervisor who is British or designated at the Bank of England, which serves both to support the pound and to fortify British influence. To guarantee against possible failure they are careful to secure the cooperation of the Federal Reserve Bank of New York. Moreover, they pass on to America the task of making some of the foreign loans if they seem too heavy, always retaining the political advantages of these operations.[51]

Moreau also recorded a fascinating report sent by his close aide in 1926 on the intentions of Montagu Norman. The aide reported that the chief objective of Norman and his group was

the setting up of links between the various Banks of Issue. . . . The economic and financial organization of the world appears to the Governor of the Bank of England to be the major task of the Twentieth Century. . . . Hence his campaign in favour of completely autonomous central banks, dominating their own financial markets and deriving their power from common agreement among themselves.[52]

Norman succeeded in getting the nations of Europe to agree to adopt the postwar gold exchange standard at the Genoa Conference,

---

51. Chandler, *Benjamin Strong*, p. 379. Norman did indeed dominate the Financial Committee of the League, particularly through three close associates, Sir Otto Niemeyer of the treasury, Sir Arthur Salter, and Sir Henry Strakosch. The major theoretician of Norman's imposed gold exchange standard was Ralph Hawtrey, director of financial studies at the treasury. As early as 1913, Hawtrey was advocating international collaboration by central banks to achieve a stable price level, and in 1919, he was one of the first to call for international central bank cooperation in the context of a European gold exchange standard. See Clay, *Lord Norman*, pp. 137–38; Rothbard, *America's Great Depression*, pp. 159–61; Paul Einzig, *Montagu Norman* (London: Kegan Paul, 1932), pp. 67, 78; Melchior Palyi, *The Twilight of Gold, 1914–1936: Myths and Realities* (Chicago: Henry Regnery, 1972), pp. 134, 155–59.

On the gold exchange standard and Britain's inducement of European countries to overvalue their currencies, see H. Parker Willis, "The Breakdown of the Gold Exchange Standard and Its Financial Imperialism," *The Annalist* 33 (16 October 1931): 626ff; and William Adams Brown, Jr., *The International Gold Standard Reinterpreted, 1914-1934* (New York: National Bureau of Economic Research, 1940), 2: 732–49.

52. Palyi, *Twilight of Gold*, pp. 134–35.

called by the Supreme Council of the Allies in April 1922. All the details of the financial world of the 1920s were agreed on then by the Financial Commission of the Conference. Britain actually adopted this standard in 1925, and the other European nations followed at about the same time. The United States had decided at the last minute not to participate at Genoa because of Soviet participation, but the administration, especially the powerful Secretary of Commerce Herbert Hoover, was enthusiastic about the idea of inter-central bank collaboration for currency stabilization.[53]

OPEN-MARKET PURCHASES IN THE 1920s

The Federal Reserve generated a monetary expansion averaging approximately 7 percent per annum in the great boom years from 1921 to 1929, an expansion propelled by an average annual increase of member bank reserves of 6 percent per year.[54] By far the most important factor in generating the increased reserves was open-market purchases by the Federal Reserve Bank of New York. The purchases came in three great bursts: in 1921–22, in 1924, and in the latter half of 1927. In the first surge, the Fed tripled its holding of government securities from $193 million in November 1921 to $603 million in June 1922. This was the Fed's famous "discovery" of the inflationary effect of open-market purchases, a discovery that the authorities were delighted to make. Before the war, there had been little government securities available on the market and almost no short-run floating treasury debt. There was therefore little scope for open-market operations as a deliberate expansionary or restrictive

---

53. On the Genoa Conference, see ibid., pp. 133–40, 148–49 (the latter for a text of the relevant resolutions); Michael J. Hogan, *Informal Entente: The Private Structure of Cooperation in Anglo-American Economic Diplomacy, 1918-1928* (Columbia, Mo.: University of Missouri Press, 1977), pp. 42–48 (on the administration's position); Stephen V. O. Clarke, *Central Bank Cooperation: 1924-31* (New York: Federal Reserve Bank of New York, 1967), pp. 34–36; and Rothbard, *America's Great Depression*, pp. 161–62.

54. What would now be considered M–2, all bank deposits and savings and loan shares increased by 6.8 percent per annum from June 1921 to June 1929, whereas M–2 plus net life insurance policy reserves increased by an average of 7.7 percent during the same period. The rationale for including the latter is that this completes the figure for all claims redeemable in dollars at par on demand. See Rothbard, *America's Great Depression*, pp. 88–96, 100–101; Board of Governors of the Federal Reserve System, *Banking and Monetary Statistics* (Washington, D.C.: Federal Reserve Board, 1943), p. 34. On time deposits as actually redeemable on demand in the 1920s, see Anderson, *Economics*, pp. 139–42; Phillips, McManus, and Nelson, *Banking*, pp. 98–101.

policy even if this method had been discovered. After World War I, however, there was suddenly a large mass of short-term floating debt on the market that needed to be rolled over.[55] The Federal Reserve purchased the massive amounts in 1921–22 largely to acquire income-earning assets during the era of business recession. It then saw to its delight that a new and powerful instrument of monetary expansion and inflation had been discovered.

That this discovery was, to an extent, anticipated by Benjamin Strong is indicated by a letter he wrote on April 18, 1922, to Undersecretary of the Treasury S. Parker Gilbert, who had wondered about the Fed's unusually large purchases of government securities. Strong explained that the policy had been designed not only to add to the Fed's income-earning assets but also "to establish a level of interest rates, or at least to maintain rates at a level, which would facilitate foreign borrowing in this country" and thus would assure "more stable conditions and [would] facilitate business improvement." This indicates that, at least to some degree, Strong bought the securities in order to push interest rates lower, to expand money and credit, and to stimulate an economic upturn.[56]

The expanded open-market operations led Governor Strong to reconvene the governors conference on a regular and systematized basis. In May 1922, the conference set up an executive committee that would henceforth centralize and execute open-market operations for the entire system; Benjamin Strong was, not coincidentally, made chairman of this governors committee.[57] From that point on, and particularly from the time of the second committee meeting in October 1922, Strong was conducting open-market purchases and sales for the entire system, instead of merely functioning as an agent processing orders from other regional Reserve Banks.

55. See Rothbard, *America's Great Depression*, p. 125; H. Parker Willis, "What Caused the Panic of 1929," *North American Review* 229 (February 1930): 178; Charles O. Hardy, *Credit Policies of the Federal Reserve System* (Washington, D.C.: Brookings Institution, 1932), p. 287. See also Esther Rogoff Taus, *Central Banking Functions of the United States Treasury, 1789–1941* (New York: Columbia University Press, 1943), pp. 182–83.

56. Chandler, *Benjamin Strong*, p. 211. See also Harold L. Reed, *Federal Reserve Policy, 1921–1930* (New York: McGraw-Hill, 1930), pp. 14–41. Gilbert, who had come to the Treasury Department from the leading Wall Street law firm of Cravath and Henderson (now Cravath, Swaine & Moore), later became a partner of J. P. Morgan & Co. (Burch, *Civil War*, pp. 298–99).

57. The full name of the committee was highly descriptive: The Committee of Governors on Centralized Execution of Purchases and Sales of Government Securities by Federal Reserve Banks (Chandler, *Benjamin Strong*, p. 215).

Strong fell ill in February 1923 and was out sick until October. Shortly after, in April, the Federal Reserve Board in Washington, prodded by Adolph Miller, took steps to try to take dominance of the system away from the absent Strong. The board dissolved the extralegal governors committee and reconstituted a new one—the Open Market Investment Committee—strictly under the control of the board. With Strong temporarily gone, the board managed to force the New York Fed to sell most of its remaining government securities, for Miller, and the treasury as well, had continued to be uneasy at the large open-market purchases the Fed had made the previous year. Strong was furious both at the loss of his power and at the sale of securities, which he feared would cause a recession. In November, however, Strong came roaring back, seizing control of the Federal Reserve from that point until his final illness in the spring of 1928. Regaining his power over the Open Market Investment Committee, Strong, as chairman, created a Special System Investment Account at the New York Fed into which committee purchases and holdings were put. He also let it be known that he would expand such purchases whenever any economic downturn loomed: "The Reserve System should not hesitate to resume open-market purchases, thereby again reducing bank borrowings and easing money rates, rather than permit an unwarranted state of mind alone to disturb the even course of the country's production and consumption."[58]

The next big burst of inflationary credit expansion came in 1924. Shortly after Strong's return, he began to purchase securities on a massive scale, buying $492 million from October 1923 through 1924. The overriding reason was the determination to help Britain and Montagu Norman return to gold at its overvalued par. To do so, the United States had to embark on an inflationary, cheap money policy to lower interest rates and raise prices relative to Britain so that Britain would not lose gold to the United States. In 1922, Norman had hailed the easy credit and drop in interest rates to match Britain's credit expansion. During that and the following year, Norman continued to pepper Strong with appeals and demands for further extensions of credit in the United States. But Strong felt that the time was not yet ripe.

Finally, in 1924, with Britain's return to the gold standard looming the following year, Strong felt that the time was ripe, and the

58. Ibid., pp. 232–33. On Strong's resumption of power, see ibid., pp. 222–34; Clark, *Central Banking*, pp. 162–74.

massive open-market purchases began. Furthermore, the pound sterling, which had risen to $4.61 by the end of 1922 with the news of the impending return to gold, had fallen sharply to $4.34 by mid-1924. Only massive inflationary pressure in the United States could raise the pound to $4.86.

Strong set forth his basic policies in a lengthy letter on May 27, 1924, to Secretary of the Treasury Andrew Mellon:

> There still remains the serious problem of the disparity of price levels in the different countries due to monetary disturbances and currency inflation, the correction of which must be undertaken before a return to actual gold payment will be safe. This may be illustrated by the case of British prices and our own. The pound sterling is, roughly, at 10 percent discount measured in our gold currency. . . .
>
> At the present time it is probably true that British prices for goods internationally dealt in are as a whole, roughly, in the neighborhood of 10 percent above our prices and one of the preliminaries to the re-establishment of gold payment by Great Britain will be to facilitate a gradual readjustment of these price levels *before* monetary reform is undertaken. In other words, this means some small advance in prices here and possibly some small decline in their prices. . . . No one can direct price changes. They will be to a certain extent fortuitous, but can be facilitated by cooperation between the Bank of England and the Federal Reserve System in the maintaining of lower interest rates in this country and higher interest rates in England so that we will become the world's borrowing market to a greater extent, and London to a less extent. The burden of this readjustment must fall more largely upon us than them. It will be difficult politically and socially for the British Government and the Bank of England to force a price liquidation in England beyond what they have already experienced in face of the fact that their trade is poor and they have over a million unemployed people receiving government aid.[59]

The inflationary open-market purchases led to a fall of interest rates in the United States below Britain by mid-1924. Sterling rose again, reaching $4.78 by the spring of 1925. Britain resumed the gold standard at the prewar par by the end of the year. This resumption was further aided by the New York Fed's loan of a line of credit of $200 million to Britain, accompanied by a similar credit of $100 million to Britain by J. P. Morgan & Co.[60]

The final great burst of inflation, and the most intense of the 1920s, came in the latter half of 1927, when the Federal Reserve

59. Chandler, *Benjamin Strong*, pp. 282–84.
60. See Rothbard, *America's Great Depression*, pp. 133–34; Robbins, *Great Depression*, p. 80; Chandler, *Benjamin Strong*, pp. 301–21.

purchased $225 million of government securities and $220 million of banker's acceptances, adding $445 million to bank reserves from these two sets of purchases alone.[61]

The problem was that Britain's return to the gold standard quickly proved an unhappy one. The sharp rise in the value of sterling put great pressure on Britain's already depressed exports, especially on the coal industry. Britain's chronic depression intensified and rigid wage rates intensified unemployment. A general strike and a lengthy coal mine strike in 1926 were the direct consequence of the return to gold at an overvalued par. Instead of deflating, therefore, to validate the $4.86, Britain insisted on inflating in a vain attempt to relieve the depression. Prices rose, the Bank of England lowered its discount rate, and the balance of payment deficit and the resulting gold outflow became much worse. The pressure on sterling intensified. Unwilling to stop inflating and tighten credit, Montagu Norman turned to Benjamin Strong, his old ally.

Benjamin Strong purchased some sterling bills to reverse the dollar flow from Britain and also sold France $60 million in gold to forestall French demands for redemption of sterling. But these were just temporary expedients. So Strong invited three top central bankers for a highly secret conference in New York in July 1927. So secret was the conclave that Strong, in his usual high-handed fashion, prevented Gates W. McGarrah, chairman of the board of the Federal Reserve Bank of New York, from attending the meeting, and the Federal Reserve Board in Washington was also kept in the dark.[62] In addition to Norman, the other European representatives were Professor Charles Rist, deputy governor of the Bank of France, and Hjalmar Schacht, governor of the German Reichsbank. Strong and Norman tried hard to get Rist and Schacht to agree on a concerted and massive four-country cheap credit and inflation, but the Europeans vigorously refused, expressing alarm at the inflationary trend. While Rist and Schacht sailed for home, the Anglo-American combine stayed to weld their pact for inflation, expanded credit, and lower interest rates. Before Rist left, however, Strong told him buoy-

---

61. Rothbard, *America's Great Depression*, pp. 102–3, 107. On the significance of the acceptance market, see "Creating the Acceptance Market," below.

62. See Anderson, *Economics*, p. 189. Gates McGarrah was a close business associate of Albert H. Wiggin, chairman of the board of Morgan's Chase National Bank (Clark, *Central Banking*, p. 267). See also ibid., pp. 313–14; Chandler, *Benjamin Strong*, pp. 440–54.

antly that he was "going to give a little *coup de whiskey* to the stock market."[63]

President Coolidge and Secretary Mellon endorsed the new inflationary policy, the only high-level objectors being Adloph Miller and Herbert Hoover. The Federal Reserve authorities stayed silent about the reasons for their sudden expansion in late 1927, with only Governor W. J. Bailey of the Kansas City Federal Reserve Bank repeating the line that Strong had told him: that the cheap credit policy—including the open-market purchases, the lowering of rediscount rates, and the lowering of Fed buying rates on acceptances—was being pursued to "help the farmers." Helping Britain—not a very popular policy in the American heartland at the time—was kept under wraps as the major reason for the inflationary surge.[64]

The importance of helping Britain in the inflationary policy of the 1920s is seen in Benjamin Strong's comments to Sir Arthur Salter, secretary of the League of Nations and a Norman associate, in Paris in May 1928. Rejecting the idea of a formal meeting of the world's central banks, Strong cited the political hostility in the United States. Then, as an aide summarized:

> To illustrate how dangerous the position might become in the future as a result of the decisions reached at the present time and how inflamed public or political opinion might easily become when the results of past decision became evident, Governor Strong cited the outcry against the speculative excesses now being indulged in on the New York market and the criticism of the Federal Reserve System for its failure to curb or prevent this speculation. He said that very few people indeed realized that we were now paying the penalty for the decision which was reached early in 1924 to help the rest of the world back to a sound financial and monetary basis.[65]

---

63. Charles Rist, "Notice biographique," *Revue d'economie politique* 65 (November–December 1955): 1006–008. See also Rothbard, *America's Great Depression*, pp. 141–42.

64. Anderson, *Economics*, pp. 189–91. See also Benjamin H. Beckhart, "Federal Reserve Policy and the Money Market, 1923–1931," in B. H. Beckhart, J. G. Smith, and W. A. Brown, eds., *The New York Money Market* (New York: Columbia University Press, 1931), 4: 45.

65. Chandler, *Benjamin Strong*, pp. 280–81. In the autumn of 1926, a leading banker admitted that bad consequences would follow the cheap money policy but added: "That cannot be helped. It is the price we pay for helping Europe"; see H. Parker Willis, "The Failure of the Federal Reserve," *North American Review* 227 (May 1929): 553. For lavish praise of Strong by English bankers and politicians, see Clark, *Central Banking*, pp. 315–16.

CREATING THE ACCEPTANCE MARKET

Nowadays there are two methods by which the Federal Reserve can add to bank reserves and therefore to the inflating process of pyramiding new money on top of reserves as a base. One is open-market operations; the other is changing the rediscount rate at which the Fed, as the lender of last resort, lends reserves to banks in trouble. But a third method was highly important in the 1920s: the intense subsidization—indeed, the very creation—of a market in acceptances.

Discount policy was inflationary during the 1920s. In the first place, rates were set below the market instead of a penalty rate above it, thus inducing banks to borrow reserves from the Fed. Second, the Fed decided to lend continuously rather than only in emergencies. As the Federal Reserve Board wrote in its annual report of 1923:

> The Federal Reserve banks are the . . . source to which the member banks turn when the demands of the business community have outrun their own unaided resources. The Federal Reserve supplies the needed additions to credit in times of business expansion and takes up the slack in times of business recession.[66]

Presidents Harding and Coolidge repeatedly pledged to lower interest rates and to keep them low during the 1920s, and each did his best to fulfill that pledge. In 1922–23, 1925, and 1928, periods when the Federal Reserve was belatedly trying to stop its inflationary policies, the discounting process, spurred by artificially low rediscount rates, came to the banks' rescue.[67] During the onrushing stock market boom in 1927, President Coolidge and Secretary Mellon stepped in whenever the boom showed signs of flagging and egged it on, predicting lower interest rates and urging higher prices. In one of these statements, Mellon assured the market that "there is an abundant supply of easy money which should take care of any contingencies that might arise."[68] Furthermore, both Harding and

---

66. Federal Reserve *Annual Report 1923*, p. 10; cited in Seymour E. Harris, *Twenty Years of Federal Reserve Policy* (Cambridge: Harvard University Press, 1933), 1: 109. See also ibid., pp. 3–10, 39–48, 108–09.

67. Rothbard, *America's Great Depression*, pp. 102–3; see also pp. 110–17.

68. Ibid., p. 117. See also Anderson, *Economics*, p. 190; Oliver M. W. Sprague, "Immediate Advances in the Discount Rate Unlikely," *The Annalist*, 1926, 493.

Coolidge appointed Federal Reserve members who would implement the low discount rate, low interest rate policy.[69]

The most unusual aspect of the Federal Reserve–generated inflation of the 1920s was its creation and subsidization of the acceptance market in the United States. Commercial paper in the United States had always been confined to single-name promissory notes, often discounted at commercial banks. By contrast, in Europe and particularly in Britain, foreign trade (not domestic) was habitually financed by the mechanism of an endorsement of the debt, or *acceptance*. The acceptance bank endorsed and purchased the note and then sold it to a "dealer," or bill broker, who in turn sold it to a commercial bank for discount.

From the inception of the system, the Federal Reserve set out to bring a thriving acceptance market into being by massive subsidization. Since there had been virtually no naturally arising acceptance market in the United States, the demand for acceptances by discount banks was extremely slight. The Federal Reserve, therefore, undertook to buy all acceptances offered to it, either by the member banks or by a tiny group of designated dealers, and to buy them at a very low, subsidized rate. Generally, this rate was lower than the discount rate for similar commercial paper. In this way, the Federal Reserve provided reserves in a way unusually favorable to the banks. First, not only was the rate cheap, but acceptances were, like discounts and unlike open-market operations, *always* there to be provided by a passive Federal Reserve. And second, the acceptances never had to be repaid to the Fed and therefore, unlike discounts and like open-market purchases, they constituted a permanent addition to the reserves of the banks.[70]

The dominance of the Federal Reserve in making a market for acceptances can be seen in the proportion of acceptances held by the Fed. On June 30, 1927, over 46 percent of bankers' acceptances

---

69. See H. Parker Willis, "Politics and the Federal Reserve System," *Bankers' Magazine* (January 1925): 13–20; idem, "Will the Racing Stock Market Become a Juggernaut?" *The Annalist*, 24 November 1924, 541–42; and *The Annalist*, 10 November 1924, 477.

70. For a lucid explanation of acceptance and the Federal Reserve's role in the market, see Caroline Whitney, "The Bankers' Acceptance Market," in H. Parker Willis and John M. Chapman, eds., *The Banking Situation* (New York: Columbia University Press, 1934), pp. 725–36. See also H. Parker Willis, *Central Banking*, pp. 201ff; Rothbard, *America's Great Depression*, pp. 117–23.

were held by the Federal Reserve, over 26 percent for its own account and another 20 percent for foreign central banks.[71]

The subsidizing of acceptances was, from the early years, highly concentrated in New York City. In the first place, the New York Fed seized control of the acceptance policy in 1922 and kept it for the remainder of the decade. Second, the bulk of acceptances were on foreign transactions, and *all* of those acceptances were purchased by the Fed from only nine very large acceptance dealers located in New York City. Third, the number of acceptance banks was also quite small: 118 in the entire country in 1932, of which 40 were located in New York City. And three-quarters of all acceptances were executed by banks in New York City. The acceptance banks were generally large commercial banks but also included the huge International Acceptance Bank of New York, the world's largest acceptance bank, which in the 1930s merged with the Kuhn, Loeb–dominated Bank of Manhattan Company.[72]

Fed policy on acceptances played an inflationary role at crucial periods during the 1920s. In late 1922, this policy supplemented the role of discounts by far more than offsetting the open-market sale of securities by the Fed. In the 1924 credit expansion, almost twice as many acceptances as government securities were purchased in the open market. And in the fateful 1927 inflationary surge, acceptances ("bills bought") were equally as powerful in adding to reserves as the Fed's purchase of securities. Furthermore, during the latter half of 1928, when the Fed stopped buying securities in an attempt to get the runaway boom under control, massive purchases of acceptances kept the boom going.

Benjamin Strong was, of course, the man who instituted and maintained the Federal Reserve creation and subsidizing of the acceptance market. Indeed, Strong often took the lead in urging cheaper and cheaper rates to intensify the subsidy. For Strong, this policy was vital for the promotion of foreign trade and for facilitating interna-

71. The Fed held the same proportion in June 1929; see Hardy, *Credit Policies*, p. 258.

72. One of the nine designated acceptance dealers, the Discount Corporation of New York, was itself organized by a group of accepting banks to deal in bankers' acceptances; see Whitney, "Bankers' Acceptance," 727–28, 732–33. See also Beckhart, *Money Market*, 3: 319, 333, 410; Clark, *Central Banking*, p. 168; H. Parker Willis, "The Banking Problem in the United States," in H. P. Willis et al., eds., "Report on an Inquiry into Contemporary Banking in the United States," 1925, 1: 31–37 (unpublished); Hardy, *Credit Policies*, pp. 100–101, 256–57; A.S.J. Baster, "The International Acceptance Market," *American Economic Review* 27 (June 1937): 298.

tional central bank collaboration and management of the world financial system.[73]

But by far the most enthusiastic and tireless advocate of ever greater Federal Reserve aid to the acceptance market was Strong's close friend Paul Moritz Warburg. From the very beginning of Warburg's promotion of a central bank in 1907, that bank's subsidization of acceptance paper was crucial to his plan. He scoffed at the prevalence of single-name promissory notes in the United States, a practice, he opined, that left the backward United States "at about the same point that had been reached by Europe at the time of the Medicis, and by Asia, in all likelihood, at the time of Hammurabi." Warburg envisioned a money supply issued by a central bank based on acceptance paper purchased by that bank.[74]

We have seen that Paul Warburg was one of the most influential founders and shapers of the Federal Reserve System. He was on the board from 1914 to 1918, when he resigned because of his German ancestry, but he continued to be highly influential through the 1920s as chairman of the Fed's Federal Advisory Council. In January 1923, Warburg boasted before the American Acceptance Council, a trade association of acceptance banks and dealers organized four years before, that he had been largely responsible for the Fed's acceptance-buying policy as well as for the repeated statutory widening of eligibility for those purchases. In 1922, Warburg demanded still lower buying rates on acceptances, and in the spring of 1929, when he began to worry about the developing boom, he still called for the Fed to create a wider acceptance market.[75]

It is certainly plausible to hold that Warburg's unremitting zeal for massive Federal subsidy of the acceptance market, as well as its cartelization in the hands of a few New York acceptance bankers and dealers, was connected to his status as a leading acceptance banker. For Paul Warburg was chairman of the board of the world's largest acceptance bank, the International Acceptance Bank of New York, from its inception in 1920. He also became a director of the impor-

73. Chandler, *Benjamin Strong*, pp. 86–93.

74. Quoted in Elgin Groseclose, *America's Money Machine: The Story of the Federal Reserve* (Westport, Conn.: Arlington House, 1980), p. 49. See also ibid., pp. 48–51, 93–98; and Warburg, *Federal Reserve*, 2: 9–25.

75. See Rothbard, *America's Great Depression*, pp. 119–20; Harris, *Twenty Years*, p. 324; *The Commercial and Financial Chronicle*, 9 March 1929, 1443–44, Warburg's speech before the American Acceptance Council is in Warburg, *Federal Reserve*, 2: 822.

tant Westinghouse Acceptance Bank and of several other acceptance houses and was the chief founder and chairman of the executive committee of the American Acceptance Council. His vaunting speech to that council in early 1923 was his presidential address.[76]

FROM BOOM TO DEPRESSION

In the spring of 1928, with Benjamin Strong ill and absent after mid-May, the Federal Reserve became alarmed by the now exploding stock market and tried to put an end to the inflationary boom. The Fed managed to contract reserves by selling securities, but its efforts were partially offset by large increases in rediscounting spurred by the Fed's failure to raise rediscount rates sufficiently and by the banks' shifting of credit from demand to time deposits, which required far less reserves. Still, the contraction of reserves took hold from May through July, and as a result, the rate of money growth leveled off sharply.[77] Stock prices rose far more slowly than before, and the gold drain out of the United States began to reverse.

The boom could have ended in mid-1928, and the resulting contraction could have been mild. But this was not to be. Instead, the Fed's massive purchases of acceptances increased reserves in the latter half of the year, and money supply growth rose again. One reason for the Fed's failure to stay its relatively less inflationary course was the great pressure it received from Europe. The short-run "benefits" of the inflationary injection of 1927 in Europe had already dissipated: The pound was sagging again, gold was flowing out of Britain, and interest rates were again higher in the United States than in Britain. With the exception of France, Europe clamored against any tighter money in the United States, and the Fed's aggravation of inflation in late 1928 eased the flow of gold from Britain.[78] And

76. Rothbard, *America's Great Depression*, pp. 120–21; Groseclose, *Money Machine*, p. 97. It is fitting that after Benjamin Strong's death, Warburg paid him high tribute by hailing him for "welding the central banks together into an intimate group" and concluding that "the members of the American Acceptance Council would cherish his memory" (Warburg, *Federal Reserve*, 2: 870).

77. M–2, which had risen at an annual rate of 7.7 percent in the latter half of 1927 (8.1 percent if net life insurance policy reserves are included), increased by only 3.2 percent in the first half of 1928 (4.3 percent if life insurance is included); see Rothbard, *America's Great Depression*, pp. 102–3.

78. See Harris, *Twenty Years*, pp. 437–38.

Benjamin Strong, though ill and traveling in Europe, kept up a stream of pressure for easier money. In mid-July, Strong looked back on his handiwork and found it good. In a letter to S. Parker Gilbert, he wrote that his policy since 1924 had

> enabled monetary reorganization to be completed in Europe, which otherwise would have been impossible. It was undertaken with the well recognized hazard that we were liable to encounter a big speculation and some expansion of credit. . . . Six months ago we faced the new year with practically all the European nations in a strong position in monetary matters. . . . Our course was perfectly obvious. We had to undertake it. The conditions permitted it, and the possibility of damage resulting abroad were [sic] at a minimum.[79]

Strong went on to express his concern at the "very high rates" then prevailing in New York and looked forward to rate reductions in the fall. On his return to the United States in August, Strong continued to express concern, not over the inflationary boom and the runaway stock market but over what he considered excessively high interest rates. He clearly wished to resume his old inflationary policy.

After Strong's retirement in August, his faithful followers tried to tread the same path. His successor as governor, George L. Harrison, led the Open Market Committee to worry about excessively high rates and asked and obtained the board's permission for the authority to engage in massive open-market purchases.

The end of Strong's reign (he died in October 1928) led to indecisive splits and fragmented power within the Federal Reserve System. Although Harrison attempted to emphasize open-market purchases, the majority of the board wanted the Fed to buy far more acceptances. Each faction wanted its own version of inflationary credit expansion.

One reason for the Fed's emphasis on acceptances was the increasing adoption in Washington of the curious theory of "moral suasion," which was to plague efforts to end the inflationary boom during the latter half of 1928 and through 1929. Until the end, President Coolidge was still trying to boost the stock market. But the new President Hoover and Governor Roy Young of the Federal Reserve Board had a different theory: that credit could remain cheap and easy for "legitimate" business but be restrictive toward the stock market. As soon as Hoover assumed office, he tried moral suasion by

---

79. Chandler, *Benjamin Strong*, p. 458; see also pp. 459–63.

intimidation, sending an old banker friend, Henry M. Robinson of Los Angeles, to New York to try to persuade the banks to restrict stock loans and calling a meeting of editors and publishers to warn them of high stock prices.[80] Moral suasion was abandoned by June 1929. The Federal Reserve, after finally shutting off the acceptance window in March by raising its buying rate above the discount rate, delayed raising the rediscount rate under pressure from Hoover. Finally, it raised the rate in August, but typically the Fed offset this check to the boom by lowering the acceptance rate at the same time. As a result of this unprecedented "straddle," large Fed purchases of acceptances from July to October drove the stock market to new heights. These acceptances were largely sterling bills purchased by the New York Fed once again to help Britain. Great Britain was trying to inflate and pursue cheap credit in the midst of a worsening depression, and the Fed was trying to stem the renewed outflow of gold in the United States.[81]

With all eyes on the stock market, however, the great American boom of the 1920s was already over. For despite, or perhaps because of, the waffling and confusion of the Fed, the money supply remained level from the peak at the end of 1928 through September 1929. A recession was now inevitable.

Unbeknownst to most Americans, the economy started turning downward around July 1929. Three months later, on October 24, the great stock market crash brought the shift from boom to depression to the attention of everyone.

The Federal Reserve did not meet the crash with any idea of laissez-faire or of allowing the economy to liquidate the malinvestments of the boom. On the contrary, its inflationist attitude during the boom was matched by a similar and even more aggravated out-

80. See David Burner, *Herbert Hoover* (New York: Knopf, 1979), pp. 246–47.

81. The grave fallacy in the efforts of 1928 and 1929 to keep credit abundant in trade and industry while restricting the stock market was pointed out in an excellent epitaph on this policy by A. Wilfred May: "Once the credit system had become infected with cheap money, it was impossible to cut down particular outlets of this credit without cutting down all credit, because it is impossible to keep different kinds of money in water-tight compartments. It was impossible to make money scarce for stock-market purposes, while simultaneously keeping it cheap for commercial use. . . . When Reserve credit was created, there was no possible way that its employment could be directed into specific uses, once it had flowed through the commercial banks into the general credit stream" ("Inflation in Securities," in Willis and Chapman, eds., *Economics of Inflation*, pp. 292–93). See also Hardy, *Credit Policies*, pp. 124–77; and Oskar Morgenstern, "Developments in the Federal Reserve System," *Harvard Business Review* 9 (October 1930): 2–3.

look during the depression. In an unprecedented act, the Fed inflated reserves wildly in one week—the week of the crash. In the last week of October, the Fed doubled its holdings of government securities and discounted $200 million for member banks, adding $350 million to total bank reserves. Almost all of these increased reserves were poured into New York in order to prevent liquidation of the stock market and to induce New York City banks to take over the brokers' loans that nonbank lenders were in the process of unloading. As a result, member banks expanded their deposits during that fateful last week in October by $1.8 billion—a monetary expansion of nearly 10 percent in one week. Almost all of this amount, totaling $1.6 billion, came from increased deposits in New York City banks. The Federal Reserve at the same time sharply lowered its rediscount and acceptance rates.

By mid-November, the great stock market break was over and, stimulated by artificial credit, began to rise again. Total bank reserves then fell, so that at the end of November they had reached precrash levels. This contraction stemmed from a decline in discounts and acceptances, a gold outflow, and increased money in circulation; the Fed tried to offset this in vain by purchasing more securities. If we compare October 23, the day before the crash, with the situation at the end of 1929, we find that bank reserves *controlled* by the Fed— all government securities—tripled in size. This expansion was offset by such *uncontrolled* factors affecting reserves as a decline in gold and an increase in cash in circulation brought on by falling public confidence in the banks and in the dollar itself. The Fed had done its best to inflate in the last quarter of 1929, but its efforts were thwarted by seasonal cash outflows and the exigencies of the gold standard. The result was that the total money supply remained level in the final quarter of 1929.

President Hoover was proud of his experiment in cheap money and, in a speech to a White House conference of several hundred business leaders in December, hailed the nation's good fortune in possessing the magnificent Federal Reserve System, which had succeeded in saving banks, restoring confidence, and lowering interest rates. Hoover also revealed that he had done his part for the cause by personally urging the banks to rediscount more extensively at the Federal Reserve. Secretary of the Treasury Mellon issued one of his by now traditionally optimistic pronouncements, stating that there was "plenty of credit available." And William Green, head of the

American Federation of Labor, hailed the Federal Reserve for its success in ending the depression. On November 22, 1929, Green opined: "All the factors which make for a quick and speedy industrial and economic recovery are present and evident. The Federal Reserve System is operating, serving as a barrier against financial demoralization. Within a few months, industrial conditions will become normal, confidence and stabilization of industry and finance will be restored."[82]

Apparently, many leading Federal Reserve officials were disposed, at the end of 1929, to "let the money market 'sweat it out' and reach monetary ease by the wholesome process of liquidation."[83] But this laissez-faire policy was not to be. Instead, Governor George L. Harrison, head of the New York Fed, led a policy of massive easy money. Rediscount rates at the Fed, buying rates on acceptances, and the call loan rate all fell drastically. At the end of August 1930, Governor Roy Young of the Federal Reserve Board resigned and was replaced by a thoroughgoing inflationist, Eugene Meyer, Jr.[84] Total bank reserves rose during the year, chiefly through large Fed purchases of government securities. But all this inflationism was to no avail, since a wave of bank failures struck toward the end of the year, and shaky banks had to contract their operations. The net result was that the total money supply remained level throughout the year. For a while stock prices rose again, but they soon fell sharply, and production and employment kept falling steadily.

Meanwhile, the New York Fed continued to lead collaborations with foreign central banks, often against the wishes of the federal administration. Thus, the new "central bankers' bank," the Bank for International Settlements (BIS), was instigated by Montagu Norman, and much of the American capital for the BIS was put up by J. P. Morgan & Co. The BIS treated the New York Fed as America's central bank, and Governor Harrison made a trip abroad in late 1930 to confer with European central bankers. Chairman of the BIS's first organizing committee was Jackson E. Reybolds, a director

82. *The American Federationist* 37 (March 1930): 344. See also Rothbard, *America's Great Depression*, pp. 191–93.

83. Anderson, *Economics*, p. 227.

84. Eugene Meyer, Jr., was the son of a partner in the great international banking firm of Lazard Frères. Like stock speculator and close friend Bernard Baruch, Meyer had made a fortune through financial association with the wealthy Guggenheim family and with the Morgans in mining investments. At the time of Meyer's appointment, his brother-in-law George Blumenthal was a partner at J. P. Morgan and Co.

of the New York Fed, and the first president of the BIS was Gates W. McGarrah, who resigned as chairman of the board of the New York Fed to assume the post. Yet there was no legislative sanction for U.S. participation in the bank.

Despite the administration's and the Fed's systemic attempts to inflate and provide cheap money, the inflationists were not satisfied with the course of events. In late October, *Business Week* thundered against the supposed "deflationists in the saddle," supposedly inspired by the large commercial and investment banks.[85]

In contrast, in the same month Herbert Hoover apparently felt that the time had come for self-congratulation. In an address to the American Bankers Association, he summed up the multifaceted intervention of the preceding year. He hailed the Federal Reserve System as the great instrument of promoting stability, and called for an "ample supply of credit at low interest," which he pointed out was now available "through the cooperation of the banks and the Federal Reserve system." Hoover proceeded to point out that the Federal Reserve was the locus of a vast system of cartelization:

> The reserve system and its member banks and the Treasury participation in fact form a widespread cooperative organization, acting in the broad interest of the whole people. To a large degree it can influence the flow of credit. Bankers themselves are represented at each stage of management. And, in addition, the various boards and advisory committees represent also industry, agriculture, merchandising, and the Government. The reserve system therefore furnishes an admirable center for cooperation of the banking business with the production and distribution industries and the Government in the development of broad and detached policies of business stability.[86]

Moreover, these broad and detached policies of cooperation had succeeded in combating the depression:

> We have all been much engaged with measures of relief from the effect of the collapse of a year ago. At that time I determined that it was my duty, even without precedent, to call upon the business of the country for coordinated and constructive action to resist the forces of disintegration. The business community, the bankers, labor and the Government have cooperated in wider spread measures of mitigation than have ever been attempted before. Our

---

85. *Business Week*, 22 October 1930. See also Rothbard, *America's Great Depression*, pp. 212–13.

86. William Starr Myers, ed., *The State Papers and the Public Writings of Herbert Hoover* (Garden City, N.Y.: Doubleday, Doran & Co., 1934), p. 379.

bankers and the reserve system have carried the country through the credit storm without impairment.[87]

The rest is history.

SUMMARY

The bleak record of accelerating inflation and recession since the inception of the Federal Reserve in 1913 may be seen in a different light if we reevaluate the purpose that this central bank was intended to serve. For the Federal Reserve was designed not to curb the allegedly inflationary tendencies of freely competing banks but to do precisely the opposite: to enable the banks to inflate uniformly without worrying about calls for redemption by noninflating competitors. In short, the Federal Reserve was designed to act as a government-sponsored and -enforced cartel promoting the income of banks by preventing free competition from doing its constructive work on behalf of the consumer. The Federal Reserve emerged in an era when federal and state governments were embarked on precisely this kind of program in many sectors of industry, and it was designed to do for the banks what the ICC had done for the railroads, the Agriculture Department for the farmers, and the FTC for general industry. These actions of the Progressive era came after widespread attempts, in the late 1890s and earlier, to cartelize or create monopolies voluntarily, attempts that almost all came to swift and resounding failure. Various large business groupings, therefore, came to the conclusion that government would have to play an active and enforcing role if cartelization was to succeed.

This paper demonstrates the unhappiness of particularly the large Wall Street banks with the "inelasticity" of the pre–Federal Reserve banking system, that is, its inability to create more money and credit. They were unhappy also with the growing decentralization of the nation's banking by the early part of the twentieth century. After the failure of attempts by McKinley and Roosevelt's secretaries of the treasury to engage in central banking, and particularly after the panic of 1907, large banking and financial groups, in particular those of Morgan, Rockefeller, and Kuhn, Loeb, began a drive to establish a central bank in the United States. Despite minor politi-

87. Ibid., p. 381.

cal disagreements, the numerous variants of Federal Reserve proposals, from the Aldrich plan to the final bill in 1913, were essentially the same.

The structure of the Federal Reserve Act was cartelizing and inflationary, and the personnel of the Federal Reserve Board reflected the dominance of the large banking groups, particularly the Morgans, in the drive for a central bank. The ruling force in the Federal Reserve System from its inception until his death in 1928 was Benjamin Strong, Governor of the Federal Reserve Bank of New York, who all his life had been firmly in the Morgan ambit.

Strong's policies were what one might expect. His willingness to inflate money and credit to purchase government deficits was critical to financing America's entry into World War I. He also moved quickly to internationalize the banking cartel by forming a close tie with the Bank of England, of which the Morgan Bank was fiscal agent. The Morgans were also closely connected with munitions and other war-related exports to Britain and France, and enjoyed the sole privilege of underwriting British and French war bonds in the United States.

Benjamin Strong was obliged to inflate money and credit during the 1920s in order to help Britain return to an inflationary form of the gold standard at a highly overvalued pound. Only by Strong's increasing the supply of dollars could his close collaborator, Montagu Norman, head of the Bank of England, hope to stem the flow of gold from Britain to the United States. Strong performed this inflationary role not only by keeping rediscount rates below the market and buying treasury securities on the open market but also by subsidizing—indeed, virtually creating—a market in bankers' acceptances, which the Fed stood ready to buy in any amount offered at artificially cheap rates. This acceptance policy, designed to promote foreign trade (especially in London), was adopted under the influence of one of the founders of the Federal Reserve, Paul M. Warburg, of Kuhn, Loeb & Co. who also became the nation's largest acceptance banker.

When the stock market crash hit, the Federal Reserve and the Hoover Administration were scarcely ready to allow free-market processes to bring about recovery. Instead, the Fed, backed strongly by Hoover, inflated reserves wildly, and interest rates fell sharply—all, of course, to no avail.

Chapter 5

STAGNATION WITHOUT 'FLATION
The 1930s Again

Jonathan R. T. Hughes

The real world is complex. Economists' models, even large ones, are relatively simple. As Sir Roy Harrod said of economic models, they describe themselves.[1] The economist's technique has always been to simplify with theory and models that are usable representations of real-world events and processes. It is the only *general* way to proceed. For some economists, the simpler the theory and the model of it the better. The problem is belief: What is a sufficient explanation? Many economists come finally to realize, though, as they grow older, that committed belief is an intellectually expensive and wearying process. This is especially true when there are several models of theoretical explanation that are mutually incompatible but that appear to explain some real-world event equally well. If the same event is subject again and again to definitive analysis, fatigue can become severe.

An enthusiastic graduate student told me recently that there was no better road to knowledge than "good theory." Maybe even as late as ten years ago I might have agreed with him. But I told him I thought he was wrong, that better than good theory is knowing what you're talking about. Any theory might be misleading. We have daily tests of this methodological position. In the commodities markets, where it *pays* to be right, theories and models of them are cheap.

---

1. Roy Harrod, "What is a Model?" in J. N. Wolfe, ed., *Value, Capital and Growth: Papers in Honour of Sir John Hicks* (Edinburgh: University of Edinburgh Press, 1968).

In January 1980, theories abounded that explained why silver, then at $50 an ounce, would soon reach $75 an ounce. A well-known California oil tycoon had better information, sold the market short, and boasted in Chicago that spring that he had profited by $114 million. When he sold short, he knew what he was doing. Just why that was so has not come out from the subsequent hearings—and apparently will not.

A great historical event is not unlike a turning point in the commodities markets, and by studying the event, economists can learn a great deal. But alas, our theoretical biases are likely also to tell us what facts to study, so that we may well see the event at the end of our study only through the theoretical lenses we were wearing in the first place. Something *did* happen. But if there is more than one explanation of an event, believing one knows what occurred often enough depends upon the prior hypotheses of the believer. It is not much different from the processes of religious commitment; what satisfies one group of worshippers is insupportable nonsense to others, who believe entirely different cosmological doctrines with equal fanaticism.

This kind of problem is everyday experience for seasoned economists and evokes no particular interest among them except on professional occasions when leading advocates of contrary theories are arrayed against each other under the lights. The lay public, by contrast, seems amazed to discover from time to time that economists cannot agree among themselves about important events. That public (judging from TV talk shows) imagines that the disagreements are due primarily to the speed of current developments, together with the awkward problem that economists are constantly being asked to foretell the future. Disagreement there might be countenanced. Few members of the public realize that economists can be equally in disagreement about events long dead. The public might lose even more of their faith in our profession if they knew what has been written and fervently believed by economists about the depression of the 1930s.

THE INTERNATIONAL SCENE

For the American economic historian, the depression of the 1930s will prove to be the kind of Golconda that the industrial revolution has been for the British. Slavery will, I predict, prove to have been only a minor detour on the way to this Mother Lode. Look at these splendid prospects:

1. We do not know what caused the huge decline in output and employment in 1929–32. Recent exchanges have only increased the mystery.[2]
2. We do not know why the depression lasted so long.
3. We do not know why unemployment remained so high after physical output recovered and exceeded the 1929 level.
4. There was a veritable explosion of government policies of all kinds at all levels designed to cure the depression, and they all apparently failed.
5. The economics profession was then and still is in total disarray in its explanations of the depression.
6. It is all directly relevant to modern problems.
7. The available data and literary information have been only sampled by recent analysts.

The heart skips and the hand trembles before such mighty vistas. A whole new generation of economic historians can be educated on this material: time series, cross sections, aggregate, micro, international, national, regional, local, theoretical—the possibilities seem endless.

The international dimension alone is almost daunting in scope. If you believe the trouble was rooted in monetary phenomena, you may begin with the characteristics of the pre-1914 gold standard, the "old financial system," and then have fun with the *Cunliffe Report* and the problems posed by the wartime disruptions and differential inflation rates.[3] American economists, typically in hot pursuit of one-cause explanations, have lately ignored this entire dazzling smorgasbord of "causes." Charles Kindleberger has again been the exception. His book *The World in Depression 1929–1938* is true to the older tradition of internationalists led by such luminaries as

---

2. Karl Brunner, ed., *The Great Depression Revisited* (Boston: Martinus Nijhoff, 1981). In this volume, the "monetarists" are aligned against the "real forces" people.

3. Sir Albert Feavearyear, *The Pound Sterling: A History of English Money*, 2d ed. (Oxford: Clarendon Press, 1963), ch. 13; E. V. Morgan, *Studies in British Financial Policy 1914–25* (London: Macmillan, 1952); D. E. Moggridge, *British Monetary Policy 1924–1931: The Norman Conquest of $4.86* (Cambridge: Cambridge University Press, 1972).

Folke Hilgerdt, Ragnar Nurkse, and W. Arthur Lewis.[4] I was once assured by an economist of high international standing that the entire depression of the 1930s was caused by the failure to find the correct exchange rates in the interwar period.

The story of the 1930s' depression seen from the vantage point of, say, London, is magnificently complex. The trail after 1918 leads obscurely past the Brussels Conference, the *Cunliffe Report*, the Genoa Conference, the German inflation, the gold exchange standard, the return to gold in Britain in 1925 at the old par value, reparations, the Young and Dawes plans, the New York stock market crash, the Hoover moratorium, the French liquidation of foreign exchange holdings, the resulting European monetary crisis of 1931, the failure of the Credit Anstalt, the British abandonment of free trade and gold, the failure of the London Monetary Conference in 1933, the rise of the 1930s' currency blocs, protectionism and the stagnation of world trade, most-favored-nation commercial policies, the Tripartite Agreement of 1937, and much else. There are also the arguments concerning the effects of World War I on the financial and technological continuity of European development, and on the terms-of-trade consequences of European deaths in 1914–18 from war and influenza, once explored by Arthur Lewis.[5] In addition to that, we have Svennilson's discussion of real forces of stagnation rooted in the European failure to modernize industry and otherwise to adapt to changes in technology and in economic conditions in the interwar period.[6] The complexity of all this is both its beauty and its curse; you finally cannot recall which part went where and how it all added up. That may be, indeed, why so many American economists have chosen just to ignore it all and concentrate on single causes— money, autonomous "real" forces, the stock market crash, the Smoot-Hawley tariff, or whatever.

---

4. See Charles Kindleberger, *The World in Depression 1929–1938* (Berkeley and Los Angeles: University of California Press, 1973); Folke Hilgerdt, *The Network of World Trade* (Princeton: League of Nations, 1942); Ragnar Nurkse, *International Currency Experience: Lessons of the Interwar Period* (Princeton: League of Nations, 1944); W. Arthur Lewis, *Economic Survey, 1919–1939* (London: Allen & Unwin, 1949).

5. For the former, see H. W. Arndt, *The Economic Lessons of the Nineteen-Thirties* (London: Oxford University Press, 1944), ch. 1; for the latter, see Lewis *Economic Survey*, pp. 151–52.

6. Ingvar Svennilson, *Growth and Stagnation in the European Economy* (Geneva: United Nations, 1954).

What difference could it make to ignore the international economy? In 1929–30, had American commodity exports fallen to zero and that product simply vanished into thin air, GNP would have been reduced, *ceteris paribus*, by 4.5 to 5 percent. That is not nothing. U.S. exports fell from $5.4 billion to $4.0 billion in 1929–30 (by 13.5 percent), accounting for $1.4 billion of the $13.3 billion fall in nominal GNP—over 10 percent of the decline.[7] But the international scene was more important than mere numbers might imply. There are capital flows to account for, "hot money" movements, and perhaps most important, the psychological impact upon American capitalists and investors of the sombre news emanating from Europe in 1930–31. Of course, the New York Fed reacted to the British abandonment of gold payments on September 20, 1931, by raising its discount rate in October from 1.5 to 3.5 percent, a rise of more than 100 percent. Elmus Wicker's study of this episode shows a narrow concentration upon foreign affairs and foreign opinion inside the Fed.[8] What difference did that increase in the rediscount rate make inside the U.S. economy? In New York, the prime rate went up from 2 to 4 percent sympathetically.[9] GNP was falling, and unemployment was rising. A doubling of interest rates cannot have been a force, at that point, in stemming the tide of contraction. Gold was flowing out, and a rise in the rediscount rate was the orthodox move in such circumstances.

But for the most part we have downplayed the foreign influence in our explanation of the origins and continuation of the depression. Perhaps instinct is right, and the international situation adds complexity without contributing to clarity. Trade expansion, after the 66 percent plunge in exports of 1929–33, did not add much fuel to the recovery of the GNP. By 1940, exports were still only three-fourths the 1929 level in value.

7. U.S. GNP in 1929 was $104.4 billion; in 1930, $91.1 billion. U.S. commodity exports in 1929 were $5.4 billion; in 1930, $4.0 billion. Data from *Historical Statistics of the United States* (Washington, D.C.: Government Printing Office, 1960), series F1, U1.

8. Elmus R. Wicker, *Federal Reserve Monetary Policy 1917-1933* (New York: Random House, 1966), pp. 163–171.

9. Board of Governors of the Federal Reserve System, *Banking and Monetary Statistics, 1914-1941* (Washington, D.C.: The Federal Reserve, 1943), table 121, p. 457.

THE HOME FRONT

Leaving aside the incredible international scene, let us consider the contending domestic arguments that have recently held the field. Major attention in the past few years has concentrated upon the spectacular beginnings. The stock market crash in 1929, the banking crisis of 1930, and the kamikaze plunge to 1932 were disasters equal to anything purely economic known to history. A roaring finale came in early 1933 with the nationwide bank holiday from which some 4000 banks never recovered.

If the fright the banks sustained produced a partial failure of confidence, the same had to be felt by bank depositors because of bank failures. Banks closing their doors to depositors had been a way of life in this country almost from the beginning of the nineteenth century. In 1914, there were about 28,000 banks and 152 failures.[10] But in 1926, 28,350 banks yielded 976 failures. Already in the 1920s the shakiness of the country's unit banking system had become obvious. After World War I, the failure rate changed an order of magnitude: 167 in 1920 to 505 in 1921. In 1922, the number dipped to 366; after that, 1928 apart, there were never fewer than 600 failures a year, about four times the rate per 1000 banks that had characterized the prewar years.

Then came the deluge. The number of failures leaped to 1350 out of 24,270 in 1930, then to 2293 out of 22,242. Between 1929 and 1933, the number of banks fell by about half—to 14,771—and there were a total of 9755 outright failures. The loss rate on total deposits sustained by the depositors themselves was about 22 percent. So a deposit in a bank in 1929–32 gave you more than a 10 percent chance of never seeing your money again, on the average. Most of the failures had been smaller banks, of course, but then most of the banks were small.

This history illuminates the sudden prosperity of the Postal Savings System. Founded in 1910 in response to the panic of 1907, it represented total safety at an unchanging 2 percent per annum.[11] Before the 1930s, 2 percent was not an attractive rate for most

10. Data to follow on number of banks, failures, loss estimates, and so on from Federal Reserve, *Banking and Monetary Statistics*, table 66, p. 283.

11. Maureen O'Hara and David Easley, "The Postal Savings System in the Depression," *The Journal of Economic History* 39, no. 3 (September 1979): 741–53.

investors and depositors. After 1932, 2 percent was a good yield compared to money market rates. Between 1929 and 1932, the deposits of the Postal Savings System jumped from $152 million to $1.2 billion.[12] As O'Hara and Easely demonstrated, this switch, due to increased bank risk, in large part helped submerge the savings and loan institutions and, along with them, the privately financed housing industry for the rest of the 1930s. The Postal Savings System *had* to pay 2 percent, and it required a 2.25 (and after 1934, 2.5) percent return if it redeposited in local banks, as the law prescribed. The law was not altered except to *raise* the required redeposit rate during the 1930s. As a result, the national banks began refusing deposits by the Postal Savings System. The only legal alternative for the Postal Savings System was treasury securities. Its entry into the market for treasury securities exacerbated the problems of all sectors of the private financial system.

Changes in consumer behavior might also be tagged to the Federal Reserve's policies, if one credits the Fed with major responsibility for the 1929 crash and subsequent disarray. Mishkin argues that the financial consequences for individuals had to include a "wealth effect."[13] For individuals, the depressing results of the contraction were not limited to such balance sheet items as stock prices. The deflation of the asset values of consumers' durables and real estate reinforced the constricting effects of straight financial losses and helped to spread retrenchment throughout the consumer sector. Although the resulting reduction in consumer activity might have cheered some analysts, such as the "Austrians" (discussed below), by helping to drive down prices and wages toward new equilibrium levels, from the conventional Keynesian viewpoint the most likely result would be declining investment and rising unemployment. With wages lagging behind the downward plunge of prices, the Austrians, in fact, would have to expect the same results.

For the economist, the problem with the crisis in the banking sector after 1929–30 is in drawing the line at the outer limit of clear spread effects. The indirect ramifications are vast. If the entire financial imbroglio, or a major part of it, can be blamed on the Federal Reserve System, there is a simplification at least in the search for

12. *Historical Statistics*, series X244.
13. Frederic S. Mishkin, "The Household Balance Sheet and the Great Depression," *The Journal of Economic History* 38, no. 4 (December 1978): 918–37.

causes, if not in the measurement of the ultimate consequences. Even if Peter Temin were considered correct in his argument against Friedman and Schwartz,[14] who bore the ultimate responsibility for the bank failures? Was it the Fed? Did the Fed's officials *at that time* consider it part of their duty to stop the bank failures? If so, of course, then there is no saving their historical reputation. But even the Bank of England in the classic monetary crises of the nineteenth century and Pierpont Morgan in 1907 practiced *triage*, saving some banks and letting others die.[15] In 1929–33, bank fatalities looked more like genocide than *triage* —unless, of course, no one was responsible except individual bank officers. In that case, the banks were like the all-too-familiar neighborhood suicide who decides to do in not only himself but his family and neighbors to boot.

The country's new central bank failed to deliver anything resembling financial or banking stability (if indeed the Fed at that time believed this to be its commission). The nominal money supply was allowed to decline, and in 1931, briefly, the rediscount rate was even raised. The Fed then sat idly by while thousands of banks failed and millions of depositors lost their savings. The Fed seemed to do little enough after that to aid recovery, but it did help the Treasury Department abort the recovery in 1937. This feckless record is the target of recent "monetarist" analyses: Friedman and Schwartz, later buttressed by Allen Meltzer, Thomas Mayer, and others.[16] The Fed did *too little*.

This interpretation of events is devastating enough, but there is another view from the money angle that is in fact quite different: the pure neoclassical, or "Austrian," view, stated most recently by Professor Murray Rothbard but sketched out earlier by Lionel Robbins.[17] In the Austrian interpretation, the 1929 stock market run-up,

14. See Peter Temin, *Did Monetary Forces Cause the Great Depression?* (New York: Norton, 1976); Milton Friedman and Anna J. Schwartz, *A Monetary History of the United States, 1867–1960* (Princeton: National Bureau of Economic Research, 1963).

15. See J. R. T. Hughes, *Fluctuations in Trade, Industry and Finance* (Oxford: Clarendon Press, 1960), app. 5, for the Bank of England's *triage* operations in the 1857 crisis. See idem, *The Vital Few* (London: Oxford University Press, 1973), pp. 439–53, for Morgan in 1907.

16. Friedman and Schwartz, *Monetary History*, ch. 7. Meltzer brings back the Smoot-Hawley tariff as an additional cause of the constriction; for samples of work by him, Mayer, and others in support of the monetarist interpretation, see Brunner, *Great Depression*, especially chapters 1, 6, 7, 17.

17. See Murray N. Rothbard, *America's Great Depression* (Kansas City, Mo.: Sheed & Ward, 1972), chs. 9–11; Lionel Robbins, *The Great Depression* (London: Macmillan, 1934).

the catastrophic "bubble on the boom," was caused by the Fed's failure to maintain a tight rein on the market in that fateful spring and summer. After the crash, the market was restrained from its normal self-correcting adjustment by *too much* Federal Reserve tinkering. As with the recent monetarist interpretation, the Fed is declared guilty, *but guilty of a different crime.* Between 1929 and 1932, the Fed raised its holdings of government securities by a factor of five, from $511 million to $2,400 million, in an unsuccessful attempt to prop up the supply of bank money by expanding the reserve base.[18]

The result was that the nominal money supply failed to fall more than prices did, and prices did not fall enough. Had prices fallen freely, faster, and farther, and had the Hoover administration not emphasized the need to maintain nominal wages as prices fell, a recovery might have occurred—and quickly too, as in 1922-24. In 1920-21, with a one-year fall in wholesale prices of nearly 40 percent, nominal GNP fell 17 percent, but real GNP fell only 3 percent, and a vigorous recovery ensued. Nominal GNP in 1930 had fallen only 13 percent from 1929 and wholesale prices a mere 10 percent, but real GNP was down 9 percent—three times the decline of real activity that had occurred, proportionately, in 1920-21.[19] Rigid prices and wages were preventing a realignment of productive resources on a free-market basis. Efforts by an activist federal government from 1933 onward to sustain and raise prices (Roosevelt: "If we can't do it one way we'll do it another")[20] killed any hope of recovery, adding meaning to the mystery recently described by Phillip Cagan: "We face in the 1930's experience the need to explain a perplexing combination of large-scale unemployment and substantial increases in wages."[21] To the Austrians, that phenomenon would be prime evidence that the necessary adjustment in wages and prices had been prohibited.[22] It had been stopped by an external force: government intervention, or at least attempted intervention. Where

---

18. *Historical Statistics*, series X249.

19. Ibid., series X267, E25, F1, F3.

20. Quoted in Jonathan Hughes, *The Governmental Habit* (New York: Basic Books, 1977), p. 162.

21. In Brunner, *Great Depression*, p. 284; Cagan comments on Michael Weinstein's chapter, "Some Macroeconomic Impacts of the National Industrial Recovery Act 1933-35."

22. In 1930, Schumpeter thought the depression had already lasted so long because wages were inflexible downward; see Joseph Schumpeter, "The Present World Depression: A Tentative Diagnosis," *American Economic Review* 21, no. 1 (1931), supplement: 177–201.

the monetarists find irresponsible inactivity, the Austrians see energetic incompetence. Either way, the Fed lost. An ambitious young econometrician who could prove that the Fed was adequate and correct would achieve overnight fame.

Peter Temin was not convinced by the Friedman-Schwartz monetarist interpretation.[23] He was struck by the downward trend of interest rates after 1929 and the scarcity of evidence that the economy was at any time suffering from a lack of "money" (thus far in agreement with the Austrians). If prices fell no faster than the supply of nominal money, then there was about the same amount of monetary command over real resources in 1932 as in 1929. Thus the crash dive from 1929 to 1932 could not have been the result of monetary forces alone. Temin found that the one factor that changed fundamentally, and independently of the rest, was nominal private consumption. It fell 9 percent in 1929–30, 8.6 percent in 1930–31, and another 8 percent in 1931–32. The total fall from 1929 to 1933 was a jarring 41 percent.[24] Americans had closed their purses and wallets after the binge of the late 1920s.

Temin's arguments raised a storm. First, the Keynesians had traditionally considered investment, not consumption, to be the volatile factor. The monetarists (both kinds) saw their villain, the Federal Reserve System, transformed into a mere accessory after the fact, perhaps even a passive witness for the prosecution. Temin's analysis revealed the great collapse if not simply as an act of God, then certainly as a voluntary act by millions of consumers pursuing (presumably) invincible self-interest. And why not? Real interest rates were falling, prices were falling, and the opportunity costs of hoarding cash were collapsing. The smart thing for income earners to do, as Joel Mokyr pointed out in conversation recently, was just to sit quietly on their hoards and earn a riskless 5 percent or more a year by watching the silver tarnish. Robert J. Gordon and James Wilcox, in a resurvey of the evidence, conclude: "The stock market collapse precipitated a drastic decline in consumption spending that interacted with and further aggravated the continuing decline in residential construction."[25] The two well-known trouble spots that had pre-

---

23. See Temin, *Monetary Forces*; see also his defense of himself, "Notes on the Causes of the Great Depression," in Brunner, *Great Depression*, pp. 108–24.

24. Data from *Historical Statistics*, series F68.

25. Robert J. Gordon and James Wilcox, "Monetarist Interpretations of the Great Depression: An Evaluation and Critique," in Brunner, *Great Depression*, p. 80.

ceded 1929 were the decline in new construction after 1925 and the blow to farm incomes and net worth produced by the 1920-21 collapse of food prices. Perhaps reluctantly, Gordon and Wilcox, brought in as *amici curiae* in this hearing, came down on Temin's side.

As we already have noted, Frederic Mishkin's study of the declining values of consumer assets lends support to the collapse of private consumption as a force operating independently of purely monetary variables.

THE REAL ISSUE

The decline in 1929-32 is only part of the problem. The big issue for most students of the 1930s' depression is, Why was the thing so bad, so deep? Why did it last so long? The decline had gone on for more than three years; then the recovery failed to reemploy the nation's work force. Ten years after 1929, despite all the great and dramatic rescue efforts and with interest rates lying dead in the water most of the time, unemployment still averaged 17 percent of the labor force — or 11 percent, counting the leaf rakers and boondogglers on Federal make-work projects as if they were employed in productive labor.[26] GNP in current prices did not reach 1929 levels again until 1941 (although real GNP surpassed that level in 1937 and was nearly 12 percent above it in 1940 — not much of a ten-year gain).[27]

In Wicksell's world, the long depression had to be caused by the market interest rate's lying persistently above or equal to the natural rate. If the market rate fell below the natural rate (given the prospective yield of investment), a potential price rise and a recovery would be indicated.[28] But what, in the world of the 1930s, could such words mean? Market interest rates were unprecedentedly low: Short rates were below 1 percent after 1934.[29]

---

26. Stanley Lebergott, "Annual Estimates of Unemployment in the United States, 1900-1954," *The Measurement and Behavior of Unemployment* (New York: National Bureau of Economic Research, 1956), pp. 213-41; Michael Darby, "Three and a Half Million U.S. Employees Have Been Mislaid," *Journal of Political Economy* 84 (February 1976): 8.

27. *Historical Statistics*, series F1, F3.

28. For a long-run application of Wicksell's system, see Jonathan Hughes, "Wicksell on the Facts: Prices and Interest Rates 1844-1914," in Wolfe, *Value, Capital and Growth*, p. 316n.

29. *Historical Statistics*, series X306, X309.

We will see shortly that Friedman and Schwartz found evidence to support the argument that even the very low Federal Reserve rediscount rates of the late 1930s were too high. Could the prospective yield on new investment be so low that record low interest rates still restrained borrowing to undertake those investments? What about Keynes's view?

To Keynes the answer was yes, but for ambiguous reasons. He saw the collapse of investment as a capital strike, and he called in the *General Theory* for a "socialization of investment" to get out of it.[30] In Chapter 22, "Notes on the Trade Cycle," he said a "sudden collapse" of the marginal efficiency of capital could yield the kind of evaporation of investment that had occurred, even with interest rates stuck at low liquidity trap levels.[31] Gross private domestic investment (current prices) fell from $16.2 billion in 1929 to $900 million in 1932, a decline of about 96 percent, and only in 1937 and 1940 did it exceed even that of 1930 ($10.3 billion). Private investment at 1929 levels never came back until the wartime economy was gearing up in 1941.[32]

How low were hopes and expectations? Apart from comments about that man in the White House and the like, such things are virtually impossible to measure with any pretense of accuracy. But consider some unpretentious data for a moment. If we take the number of corporate mergers and new corporate issues as representatives of the animal spirits of our depression entrepreneurs, it was clearly vacation time. There were 1245 mergers in 1929 and 101 in 1934, a decline of 92 percent. From 1934 to 1941, corporate mergers never numbered as many as 12 percent of the 1929 figure. New capital issues, $8.0 billion in 1929, were $161 million in 1933, a decline of 98 percent. Before the Japanese attacked Pearl Harbor, new issues never totaled as much as 15 percent of 1929 in any year. Even patents applied for, surely a measure of hope at the thinnest margins, fell from 89,700 in 1929 to 56,100 in 1933, down 37.5 percent. They recovered to 66,900 in 1938, but by 1941, after a renewed onslaught of depression, they sank to 52,300.[33] In short, expectations were flat, to say the least. Henry Ford may have thought that

30. John Maynard Keynes, *The General Theory of Employment, Interest and Money* (New York: Harcourt Brace, 1936), p. 378.

31. Ibid.

32. Data from *Historical Statistics*, series F68.

33. Ibid., series X367, V30, W66.

Table 5-1.   Excess Reserve Measures, 1929-1940.

	Excess Reserves as Percentage of	
Year[a]	*Total Reserves*	*Required Reserves*
1929	2.2	2.3
1930	1.8	1.9
1931	5.2	5.2
1932	1.4	1.8
1933	22.6	32.1
1934	21.4	37.8
1935	35.1	74.4
1936	45.5	65.7
1937	30.4	36.0
1938	15.5	24.5
1939	30.4	53.9
1940	54.6	73.8

a. Ratios for the end of December each year.

Source: Federal Reserve, *Banking and Monetary Statistics*, table 105, p. 396.

"these are the best times we ever had" heading into the 1930s, but his fellow entrepreneurial types hardly agreed with him.[34]

Conceivably, the strange behavior of bank reserves in the 1930s tells us something about someone's expectations. To Keynesians, the data transparently reflect the "liquidity trap," but others deny such an interpretation. We will merely note that reserves in excess of the legal minima are not earning any money for the bankers, nor are they being invested by the borrowers, and it is passing odd that they should have remained idle in such volumes for so long and that this strange behavior was precisely coterminous with the administration of FDR. According to the Fed's own estimates, "excess reserves" rose to astonishing levels from 1934 to 1941 (see Table 5-1). The ratio of cash to total deposits in the national banks rose from an average of 19.9 in 1929 to 21.5 in 1929-33 to 42.5 by 1940, averaging 32.8 from 1933 to 1940. This average increase of more than 50 percent, year after year, represents a disinclination either to lend or to borrow, or some even stranger aberration. By 1944, under the stimulus of wartime prosperity, the number was back down to 24.4.

34. By 1933, Ford denied that there was a depression at all. And he wasn't even a professor of economics. See Hughes, *Vital Few*, p. 347.

Huge excess reserves with these high ratios were a strictly New Deal phenomenon.

It is worth dwelling a moment on this curiosity of the 1930s. In Table 5-1 we see measures of member bank reserves from 1929 to 1940. Excess reserves in this data are cash reserves held by member banks over and above their legal reserve requirements. Apart from 1938, excess reserves as a proportion of total reserves ranged from a factor of ten to a factor of twenty higher than the levels of 1929-30 or of 1932. Excess reserves as a percentage of required reserves were of course far higher. If we assume that bankers did not develop a phobia against loans and investments, how do we account for these numbers? Normal risk? What would we think today if the member banks held excess reserves of 30 to 40 percent instead of the normal 5 percent or less? If the numbers of the 1930s measured normal risk, it is clear that the New Deal, whatever its other triumphs, hardly inspired confidence in the banking sector.

Friedman and Schwartz have a go at these numbers. They argue that the huge increases in excess reserves over normal levels reflected the relative tightness of monetary policy; the rediscount rate, however low, was too high compared to other rates. Actually, this argument is believable and is in accord with the facts, but *can it be the major explanation* of them? The Federal Reserve Bank of New York's rediscount rate was less than 2 percent from 1934 to 1937 and a mere 1 percent from 1937 onward. Yet the relevant measure is the discount rate relative to other market rates, and as Friedman and Schwartz point out:

> With discount rates so high relative to market rates, discounting was an expensive way to meet even temporary needs for liquidity. Banks, therefore, had an incentive to rely on other sources for liquidity, including the accumulation of larger than normal reserves.[35]

But "larger than normal" might be 100 percent or 200 percent. Does the phrase stretch to 1000 or 2000 percent?

As I have argued elsewhere, the Bank of England probably made a similar contribution to the Great Depression of the 1873-96 period in Britain.[36] In that case, the bank rate of 2 percent lay above market rates for years. However, neither I nor anyone else blamed a

---

35. Friedman and Schwartz, *Monetary History*, p. 514.
36. Hughes, "Wicksell on the Facts," in Wolfe, *Value, Capital and Growth*.

major part of the Great Depression on the Bank of England, nor is it clear that a reversal of these policies could by itself have ended the Great Depression.[37] Friedman and Schwartz could be entirely correct about the depressing consequences of the rediscount rate and still have only chipped the edge of an explanation of the excess reserve phenomenon.

The Fed's activities no doubt inspired member banks to be cautious. After all, the Fed might suddenly raise reserve requirements in a depression out of fear that the New Deal had succeeded and there would be an inflation. It was this situation in 1936–37 that inspired Keynes's famous jibe: "They profess to fear that for which they dare not hope." Raising the reserve requirements in August 1936 and again twice in 1937 did temporarily reduce the excess reserve ratios, but in 1938 they were still ten times as large as in 1932. In April 1938, with the threat of runaway inflation apparently gone, reserve ratios were reduced slightly (by about 12.5 percent on average), but excess reserves ballooned to the highest levels ever. Whatever the trouble was, the medicine of 1936–37 did not cure it.

It hardly matters what the Fed thought it was doing in 1936–38; what it was not doing was aiding anyone's recovery effort, which, one supposes, was somehow the object of government policy in 1929–41. Were bankers afraid? And if so, of what?

Cary Brown said in his famous essay on New Deal fiscal policy that "it was not tried."[38] He did not dwell on its negative effects: the adverse psychological impact upon the business community of the militantly hostile Roosevelt Administration (especially after 1936), which presided over the depression from 1933 until it ended in World War II. Conceivably, one reason the private entrepreneur might not reenter the arena of risk-taking investment was the prospect of confiscation. In the 1930s, the European world was full of autocracy, and there was no guarantee that Roosevelt would not follow the leaders of other major nations in placing a firm hand on economic life. To be an "economic royalist" in the 1930s could not have been a comfortable social position, at least psychologically. Indeed, Larry Peppers published a study in 1973 showing that New Deal fiscal policy was less helpful than even Professor Brown had

37. For a reconsideration of Wicksell and the essay cited in n. 28, see Sir John Hicks, *Economic Perspectives: Further Essays on Money and Growth* (Oxford: Clarendon Press, 1977), ch. 3, pt. 2.

38. Cary Brown, "Fiscal Policy in the Thirties: A Reappraisal," *American Economic Review* 46, no. 5 (December 1956): 879.

found. Reworking Brown's figures on different assumptions, Peppers found that the New Deal, by its small deficits, was fine-tuning a full-employment surplus throughout.[39]

In Schumpeter's considered opinion, a concatenation of cyclical forces during the depression of the 1930s is what made the downswing so severe and so long lasting. All three of his cycles came down together.[40] He believed the depression itself to be a great waste and not the useful burning away of inefficient economic practices and combinations he celebrated in his grand design of historical capitalist growth and development. The Schumpeterian vision of capitalist growth was generally supported by Thomas Wilson, who found massive excess capacity created in the American manufacturing industry by the investment of the 1920s.[41] It overhung the depressed economy of the 1930s, rendering largely nugatory any further industrial investment. Obsolescence and depreciation had to work themselves out before a new wave of Schumpeterian innovation could resume its historic role. (Meanwhile, Schumpeter himself decided that capitalism was doomed to be replaced by socialism.)[42] Later theories of growth and cycles by Evsey Domar and Arthur Smithies would incorporate at their cores the Schumpeter-Wilson ideas about excess capacity.[43]

Schumpeter was partly involved also in Alvin Hansen's interpretation of the 1930s, the theory of secular stagnation. The drying up of investment opportunities played a role coequal with the end of the physical frontier and the nation's declining vitality (population growth) in the combination of forces that Hansen believed would make the deflationary stagnation of the 1930s long-lasting.[44]

---

39. Larry L. Peppers, "Full Employment Surplus Analysis and Structural Changes: The 1930s," *Explorations in Economic History* 10, no. 2 (Winter 1973): 197–210.

40. Joseph Schumpeter, *Business Cycles* (New York: McGraw-Hill, 1939), 2: 788–94, 907.

41. Thomas Wilson, *Fluctuations in Income and Employment* (New York: Pitman, 1949), pp. 114–26.

42. Joseph Schumpeter, *Capitalism, Socialism and Democracy* (London: Allen & Unwin, 1943), pt. 3.

43. See Evsey Domar, *Essays in the Theory of Economic Growth* (New York: Oxford University Press, 1957), ch. 1; Arthur Smithies, "Economic Fluctuations and Growth," *Econometrica* 21 (January, 1957): 1–52.

44. For a roundup of Hansen's several statements of his thesis, see Benjamin Higgins, "Concepts and Criteria of Secular Stagnation," in *Income, Employment and Public Policy: Essays in Honor of Alvin H. Hansen* (New York: Norton, 1948), pp. 82–107.

It is a distortion of history to view the New Deal primarily as a set of economic policies, successful or not. The New Deal in American history was primarily party politics. Roosevelt came into office pledged to stop the deficits. After that, all was makeshift, as Otis Graham sadly observed after examining the Roosevelt administrations for signs of economic planning.[45] A goodly proportion of the New Deal legislation was really just warmed-over populism called back to the stage of history by hard-pressed men anxious to "do something" to advance their own designs, including reelection. It is almost unfair to evaluate the New Deal's economic policies in terms of their economic consequences. We are economists, and we naturally tend to do that. But the result is a crabbed vision of what the New Deal really was. Hence, to argue from the New Deal experience that federal economic policies cannot be effective ought to include a further statement about the *normal* ambitions and procedures of American politics. When Rexford Tugwell complained to Roosevelt that the social security taxes were, among other things, utterly regressive, the great politician answered that "those taxes were never . . . economics. They are politics all the way through."[46] He probably was surprised at the naïveté of Tugwell to suppose it could be otherwise. The Social Security Act was a vehicle for other things besides social justice.

If the only objects of the New Deal had been full employment, the restoration of business confidence, and the achievement of high economic growth, there might have been suitable policies devised. But when you mix in social reform, income and wealth redistribution, reforestation, free silver, greenbackism (Federal Reserve Bank Notes), public power, moral regeneration in Wall Street, and a host of other causes, new, old, and lost going back to Andrew Jackson and beyond, it is not surprising that the outcomes of any policy initiatives were a mixed bag. Viewed as electoral politics, the New Deal was an extraordinary triumph for the Democratic Party; that is what it was supposed to be, and that is why political historians have celebrated it. When we view the New Deal as economics, we are appalled. But the same thing is true of modern economic policies. We should hardly be surprised. What optimal central bank policy might have

45. Otis L. Graham, Jr., *Toward a Planned Society: From Roosevelt to Nixon* (New York: Oxford University Press, 1976), ch. 1.

46. Arthur H. Schlesinger, Jr., *The Age of Roosevelt: The Coming of The New Deal* (Boston: Houghton Mifflin, 1959), p. 308.

been in a political vacuum is a reasonable question. What it could have been in the New Deal is something else. Presumably, when Marriner Eccles took over the Board of Governors in 1934, the Fed produced mainly what the treasury wanted, at least until World War II. Whatever that might have done for full employment, economic growth, or business confidence was either a vast failure or not really the primary aim of the policy.

BEYOND SINGLE CAUSES

One need not go further with the issue of our understanding, as economists, of the Great Depression. There is much more—for example, the entire vast (and unread) literature on business cycle theory—that I have mainly ignored. The point is obvious: If you ever get that many different opinions from your private physician, you should call for a priest and a lawyer and put your affairs in order.

I have often wondered: If we accepted *all* the explanations, would they make a convincing panorama? Perhaps if the contradictions would somehow cancel each other out and not reduce the algebraic sum of the explanations to zero. When your seventeen-year-old dog expires, the vet does not usually try to pinpoint a single cause. If you add up the international, national, regional, local, macro- and microeconomic explanations of the 1930s, you certainly have one thing on your desk that is unambiguous: a worldwide depression. No one of note except perhaps Henry Ford would deny it. So far, at least, no revisionist historian has come along with an article called "The Great Prosperity, 1929–1940." But editors beware! The pressure to publish has become intense.

The celebrated "reforms" and institutional innovations and revisions of the 1930s have the curious reputation of having saved capitalism. Others have written extensively on that, and so have I;[47] we need not rehash it all again on this occasion. It is only worth noting here that the New Deal did *not* end the depression of the 1930s. The Japanese did. It is no problem to solve unemployment if you put the unemployed into military service, cut civilian output of durables to

---

47. See Hughes, *Governmental Habit*, ch. 5; idem, "Roots of Regulation: The New Deal," in Gary M. Walton, ed., *Regulatory Change in an Atmosphere of Crisis: Current Implications of the Roosevelt Years* (New York: Academic Press, 1979), pp. 31–55.

the bone, and create a military force big enough to conquer the world. You may have problems, but unemployment is not likely to be one of them. We did that in 1942–45. Big problems of stagnation came back a generation later, accompanied this time by the worst peacetime inflation we ever knew. But that is a very different story. The amazing thing about the 1930s depression is that we never found our way out of it in peacetime and we still do not understand the entire experience the way we would like to understand it. The Great Depression remains a challenge to scholarship and a mystery for policymakers. Despite all that fantastic experimentation, jiggering and fooling around with everything from the price of gold to free farm outhouses, we never did find the handle.

In the 1930s jiggering around. failed to solve the problem of unemployment. There finally was a bit of real growth, but the big problem remained unsolved. In the 1970s, we were back at it again. This time the problem was to find economic growth and stop unemployment without inflation. We failed again.

So the lack of unity among economists about the 1930s is equaled by more recent events. As Robert J. Gordon shows in a recent essay, the policy prescriptions of 1945–80, together with their real-world outcomes, make a powerful cautionary tale.[48] For an economist, all this might be distressing. Our problem is the real world's stubborn refusal to behave as we want it to behave. In recent years, various supply shocks have added to the ordinary hazards of forecasting as well as of policymaking and have given the economics profession several black eyes.

Some argue that we should just forget the shortcomings of the 1930s, since even now we are not in agreement about the primary causes of that extraordinary episode. This certainly will not happen. The public and its political leaders expect economists to understand economic reality, and some economists, at least the ones who actually study the real-world economy, also want to understand reality. But more important than public pressure is the fact that the expansion of the government's role in the economy in the 1930s set a tradition for later years. We still live with the institutional consequences. At least for those whose only hope to escape modern stagflation is government action, it is crucial to know what the results of

48. Robert J. Gordon, "Postwar Macroeconomics: The Evolution of Events and Ideas," in Martin Feldstein, ed., *The American Economy in Transition* (Chicago, Ill.: University of Chicago Press, 1980), pp. 156–58.

past government actions actually were. The record of the 1930s should act as a brake upon such hopes, unless American politics change remarkably. As for those who believe monetary policy is decisive, the record of the 1930s seems to be the definitive catalogue of what not to do.

Chapter 6

EXPECTATIONS AND BUSINESS CONFIDENCE DURING THE GREAT DEPRESSION

Stephen J. DeCanio

Historians of the Great Depression of the 1930s have commonly ridiculed the expressions of confidence and optimism voiced by economists, businessmen, and politicians just after the economy began its long downward slide. For example, John Kenneth Galbraith, in *The Great Crash 1929*, cites with wry amusement a profusion of statements by leading figures all declaring that the "fundamental business of the country was sound."[1] According to Samuel Eliot Morison:

> No nation ever faced a business decline more optimistically than America did this one. Nobody highly placed in government or finance admitted the existence of a depression for six months or more after the crash. Everyone wanted to stop the decline, but nobody knew how. Incantation was the favorite method for the first six months.... [But] more than talk was needed to swell the shrunken gourd and plump the shriveled shell.[2]

The attempts by contemporary leaders to reassure the public (and each other) after the initial wave of panic on Wall Street have been interpreted as evidence of the primitive state of economic knowledge then prevailing. The whole range of national and individual

---

1. John Kenneth Galbraith, *The Great Crash 1929* (Boston: Houghton Mifflin, 1972), pp. 123–124, 126, 141–143, 147–151. The quotation is President Hoover's.
2. Samuel Eliot Morison, *The Oxford History of the American People, Vol. III, 1869–1963* (New York: New American Library, 1972), p. 291.

responses to the depression prior to the New Deal have become, in the popular mind, synonymous with helplessness and incompetent do-nothingism.

Modern economists in particular have been skeptical of the perspicacity and theoretical sophistication of those who observed or participated in the slump itself. It must be said that there is some basis for such distrust, since economic understanding does advance. However, the macroeconomic problems and policy failures of the 1970s have shaken the endemic smugness of the academic profession and have galvanized a reaction against the technocratic and interventionist attitude permeating economic theory and practice. In reexamining the full implications of rationality in economic behavior, economists have been forced to acquire a certain respect for the acumen of practical men working within actual markets. The new industrial organization recognizes that most of the unusual things firms do have a sensible business basis. Financial economics has developed the theory of efficient markets and has begun to grapple with the paradoxes that that concept involves.[3] In macroeconomics, of course, the theory of rational expectations has made economists realize that the agents in the economy are not merely passive or mechanical responders to all-knowing policymakers but rather usually possess more and better information about the structure and operation of the economic system than either bureaucrats or econometricians.[4]

A natural outgrowth of this new humility should be to take somewhat more seriously the responses of the businessmen and commentators whose wealth and reputations were at stake at the onset of the Great Depression. Rather than dismiss their attempts to reassure the public of the underlying health of the economy as economic Babbittry, we should try to understand why confidence and optimism seemed at the time to be so vital for stability.

3. For example, the competition inherent in certain financial markets would seem to eliminate speculative profit opportunities. Yet only the continued existence of such opportunities provides the incentive for speculative traders to collect information and to act in a way that makes the markets "efficient." See Sanford J. Grossman and Joseph E. Stiglitz, "On the Impossibility of Informationally Efficient Markets," *American Economic Review* 70 (June 1980): 393–408.

4. These instances are not exhaustive; for example, nineteenth-century American farmers were aware of most "modern" techniques for predicting movements in crop prices. See Adam Rome, " 'Growing Crops for Profit': American Farmers as Entrepreneurs, 1870–1900" (Paper for the Symposium on the History of Agricultural Trade and Marketing, University of California, Davis, June 24–26, 1981).

THE ROLE OF EXPECTATIONS

It is not unusual nowadays to grant a central role to expectations in the theory of economic dynamics, nor is this emphasis new.[5] Economic forecasting or expectation formation involves more than the GNP projections of purchased econometric models and the market analyses of firms' own economics departments. It also includes seat-of-the-pants impulses and entrepreneurial intuitions which matter more than economists (or executives) care to admit. Expectation formation is ubiquitous because of the irreducible uncertainty that permeates economic planning. No one can be quite certain what the future holds, but decisions bearing consequences extending over time still have to be made. If it were possible to specify in advance every possible state of the world, if markets in "contingent contracts" could be developed that specified the payoffs in every alternative state, and if the time and information costs of transacting in all these markets were sufficiently low, then it would be possible to insure against all risks and to take account of all possibilities in formulating one's plans. "Futures contracts" would be available for every eventuality. Yet even the statement of the conditions necessary to have such a complete set of markets indicates why this solution to the uncertainty problem will never be obtained.

The actual situation is that agents form expectations about the future and that they make predictions, guesses, or estimates to reduce the problem of contingency planning to a humanly manageable scale. The requirement that agents make plans based on incomplete knowledge does not mean that information is unimportant—quite the contrary. The difference between business success and business failure usually depends on the quality of information the entrepreneur or managers possess and their skill in translating that information into an appropriate operational plan. But the possibility of disappointed expectations—that is, of disequilibrium—means that real economies are subject to a coordination problem. Mistaken forecasts can mean warehouses full of unsold goods and, ultimately, bankruptcy. There is no market mechanism, other than the natural selection of competition, that forces everyone's expecta-

---

5. Friedrich A. Hayek, "Economics and Knowledge," *Economica* 4 (new ser., 1937), reprinted in *Individualism and Economic Order* (Chicago: University of Chicago Press, 1969), pp. 41–45.

tions to be consistent. During normal times, learning from experience tends to stabilize expectations, but if conditions change rapidly and dramatically, there may be no expectational equilibrium in the short run. Centralized planning is no solution to this coordination problem because even a totalitarian state cannot control the weather, the strength of foreign markets, or the reproductive urges of the anchovy. More importantly, the information losses and coercion involved in replacing individual decisionmaking by central planning are so extensive that they make the "solution" far worse than the original macroeconomic problem. (Compare the "full-employment" USSR or Nazi Germany of the 1930s with the depression-wracked democracies.)

The fact that expectations are involved at every stage of the firm's decisionmaking process implies that changes or movements in expectations have real consequences. Every investment decision, whether it involves the commitment of fixed or working capital, involves projections of the expected future stream of earnings from the project. Movements in expectations, therefore, may be critical to the short-run dynamics of an economy in crisis. A necessary first step in understanding the Great Depression, or any major transitional episode, is to have some notion of the pattern of expectations over time and across sectors. Any complete model, of course, would need to specify the feedbacks between the more tangible variables in the economy and expectational factors, but the prior task of describing the course of expectations is still worthwhile. It can be seen that in the case of the Great Depression, expectations did appear to have a life of their own—at least they moved quite differently from the overall path of output and employment. Furthermore, the timing of changes in the direction and level of expectations in the U. S. manufacturing sector suggests that news, outlook, and particularly political events exerted a major influence on the course of the economy.[6]

AN ECONOMIC MODEL OF DECISIONMAKING

Theory

Suppose the production process of a manufacturing firm requires time: a commitment to produce must be made at the beginning of

6. Jude Wanniski, in *The Way the World Works: How Economies Fail—And Succeed* (New York, Basic Books, 1978), ch. 7, asserts that the Smoot-Hawley Tariff of 1930 (and foreign retaliations to it) caused the general economic decline because the tariff increased the tax "wedge." While this tariff was surely a negative factor, it was not the only bad news of the early 1930s. The argument I am making here is more general.

the period of production, but no finished output is realized until the end of the process. Thus in period t, workers are hired, raw materials are purchased, and physical production takes place. In period $t+1$, the finished output is sold, and revenues are realized. (Production and sale occur repeatedly over time, of course.) This stylized characterization of the production process is "Austrian" in spirit and highlights the working capital aspect of both payroll and goods in process. To emphasize this even more, assume that the firm is operating in the short run, during which the plant and equipment are fixed, so that there are no changes in capital as neoclassically defined.

Since the focus of attention here is on changes in employment, further simplification can be achieved by ignoring the raw materials component and concentrating exclusively on the demand for labor by the firm. Given these preliminaries, the real costs incurred by the firm in period t are $W(t)L(t)/P(t)$, where $W(t)$ is the nominal wage rate in t, $L(t)$ is the amount of homogeneous labor hired, and $P(t)$ is the appropriate general price level. Total revenue in $t+1$ will be $[V(t+1)/P(t+1)]Q(t)$, where $V(t+1)$ is the price received by the firm for its output in $t+1$, $P(t+1)$ is the general price level prevailing then, and $Q(t)$ is the quantity of output produced in t. Note that V is distinct from P, since the firm is only one out of many making up the economy.

The present value of this production process is

$$PDV(t) = -[W(t)/P(t)]L(t) + [V(t+1)/P(t+1)][Q(t)/(1+r)]$$

(1)

where r is the real discount rate prevailing at t. (For the moment, r will be treated as being independent of t. This assumption will be relaxed subsequently.) However, $V(t+1)/P(t+1)$ cannot be known with certainty at the time the commitment to production must be made, and so the firm maximizes its expected profit $EPDV(t)$, given by

$$EPDV(t) = -[W(t)/P(t)]L(t) + [[V(t+1)/P(t+1)]^*][Q(t)/(1+r)]$$

(2)

where $[V(t+1)/P(t+1)]^*$ is the forecast or expected value of the price ratio formed by the firm at time t.[7]

---

7. The firm is assumed to be risk neutral, which is the appropriate assumption if shareholders are able to diversify their holdings across lines of production.

To round out the model of the firm's decision, assume that the demand for the firm's product is inversely related to the real price of the product, so that

$$[V(t+1)/P(t+1)]^* = X(t)[Q(t)^g] \quad . \qquad (3)$$

Here, $X(t)$ is a demand shift factor related to the firm's expectations about its market and includes forecasts of the general level of income and aggregate demand, the relative prices of competing products, and so on. The g parameter is the reciprocal of the price elasticity of demand.

In this model, the firm may have market power (if g does not equal 0), but its ability to set the price of its output is exercised only *ex ante*, prior to completion of the production process. The firm decides how much to produce (how much labor to hire in t) based on its best estimate of future demand; production then occurs and the resulting output is sold at whatever price clears the market. There are no inventories, but this is only a matter of expositional convenience. Inventories could easily be added as one of the factors influencing expectations, but the subsequent discussion would be unduly complicated as a result.

Given these preliminaries, the firm maximizes expected profit with L in period t as the control variable. The first-order condition for a maximum is given by

$$[W(t)/P(t)] = [[V(t+1)/P(t+1)]^*] [(1+g)/(1+r)] [dQ(t)/dL(t)] \quad . \qquad (4)$$

The first of the three bracketed terms on the right-hand side of equation (4) is the expectational shift term that will be the focus of attention here; the second is a constant depending on the interest rate and the elasticity of demand for the firm's product, and the third is the marginal physical product of labor determined by the (fixed) technology of the production process.

If the model were cast in terms of the conventional labor demand curve of the firm, equation (4) says that the real wage is directly proportional to the marginal physical product of labor. The form of the production function determines the shape of the labor demand curve as usual, but the location of the labor demand curve is determined by the firm's expectations of the strength of the market for its output when the finished product becomes available for sale.

Equation (4) shows that changes in the level of employment can be broken down into two components from the demand side: changes due to shifts in the labor demand curve that are associated with shifts in expectations, and changes due to movements along the labor demand curve that are associated with movements in the real wage. It should be emphasized that a decomposition of this type is not by any means a full explanation of why unemployment or a depression occurs. A complete model would require at least two additional components: (1) a description of the supply side of the labor market and (2) a mechanism for determining expectations as a function of the other variables in the economy. Thus, if sales expectations are volatile and subject to feedbacks from aggregate income, employment could change even without the appearance of involuntary unemployment. For present purposes, however, both of these issues are deferred.

It should also be pointed out that the expectational mechanism developed here is not inconsistent with other accounts of the depression. For example, Temin emphasizes an (unexplained) fall in consumption as the major causative factor.[8] But a fall in employment due to falling expectations could be closely linked to a decline in consumption, particularly if consumption is income-constrained, and income depends on employment.[9] Causation can operate in the other direction as well, since declines in consumption demand are one obvious source of declining sales expectations as firms monitor their inventories and market-clearing output prices. Temin argues most forcefully that there is probably insufficient data ever to permit definitive statistical testing of the many competing hypotheses of causation.[10] The purpose of the decomposition based on equation (4) is more modest: to calculate shifts in the labor demand curve from changes in observable variables. Given this conjectural measurement of expectations, it is possible to suggest connections between them and underlying economic or political forces, but no claim can be made to a complete explanation either of the expectations themselves or of the larger panorama of the depression.[11]

8. Peter Temin, *Did Monetary Forces Cause the Great Depression?* (New York: Norton, 1976).

9. For a theoretical treatment of income-constrained demand, see R. W. Clower, "The Keynesian Counter-Revolution: A Theoretical Approach," in R. W. Clower, ed., *Monetary Theory—Selected Readings* (Baltimore: Penguin Books, 1970), pp. 270–97.

10. See Temin, *Monetary Forces*, especially ch. 2 and pp. 177–178.

11. The framework of equation (4) can also include the effects of credit stringency. Like a deterioration in expectations, an increase in the discount rate r would shift the labor demand curve to the left. Available data on interest rates, however, do not provide a simple way of estimating the impact of bank failures and other monetary phenomena on the

Data and Results

To make the decomposition of employment changes operational, it is required to have time series information on real wages and levels of employment for periods corresponding roughly to the period of production expressed in the model by the length of the time interval t. This information, combined with knowledge of the form of the production function (so that the value of the marginal physical product of labor can be estimated) enables the expectations index $[V(t+1)/P(t+1)]^*$ to be traced out period by period.

Monthly wage and employment data for the manufacturing sector as a whole (and for twenty-five manufacturing industries within the sector) over the period 1920–36 have been collected and published by the National Industrial Conference Board.[12] The Conference Board data include an index of average real hourly earnings and an index of total man-hours worked. Total man-hours, rather than number of workers employed, is the appropriate measure of employment because average hours per week varied considerably over the period. (The Conference Board's index of hours per week per wage earner in manufacturing fell from a level of 100.2 in October 1929 to as low as 65.2 in March 1933.)[13] The data were collected by mail survey, and the Conference Board made a serious effort to obtain responses from a representative sample of manufacturing firms:

> In the middle of 1936, 1,886 plants were reporting directly to the Conference Board.... The total number of workers employed by the companies represented in the survey was 1,532,000 in June, 1936. This constitutes approximately 35 percent of the total number of workers in the twenty-five industries and 20 percent of the total number of workers in manufacturing as a whole.
>
> The plants included in the survey range in size from very small establishments employing only a few workers to very large ones employing thousands of workers, in order to assure proper representation of all types of establish-

---

demand for labor. The problem faced by the firm whose loans were called in by a failing bank was not that credit was then available at too high a price, but that it was not available at all. Aggregate time series on market interest rates will not reflect this type of pressure and hence cannot be used to compute an interest rate–driven analogue of the expectations index.

12. M. Ada Beney, *Wages, Hours, and Employment in the United States 1914–1936* (New York: National Industrial Conference Board, 1936).

13. Ibid., table 2, pp. 46–47.

ments. . . . It will be noted that all states except Arizona, Florida, Nevada, and North Dakota are represented in the study.[14]

Data were collected from the following industries: agricultural implements, automobiles, boots and shoes, chemicals, cotton (North), electrical manufacturing, foundries and machine shops (of which there are five subcategories), furniture, hosiery and knit goods, iron and steel, leather tanning and finishing, lumber and millwork, meat packing, paint and varnish, paper and pulp, paper products, printing (book and job), printing (news and magazine), rubber, silk, and wool.[15] The monthly timing of the Conference Board data is ideal for measuring short-term expectations as specified in the theoretical model because the period of production in U.S. manufacturing during the 1930s was approximately one month in length.[16]

Two approaches to the determination of dQ/dL, the production function segment of equation (4), are possible. The first would be to attempt to estimate the production function statistically from the available time series data. This approach, pioneered by Arrow et al. and followed by others,[17] involves estimating some form of the first-order condition for profit maximization relating the wage rate and the level of activity of the firm. To do this, however, requires an identifying assumption that is not appropriate in the present application. The Arrow et al. approach assumes that there is no expectations shift term in the first-order condition, or if there is a shift in the production function, that it can be described by some simple function of time such as exponential growth. (This shift term is what is conventionally designated "technical change" or "productivity growth.") Such an assumption may be justified if steady-state growth is taking place, but it is clearly mistaken if the observations on wages and employment or output are drawn from a period of extreme short-term fluctuations.

In such a case, constraining the shift term to be constant or to take the form of smooth geometric growth is a misspecification, and

---

14. Ibid., p. 16.

15. Ibid., p. 17.

16. Moses Abramovitz estimates that the length of the production period in U.S. manufacturing as a whole in 1939 was approximately 25 days; see *Inventories and Business Cycles* (New York: National Bureau of Economic Research, 1950), pp. 171–73.

17. Kenneth Arrow et al., "Capital-Labor Substitution and Economic Efficiency," *The Review of Economics and Statistics* 53 (August 1961): 225–50; for a study in the same tradition, see P. A. David and Th. van de Klundert, "Biased Efficiency Growth in the U.S.," *American Economic Review* 55 (June 1965): 357–94.

any statistical estimates of the shape of the production function obtained from such a misspecified model would be suspect. The need to make an identifying assumption to distinguish shifts in a production function from movements along the function has led Nelson to doubt the feasibility of estimating production functions from time series data altogether.[18] Although Nelson's pessimism may be justified in the case of long-term studies where steady-state growth cannot be presumed, for the short run another approach is possible. Since the technology is fixed in the short run, a particular production function can simply be assumed, and the expectations shift term can be calculated directly from equation (4). Given the known shape of the labor demand curve derived from the production function, the location of the curve is computed so as to make the observed values of the real wage and employment lie on it.

The production function chosen for the empirical estimates of the expectations index was of the simplest possible form: Cobb-Douglas with a labor elasticity equal to labor's overall share in manufacturing.[19] This labor share was 0.477. The particular choice of a production function is not the determinant of the qualitative results obtained. The expectations index was also calculated by assuming a constant elasticity of substitution (CES) production function with the same distribution parameter as in the Cobb-Douglas case and with an elasticity of substitution of 0.5, and the results were essentially indistinguishable from those reported here.

By some simple algebraic manipulations, it is easy to show that an index of expectations derived from equation (4) can be expressed in the Cobb-Douglas case solely in terms of the real wage and employment indexes and the value of the labor elasticity:

$$E(t)/E(0) = [[W(t)/P(t)]/[W(0)/P(0)]] [[L(t)/L(0)]^{1-a}] \quad . \quad (5)$$

In equation (5), a is the labor elasticity from the production function, $E(t)$ and $E(0)$ are the values of the expectations terms at time t and time 0 respectively, $L(t)$ and $L(0)$ are the levels of the employ-

18. Richard R. Nelson, "Recent Exercises in Growth Accounting: New Understanding or Dead End?" *American Economic Review* 63 (June 1973): 462–68.

19. Labor's share in manufacturing was calculated as the ratio of wages and salaries in all manufacturing to total value added in manufacturing, from U.S. Department of Commerce, Bureau of the Census, *Fifteenth Census of the United States, Manufactures: 1929, Vol. II, Reports by Industries* (Washington, D.C.: Government Printing Office, 1933), table 5, p. 20.

ment index in the periods t and 0, and W and P are as defined previously.

Taking October 1929 as the base, Figures 6-1, 6-2, and 6-3 show the time path of the expectations index $E(t)/E(0)$, the Conference Board index of the real wage, and the Conference Board index of the level of employment. Figure 6-1 shows that expectations deteriorated almost monotonically after the stock market crash until they reached their lowest ebb in late 1932. Expectations then rapidly recovered beginning in 1933 and never after that suffered the decline associated with the first years of the depression. The real wage, on the other hand, rose only modestly during the first years of the depression, and by mid-1933 had fallen back almost to its 1929 level. Despite the 25 percent fall in the general price level from 1929 to 1933, money wages were flexible enough to preclude any substantial rise in the real wage due to wage stickiness.[20] The man-hours index in manufacturing, on the other hand, fell to its lowest level in late 1932, and although it recovered somewhat after that, it remained substantially below its 1929 level well into 1936, never attaining more than about two-thirds of its October 1929 level.

Another way of looking at the results is presented in Figure 6-4. This graph traces the fraction of the change in employment attributable to the decline in expectations. This proportion is obtained by comparing the level of employment actually prevailing with the level that would have prevailed had the expectations index not fallen. (Both levels assume the same real wages.) It is evident from Figure 6-4 that until mid-1933, most of the decline in employment is attributable to the decline in expectations. From that point onward, however, the proportion of unemployment due to weakened expectations falls drastically, until by the end of the period virtually all the reduction in employment is due to the increased real wage level rather than to the level of expectations.

The gross timing of the changes in expectations given in Figure 6-1 is similar to the time pattern of expectations found by Peter Temin from a survey of the business press and an analysis of corpo-

---

20. The price index used is from M. Ada Beney, *Cost of Living in the United States, 1914-1936* (New York: National Industrial Conference Board, 1936). Michael N. Weinstein's estimation of wage and price adjustment equations for the early depression period leads him to conclude that "no support is provided for any theory that attributes wage and price rigidity to the private economy of the early and middle 1930s" (*Recovery and Redistribution under the NIRA* [Amsterdam: North-Holland, 1980], p. 29).

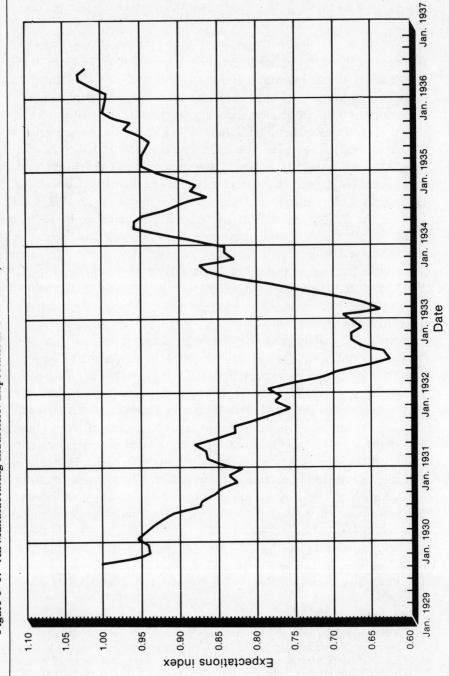

Figure 6-1. All Manufacturing Industries: Expectations Over Time, October 1929 – June 1936.

Figure 6-2. All Manufacturing Industries: Real Wage Index Over Time, October 1929–June 1936.

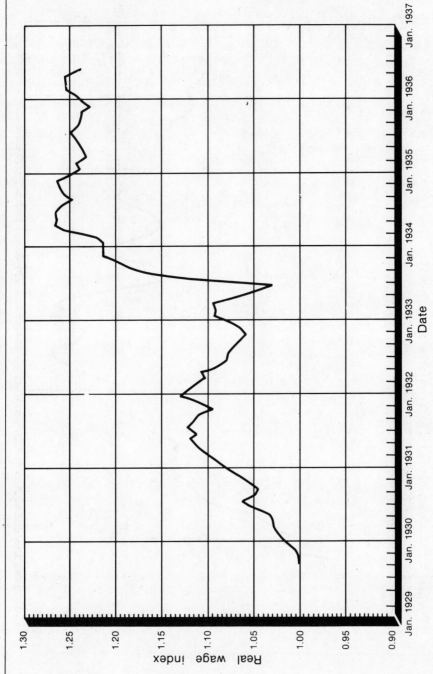

Figure 6-3. All Manufacturing Industries: Manhour Index Over Time, October 1929–June 1936.

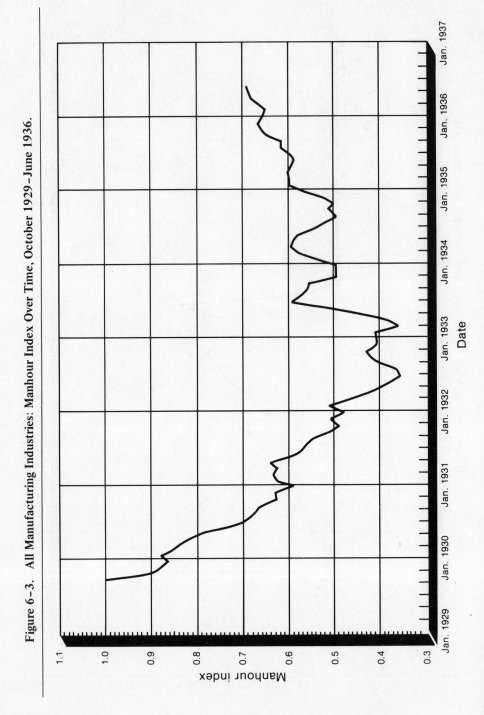

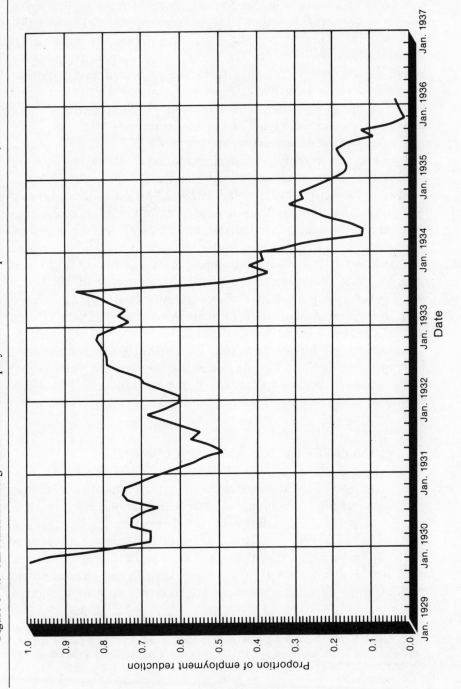

Figure 6–4. All Manufacturing Industries: Unemployment Due to Expectations Over Time, October 1929–June 1936.

rate bond reclassification. He found a large increase in the down-grading of corporate bonds in 1930 and especially in 1931 and 1932. Beginning in 1933, the heavy downgrading ended, but bond ratings did not fully recover.[21] Since bond ratings embody predictions of the overall survival prospects of the firms, the continued unemployment after 1933 would have had a continued depressing effect on bond ratings, even though the pure expectations component of labor demand (as measured in Figure 6-1) was improving.

It is also interesting to compare the movements of expectations, real wages, and employment during the brief, sharp recession of 1920-22 with the patterns shown in Figures 6-1 through 6-3. Analogous graphs constructed for the 1920-22 period (not reproduced here) show that the expectations index and the change in employment moved in almost parallel fashion during the earlier recession. The reason is that real wages hardly changed at all. The downward turning point in manufacturing employment was August 1920, and until the time employment had essentially recovered in 1923, real wages never rose more than 11 percent above their July 1920 level. Over the period August 1920 through December 1922, the average ratio of the real wage to its base level of July 1920 was only 1.05.[22] Expectations fell for a longer time during the 1930s, but the main difference between the two slumps is the very large increase in real wages occurring when expectations began to recover in 1933. This rise in real wages had no counterpart in the 1920-22 recession.

INTERPRETATION AND CONCLUSIONS

What accounts for the divergence between the paths of expectations and manufacturing employment after expectations reached their nadir in late 1932? The timing of the divergence suggests that the election of 1932 was the critical event in the story. Expectations moved downward almost without interruption until July 1932 (just after Roosevelt's nomination). Indeed, virtually all the economic news prior to that time was bad. Major events such as the initial

21. See Temin, *Monetary Forces*, pp. 76-82.
22. Beney, *Wages, Hours, and Employment*, table 2, p. 44. The Conference Board data are missing for the first six months of 1922, but since real wages were slightly below their July 1920 level at the end of 1921 and during July and August of 1922, the average ratio of 1.05 calculated in the text is probably an overstatement of the ratio.

stock market crash, the failure of the *Credit Anstalt* in May 1931, and Britain's departure from the gold standard in September 1931 may have accelerated the decline in confidence, but it is not really possible to assess the fine effects of news and other information on expectations without a complete specification of the forecasting mechanism. This is particularly so because a firm's expectations are influenced by its own data on sales, inventories, and product prices independent of the news of national or world economic events. The Conference Board data on the individual industries may enable the effects of news and political events to be separated from industry-specific influences, and research in that direction is indicated.

Beginning with Roosevelt's nomination, however, a new element of hope began to suffuse the prevailing gloom. This hope may have been generated more by FDR's style than by the content of his campaign promises. As Leuchtenburg observes:

> If Roosevelt's program lacked substance, his blithe spirit – his infectious smile, his warm, mellow voice, his obvious ease with crowds – contrasted sharply with Hoover's glumness. While Roosevelt reflected the joy of a campaigner winging to victory, Hoover projected defeat. From the onset of the depression, he had approached problems with a relentless pessimism.[23]

Interestingly, the *Commercial & Financial Chronicle*, in commenting on the presidential campaign, took the occasion to attack both parties – the Hoover campaign in particular – for undermining public confidence through campaign excesses. The *Chronicle*'s concerns are worth quoting at length:

> The Presidential campaign has reached a stage where it has become the paramount topic not only of popular discussion but also as an influence affecting the business world. The result is that for the time being it is exercising a decidedly repressing effect upon the ordinary course of business activity. It is not alone that it involves an uncertain element in the situation, but that in the heat of the controversy statements are being made, on behalf of one of the great political parties or the other that deal with matters of vital concern in relation to economic affairs which, if they be accepted as accurate, cannot but arouse the deepest misgiving as to the soundness of the whole industrial and financial structure. It accordingly happens that they serve to undermine

23. William E. Leuchtenburg, *Franklin D. Roosevelt and the New Deal 1932-1940* (New York: Harper & Row, 1963), p. 13. Of course, it is possible that Roosevelt's optimism had the greatest impact on those segments of industry, labor, and agriculture that stood to gain from the output-restricting policies of the New Deal.

that confidence which alone can insure enduring activity and prosperity in
the business world. . . .

All the President's recent speeches and addresses have been directed towards
creating a belief that though things may have been intolerably bad during the
last three years, they may easily be rendered a great deal worse, and that if
the voters choose to put the Democrats into control they run a good chance
of having it worse.

Many of the President's most ardent supporters go a great deal further and
seek to instill a feeling of fear in the minds of the voters. For ourselves we
have no patience with tactics of this kind.[24]

Of course, FDR's ability to restore the public's faith in the future
is an integral part of the Roosevelt legend. The cynicism of hindsight
should not obscure the galvanizing impact of FDR's rhetoric, exem-
plified by his inaugural theme that "the only thing we have to fear is
fear itself—nameless, unreasoning, unjustified terror which paralyzes
needed efforts to convert retreat into advance."[25] Yet, Roosevelt's
ability to restore confidence had a high price. The policies that constituted the economic core of the New Deal and that captured the
imagination of the public moved the economy in a direction that
made recovery more difficult. It is well known that the net effect of
the fiscal policies of government at all levels during the New Deal did
not stimulate aggregate demand in any substantial way.[26] The most
effective New Deal policies were the ones that reduced the allocative
flexibility of the economy—policies of which the National Industrial
Recovery Act (NIRA) was the prototype. By promoting restrictive
unionization and establishing minimum wages and maximum hours
provisions, the NIRA succeeded in raising real wages in industry; by
exempting industry from the antitrust laws and by fostering price
and production agreements between firms, the legislation created or
enhanced monopoly power.[27]

Figure 6-2 shows that the dramatic increase in real wages in the
manufacturing sector coincided with the passage of the NIRA. President Roosevelt signed the bill on June 16, 1933, and the low point

24. *Commercial & Financial Chronicle*, 15 October 1932, pp. 2529, 2531.

25. Quoted by Morison, *History of the American People* 3: 297.

26. See E. Cary Brown, "Fiscal Policy in the Thirties: A Reappraisal," *American Economic Review* 46 (December 1956): 857-79. According to Brown, federal fiscal policy was
more expansionary than that of state and local governments but "the primary failure of
fiscal policy to be expansive in this period is attributable to the sharp increase in tax structures enacted at all levels of government."

27. Weinstein, *Recovery and Redistribution*, pp. 1-4, 29-30.

in the real wage series is July 1933. Of course, it took some time for the codes to be approved and implemented, but by January 1934, 80 percent of industry was codified and by December 1934, only a small fraction of the eligible industries were not codified.[28] The second half of 1933 corresponds to the period of steepest increase in the real wage rates shown in Figure 6-2. The cartelization and the increase in monopoly power of firms encouraged by the NIRA must also have had an adverse effect on industrial recovery. A restriction of output associated with the exercise of market power would necessarily be associated with an inward shift in the demand for labor in manufacturing. These allocational effects were compounded by the real wealth reduction caused by the NIRA-induced increase in industrial prices.[29]

Thus, the Roosevelt administration undermined the positive effects of its restoration of confidence by implementing a set of policies that actually prolonged the depression. The leaders who attempted to reassure the business community and the public during the first dark days of the crash were not the simpletons they have been portrayed to be. They recognized, with a perception grounded in their practical experience, that expectations in the short run are volatile, sensitive, and very powerful in influencing the course of events. When Hoover's initial prescriptions and exhortations failed to halt the decline, the effect was to dissipate the reservoir of credibility attached to the office of the presidency.[30] FDR offered the beleaguered nation a New Deal, and in large measure he succeeded in restoring the people's shattered confidence. The tragedy of the New Deal is that the recovery of expectations was built on a foundation of harmful and misguided policies, the aftereffects of which are still being felt today.

28. Ibid., p. 9, citing Research and Planning Division of the National Recovery Administration, *Charts on the Operation of the National Industrial Recovery Act* (Washington, D.C.: Government Printing Office, 1935), chart 36.

29. Weinstein, *Recovery and Redistribution*, pp. 128-34.

30. It should not be assumed that Hoover was in any sense a noninterventionist. See Murray N. Rothbard, *America's Great Depression* (Los Angeles: Nash, 1972).

Chapter 7

FEDERAL RESERVE POLICY SINCE 1945
The Results of Authority in the Absence of Rules

Richard H. Timberlake

The enemies of liberty have always based their arguments on the contention that order in human affairs requires that some should give orders and
others obey. Much of the opposition to a system of freedom under general laws arises from the inability to conceive of an effective co-ordination
of human activities without deliberate organization by a commanding
intelligence.[1]

THE RELATIONSHIP BETWEEN MONETARY
POLICY AND STAGFLATION

The relationship between monetary policy and stagflation arises from
the effect of monetary excesses on the price level. The current inflation, which has resulted from the creation of money at rates incompatible with the growth of real product during the last fifteen years,
has demonstrated a number of truths. First, it has provided empirical
verification again that changes in the quantity of money do indeed
initiate price level movements. Second, it has shown that monetary
policies can have only an ephemeral effect on interest rates, and that
interest rates, therefore, are both mercurial targets and fickle indica-

1. Friedrich A. Hayek, *The Constitution of Liberty* (Chicago: University of Chicago
Press, 1960), p. 159.

tors for central bank decisionmaking. Third, the increases in unemployment and declines in general productivity over this period imply that inflation not only has no beneficial effects on the real economy but, if anything, is positively counterproductive.

The continuing, persistent inflation suggests that U.S. central bank policies, which are supposed to provide high levels of employment, reasonable growth of real product, and stable prices, have failed. To treat this issue at its source requires an analysis of central banking development from its beginnings in order to determine what factors move this institution to contravene the very mission set out for it.

This paper first examines the character of the original Federal Reserve System (the central bank in the United States) and the course of events that led to its mutation from a limited-function institution subordinate to a gold standard into an all-powerful central bank. Possible reformulations for monetary policy are discussed at the conclusion.

ORIGINAL STRUCTURE OF THE FEDERAL RESERVE SYSTEM

The Federal Reserve System was created by an act of Congress in 1913. It was to be a largely self-regulating adjunct institution to the self-regulating gold standard for determining the monetary substance of the United States. When the act was passed, it contained a section disclaiming any intention to subvert the gold standard: "Nothing in this act shall be considered to repeal the parity provisions contained in [the Gold Standard Act of 1900]."

The original institution was limited to the discounting of notes for commercial member banks at their initiative during times of financial stress. Its only discretion was manipulation of the discount rate that it charged for this service. Such lending operations were supposed to be regulated as well by the "eligibility" of the bank paper presented for discount and of the collateral obligations that might secure such paper. The power of the Fed was thus limited to sometime support of the credit market when commercial bank reactions reflected liquidity problems, whereas the gold standard remained the dominant monetary institution.

By 1934, just twenty years after the passage of the Federal Reserve Act, the gold standard was defunct for all practical purposes. Gold was no longer allowed by federal law to be used as money, and it exerted no significant control over the Fed's monetary policies.

FEDERAL RESERVE POLICY AND INSTITUTIONAL CHANGES IN THE 1950s

The Federal Reserve's failure to use its discretion in the mode presumed for it significantly aggravated the Great Depression of the 1930s.[2] Bureaucratology requires that a bureau, when it has failed to carry out the mission assigned it, blame its failure on "special factors" over which it alleges it has no control and then petition the appropriate legislature for enough additional powers to handle all such special factors that might appear in the future. This procedure was manifest in the monetary laws passed in the 1930s, particularly in the Banking Act of 1935.

The 1935 act permitted the Federal Reserve to initiate policy by buying and selling government securities at its discretion. The power base, which had been diffused among the separate Federal Reserve Banks, was now centered in the Federal Reserve Board in Washington. All policy from this time on was to be conducted on a system-wide basis. Discretion over policy was vested in the Federal Open Market Committee (FOMC), which was composed of the Federal Reserve Board (seven members) and five of the twelve Federal Reserve Bank presidents. The board thus constituted a majority of the FOMC.

The New Deal approach toward money was to quarantine it. The view was that money left on its own could do mischief. Therefore, it had to be controlled. At the same time, control over it was seen to have no political advantages, and so monetary policy was not included as a strategic factor in the New Deal program. A positive spending policy—public works and the like—was judged to be more important by the administration of the time. Consequently, monetary policy slipped into limbo.

During this period, nevertheless, significant changes occurred in the institutional character of the Federal Reserve System. First, the Fed was allowed to escape the constraint of gold. Second, it was

2. See Milton Friedman and Anna J. Schwartz, *A Monetary History of the United States, 1867-1960* (Princeton: Princeton University Press, 1964), pp. 407–19.

given a different mission to perform. Its original function had been to "furnish an elastic currency, [and] to afford means of rediscounting commercial paper." Now it was charged with supporting the prices of government securities in order to effect a prescribed pattern of yield rates. No logic can connect such disparate goals. Third, the Fed's new directive was not prescribed by Congress, wherein rests the limited constitutional authority over the monetary system, but by executive pressure.[3]

Concentration on the prices and yield rates of government securities as the targets of Fed policy had no theoretical or empirical economic justification. It began as political pragmatism in the 1930s (maintain an orderly market in government securities to accommodate treasury financing of deficits), continued on a similar note during the war years (keep interest rates "low" to facilitate treasury financing of the war effort), and was extended in the postwar period (prevent a postwar recession by keeping interest rates down). Quite obviously, a rationale for low interest rates can be found to suit virtually any current condition. Low interest rates are always a political desideratum.

When Congress finally freed the Fed from Treasury control in 1951, it also provided a new goal of sorts for Federal Reserve action. The resolution at that time from the Joint Committee on the Economic Report stated that Federal Reserve policy should "be guided primarily by considerations relating [the effects of its policies] on employment, production, purchasing power and price levels, and that such policies shall be consistent with and shall promote the purpose of the Employment Act of 1946."[4] Thus, the Fed was relieved of both statutory and political constraints from this time on. It still faced gold reserve requirements of 25 percent against its monetary obligations, but its "excess" gold holding rendered this constraint practically irrelevant to its policy operations.

3. See Marriner S. Eccles, *Beckoning Frontiers* (New York: Knopf, 1951), reprinted in Lawrence Ritter, ed., *Money and Economic Activity* (New York: Houghton Mifflin, 1957), pp. 157–66.

4. *Monetary, Credit and Fiscal Policies: Report of the Subcommittee Joint Committee on the Economic Report*, 81st Congress, 2d sess., 1950, S. Doc. 129.

FEDERAL RESERVE POLICY FROM 1951 TO 1965

The technical monetary function of the original Federal Reserve System was to promote form-seasonal elasticity—that is, to facilitate the public's desire to convert one form of money into another while allowing only minimal change in the total stock of money. Secular increase in the money supply was left to the functioning of the gold standard. As the gold standard was deactivated, the power to increase or decrease the money stock over time was also given to the Federal Reserve System. The power lost by the gold standard was gained by the Federal Reserve. The removal of political constraints by the Federal Reserve–Treasury Accord of 1951 was the last step in the Fed's development as an omnipotent central bank.

During the 1950s, the operational norm that the Federal Reserve adopted was to keep increases in the money stock consistent with the growth in the economy's real output.[5] It used its reserve requirement powers to further this policy—gradually reducing these requirements for the member commercial banks throughout the decade. For short-run operations, the Fed reinstituted the traditional discount rate policy of earlier eras.

Even though gold had been forbidden in domestic monetary transactions by legislation passed in 1933, it was still a vehicle for clearing international balances among the world's central banks and treasuries. Because of deficits in the U.S. balance of payments to other countries, the Federal Reserve System lost title to gold in the 1960s—just the reverse of the circumstances by which it had gained gold in the 1930s. The Fed then increased its purchases of government securities in order to prevent any declines in the money stock and associated declines in prices, incomes, and employment.[6] By the mid-1960s, this policy had reduced by 50 percent the ratio of gold to the monetary obligations (the monetary base) that the Fed had created. Congress thereupon abolished the legal gold reserve requirements over the Fed—against member bank reserve accounts in 1966, and against its issues of Federal Reserve notes in 1968—thus removing the last discipline that gold could exert over the monetary system. From this

5. Friedman and Schwartz, *Monetary History*, pp. 628–30.
6. Much of the actual gold remained in the United States held under earmark to the credit of foreign central banks and governments.

point on, the stock of monetary gold, under title to the Federal Reserve System but under the operational jurisdiction of the U.S. Treasury, became simply a metal—one could hardly call it strategic—that the government stockpiled at a significant real cost.

INFLATION, 1967–1981

The cause of the recent fifteen-year inflation in the United States economy was an outsize rate of growth in the monetary base that in turn generated an unduly large rate of increase in the stock of conventional money. The rates at which the Fed has increased the base, and thereby common money, have tended to be cyclical. (See Table 7–1.) Each periodic ebb and peak had generally higher growth rates

Table 7-1. Patterns of Monetary Growth, 1965–1980.

Year	Growth Rate in Monetary Base	Growth Rates In	
		$M - 1 - B^a$	$M2^b$
1965	6.1	4.4	8.0
1966	4.4	2.7	4.9
1967	6.0	6.3	9.3
1968[c]	7.5	7.4	8.0
1969	4.2	3.8	4.2
1970	6.5	4.8	5.8
1971	7.1	6.6	13.5
1972[c]	8.8	8.5	12.9
1973	8.0	5.8	7.3
1974	9.5	4.7	6.0
1975	5.8	4.9	12.3
1976[c]	6.8	6.0	13.7
1977	8.5	8.1	11.5
1978	9.0	8.2	8.4
1979	7.9	8.0	8.8
1980[c]	8.5	7.2	9.4

a. M – 1 – B includes (1) demand deposits at all commercial banks, (2) hand-to-hand currency outside of commercial banks and the U.S. Treasury, (3) travelers checks of nonbank issuers, and (4) checkable deposits at all other financial institutions, including NOW and ATS accounts, credit union share drafts, and demand deposits at mutual savings banks.

b. M2 includes everything in M – 1 –B plus savings and small-denomination time deposits at all depository institutions, overnight repurchase agreements at commercial banks, a limited number of Eurodollars, and money market mutual fund shares.

c. National election year.

Sources: For data on monetary base, see John A. Tatom, "Issues in Measuring an Adjusted Monetary Base," Federal Reserve Bank of St. Louis *Review* 62, no. 10 (December 1980): 22. For data on M – 1 – B, see Thomas D. Simpson, "The Redefined Monetary Aggregates," *Federal Reserve Bulletin* 66 (February 1980): 112.

Table 7-2.   Average Annual Percentage Change in the Stock of Money
(M2)^a and Prices in the United States over Four Periods, 1867-1980.

Period	Years in Period	Average Annual Percentage Change			
		Gross M2^b	Net M2^c	Gross Price^b	Net Price^c
1867-1915	48	7.17	5.73	4.87	-1.07
1882-1915	33	7.59	6.55	4.46	-0.07
1928-1980^d	47	7.23	5.13	5.55	2.79
1947-1980	33	6.06	6.03	4.55	3.93

   a. M2 is the stock of money that includes hand-to-hand currency outside banks and all commercial bank deposits adjusted for interbank holdings.
   b. Computed without regard to sign.
   c. Positive changes net of negative changes.
   d. Excluding 1942-46.

Sources: For data on money stocks, Friedman and Schwartz, *Monetary History*, app. A, table A-1, pp. 704-22, and *Federal Reserve Bulletins*, 1965-81. For data on prices, U.S. Department of Commerce, *Historical Statistics of the United States* (Washington, D.C.: Government Printing Office, 1960), series E-1; Wholesale Prices (Warren and Pearson), pp. 115-16; and *Federal Reserve Bulletins*, 1960-81.

than were seen in the preceding cycle—all of which suggests very high inflation rates indeed if some means is not soon devised to divorce money creation from political influences.

MONEY AND PRICES UNDER A GOLD STANDARD AND UNDER A FEDERAL RESERVE SYSTEM

The principal argument for central banking has always been that it offers a humanly controlled improvement to a market monetary system that otherwise is subject to disorder and chaos.[7] If central bank policy is indeed stabilizing, data on the rates of growth in money and prices in an economy with a central bank should show less variation than in an economy operating on a gold standard without a central bank. In order to help resolve this issue, summaries of annual average percentage variations in money and prices for four historical periods are shown in Table 7-2.

   This table includes two long periods, each close to fifty years, and two shorter periods within the long periods, each thirty-three years. The earlier long-period data (1867-1915) reflect a mixture of post-

   7. Sherman J. Maisel, *Managing the Dollar* (New York: Norton, 1973), p. 24.

Civil War paper money and gold standard policies. The shorter period (1882–1915) witnessed a fully operational gold standard, albeit with some disruptive effects from the free silver movement.

The later long period average summarizes contemporary data that exclude values for the years covered by World War II. Although the Federal Reserve operated throughout this forty-seven-year period, only in the post–World War II period (1947–80) did it function as a completely discretionary central bank. These two pairs of period data thus give a picture of money and price variations over comparable time spans—before the Federal Reserve existed, and after it had become a seasoned institution.

The data would seem to indicate that annual variations in both gross and net money stocks were approximately the same under the two institutions. Price level variations were also similar. The gold standard system, however, tended to force prices that had risen to decline subsequently, whereas the usual strategy of the Federal Reserve has been to allow price increases to remain in the system. If price level increases are not matched by later decreases, an inflationary secular trend develops. This pattern is visible in the line showing price changes. For the 1947–80 period, the average annual net variation in prices was a stout 3.93 percent, whereas for the gold standard period (1882–1915), it was almost zero: –0.07 percent.[8] Thus, the gold standard data reflect monetary flexibility conducive to price level stability, whereas the data for the post–World War II period indicate the presence of a pervasive inflationary bias in policies inspired by human management.

CHARACTERISTICS OF THE POSTWAR FED

Since the original Federal Reserve System was supposed to have limited powers and to be independent of political influences, it was not subjected by law to conventional checks and balances. Then, when it underwent fundamental structural changes in the 1930s, all of the conventional principles for establishing operational scope, goals, targets, accountability, and personnel replacement were im-

8. Even the shorter period, 1947–80, includes very disparate rates of monetary growth and price level change. Only the years between 1954 and 1965 show especially stable growth rates in these variables.

properly left unchanged, and "independence" was advertised even more pointedly as a sacrosanct principle of central bank operations.

Independence is an attribute that could only be justified while the Fed's powers were limited. Allowing the Federal Reserve to function in such a mode with its current powers is no more logical than giving the same status to the State Department. In addition, the Federal Reserve has not been independent when a willful executive wanted it otherwise. During and after World War I, again in the 1930s, and for several years after World War II, either the current president or his secretary of the treasury had a dominating influence on Fed policies.[9]

The lagged schedule, by which presidential appointments to the Board of Governors occur only every other year, is another aspect of the independence principle. It was conceived originally as a method of limiting the influence of any one executive. For a limited-function, apolitical central bank, it may have had merit; but for a central bank that has complete day-to-day control over the monetary system, it is a dangerous anachronism. What it means in practice can be seen in the personnel on the current board: Five of the seven members were appointed by former President Carter and the other two by former President Ford.

The arithmetic of the staffing provision means that in the first three years of his administration, President Reagan will have only one appointment to make to the board unless some other incumbent member resigns. Consequently, the Reagan administration may have to tolerate an agency that bespeaks an economic ideology at odds with the rest of the Reagan economic program. All of the other departments and offices that have a bearing on economic affairs are routinely staffed with people in harmony with the president's economic principles. Yet, to assume this same logical method for implementing monetary policy is met with the cry that it violates the independence of the board. In point of fact, monetary norms are extremely varied and highly controversial. Nothing is gained by pretending otherwise. To do so simply denies the majority faction the ability to get its will into action and thus subverts a fundamental principle of the democratic process. Resignations of current board members may, of course, eliminate this potential dichotomy. But such a solution can only be happenstance.

9. See Eccles, *Beckoning Frontiers*, pp. 157–66.

Another possibility is that the board in chameleonlike fashion will adapt itself to the administration's political philosophy. Although this tendency has been observed before, it is not a solution. Its net effect is likely to make monetary policy even more uncertain. If policymakers can shift their principles this easily in one direction today, they can just as easily shift them back the other way tomorrow.

Thus, the presence of the Federal Reserve System in current polity poses a constitutional dilemma. If the Fed's management is brought squarely into cabinet-level status to serve at the pleasure of the executive, the constitutional control of Congress over norms for the monetary system is abrogated. But if monetary policy is kept out of executive reach, an undesirable, and even dangerous, discord may arise between monetary policy and all other economic policies.

FEDERAL RESERVE TRAITS
IN POLICYMAKING

Congressional directions for Federal Reserve operations have not been encouraged by the Fed's managers, who have traditionally belittled their monetary powers. By and large, appointees chosen for positions on the Federal Reserve Board have emphasized caution and have reflected this trait in their rare confrontations with the executive branch. Certainly, they do not have the case-hardened tenacity of people who have successfully run for political office.

Complementary to the caution principle is the Fed's embrace of an eclectic approach—first in its analysis of economic conditions, which is fair enough, but also in the policies it espouses in order to deal with these conditions. The implication here, however, is invalid: Just because economic variables are numerous does not mean that a central bank can (or should try to) treat them all, no matter what policy weapons it has at its command.

A clear statement of the Fed's eclectic philosophy is seen in an official statement made in 1973 by Arthur Burns, who was at that time chairman of the Board of Governors. First, Burns denied the inherent stability of the market economy. "Reliance on the self-correcting properties of our economic system," he stated, "can lead to serious trouble. Discretionary economic policy, while it has at times led to mistakes, has more often proved reasonably successful."[10] This dogma, if based on the performance of the contemporary Federal Reserve System, is contradicted by the data in Table 7-2.

Burns next raised the bugaboo of a capriciously unstable velocity of money. Yet, empirical data on velocity show beyond question that it is a passive variable conditioned by other, more forceful factors.[11] People's money-holding habits are secularly stable. They only change when some institution, such as a central bank, fosters a much too generous, or too stingy, rate of growth in the community's stock of money units. In spite of all the evidence that must have been available to him, Burns simply asserted that the public's "willingness to use the existing stock of money . . . is a highly dynamic [i.e., unstable] force in economic life."[12]

These instabilities in the market and monetary systems, Burns argued, require

> the Federal Reserve [to] use a blend of forecasting techniques. Evidence from all these sources is weighed. . . . An eclectic approach is [then] taken by the Federal Reserve in recognition of the fact that the state of economic knowledge does not justify reliance on any single forecasting technique. As economic research has cumulated, it has become increasingly clear that money does indeed matter. But other financial variables also matter.[13]

This doctrine is yet another facet of bureaucratology. It excuses all sorts of discretion. The more eclectic the approach to a policy decision, the more torturous and the more difficult seems the task of resolving the different implications of the eclectic analysis. It thus lends itself to the enlargement of the bureau's staff and resources. It also helps to explain the Fed's secretive attitude with respect to its policy decisions. This cloak-and-dagger approach, in conjunction with prescribed doses of central bank priestcraft, has furthered the Fed's self-styled image of complexity and mysticism.

All of these factors—the presumption of "natural" instability, eclecticism, complexity, and secrecy—foster the implication that only

10. Arthur F. Burns, "Money Supply in the Conduct of Monetary Policy," Board of Governors of the Federal Reserve System, *Federal Reserve Bulletin* 59, no.11 (November 1973): 792.

11. See, for example, Milton Friedman and David Meiselman, "The Relative Stability of Monetary Velocity and the Investment Multiplier in the United States, 1897–1958," Commission on Money and Credit, *Stabilization Policies* (Englewood Cliffs, N.J.: Prentice-Hall, 1963), pp. 165–268.

12. Burns, "Money Supply," p. 793.

13. Ibid.

a discretionary authority can acquire the expertise to deal with them and to bring some semblance of order into the monetary system. Of course, no human being or group of human beings could handle so intricate a task perfectly; but if authorities cannot do the job, the legend goes, the task is impossible.

Another economist, Sherman J. Maisel, who was contemporary with Burns on the Board of Governors, shared Burns's view on the necessity to manage money. "Like fire," he wrote, "money is useful under control; but running wild, it can do great harm." And: "Millions of independent decisions made daily at all levels of our banking and credit structure operate to create and cancel money. If they are not properly orchestrated, the result is chaos," Yet he admitted that even with the data provided by the Fed's excellent economic intelligence system, there remain "large gaps and many possibilities of error. The inescapable fact is that our economy is so immense and diverse that we are far from achieving accurate or complete measurement. Nevertheless, monetary policy must be made, even with less than perfect information." [14]

But must policy be *made?* And can it be made competently? Maisel seemed to imply otherwise in another section in which he discussed Federal Reserve policies in the latter half of the 1960s. "Our initial conception of what could be accomplished through monetary policy may have been wrong," he wrote. "Choices looked clearer than they turned out to be in practice; problems were oversimplified, and many elements were neglected. . . . We knew less than we thought we did, both as to what had to be accomplished and how to do it." [15]

RECONSTITUTING MONETARY POLICY

The need that Burns and Maisel perceive for intervention ignores the force of the *undesigned order* that manifests itself in the economic activity of free individuals. What the authorities "lightly pass over as chaos," to use the words of Leonard Read, "is but a reflection of [their] failure to comprehend." Maisel's last statement, indeed,

---

14. Sherman J. Maisel, *Managing the Dollar* (New York: Norton, 1973), pp. 24, 25, 47–48.
15. Ibid., p. 22.

demonstrates that man "can no more mastermind market data than he can the data of his own being."[16]

The proper beginning for monetary or any other public policy meant to function in a free society is well described by Hayek in his *Constitution of Liberty*:

> We can produce the conditions for the formation of an order in society, but we cannot arrange the manner in which its elements will order themselves under appropriate conditions. In this sense the task of the law-giver is not to set up a particular order but merely to create conditions in which an orderly arrangement can establish and ever renew itself.[17]

The gold standard was a law that fit this prescription. It required that Congress specify the relationship between a quantity of gold and some number of the unit of account, and do nothing more. It worked well in several countries for over a hundred years. Its implementation in the United States resulted in exceptional price level stability. In fact, most of the monetary instability during the tenure of the gold standard resulted from occasional issues of paper money by the U.S. Treasury.

A gold standard system is not out of the question today. It would require, however, three prior conditions: (1) political acceptance; (2) ubiquitous redistribution of the gold stock held in the U.S. Treasury; and (3) abolition of the Federal Reserve System. These obstacles are formidable. The worst option would be to reestablish a gold standard on paper while allowing actual control of the monetary system to remain with the Federal Reserve System (or the treasury).

A second option is to constitutionalize the Federal Reserve System, that is, defrock it of its activist discretionary role by putting its operations under a framework of rules. Since it is largely single-functioned, it should have just one rule. The one thing it can do precisely is to create one of the monetary aggregates—specifically, the monetary base. Congress, therefore, should commission the Federal Reserve to generate a constant rate of increase in the monetary base equal to the historical rate of growth in real output.[18] The rate of

---

16. Leonard E. Read, *The Free Market and Its Enemy* (New York: Foundation for Economic Education, 1965), pp. 54, 55. See also the epigraph at the beginning of this paper.

17. Hayek, *Constitution of Liberty*, p. 161.

18. This prescription follows a well-known monetarist doctrine. For simplicity, I suggest as a "golden constant" the rate of 3.65 percent per year for the triennium between leap years and 3.66 percent per year for leap years. These rates are 0.01 percent per day and very close to the historical rate of growth in real transactions.

growth in common money—hand-to-hand currency and checkable deposits—could then be left safely to banks and other financial institutions, which would treat the base money as if it were gold. Where the gold standard looked toward a growth rate in the money stock by implication—with the actual growth rate subject to some uncertainty due to the fortuitous nature of gold discoveries—the rule of a growth rate in the monetary base would be prescriptive and certain.

The Federal Reserve's function would become entirely custodial: It would simply oversee the technical creation of monetary base material at the prescribed rate. It might be given upper and lower tolerances on a month-to-month basis, but no other discretion for its operations would be either necessary or desirable. All of its other activities—clearing checks, passing judgment on the entry and exit of member banks, discounting paper for member banks, fixing reserve requirements, and administering regulations O, P, Q, R, S, T, U, V, W, X, Y, and Z—would be eliminated. The market system would see to these functions just as it does for nonbank industries.

This much-simplified structure for the central bank would render irrelevant the dilemma of whether the president or the Congress should control the monetary system. Neither would have any control beyond the initial specifications by Congress of the monetary base growth rate. Therefore, the privilege of staffing the Federal Reserve Board could be safely left with the president. In fact, it would probably be logical to make the board and the Council of Economic Advisors a single agency. However, the actual administrative organization is a detail that could be worked out at any time.

A MONETARY SYSTEM WITHOUT POLICY

No matter how tightly legislative rules appear to limit the policies of a regulatory agency, its very existence implies a compulsion to expand beyond statutory boundaries.[19] The growth of the Federal Reserve System reflects this principle. Consequently, if the Fed's activities were scaled back to a simple monetary growth operation while leaving its administrative structure in place, it might again usurp functions for which it was not designed or intended. In view

19. The original Federal Reserve System, for example, began engaging in open-market operations in government securities as early as 1923, although such activities were virtually proscribed by the Federal Reserve Act as it was conceived in 1913.

of this danger, the question should be raised and, as far as possible answered: Can a monetary system operate satisfactorily in the absence of *any* governmental policy—say under the same constitutional safeguards that apply to grocery stores or any other business enterprises? [20]

An unregulated monetary system implies the abolition of the central bank. Not only would its ordinary functions, such as the clearing of checks, be left to private institutions (where they originated), but so also would its power of creating money. Only the creation of money is an issue; free market institutions already handle the other activities currently performed by central banks, or they would do so if permitted by law. [21]

Provision of money by private enterprise would seem at first to be a momentous step. The lay person's immediate reaction is that such indulgence would promote hyperinflation and chaos. For even though commercial banks and other institutions now create money, they do not initiate the process. So where would be the check and balance to a private enterprise monetary system? This question is especially pertinent in view of the fact that very few, if any, unregulated and unrestricted monetary systems have ever existed. Thus, empirical evidence to validate the efficacy of such a system is almost nonexistent. [22]

Intuition and inference, however, provide a beginning rationale. A monetary system, like highway and communication systems, is an economizing device. It greatly reduces many real costs, increases productivity, and therefore contributes to a higher real standard of living. Even a poor system—one in which the value of the monetary unit is highly unstable—is much more productive than no monetary system at all.

The widespread awareness of the utility to be derived from a payments system suggests that even if the government did not furnish

20. That is, essentially, protection of life, liberty, and property against coercion and fraud.

21. The federal funds market, for example, is composed of commercial banks and other institutions that borrow and lend reserves from and to each other. This market renders superfluous Federal Reserve discounting operations. Check-clearing operations are another function that could be and were handled completely by private institutions. The history of clearinghouse associations supports this contention.

22. See Lawrence White's contribution to this volume, "Free Banking as an Alternative Monetary System." See also Richard Timberlake Jr., "The Significance of Unaccounted Currencies," *Journal of Economic History* 41, no. 4 (December 1981), pp. 853-66.

one, human creative talents would ensure that one emerged. Certainly this inference is valid for our other conventional requirements, such as food, clothing, shelter, transportation, and communication.

To proceed, however, from an appreciation of the probability of a workable and stable private monetary system to a concrete set of conditions "in which an orderly arrangement can establish and ever renew itself" requires some cerebral attention to details. First, the notion of hyperinflation and chaos should be dismissed. The fallacy here results from the specious thought that everyone would immediately be an issuer of money.

This behavior on the supply side is no more likely from a private monetary system than a similar reaction from, say, a private shoe industry. Not everyone supplies shoes, even under a system of complete laissez-faire, because not everyone can produce good shoes. The watchdogs for quality in shoes are the people on the demand side of the market who only buy shoes they think are good. Similarly, on the demand side of the money market (and here I mean *all* the markets in which money is exchanged), discriminating consumers of money would only accept money that is good.[23]

A complementary question is, What could private suppliers do to make their money good? Governments impose legal tender coercion to make their bad moneys acceptable; but private enterpreneurs do not have this power. So what could they do?

One sufficient answer to this question is that any money would be acceptable if it promised and delivered redemption in a readily marketable commodity (or set of commodities). The list of possible articles used for redemption could include precious metals, of course, and also primary staples marketed on commodity exchanges. But it could also include bundles of common stocks and other short-term financial instruments—that is, the items the money market mutual funds use as the basis for the deposits they now issue. Other possibilities would undoubtedly be suggested as the practicability of such a system became more apparent.

One final question needs to be answered: Where would the monetary system *begin*? A gold standard features an operational rule that requires governmental specification of a unit of account (the dollar) that is equated with a weight of gold. The gold is then legal tender on

23. See F. A. Hayek's contribution to this volume, "The Future Monetary Unit of Value."

this basis and determines the equilibrium quantity of money for the economy.

A monetary system based on monetarist principles would forego the gold rule and adopt one that fixed the rate of increase in the quantity of money directly. This operation would anticipate a constant rate of increase in the monetary base furnished by the central bank. Of necessity, the rate would also be nominal, aiming at the historic growth rate in the economy's real output.

A free market monetary system must also include an operational starting point. Since the monetary base material—the currency and bank reserve accounts created by the Federal Reserve System— already exists, the most expedient, least costly, and least harmful policy would be to freeze the existing monetary base and allow all private monetary institutions to produce any media of exchange they wished on free market terms using these base money dollars or gold or some combination of assets. The stock of legal tender base money would ensure continuation of a set of money prices and would thereby determine a beginning value for the dollar as well as a legal label for the unit of account.[24]

The details of the monetary system that would emerge from this basic scheme are not predictable. All that can be expected with any confidence is that specialists in producing money would appear and compete in supplying money. On the demand side, the holders and users of money would only accept good money—money whose real value was assured by redemption in something of marketable value. After incorporating such a system, social observers would look back to discretionary central banking as an authoritarian use of state power similar to, and just as objectionable as, taxation without representation.

24. Sometimes the objection is raised that this scheme would allow the government to retain a foot in the door of the monetary system. But this objection is just as valid for a gold standard where the government can change the gold rule (devalue the dollar).

PART III
MONETARY REFORM

Chapter 8

THE GOLD STANDARD
Myths and Realities

Michael David Bordo

Recently, there has been considerable interest in the United States' returning to some form of gold standard or at least restoring some role for gold in the U.S. monetary system. Proponents of a return to a gold standard argued that such an action would quickly restore price stability both by providing an effective brake on monetary expansion and by reducing inflationary expectations.[1] Indeed, Congress even established a commission to examine the role of gold in the U.S. monetary system.[2]

This paper was written while I was research staff member to Anna J. Schwartz, executive director of the Gold Commission. I would like to thank the following for helpful suggestions: Anna J. Schwartz, Anatole Balbach, and Daniel Landau. Parts of this paper are based on my article "The Classical Gold Standard: Some Lessons for Today," in the *Federal Reserve Bank of St. Louis Review* 63, no. 5 (May 1981), pp. 2–17. For able research assistance, I am indebted to Glen Vogt, Michael Hollihan, and Fernando Santos.

1. See, e.g., Robert Bleiberg and James Grant, "For Real Money: the Dollar Should Be as Good as Gold," *Barron's*, 15 June 1981; Robert A. Mundell, "Gold Would Serve into the 21st Century," *Wall Street Journal*, 30 September 1981; and Arthur E. Laffer and Charles Kadlec, "The Point of Linking the Dollar to Gold," *Wall Street Journal*, 13 October 1981.

2. The Gold Commission, headed by Treasury Secretary Donald Regan and consisting of members of both houses of Congress as well as representatives from the Federal Reserve Board, the Council of Economic Advisers, the Treasury Department, and the private sector, submitted its report in two volumes on March 31, 1982. See *Report to the Congress of the Commission on the Role of Gold on the Domestic and International Monetary Systems. March 1982.* U.S. Treasury (processed). Also see Anna J. Schwartz, "Reflections on the Gold Committee Report," *Journal of Money, Credit and Banking* 14, no. 4 (March 1982), pp. 538–51.

In considering the case for a return to some form of gold standard, three important questions must be answered. First, what type of gold standard should we return to? Second, and more fundamentally, what can and what cannot a gold standard do to maintain overall economic stability? An answer to this question would involve understanding both the theory of the gold standard and evidence on the actual performance of the economy under various forms of the gold standard in the past. Third, would returning to some form of a gold standard be a feasible option for the future?

In this paper, we attempt to provide answers to these questions. The first section presents a brief classification of types of gold standards (and other monetary standards). The second section summarizes the theory of the gold standard as a form of commodity money, as a national monetary standard, and as an international monetary standard. The third section discusses the operation of a managed gold standard—the system that has prevailed over much of the period since the Napoleonic Wars. The fourth section presents a brief chronology of the gold standard from 1821 to 1971. The fifth presents empirical evidence for the economies of the United States and the United Kingdom on the price and output stabilization properties of the classical gold standard compared to those of "managed fiduciary money." The sixth examines some of the issues connected with a possible return to gold. Finally, the seventh section presents a brief conclusion assessing the costs and benefits of the gold standard.

TYPES OF GOLD STANDARDS

We can discuss a number of variants of the gold standard in its long history. Under a gold standard, of whatever type, the monetary authority must maintain a fixed price of gold by purchase and sale. That price must rule not only in transactions by the monetary authority, but also in market transactions in which private participants are free to engage.

The types of gold standard are:

1. A gold coin standard with 100 percent gold cover for nongold money and no central bank.

2. A gold coin standard with fractional reserves held by the government against its note issues and by commercial banks against

their deposits, with or without a central bank, with convertibility for all holders of nongold money in gold coin.

3. A gold bullion standard with fractional reserves against the central bank's monetary base (currency plus bank reserves), with no gold coin circulation, and with convertibility for all holders of nongold money limited to large amounts.

4. A gold exchange standard with fractional reserves and with a central bank tied to a currency of a center country that has a gold-coin or gold-bullion standard.

5. The Bretton Woods dollar-gold exchange standard, with convertibility limited to official institution dollar assets "for the settlement of international balances or for other legitimate monetary purposes."[3]

The first type of gold standard existed only in premodern times; as we argue below, the classical gold standard that held sway before 1914 was a combination of types 2 to 4 and is frequently referred to as a managed gold standard.[4]

These various gold standards must be contrasted with the type of standard in use today: an inconvertible paper standard, with a central bank free to exercise discretion or else subject to a prescribed rule with respect to the quantity of money outstanding.[5]

THE THEORY OF THE GOLD STANDARD: THE STYLIZED FACTS

Economists from Cantillon to Keynes have formulated a theory of the gold standard with three dimensions: the gold standard as a com-

---

3. Milton Friedman refers to type 1 as a "real" gold standard and to all the others as "pseudo" gold standards, in "Real and Pseudo Gold Standards," *Journal of Law and Economics* 14 (October 1961), pp. 66–79.

4. Over the history of the gold standard, numerous writers have proposed the use of commodity standards based on commodities other than gold, with convertibility for all holders of noncommodity money in the designated basket of commodities.

5. The recent proposal by Robert E. Weintraub, "Restoring the Gold Certificate Reserve," *Joint Economic Committee U.S. Congress Study* (1981), for the U.S. to tie its monetary base to the monetary gold stock valued initially at a price to be determined, and then to allow it to grow only in accordance with the value of the monetary gold stock, with growth in the latter determined by a rise in the price of gold equal to the growth of real economic activity, is not really a gold standard, since it does not allow convertibility of

modity money standard, ensuring long-run price stability; the gold standard as a national monetary standard, regulating the quantity and growth of a nation's money supply; and the gold standard as an international monetary standard, ensuring the external value of a nation's currency.[6]

The Gold Standard as a Commodity Money Standard

The gold standard is a form of commodity money standard. Of the numerous commodities that served as money in world history, gold emerged as the most widely accepted. Gold has the desirable properties of money that have been stressed by early writers in economics. It is durable, easily recognizable, storable, portable, divisible, and easily standardized. Especially important, changes in the stock are limited, at least in the short run, by high costs of production, making it costly for governments to manipulate.[7] Because of these physical attributes, it emerged as one of the earliest forms of money.

Through the operation of the competitive market mechanism, a commodity money standard, regardless of the commodity involved, ensures a tendency toward long-run price stability.[8] Under any commodity money standard, the purchasing power of a unit of commodity money, or what it will buy in terms of all other goods and services, will always tend toward equality with its long-run cost of production.

The simplest example of a gold standard is a pure gold coin standard with gold coins serving as the only money. Under such a standard, government's role in the money system is restricted to certify-

gold. It is rather a form of monetary rule based on gold. See also "The New Role for Gold in U.S. Monetary Policy," Weintraub's contribution to this volume (Chapter 9).

6. For a historical survey of the literature on the gold standard, see Michael David Bordo, "The Gold Standard: The Traditional Approach," in Michael D. Bordo and Anna J. Schwartz, eds., *A Retrospective on the Classical Gold Standard, 1821 to 1931* (Chicago: University of Chicago Press, 1984).

7. Of course, in earlier times governments manipulated gold by debasement, clipping, and so on. Such practices, however, were the exception. See Anna J. Schwartz, "Secular Price Change in Historical Perspective," *Journal of Money, Credit and Banking* 5 (February 1973): 243–69.

8. For a lucid discussion of the theory of commodity money, see Milton Friedman, "Commodity-Reserve Currency," in Milton Friedman, ed., *Essays in Positive Economics* (University of Chicago Press, 1953), pp. 204–50.

ing coins of a fixed weight in gold or, to put it another way, to maintaining a fixed price of its currency in terms of gold. Thus the government would be committed to purchasing gold from the public on demand at a fixed price and to converting it into gold coin. Similarly, the government would sell gold to the public at the fixed price.[9]

The supply of money and the prices of goods in terms of that money would be determined in the market by the demand for gold for monetary and nonmonetary uses and by the supply of gold, which would be governed by the opportunity cost of producing gold. The demand for gold for nonmonetary use would be governed by the relative price of gold and all other commodities. The demand for monetary gold would be governed by (1) total wealth available to hold in asset form, (2) the total amount of goods and services produced, (3) the average price of these goods and services, (4) the return on holding monetary gold relative to the return available on alternative assets, and (6) the tastes and preferences of holders of money.

In such a system, the money supply would vary automatically with the profitability of producing gold. A rapid increase in the output of gold due to gold discoveries or technological improvements in gold mining would raise the prices of all other goods in terms of gold, making them more profitable to produce than gold and thus ultimately leading to a reduction in gold output. Moreover, the initial reduction in the purchasing power of gold would lead to a shift in the demand for gold from monetary to nonmonetary use, thus reinforcing the output effects. Conversely, a decline in prices of goods and services due to technological improvement in the nongold sector would increase the profitability of gold production, encouraging increased gold output, and this would ultimately tend to return prices to their initial level. The initial increase in the purchasing power of gold would also lead to a shift in the demand for gold from nonmonetary to monetary use, thus reinforcing the output effects. This would ensure long-run price stability.

---

9. In actuality, the buying and selling prices will differ, reflecting the cost of certifying and minting coins. This difference is referred to as brassage.

The Gold Standard as a National Monetary Standard

In a closed economy, the free convertibility of gold coin into bullion would ensure a limit to the money supply, since any divergence of the real price or purchasing power of gold from its fixed official value would lead to conversion of coin into bullion or vice versa and would also affect gold production.

The Gold Standard as an International Monetary Standard

The international gold standard is a mechanism to ensure uniformity of price level movements between countries and hence to constrain the money supply of any one country. Under an international gold standard, each country defines the monetary unit as a specific physical quantity of gold, fixing the value of all national monetary units to each other and thus establishing fixed exchange rates. The fixed exchange rate determined by the gold weight in each country is referred to as the par exchange rate. The costs of shipping, packing, and insuring gold set the gold points—the upper and lower limits to fluctuations around the par exchange rate.

Thus, for example, before World War I, the dollar was defined as 23.22 grains of fine gold and a pound sterling as 113.0011 grains of fine gold; hence the par exchange rate of 4.8166 was the multiple of the weight of gold in a pound sterling compared with the weight of gold in a dollar. This represented a fixed exchange rate because the gold weight of each currency was fixed or, equivalently, the price of gold per ounce was fixed.[10]

In addition, countries under the gold standard allow both unlimited convertibility of their currencies at the fixed price and the free export and import of gold.[11] Under the gold standard, in addition to serving as domestic currency, gold is the international medium of

10. The United States fixed the price of an ounce of gold at $20.67, and the United Kingdom set it at £3. 17s. 10½d. The U.K. definition of an ounce of gold was 11/12 of the U.S. definition.

11. It is important to note that a monetary standard such as the gold standard has two aspects: a domestic one and an international one. The domestic aspect applies to the arrangements regulating the quantity and growth rate of the domestic money supply, whereas the international aspect applies to the arrangement by which the external value of the currency is determined. Thus, it is possible to have a domestic gold standard where the

exchange, providing the means for setting imbalances in international payments. If the demand for and supply of a national currency do not balance, gold flows are activated. Thus, whenever the dollar price of a British pound at the official or par exchange rate of \$4.86 deviated by more than 1 or 2 percent above or below par, it paid either to convert U.S. dollars into gold and transfer it abroad or else to convert British pounds into gold and transfer it here. If U.S. demand increased, for example, for cheaper British goods, this raised the dollar price of the pound. Once the dollar price of the pound reached \$4.92, referred to as the U.S. gold export point, it paid to convert U.S. dollars into gold, ship the gold to England, and purchase pounds at \$4.86. Conversely, at the U.S. gold import point of \$4.83, it paid to convert pounds sterling into gold, ship the gold to the United States, and purchase dollars. Gold shipments in either direction then acted to restore the price of foreign exchange to parity.

Gold flows require internal adjustments under the gold standard. Thus, a deficit in the balance of payments is paid in gold; the outflow reduces the country's domestic money supply and ultimately its price level, hence enhancing the country's appeal as a source of goods and services to foreigners and reducing the domestic demand for foreign goods and services. The surplus country experiences an inflow of gold that raises its domestic money supply and ultimately its price level, hence diminishing that country's appeal as a source of goods and services to foreigners and increasing domestic demand for foreign goods and services. As a consequence of this automatic adjustment process, the duration and size of imbalances is self-limiting.

Under the gold standard, a fixed price of gold acts to constrain the ability of any one country to allow its price level to differ markedly from the price level in the rest of the gold standard world so that price increases in excess of the world average or price declines below the world average are reversed in response to movements in the country's monetary gold stock. The worldwide movement might be deflationary, as it was from 1879 to 1896, or inflationary, as it was from 1896 to 1913. Adherence to the gold standard imposes the requirement that each country accept the world price level.

---

monetary authorities of one country fix the weight of gold in domestic currency and allow free convertibility, but where other countries base their currencies on other commodities, such as silver, or on inconvertible paper. In that case the external value of the currency would be determined by the open-market price of the two currencies, and a flexible exchange rate would prevail.

By the same token, the gold standard fixed exchange rate system makes individual countries vulnerable to disturbances in economic activity that are transmitted from one country to another. A country can ultimately protect itself from a foreign disturbance or from deflationary or inflationary effects on its domestic prices only by cutting the gold link.

THE MANAGED GOLD STANDARD

The simple theory of the gold standard just described was seldom followed in practice. The pure gold coin standard had two features that caused most countries to modify its operation: Very high resource costs were required to maintain a full commodity money standard, and strict adherence to the "iron discipline" of the gold standard required each country to subsume its internal balance (domestic price and real output stability) to its external balance (balance of payments equilibrium). Thus, if a country was running a balance of payments deficit, the "rules of the game" required it to deflate the economy until "purchasing power parity" was restored at the par exchange rate. Such deflation was often accompanied by a reduction in real output and employment. Consequently, a meaningful discussion of how the gold standard actually operated requires a discussion of the ways in which nations modified the gold standard to economize on gold and to shield domestic economic activity from external disturbances.

The Use of Fiduciary Money

As mentioned above, very high resource costs are required to maintain a full commodity money standard. Discovering, mining, and minting gold are extremely costly activities.[12] Consequently, as nations developed, they evolved substitutes for pure commodity money. These substitutes encompassed both government-provided paper money, referred to as fiat money, and privately produced fiduciary money—bank notes and bank deposits. As long as governments main-

12. Friedman estimated the cost of maintaining a full gold coin standard for the United States in 1960 to be in excess of 2½ percent of GNP. See Milton Friedman, *A Program for Monetary Stability* (New York: Fordham University Press, 1959), p. 105.

tained a fixed ratio of their notes to gold, and commercial banks kept a fixed ratio of their liabilities to gold (or to government notes and gold), a gold standard could still be maintained. This type of standard prevailed throughout the world before World War I.

One aspect of this "mixed" gold standard system was that one unit of a country's gold reserves could support a number of units of domestic money; for example, the U.S. ratio of money to the monetary gold stock was 8.5 in the 1880-1913 period. This meant that gold flows had powerful effects, in the short run, on the domestic money supply, spending, and prices.[13]

International Capital Flows

In the pre–World War I gold standard era, most international trade was financed by credit—the issuing of short-term claims in the London money market.[14] In addition, economic projects in the less developed economies were generally financed by long-term loans from investors in England, France, and other advanced countries.[15] The influence of these capital flows significantly reduced the burden of gold flows in the adjustment mechanism.

Thus, for example, if a gold discovery raised the domestic quantity of money, interest rates would tend to decline in the short-run, inducing investors to shift short-term capital to foreign money markets. The size of the change in export prices relative to import prices that would otherwise have occurred would be reduced by the resulting gold outflow. Also, to the extent that short-term capital substituted for gold as an international reserve asset and domestic financial intermediaries held balances with correspondents abroad, smaller gold flows would be required to settle international imbalances of payments.

Finally, long-term capital flows enabled developing countries to borrow real resources from developed countries by running a persis-

13. It also meant that changes in the composition of the money supply between the monetary base (gold coins and government paper) and bank-provided money (notes and deposits) could be a source of monetary instability.

14. See A. I. Bloomfield, *Short-Term Capital Movements Under the Pre-1914 Gold Standard*, Princeton Studies in International Finance no. 11 (Princeton: Princeton University Press, 1968).

15. See A. I. Bloomfield, *Patterns of Fluctuation in International Investment before 1914*, Princeton Studies in International Finance no. 21 (Princeton: Princeton University Press, 1968).

tent excess of imports of goods and services over exports of goods and services without entailing gold flows.

The Role of Central Banks in the Gold Standard

Under a strict gold standard, there is no need for a central bank. All that is required is for some governmental authority to maintain the fixed domestic currency price of gold by buying and selling gold freely. Indeed, many countries on the gold standard prior to World War I (such as the United States and Canada) did not have central banks. Most European countries, on the other hand, have had central banks that predated the gold standard. These institutions, in most cases, evolved from large commercial banks serving as bankers to the government (for example, the Bank of England was founded in 1697) to institutions serving as lenders of last resort to the banking community.

Under the classical gold standard, central banks were supposed to follow the rules of the game—to speed up the adjustment of the domestic money supply and price level to external gold flows. Whenever a country was faced with a balance of payments deficit and the central bank saw its gold reserves declining, it would raise its discount rate. By causing other interest rates to rise, the rise in the discount rate was supposed to produce a reduction in holdings of inventories and a curtailment of other investment expenditure. The reduction in investment expenditure would then lead to a reduction in overall domestic spending and a fall in the price level. At the same time, the rise in bank rates would stem any short-term capital outflow and attract short-term funds from abroad.

For most countries on the pre–World War I gold standard, with the possible exception of Great Britain, there is evidence that interest rates were never allowed to rise enough to contract the domestic price level—in other words, that they did not follow the rules.[16] Also, many countries frequently followed policies of sterilization of gold flows—of attempting to neutralize the effects of gold flows on

16. Noted examples are France and Belgium. See P. B. White, "The Working of the Pre-War Gold Standard," *Economica* (February 1937): 18-32; and A. I. Bloomfield, *Monetary Policy Under the International Gold Standard* (New York: Federal Reserve Bank of New York. 1959).

the domestic money supply by open-market purchase or sales of domestic securities.[17]

Reserve Currencies and the Role of Sterling

Many countries under the pre-World War I gold standard held their international reserves in the form of gold and in the currencies of several major countries—key currencies.[18] The center of the international payments mechanism was Britain, with the Bank of England maintaining its international reserves primarily in gold. Most other countries kept reserves in the form of gold and sterling assets. Two other major European capitals also served as reserve centers in the period between 1900 and 1914: Paris and Berlin, each of which held reserves in gold, sterling, and each of the other country's currency, while a number of smaller European countries held reserves in the form of francs and marks. Thus, by 1914, for many countries the gold standard was a gold exchange standard.

In addition to the use of other currencies as reserve assets, an elaborate network of short-term financial arrangements developed between private financial institutions centered in the London money market. This extensive network of reserve currencies and short-term international finance had two important results. First, the Bank of England could act as manager of the world's gold standard system without having to hold excessive gold reserves.[19] By altering its bank rate, the Bank of England produced major repercussions around the world.[20]

17. Usually gold outflows were offset by open-market purchases of domestic securities. For U.S. experience, see Milton Friedman and Anna J. Schwartz, *A Monetary History of the United States, 1867–1960* (Princeton: Princeton University Press, 1964). For other countries, see Bloomfield, *Monetary Policy*.

18. Much of this discussion derives from Peter H. Lindert, *Key Currencies and Gold, 1900–1913*, Princeton Studies in International Finance no. 24 (Princeton: Princeton University Press, 1969).

19. Indeed, Britain's total gold reserves in 1913 accounted for only 9.5 percent of the world's monetary gold stock, whereas the Bank of England's holdings accounted for 3.5 percent. See John Maynard Keynes, *A Treatise on Money: 2, The Applied Theory of Money*, vol. 6 of *The Collected Writings of John Maynard Keynes*, ed. Elizabeth Johnson and Donald Moggridge (London: Macmillan, Cambridge University Press for the Royal Economic Society, 1971).

20. It probably caused monetary crises in the United States in the 1837–43 period and again in 1873. See Peter Temin, *The Jacksonian Economy* (New York: Norton, 1969), and Friedman and Schwartz, *Monetary History*.

Second, much of the balance of payments adjustment mechanism before World War I did not require actual gold flows. Instead, the adjustment consisted primarily of transfers of sterling and other currency balances in the London, Paris, Berlin, and New York money markets.[21] In addition, short-term capital flows accommodated the balance of payments adjustment mechanism in this period.[22] Indeed, the pre–World War I gold standard has often been described as a sterling standard.[23]

In sum, the gold standard that emerged before World War I was very different from the pure gold coin standard outlined earlier. Unlike the pure gold coin standard, countries economized on the use of gold both in their domestic money supplies and as a means of settling international payments imbalances. In addition, to avoid the iron discipline of the gold standard, central banks in some countries did not follow the rules of the game, and some countries even abandoned the gold standard periodically.[24] The final modification of the pure gold standard was the key role the Bank of England played as manager of the system. The result was a "managed gold standard." Indeed, most of the characteristics of this managed standard were carried forward to the post–World War I gold exchange standard.

CHRONOLOGY OF THE GOLD STANDARD, 1821-1971

This section briefly sketches the chronology of the gold standard from the end of the Napoleonic Wars to the collapse of Bretton Woods.

21. Also, the period after 1900 marked a growing trend toward earmarking gold holdings in major centers, rather than transporting gold between centers.

22. See Bloomfield, *Short-Term Capital Movements*, p. 44.

23. See Melchior Palyi, *The Twilight of Gold 1914 to 1936: Myths and Realities* (Chicago: Henry Regnery, 1972); and David Williams, "The Evolution of the Sterling System," in C. R. Whittlesey and J. S. G. Wilson, eds., *Essays in Money and Banking in Honour of R. S. Sayers* (Oxford: Clarendon Press, 1968).

24. Argentina and other Latin American countries did so, for example. See Alec George Ford, *The Gold Standard 1880-1914, Britain and Argentina* (Oxford: Clarendon Press, 1962).

The Classical Gold Standard, 1821-1914

In the eighteenth century, England and most countries were on a bimetallic standard based primarily on silver.[25] When Great Britain restored specie payments in 1821 after the inflation episode of Napoleonic Wars, the gold standard was restored. From 1821 to 1880, the gold standard steadily expanded as more and more countries ceased using silver.[26] By 1880, the majority of countries in the world were on some form of a gold standard.

The period from 1880 to 1914, known as the heyday of the gold standard, was a remarkable period in world economic history. It was characterized by rapid economic growth, free flow of labor and capital across political borders, virtually free trade, and, in general, world peace. These external conditions, coupled with the elaborate financial network centered in London and the role of the Bank of England as manager of the system, are believed to be the sine qua non of the effective operation of the gold standard.[27]

The Gold Exchange Standard, 1925-1931

The gold standard broke down during World War I,[28] was succeeded by a period of managed fiduciary money, and then was briefly reinstated from 1925 to 1931 as the gold exchange standard. Under the gold exchange standard, the United States and Great Britain held reserves only in gold, whereas other countries could hold both gold and dollars or pounds as reserves. In addition, most countries en-

25. Under a bimetallic standard, each of two precious metals, gold and silver, serves as legal tender, and the two metals are kept by the mint in a fixed proportion to each other. The relationship between the official exchange rate of gold for silver and the market rate determines whether either one or both metals are used as money. Thus, for example, in 1834, the United States raised the mint ratio of silver to gold from 15:1 to 16:1, hence valuing silver slightly lower relative to gold than the world market. As a result, little silver was offered for coinage, and the U.S. was in effect on the gold standard. See Leland B. Yeager, *International Monetary Relations: Theory, History and Policy*, 2d ed. (New York: Harper & Row, 1976), p. 296.

26. The switch from silver to gold reflected both changes in the relative supplies of the two precious metals, brought on by the gold discoveries of the 1840s and 1850s, and a growing preference for the more precious metal as world real income rose.

27. See Palyi, *Twilight of Gold*; and Yeager, *International Monetary Relations*, ch. 15.

28. The United States alone remained on the gold standard, except for a brief embargo on gold exports from 1917 to 1919.

gaged in active sterilization policies to protect their domestic money supplies from gold flows.

Following Britain's departure from gold in the face of massive gold and capital flows, the gold exchange standard broke down in 1931 and was again succeeded by managed fiduciary money. The reasons usually cited for the failure of the gold exchange standard include (1) the general unwillingness of countries to subsume internal economic conditions to the external discipline of the gold standard and to frequently sterilize gold flows; (2) an imbalance in the world's distribution of gold caused by Britain's decision to return to gold at an overvalued exchange rate, which led to a chronic gold outflow, France's decision to return to gold at an undervalued exchange rate, which led to persistent gold inflows, and the frequent sterlization of gold inflows by the Federal Reserve System; (3) the inability of London and the unwillingness of New York to act as manager of the system; and (4) German reparations, which disrupted the international payments mechanism.[29]

The Bretton Woods System, 1946–1971

The Bretton Woods system was an attempt to return to a modified gold standard using the U.S. dollar as the world's key reserve currency. All countries other than the sterling bloc settled their international balances in dollars. The United States maintained the fixed price of gold at $35 per ounce, maintained substantial gold reserves, and settled external accounts with gold bullion payments and receipts.

After World War II, persistent U.S. balance of payments deficits helped finance the recovery of world trade from depression and war. However, the steady growth in the use of U.S. dollars as international reserves and persistent U.S. balance of payments deficits steadily reduced U.S. gold reserves and the gold reserve ratio, reducing public confidence in the ability of the U.S. to redeem its currency in gold.[30] This confidence problem, coupled with many nations' aver-

29. See W. A. Brown, *The International Gold Standard Reinterpreted, 1914–1934* (New York: National Bureau of Economic Research, 1940); and Yeager, *International Monetary Relations*, ch. 17.

30. See H. G. Johnson, "Theoretical Problems of the International Monetary System," *Pakistan Development Review* 7: 1–28.

sion to paying both seigniorage and an "inflation tax" to the United States after 1965, led ultimately to the breakdown of the Bretton Woods system in 1971. The U.S. decision in 1971 to stop pegging the price of gold represented the final demise of the gold standard.

THE RECORD OF THE GOLD STANDARD

This section briefly examines some evidence for the United Kingdom and the United States over the period 1800-1979 on the stability of the price level and of real output under both gold and managed fiduciary money standards.[31] Figures 8-1 and 8-2 portray the behavior of the wholesale price index from 1800 to 1979 for both countries.

From 1797 to 1821, during and immediately following the Napoleonic Wars, the United Kingdom was on a fiat (or paper) standard; it officially joined the gold standard in 1821 and maintained a fixed price of gold until 1914. There is very little difference in the U.K. price level between the first year of the gold standard and the last, but over the whole period there was a very slight downward trend in prices averaging 0.4 percent per year. Within that approximate one hundred-year span, however, periods of declining price levels alternated with periods of rising price levels—a pattern consistent with the commodity theory of money. Prices fell until the mid-1840s, reflecting the pressure of rising real incomes on the limited stock of gold. Following the California and Australian gold discoveries of the late 1840s and early 1850s, prices turned around and kept rising until the late 1860s. This was followed by a twenty-five-year period of declining prices, again reflecting both rising real income and an expanding number of countries on the gold standard. This deflation ended after technical advances in gold processing and major gold discoveries in the late 1880s and 1890s increased world gold supplies.

31. Managed fiduciary money is a monetary standard where the government is not committed to maintaining a fixed price of gold. The United States had such a standard from 1861 to 1879 and has been on one since 1971. Under such a standard, the monetary authorities have complete control over the domestic money supply. An alternative situation, often called managed money, occurs when the monetary authorities, though committed to maintaining a fixed price of gold, engage in a systematic policy of sterilizing (or neutralizing), using offsetting open-market operations, the influence of gold flows on the domestic money supply. Thus the period from 1914 to 1933 in U.S. monetary history can be viewed as a period of managed money because of the frequent sterilizing activity of the Federal Reserve System. See Friedman and Schwartz, *Monetary History*, pp. 462-92.

Figure 8–1.   Wholesale Price Index, United Kingdom, 1800–1979.

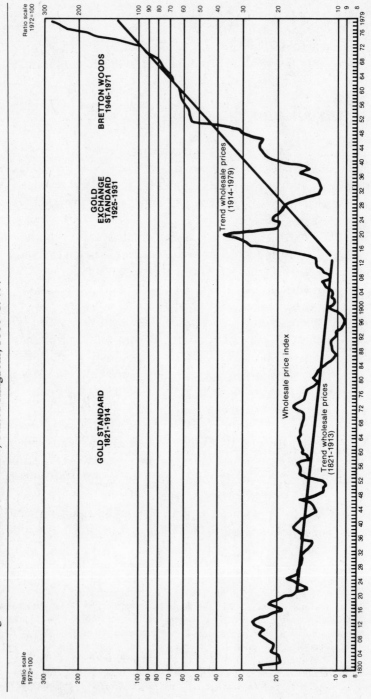

Note: Prepared by Federal Reserve Bank of St. Louis.

Figure 8-2. Wholesale Price Index, United States, 1800-1979.

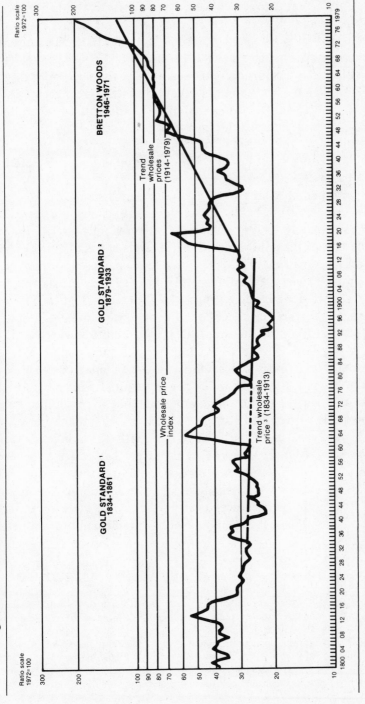

1. Excludes 1838–1843 when spacie payments were suspended.

2. United States imposes gold export embargo from September 1917 to June 1919.

3. Broken line indicates years excluded in computing trend.

Note: Prepared by Federal Reserve Bank of St. Louis.

The United States followed a similar pattern to the United Kingdom, experiencing a very slight downward trend in the price level averaging 0.14 percent per year from 1834 to 1913. The country adopted the gold standard in 1834 (it had been on silver for the preceding thirty-five years) and remained on it at the same price of gold until World War I, with the noted exception of the greenback episode from 1861 to 1878.[32] During that period, the country abandoned the gold standard, and prices increased rapidly until 1866. To restore convertibility to gold, prices had to fall sufficiently to restore the prewar purchasing power parity. This occurred in the rapid deflation of 1869 to 1879.

The period since World War I has not been characterized by price stability except for the 1920s, under the gold exchange standard, and the 1950s and early 1960s, under the Bretton Woods system. Indeed, since the end of the gold standard, price levels in both countries have on average been rising. The U.K. price level increased at an average annual rate of 3.81 percent form 1914 to 1979, whereas the U.S. price level increased by an average of 2.2 percent. Figures 8-3 and 8-4 present further evidence of the operation of a commodity money standard and of the long-run price stability characteristic of the gold standard. Figure 8-3 compares the purchasing power of gold in the world (measured by the ratio of an index of the price of gold to the wholesale price index for the United Kingdom) in relation to trend, to the world monetary gold stock in relation to trend, over the period 1821-1914.[33] The index of the purchasing power of gold presented here varies inversely with the wholesale price index presented in Figure 8-1. This inverse association between the two series reflects the fixed price of gold over this period.[34] The trends of both series were rising over the whole period. The upward trend in the purchasing power of gold series reflects a more rapid growth of world real output and, hence, of the demand for monetary

---

32. Also excluded from the gold standard are the turbulent years 1838-43, during part of which period specie payments were suspended.

33. The United Kingdom was chosen as representative of the pre-1914 world because it was a large, open economy with few trade restrictions; hence, its wholesale price index was dominated by internationally traded goods.

34. Indeed, this inverse relationship prevailed virtually until the late 1960s. Since the freeing of the price of gold in 1968, the purchasing power of gold has varied directly with the wholesale price index. This reflects primarily the rising demand for gold as a hedge against inflation and increasing world political and monetary instability.

Figure 8–3. Monetary Gold Stock and Purchasing Power of Gold Index, World, 1821–1914.

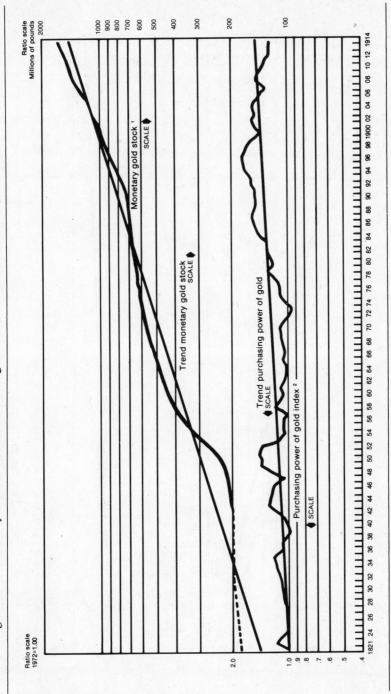

1. Broken line indicates interpolated data.

2. Measured by the ratio of an index of the price of gold to the wholesale price index for the United Kingdom.

Note: Prepared by Federal Reserve Bank of St. Louis.

Figure 8–4.   Monetary Gold Stock and Purchasing Power of Gold Index, United States, 1879–1914.

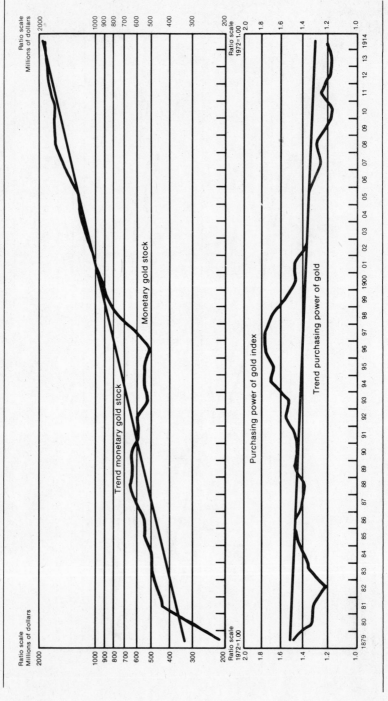

Note: Prepared by Federal Reserve Bank of St. Louis.

gold than could be accommodated by growth in the world's monetary gold stock.

In comparing deviations from trend in the purchasing power of gold to deviations from trend in the world monetary gold stock, one would expect the latter to produce corresponding changes in the price level and, for a given nominal price of gold, to affect inversely the purchasing power of gold. A comparison of deviations from trend of both series reveals this negative association, with deviations from trend in the world monetary gold stock leading deviations from trend in the purchasing power of gold.[35]

In addition, according to the operations of a commodity money standard, movements in the purchasing power of gold would be expected to precede movements in the monetary gold stock, since a rising purchasing power of gold would induce both a shift from nonmonetary to monetary uses of gold and increased gold production. Such a positive association between deviations from trend of the two series is observed.[36] Thus, during the 1830s and 1840s the purchasing power of gold largely exceeded its long-run trend. This was followed by a rapid increase in the world monetary gold stock after 1848 as the output of the new California and Australian mines was added to the existing world's stock. Subsequently, the purchasing power of gold declined from its peak above trend in the mid-1850s and was succeeded by a marked deceleration in the monetary gold stock after 1860. The same pattern arises when comparing the rise in the purchasing power of gold in the 1870s and 1880s with the subsequent increase in the monetary gold stock in the mid-1890s.

Table 8–4 compares the United States' purchasing power of gold with the U.S. monetary gold stock over the 1879 to 1914 gold standard period.[37] In this period the trends of the two series moved in

35. The highest statistically significant negative correlation in the 1821 to 1914 period occurred when deviations from trend in the monetary gold stock led deviations from trend in the purchasing power of gold by two years. The correlation coefficient, –0.644, was statistically significant at the 1 percent level.

36. The highest statistically significant positive correlation in the 1821–1914 period occurred with deviations from trend in the purchasing power of gold leading deviations from trend in the world monetary gold stock by twenty-five years. The correlation was 0.436, statistically significant at the 1 percent level.

37. An important difference between the behavior of the U.S. monetary gold stock and that of the world as a whole is that short-run movements in the United States series reflect not only changes in gold production and shifts between monetary and nonmonetary uses of gold but also gold movements between the United States and other countries.

opposite directions. The declining trend in the purchasing power of gold series reflects the more rapid growth in the U.S. monetary gold stock than in real output over the whole period. This rapid growth resulted from (1) the accumulation of monetary gold from the rest of the world early in the period after the resumption of specie payments and (2) the effects of gold discoveries in the 1890s.

As in Figure 8–3, Figure 8–4 shows a negative association between concurrent deviations from trend in the monetary gold stock and in the purchasing power of gold.[38] Also as in Figure 8–3, deviations from trend in the purchasing power of gold preceded deviations from trend in the monetary gold stock.[39] Thus declines in the purchasing power of gold from 1879 to 1882 preceded declines in the monetary gold stock below trend in the late 1880s and early 1890s, whereas rises in the purchasing power of gold after 1882 can be associated with a rising monetary gold stock after 1896. Finally, the declining purchasing power of gold in the mid-1890s can be associated with the declining growth of the monetary gold stock after 1903.

One important implication of the tendency for price levels to revert to a long-run stable value under the gold standard is that it ensured a measure of predictability with respect to the value of money: Though prices would rise or fall for a few years, inflation or deflation would not persist.[40] Such belief in long-run price stability

38. The highest statistically significant negative correlation from 1879 to 1914 occurred with the contemporaneous relationship between deviations from trend in the monetary gold stock and deviations from trend in the purchasing power of gold. The correlation coefficient, –0.656, was statistically significant at the 1 percent level.

39. The highest statistically significant positive correlation from 1879 to 1914 occurred when deviations from trend in the purchasing power of gold led deviations from trend in the monetary gold stock by fourteen years. The correlation coefficient was 0.793, statistically significant at the 1 percent level. The highest statistically significant positive correlation in this period occurred when deviations from trend in the *world* purchasing power of gold led deviations from trend in the *world* monetary gold stock by sixteen years. The correlation coefficient was 0.863, statistically significant at the 1 percent level. The considerably longer lead observed over the 1821–1914 period (see n. 36 above) likely reflects a longer adjustment period in the early part of the nineteenth century.

40. See Benjamin Klein, "Our New Monetary Standard: The Measurement and Effects of Price Uncertainty, 1880–1973," *Economic Inquiry* 13, no. 4 (December 1975): 461–84, for evidence of long-run price stability in the U.S. under the gold standard. His evidence that positive (or negative) autocorrelations of the price level are succeeded by negative (or positive) autocorrelations is consistent with the hypothesis that the price level reverted back to its mean level. As a consequence of this mean reversion phenomenon, year-to-year changes in the price level were substantial for each country. However, the standard deviations of year-to-year changes in the wholesale price index were still considerably lower in

would encourage economic agents to engage in contracts with the expectation that, should prices of commodities or factor services change, the change would reflect real forces rather than changes in the value of money.

Belief in long-term price level stability has apparently disappeared in recent years, since people now realize that the long-run constraint of the gold standard has vanished.[41] As a consequence, it has become more difficult for people to distinguish between changes in relative prices and changes in the price level. Such absolute vs. relative price confusion has increased the possibility of major economic losses, since people fail to respond to market signals.[42]

Finally, we present evidence on real output stability for the United Kingdom and the United States. It is frequently argued that under the gold standard, when countries had to subordinate internal balance considerations to the gold standard's discipline, real output would be less stable than under a regime of managed fiduciary money. Figures 8-5 and 8-6 show the deviations of real per capita income from its long-run trend over the period 1870-1979.

For the United Kingdom, Figure 8-5 shows both a single trend line for the 1870-1979 period as a whole and separate trend lines for each of the pre- and post-World War I subperiods. The U.K. data were split into two subperiods because the trend line for the entire period puts real output after 1919 virtually always below trend. World War I drastically reduced the level of real per capita income and was followed by a lengthy period of recovery. This suggests that the two periods should be handled separately. Examining the deviations from trend (using the subperiod trends) suggests that real per capita income was less variable in the pre-World War I period than

---

the pre-World War I gold standard era than in the post-World War I managed fiduciary money era. For the United Kingdom, the standard deviations are: 1821-1913, 6.20; 1919-79 (excluding 1939-45), 12.00. For the United States, the standard deviations are: 1834-1913 (excluding 1838-43 and 1861-79), 6.29; 1919-79 (excluding 1941-45), 9.28.

41. Indeed, evidence presented in Klein, "New Monetary Standard," shows a marked decline since 1960 in long-term price level predictability—the belief in long-term stability measured by a moving standard deviation of changes in the price level. At the same time, short-term price level predictability—the belief about price level behavior in the near future—has improved in the postwar period. See pp. 461-84.

42. See Friedrich August von Hayek, *A Tiger by the Tail*, Hobart Papers (London: Institute of Economic Affairs, 1972); Milton Friedman, "Nobel Lecture: Inflation and Unemployment," *Journal of Political Economy* 85 (June 1977): 451-72; Axel Leijonhufvud, "Costs and Consequences of Inflation," *Information and Co-Ordination: Essays in Macro Economic Theory* (London: Oxford University Press, 1981).

Figure 8–5.   Real Per Capita Income, United Kingdom, 1870–1979.

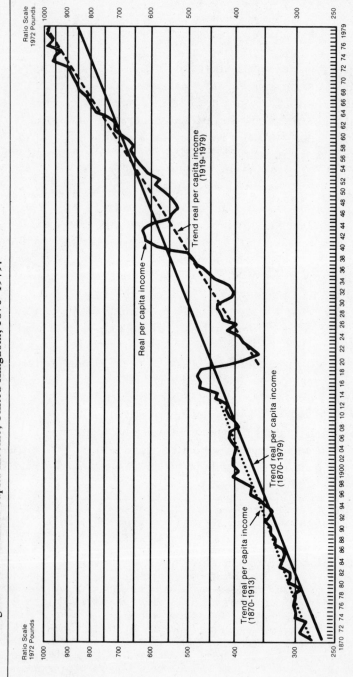

Note: Prepared by Federal Reserve Bank of St. Louis.

Figure 8-6. Real Per Capita Income, United States, 1870–1979.

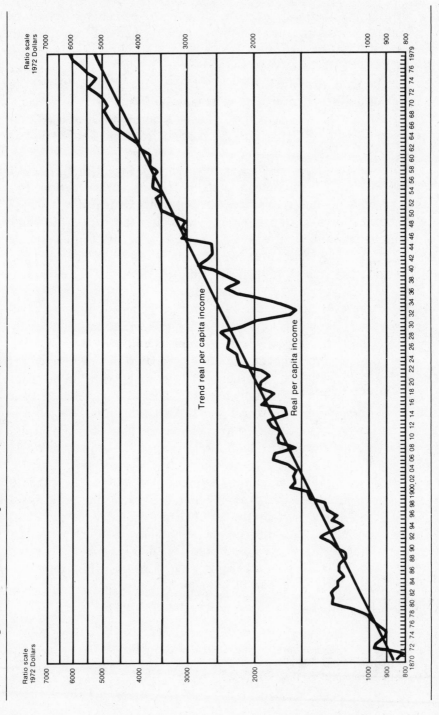

Note: Prepared by Federal Reserve Bank of St. Louis.

subsequently. The mean absolute value of the percentage deviations of real per capita income from trend was 2.14 percent from 1870 to 1913 and 3.75 percent from 1919 to 1979 (excluding 1939–45).

As in the U.K. case, U.S. real per capita income was more stable under the gold standard from 1879 to 1913 than during the entire post–World War I period. The mean absolute values of the percentage deviations of real per capita income from trend were 6.64 percent from 1879 to 1913 and 8.51 percent from 1919 to 1979 (excluding 1941–45).

Moreover, unemployment was on average lower in the pre–1914 period in both countries than in the post–World War I period. For the United Kingdom, the average unemployment rate over the 1888–1913 period was 4.30 percent, whereas over the period 1919–79 (excluding 1939–45) it was 6.52 percent. For the United States, average unemployment rates by subperiod were 6.78 percent from 1890 to 1913 and 7.46 percent from 1919 to 1979 (excluding 1941–45).

Thus, the evidence for the two countries suggests that the managed fiduciary money system superseding the gold standard generally has been associated with less real economic stability.

One dominant feature of the classical gold standard period was long-run price stability. This contrasts favorably with the behavior of the price level under the managed fiduciary money standard for much of the period since World War I. Also, though real output varied considerably from year to year under the gold standard, it did not vary discernibly more than it has in the entire period since World War I.[43]

One problem with comparing the pre–World War I gold standard with the managed fiduciary money standard over the entire post–World War I period is that the latter period includes the turbulent interwar years, and including such a period may bias the case against managed fiduciary money. To account for this, Table 8-1 presents a comparison for both countries of several measures of performance of the price level, real output, and money growth for three time

43. The standard deviations of year-to-year percentage changes in real per capita income for the United States were: 1879–1913, 5.79; 1919–79 (excluding 1941-45), 6.1. For the United Kingdom, they were: 1870-1913, 2.62; 1919–79 (excluding 1939–45), 3.24.

Table 8-1. A Comparison of Three Major Periods: the Gold Standard, the Interwar Period, and the Post-World War II Period.

	Gold Standard[a]		Interwar Period		Post-World War II	
	U.K.	*U.S.*	*U.K.*	*U.S.*	*U.K.*	*U.S.*
	1870–1913 (1821–1913)	*1879–1913 (1834–1913)*	*1919–39*	*1919–41*	*1946–79*	*1946–79*
1. The average annual percentage change in the price level	-0.7 (-0.4)	0.1 (-0.1)	-4.6	-2.5	5.6	2.8
2. The coefficient of variation of annual percentage changes in the price level (ratio)	-14.9 (-16.3)	17.0 (6.5)	-3.8	-5.2	1.2	1.3
3. The coefficient of variation of annual percentage changes in real per capita income (ratio)	2.5	3.5	4.9	5.5	1.4	1.8
4. The average percentage level of unemployment	4.3[b]	6.8[c]	13.3	11.3	2.5	5.0
5. The average annual percentage change in the money supply	1.5	6.1	0.9	1.5	5.9	5.7
6. The coefficient of variation of annual percentage changes in the money supply (ratio)	1.6	0.8	3.6	2.4	1.0	0.5

a. Data for the longer periods were available only for the price level.
b. 1888–1913.
c. 1890–1913.

Notes by row: Rows 1 and 5 were calculated as the regression coefficient of a regression of the log of the variable on a time trend. Rows 2, 3, and 6 were calculated as the ratio of the standard deviation of annual percentage changes in the variable to its means.

Sources: See Michael D. Bordo, "The Classical Gold Standard: Some Lessons for Today," *Federal Reserve Bank of St. Louis Review* 62, no. 5 (May 1981): Appendix pp. 16–17.

periods: the pre–World War I gold standard, the interwar period, and the post–World War II period.[44]

First, evidence is presented in row 1 on long-run price level stability measured by the average annual rate of change in the price level over the period. This shows that the interwar period in both countries was characterized by substantial deflation, whereas the post–World War II period has been characterized by inflation. This performance is in marked contrast to the near price stability of the gold standard period. However, price variability, measured in row 2 by the coefficient of variation of percentage year-to-year changes in the price level, reveals a slightly different picture. Prices were more variable under the gold standard than during both post–gold standard periods, with the least variability occurring in the post–World War II period.

Second, evidence is presented in row 3 on real output stability measured by the coefficient of variation of year-to-year percentage changes in real per capita output. Real output was considerably less stable in both countries in the interwar period than it was either under the gold standard or in the post–World War II period, with the latter period having the best record. In addition, the evidence on average unemployment rates presented in row 4 agrees with the evidence on real output stability: Unemployment was by far the highest in the interwar period,[45] and by far the lowest in the post–World War II period in both countries.

Finally, comparisons are made across periods in the average annual rate of monetary growth in row 6, and in the variability in monetary growth (measured by the coefficient of variation of percentage year-

44. Both world wars are omitted from this comparison for two reasons. First, both wars were accompanied by rapid inflation in both countries, and in each case wartime government expenditures were largely financed by the issue of government fiat money. Hence, a comparison of the price-stabilizing characteristics of the two monetary standards that included two major wars in the case of the managed fiduciary money standard and none in the case of the gold standard would bias the case against the former. Second, measured real output would tend to be higher than otherwise in wartime to the extent that resources (both employed and other unemployed) are devoted to nonproductive wartime use. Hence, including wartime real output would bias the case in favor of managed fiduciary money.

45. Comparing the two countries' unemployment rate with the measure of real output stability reveals an interesting difference. Real output was less stable in the United States, but unemployment was higher in the United Kingdom. The high and persistent unemployment in the United Kingdom in the interwar period is attributed by some to significant increases in the ratio of unemployment benefits to wages. See Daniel K. Benjamin and Levis A. Kochin, "Searching for an Explanation of Unemployment in Interwar Britain," *Journal of Political Economy* 87 (June 1979): 441-78.

to-year changes in the money supply) in row 7. According to monetary theory, a reduction in monetary growth below the long-run trend of real output growth will produce deflation, whereas a rise in monetary growth above the long-run trend of real output growth will lead to inflation. In the transition between different rates of monetary growth, both the levels and growth rates of real output will deviate considerably from long-run trends. Thus, monetary variability will lead to real output variability.[46]

The rate of monetary growth was lower in both countries in the interwar period than in both the post–World War II and the gold standard periods. In the case of the United Kingdom, the post–World War II period exhibits more rapid monetary growth than under the gold standard, whereas for the United States, monetary growth rates are very similar in both the post-war and gold standard periods. Finally, monetary growth was more variable in both countries in the interwar period than in the other two periods, with the post–World War II period displaying the least variability in monetary growth.

The poor economic performance of the interwar period compared to either the preceding gold standard period or the post–World War II period has been attributed to the failure of monetary policy. Indeed, the Bank of England's attempt to restore convertibility to gold at the prewar parity has often been blamed for British deflation and unemployment in the 1920s.[47] The failure of the Federal Reserve System to prevent the drastic decline in the U.S. money supply from 1929 to 1933 has likewise been blamed for the severity of the Great Depression in the United States.[48] One could argue that the greatly improved performance of monetary policy and the economic stability in the two countries in the post–World War II period reflects learning from past mistakes. This suggests that in weighing the historical evidence in favor of a return to the gold standard, a meaningful comparison should be made between the post–World War II period and the gold standard. In such a comparison, the gold standard did provide greater *long-run* price stability, but at the expense of both short-run real output and short-run price stability. The higher rates of inflation, lower variability of real output, and lower

46. See Milton Friedman, *A Theoretical Framework for Monetary Analysis*, Occasional Paper no. 112 (New York: National Bureau of Economic Research, 1971).

47. See John Maynard Keynes, *The Economic Consequences of Mr. Churchill*, vol. 9 of *Collected Works*.

48. See Friedman and Schwartz, *Monetary History*.

unemployment in the two countries in the recent period compared to the preceding periods probably reflects a shift of policy preferences away from the goal of long-run price stability and toward that of full employment. Indeed, the strong commitment to full employment in both countries probably explains the worsening of inflation in the postwar period.[49]

A RETURN TO THE GOLD STANDARD: SOME UNRESOLVED ISSUES

Before seriously considering a return to a gold standard, we must resolve a number of important issues.

The Type of Gold Standard

The issue of the type of gold standard raises a number of questions. First, does the United States want a national or an international standard? It is conceivable for the United States to return unilaterally to a gold standard, that is, to determine its domestic money supply by a gold standard rule of a fixed price of gold. This would be equivalent to having a flexible exchange rate with all countries not on the gold standard. Indeed, a historical precedent for such a standard was the silver standard maintained by China until 1935 in a world where most countries were on a gold standard. However, like China in the period 1933–35, the United States would run the risk of a major external disturbance, which could produce an unwanted inflation or deflation equivalent to the disturbance China suffered following the U.S. silver purchase policy of 1933.[50] However, if other industrialized countries returned to gold along with the United States, then the effect of random disturbances in the gold market would be dissipated across all countries, reducing its impact on any one country.

49. Friedman forcefully argued this point in his 1968 presidential address to the American Economic Association. See Milton Friedman, "The Role of Monetary Policy," *The American Economic Review* 58 (May 1968): 1–17.

50. The U.S. silver purchase program beginning December 21, 1933, trebled the market price of silver in two years, caused a massive silver outflow from China and severe deflationary pressure in that country, and ultimately forced China to abandon the silver standard in November 1935. See Friedman and Schwartz, *Monetary History*, pp. 489–91.

Thus, ultimately we would want an international gold standard, which would require an international agreement and an amendment to the IMF rules.[51] However, for an international gold standard to be reestablished, the first requirement would be the removal of the forces that caused it to break down. Disparate inflation rates among the industrialized countries led to the collapse of the Bretton Woods system. The gold standard compels countries adhering to it to adjust their price levels to the world level through the operation of the fixed exchange rate. The unwillingness of low inflation countries to subordinate their domestic monetary policies to the requirements of the fixed exchange rate system led to the breakdown of the Bretton Woods arrangement. This means that before the restoration of an international gold standard could be seriously contemplated, the disparity among rates of inflation would need to be reduced, if not eliminated.

Second, what type of gold standard is wanted? A gold coin standard with free convertibility of fiduciary money? A gold bullion standard with free export and import of gold but without a gold coinage? A return to Bretton Woods? As discussed above, all these options in the past led to serious difficulties and were ultimately abandoned. However, this is not to say that feasible arrangements are impossible.

Restoring a Gold Standard

Holding in abeyance the issues just raised, two key issues remain: choosing the right price and determining whether there is sufficient gold to maintain long-run price stability.

Choosing the Right Price. In the past, when the United States and other countries decided to return to a gold standard, they returned to a standard that still existed, and they invariably attempted to restore payments at the old price.[52] However there is no comparable

51. According to the second amendment to the IMF Charter, members are not obliged to maintain an official price of gold or to use gold in transactions with the fund. See Sir Joseph Gold, "Gold in International Monetary Law: Change, Uncertainty, and Ambiguity," *Journal of International Law and Economics* 15, no. 2 (1981): 323-69.

52. Thus Great Britain returned to gold at £3 17s. 10½d. after a period of wartime inflation in 1821 and again in 1925. In both cases, it underwent internal deflation. And in

old price today. The last official price of an ounce of gold, $42.23, is so out of line with current market prices that it provides no guidance. The risk involved in choosing the wrong price is considerable. If the price were set too high, it would produce a massive gold inflow and inflation; if too low, a massive gold outflow and deflation.

Since 1968, the price of gold has been determined in the free market.[53] Hence, a solution to the question of the right price may lie in isolating the determinants of supply and demand for gold. The total supply of gold consists of gold production in market economies, the flow from centrally planned economies, official sales (net), jewelry sales by developing countries, and dishoarding of private bullion holdings. The total demand for gold consists of two components: industrial demand (the fabrication demand for gold for jewelry, electronics, and dentistry), and investment or asset demand (the holding of gold in portfolios as a hedge against both inflation and uncertainty).

Table 8-2 displays the components of the supply and demand for gold as well as the behavior of the price of gold and the real price of gold from 1968 to 1980. On the supply side, production in market economies, representing the largest component of total supply, declined steadily throughout the period, whereas both the flow from centrally planned economies and net official sales varied considerably over the period. The flow from centrally planned economies does not seem to be related to either the nominal or the real price of gold over the period, whereas official sales increased with rising gold prices in the 1976–79 period.

On the demand side, both components are highly variable, with asset demand the more variable component. Also, as theory would predict, industrial demand varied inversely with movements in the real price, whereas asset demand varied directly.[54]

Finally, both nominal and real price series are dominated by two major increases, the first running from 1972 to 1975 and the second from 1977 to 1980, both likely reflecting expectations of a rise in world inflation.

---

both cases, there was a major controversy over the choice between devaluation and deflation. The United States returned to gold in 1879 under similar circumstances.

53. With the adoption of the two-tier system in 1968, governments maintained the fixed price of $35.00 per ounce only for official transactions.

54. In this breakdown, medallions and coins are included under industrial demand; however, even if they had been included as part of asset demand, the behavior of the two components would not be much different.

Table 8-2. Fundamentals of the World Gold Market, 1968–1980.

Year	Demand[a]			Supply[b]			Price	
	Industrial Demand	Asset Demand	Total Demand	World Production (in market economies)	Net Sales From Stocks	Total Supply	Price of Gold (London price)	Real Price of Gold[c]
1968	39.3	20.7	60.0	40.1	19.9	60.0	38.64	37.70
1969	38.6	3.4	42.0	40.3	1.7	42.0	41.12	38.61
1970	44.3	7.7	52.0	40.9	11.1	52.0	35.94	32.55
1971	44.7	—	44.7	39.7	5.0	44.7	40.81	35.83
1972	43.2	4.9	48.1	38.1	10.0	48.1	58.16	48.83
1973	27.2	17.2	45.1	36.0	9.1	45.1	97.32	72.25
1974	25.4	16.5	41.9	32.4	9.5	41.9	159.26	99.48
1975	31.6	4.1	35.7	30.7	5.0	35.7	160.90	92.00
1976	44.5	1.8	46.3	31.2	15.1	46.3	124.84	68.22
1977	45.6	7.1	52.7	31.2	21.5	52.7	148.11	76.27
1978	51.3	5.0	56.3	31.5	24.8	56.3	193.36	92.38
1979	42.3	12.5	54.8	30.9	23.9	54.8	307.82	130.65
1980	21.0	16.4	37.4	30.3	7.1	37.4	613.67	228.44

a. Millions of fine troy ounces.
b. Dollars per ounce.
c. London price of gold divided by U.S. WPI (1967 = 100).

Sources: See tables 4–1, 4–2, and Sc–16, *Report to the Congress of the Commission on the Role of Gold in the Domestic and International Monetary Systems* 1 (March 1982): 157–67, 219–25.

The price of gold at any given moment is determined by total demand and supply; however, it is important in the short run to distinguish between the influence of stocks and flows. It has been argued that in the short run, conditions in the stock (asset) market prevail, since within short periods the effects of net additions to the gold stock on the total stock are small. Thus, the key determinant of price would be factors shifting the asset demand for gold. As the time period lengthens, flow factors become more important until in the long run the key determinants of price would be the independent variables in the flow demand and supply functions.[55]

Accounting first for the determinants of the flow demand for gold, economic theory suggests that the industrial demand for gold would be a function primarily of the real price of gold, world real income, and the real price of close substitutes. In accordance with theory, recent studies have found the own price elasticity to be negative and close to one, with the real income elasticity greater than one.[56]

On the supply side, gold production in market economies should be a positive function of the real price, the price of key inputs and technology. However, recent studies have found the price elasticity of market economy gold production to be negative and quite low.[57] This result is largely explained by the behavior of South African gold production, which in 1980 accounted for 71 percent of total market economy production.[58]

55. See Leslie Lipschitz and Ichiro Otani, "A Simple Model of the Private Gold Market, 1968-1974: An Exploratory Econometric Exercise," *IMF Staff Papers* 24 (March 1977): 36-63.

56. In a recent study by the International Gold Corporation using annual data over the period 1970-80, the real price elasticity was found to be -1.2 and the real income elasticity, 2.9. See International Gold Corporation Limited, "A Gold Pricing Model" (August 1981), p. 6. (Mimeo.) Using quarterly data over the 1968-74 period, Lipschitz and Otani found a price elasticity of -0.7 and an income elasticity of 0.6; they also found an elasticity of -0.11 over the 1968-74 period ("Simple Model," p. 50). In a log linear regression of industrial demand for gold, using annual data over the period 1950-80, I found the price elasticity to be -0.8, the income elasticity to be 2.3, and the silver price coefficient to be insignificant. Similar results were produced using the world CPI over a similar period. By contrast, a similar regression run over the 1969-80 period yielded own price elasticities closer to 1 and a real income elasticity closer to 4.

57. Using annual data over the 1950-80 period, I found a current period elasticity of -0.07 based on a loglinear regression of market economy production as the real price and a time trend. Using the real price of gold lagged one year as an independent variable produced an elasticity of -0.10. Similar results were obtained for the 1969-80 period.

58. In 1980, South Africa accounted for 55.6 percent of the world's total output, with the USSR second at 21.3 percent, Canada third at 4.1 percent, Brazil fourth at 2.8 percent,

In South Africa, the rapid increase in the real price of gold since 1968 has led to a considerable expansion in milling capacity, but the number of ounces produced has steadily declined, reflecting a decline in the average grade of ore milled.[59] This phenomenon largely reflects official South African policy to preserve its reserves of gold. The calculation of South African reserves depends critically on the concept of pay limit, which is the minimum quantity of metal in a ton of rock sufficient to yield the revenue to cover the costs of mining, processing, and marketing gold. The reserves usually include ore available for extraction within a year. All gold mines in South Africa lease mines from the state subject to the restriction that the company must mine to the average value of its published ore reserves. When the price of gold was fixed, the pay limit rose as mining costs increased; since the 1970s, the pay limit has declined when the price of gold has risen and vice versa.[60]

Thus, the determinants of flow supply and demand should be important in explaining movements in the real price of gold. Indeed, on the basis of a very simple model both of industrial demand as a function of the real price of gold, the real price of silver, and world real income, and of market economy production as a function of the real price of gold (current and lagged by one year) and a time trend as a proxy for technological progress, I found that the independent variables of the demand and supply functions explained 95 percent of the variation in real price in the 1969–80 period. The remainder of the movements in the real price must be explained by the net asset demand for gold and by sales by Western and Communist bloc official sources.[61]

The net asset demand for gold should be a function of, among other things, the opportunity cost of holding real financial assets, the expected rate of inflation, and variables reflecting world economic and political instability. Indeed, consistent with a number of other

---

and the United States fifth at 2.4 percent; see J. Aron, *Gold Statistics and Analysis* (New York: n.p., January 1981).

59. A similar phenomenon has been observed in Canada and the United States.

60. See Lipschitz and Otani, "Simple Model," p. 50; see also F. Hirsch, "Influences on Gold Production," *IMF Staff Papers* 15 (November 1968): 405–70. In addition, South Africa, like Canada, subsidizes gold mines that are no longer profitable, thus enabling marginal mines to remain in operation. If the price of gold should decline, the amount of state assistance, which has been negligible recently, could rise again.

61. Net asset demand for gold is defined as the sum of net private bullion purchases, coins, and medallions less net dishoarding of private bullion holdings.

studies, I found proxies for these variables to explain much of the variation in the net asset demand for gold.[62] Moreover, accounting for these factors adds 3 percent further to the explanation of the variation in the real price of gold.

The final factors to be accounted for are the flows of gold to the market economies from the Communist bloc, which are believed to fluctuate with its real need for foreign exchange, and net official sales by Western monetary authorities, which would be explained by different factors in each instance.[63]

Putting all the information together suggests that choosing a "correct" official price may be a difficult task. Even accounting for the volatile factors affecting the net asset demand for gold as well as for net sales from the Communist bloc, we cannot be sure that these factors are sufficiently stable or predictable to maintain such a price for long.[64]

62. Lipschitz and Otani found their hoarding demand for gold to be significant functions of Eurodollar and Euromark interest rates, expected inflation and wealth over the 1968–74 period ("Simple Model," p. 50). The International Gold Corporation study, using monthly data, found measures of the real rate of interest, lagged world money growth, and world political tension to explain most of the variation in the price of gold ("Gold Pricing Model," p. 15). Using annual data over the 1969–80 period, I found the net asset demand to be significantly related to the real rate of interest (measured by the ninety-day Eurodollar rate on an annual basis less the annual rate of change of the world CPI), the annual rate of change of the world CPI, and world real income. Similar results were found using the U.S. ninety-day T-bill rate and the U.S. CPI.

63. See S. W. Salant and D. W. Henderson, "Market Anticipation of Government Policies and the Price of Gold," *Journal of Political Economy* 86, no. 4 (August 1978): 627–48; they regard speculation on the timing of official sales as an important determinant of fluctuations in the price of gold in the 1970s.

64. Robert Aliber suggests an interesting method to arrive at an equilibrium gold price. He takes the price of $35 per ounce in 1961, a year when the United States had virtual price stability, as an initial equilibrium price. Assuming that no other factors affected the real price, the nominal price of gold should have increased to the same extent as the increase in the U.S. price level since 1961. Since the U.S. CPI tripled between 1961 and 1980, the nominal price of gold should have been $105 in 1980; using the increase in the world CPI (based on IMF data), it should have been $155. However, other factors would have affected the real price of gold in addition to the increase in the general price level. If the world real income elasticity is about 2 (based on the results discussed in n. 56) and the increase in world income about 80 percent (based on the IMF index of world real GNP), then the demand for gold would have increased by 160 percent over the period 1961–80. Over the same period, the total world gold stock increased by 35 percent (based on U.S. Bureau of the Mines data). Thus, the excess demand for gold amounted to about 125 percent since 1961. If we take the price elasticity of demand for gold to be –1 and the price elasticity of supply to be close to zero, then the real price would have increased (other things being equal) by about 120 percent since 1961. On this calculation, the equilibrium price of gold in 1980 would have been between $230 and $350. This exercise assumes that factors affect-

Is There Sufficient Gold to Maintain Long-run Price Stability? Even if we choose the "correct" price for establishing a gold standard, we still must ascertain whether gold production will be sufficient in the future to ensure a growth rate of the world's monetary gold stock, and hence the world money supply, sufficient to match the growth of real per capita output and population and to account for underlying trends in velocity.[65]

As background to the discussion, Figure 8–7 displays annual data on world gold production since 1800. Most of the world's gold has been produced since 1850; indeed, two-thirds of it has been produced in the past fifty years. In addition, there is evidence of a direct relationship between the real price of gold and gold production with a long lead—at least until World War II.[66] Thus, the large increase in production from the mid-1930s to the 1960s reflects the U.S. response to the rise in the official price of gold in 1934 from $20.67 to $35.00 per ounce. Subsequently, with a declining real price of gold in the 1960s in the face of worldwide inflation and a fixed gold price, production peaked in 1970 and has followed a declining trend since then.

Since South Africa currently accounts for over half of world production and is believed to possess at least half of the world's proven reserves of 1 billion ounces, the prospect for world production hinges largely on the South African industry.

A number of factors suggest that South African production will not increase in the near future. These include high capital costs—which deter both the expansion of existing mines mining lower grade ores and the reopening of mines that were uneconomical when the

---

ing the net asset demand for gold are transitory and would vanish once price stability is restored. See Robert Aliber, "Inflationary Expectations and the Price of Gold" (Paper for the World Conference on Gold, Rome, February 5, 1982).

65. The same question was asked by both G. Cassel and J. Kitchin in their contributions to the *Interim Report of the Gold Delegation of the League of Nations* (Geneva: League of Nations, 1931).

66. Over the period 1800–1913, the highest statistically significant positive correlation occurred with the real price of gold leading world gold production by fourteen years. The correlation coefficient was 0.724, significant at the 1 percent level. Over the period 1914–45, the highest statistically significant positive correlation occurred with the real price of gold leading world gold production by two years. The correlation coefficient was 0.924, significant at the 1 percent level. Finally, over the period 1946–80, correlations with the real price of gold leading world gold production were negative and significant, with the highest significant correlation of −0.917 reached after thirteen years. This undoubtedly reflects the South African government's gold policy, as outlined above.

Figure 8-7. World Gold Production, 1800–1980.

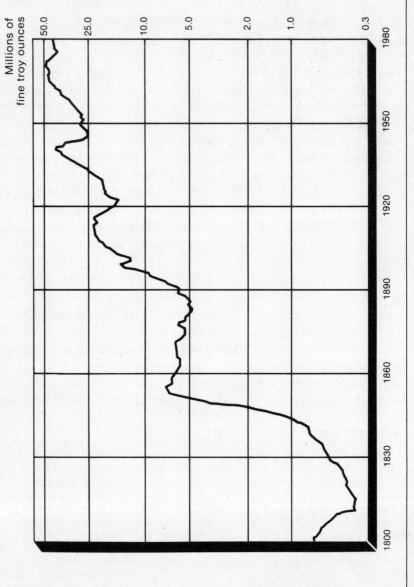

Source: Report to the Congress of the Commission on the Role of Gold in the Domestic and International Monetary Systems 1 (March 1982): 170.

gold price was fixed—and rising labor costs.[67] In addition, gold mining in South Africa is a labor intensive industry: Mechanization of the gold fields is impractical because of the depth at which mining is carried out, the hardness of the rock that has to be excavated to develop access tunnels, the high temperature of the rock, and the narrowness of the ore body. The final factor is the government-mandated shift to lower grade ores when the average gold price rises.[68]

Indeed, Consolidated Gold Fields project that South Africa's annual gold output will total 22.5 million ounces until 1987 (in 1980 it was 21 billion ounces) and then gradually decline to 11.25 million ounces by 2000, assuming a current gold price of $450, rising to $554 in 1984 and then remaining constant in real terms until 2000.[69]

The country with the next largest share in world output and in proven reserves is the USSR. Its current output is estimated at between 8 and 11 million ounces and is not expected to increase dramatically in the future. Also, since it does not seem to gear its sales to production but rather to balance of payments needs, it is unclear how steady a source of supply it would be.[70]

Finally, gold production in the United States and Canada has displayed a negative postwar trend, although the recent rise in gold prices has encouraged a reopening of mines and exploration.[71]

Thus, barring a major gold discovery, it is doubtful whether rising gold production in Brazil and elsewhere would be sufficient to offset the declining trend. Since 1970, world gold production has decreased on average by 1.5 percent per year, whereas total world real output has increased in excess of 3 percent per year. Even if outstanding private gold hoards, estimated to be 662 million ounces, could be attracted to the existing world monetary gold stock of 1132.3 million ounces,[72] it is unlikely that they would be sufficient in the

67. Related to this is inelasticity in the supply of skilled labor, since most of the people employed in the industry are unskilled black migrant workers whose families must stay in the tribal "homelands" and whose movement into skilled work is opposed by white trade union members.

68. See Consolidated Gold Fields, Inc., *Gold 1981* (New York: 1981), app. 4, pp. 71-85.

69. Ibid., p. 77.

70. Ibid., p. 18-21.

71. J. Aron, *Gold Statistics and Analysis* (Precious Metals Research Department, J. Aron Commodities Corporation, January 1981).

72. Ibid., p. 14.

long run to offset the shortfall in production. This suggests that return to a gold standard would ultimately be associated with deflation.

A declining price trend may seem desirable after decades of rising prices, but deflation also imposes costs on the economy. These include the transition cost of moving from an inflationary to a deflationary environment in a world of long-term contracts as well as distribution effects, to the extent that the deflation is not fully anticipated—costs that may be as severe in their social consequence as those associated with inflation.

CONCLUSION: BENEFITS AND COSTS OF RETURNING TO A GOLD STANDARD

In assessing the case for a return by the United States and the rest of the world to a gold standard, we must weigh the benefits of such a policy against the costs.

The key benefit to a return to a gold standard would be a return to long-run price stability. This would create an environment where private market participants would have incentives to make long-term contracts, which are necessary for the efficient operation of a market economy. In addition, it would minimize the confusion between relative and absolute price level movements, reducing the incidence of false signals with regard to real economic decisions. An additional benefit would be a limited role of government intervention in the determination of the price level and overall economic activity.[73]

The costs, however, are not inconsiderable. These include the high resource costs of maintaining the standard; short-term instability in the price level, real output, and employment; and the subordination of monetary independence to international considerations. In addition, there is the risk of choosing the wrong fixed price of gold and the likelihood that in the long run instead of a stable price trend we would have deflation.

---

73. The history of the pre-World War I gold standard suggests that it worked because it was a "managed" international standard. In addition, the concentration of world capital and money markets in London and the use of sterling as a key currency enabled the system to function smoothly with very limited gold reserves and to withstand a number of severe external shocks. Perhaps of paramount importance for the successful operation of the managed gold standard was the tacit cooperation of the major participants in ultimately maintaining the gold standard link and its corrollary—long-run price stability as the primary goal of economic policy.

The question then remains, How can we attain the benefits of a gold standard without the costs? Irving Fisher offered one solution to the problem sixty years ago: that we adopt a tabular standard. By a tabular standard he meant varying the gold content of the dollar to keep the purchasing power constant. In the face of a rising price level, he recommended raising the gold content of the dollar—thus lowering the price of gold. In the face of a declining price level, he recommended lowering the gold content of the dollar—thus raising the price of gold.[74] Such a scheme could be applied to any type of gold standard.[75]

Another solution, advocated by many economists, is to follow a fiduciary money standard based on a monetary rule of a steady and known rate of monetary growth. The key problem, however, with such a standard is to ensure that the rule is maintained and that a commitment is made to the goal of long-run price stability.

74. See Irving Fisher, *Stabilizing the Dollar* (New York: n.p., 1920), p. 498. He proposed changing the dollar value of gold by a simple formula: Every month, change the dollar price by 1 percent downward for each percent increase in the price level above a target; change the dollar price by 1 percent upward for each percent decrease in the price level below a target.

75. Such a standard could also be applied to a wider basket of commodities. See Robert E. Hall, "Explorations in the Gold Standard and Related Policies for Stabilizing the Dollar," in Robert E. Hall, ed., *Inflation: Causes and Effects* (Chicago: University of Chicago Press, 1982).

Chapter 9

THE NEW ROLE FOR GOLD IN U.S. MONETARY POLICY

Robert E. Weintraub

The gold standard as it was implemented in the United States had three elements. First, the treasury bought gold from and sold gold to all comers at a fixed dollar price, and international claims were settled by gold transfers. Second, gold was used as money—as the medium of exchange. Third, after their creation in 1913, the Federal Reserve Banks were required to hold gold certificate reserves behind their currency or note liabilities and behind their deposit liabilities in ratios set by law. Today, none of these provisions is in effect. In this paper, I propose that the United States immediately return to the use of gold as money—of so-called full-bodied money coins—and immediately reinstate a certificate reserve requirement for Federal Reserve notes. However, I would delay, possibly for eight or nine years, deciding whether or not to return to convertibility at a fixed price.

THE CERTIFICATE RESERVE REQUIREMENT

The certificate reserve plan, the most complicated part of my proposal, would require that fractional gold certificate reserves be held for all Federal Reserve notes in the hands of the nonbank public. These reserves would cover only this currency component of our money supply. It would be easy to amend the plan to cover Federal

Reserve deposit liabilities as well, and therefore what is sometimes called the monetary base, but I believe that a certificate reserve requirement for Federal Reserve notes is sufficient.

The purpose of the certificate reserve plan is to put a lid on the growth of the nation's transactions balances and thereby on inflation. Our transactions balances are accurately measured by the sum of publicly held currency, nonbank traveler's checks, and fully checkable deposits in depository institutions. The Federal Reserve calls this sum M1.

Some will assert that it is unwise to focus monetary policy on constraining the growth of M1. I believe that it is unwise *not* to do so for reasons I will develop below.

SPECIFICATIONS OF THE PLAN

The limitation on M1 growth in the certificate reserve requirement plan is enforced by tying the maximum allowable growth of the currency component of M1 to a programmed increase in the value of the Federal Reserve's gold certificates.[1] The value of the certificates would be raised every twelve-month period, that is, from January of one year to January of the next year, from February of one year to February of the next year, and so on. The official price of gold, which is now $42.22 per ounce, and the value of the Fed's gold certificates, which is pegged to the official price, will be programmed to increase in each twelve-month period by exactly enough percentage points to offset (1) a predetermined increase in the certificate requirement, starting at 9 percent, (2) the maximum desired growth in M1, and (3) an adjustment for changes in the ratio of checking deposits to currency.

I will stipulate these three adjustments in order. First, for reasons that will become apparent, the certificate requirement will be raised 33 percent each year, from 9 percent to 12 percent to 16 percent and so on. To compensate for these increases, the official price of gold will also be raised 33 percent each year. Second, the maximum desired yearly growth of M1 will be 3 percent. To adjust for this factor, the official price of gold will be raised another 3 percent each

1. Necessarily, it is the growth of Federal Reserve notes that will be constrained by law. The difference between this component of currency and total currency, which includes coin and remnants of greenbacks and silver certificates, is ignored.

year less, however, the difference between 3 percent and actual M1 growth in years following years when M1 grows less than the 3 percent upper limit. Third, the adjustment for changes in the ratio of checking deposits to currency will be made by applying a formula that will permit reaching but not exceeding the maximum desired growth of M1 in the event that the ratio of deposit to currency changes. Specifically, the official price of gold will be adjusted by

$$1/(1+g)-1$$

where g is the percentage change (divided by 100) in the ratio of checkable deposits to currency. In essence, if the public prefers to hold more exchange media in the form of currency, the official price of gold will be increased faster than the programmed 33 percent increase in the certificate requirement plus the 3 percent limit on M1 growth. It will rise more slowly if there is an increase in the ratio of checking deposits to currency—that is, if the public decides to return currency to banks and to take out additional check deposits.[2]

With the adjustment for changes in the ratio of deposits to currency, the plan is flexible enough to allow the Federal Reserve to limit money growth and at the same time to allow the public to hold in the form of currency any fraction of total exchange media that it wants to. The proposal will in no way prevent the Federal Reserve from meeting all demands for liquidity or from carrying out its responsibility under the law to furnish an elastic currency.

Moreover, the plan does not require or provide for treasury sales of gold at a fixed price now or in the next few years. However, it paves the way for the question to be considered when the official price of gold equals or exceeds the market price. As I noted above, my plan provides for yearly increases in the official price or book value of gold, which is now $42.22 per ounce. The certificate reserve requirement is programmed to rise 33 percent a year. To offset these yearly increases, the official price of gold will also rise automatically 33 percent every year. And the official price will be allowed to rise another 3 percent a year to allow for 3 percent per year growth in M1 plus an adjustment for changes in the ratio of checking deposits to currency. Thus, in a period of eight years or so, the official

---

2. An adjustment also must be made for changes in the ratio of nonbank traveler's checks to currency. The procedure would be the same as in the case of the more important ratio of deposits to currency.

price will equal the market price. (Capital gains accruing to the treasury from raising the official price would be used to retire Federal Reserve–held treasury debt; thus, increasing the official price would not change the monetary base or M1. The increases serve only to *authorize* increases in Federal Reserve notes – that is, in currency – to permit 3 percent increases in M1 each year. The Fed could focus on reserves, the base, or some interest rate, as it prefers, to keep money growth at or below the 3 percent per year lid.)

The timetable for increasing the official price of gold can be changed if desired. But whatever timetable is adopted – and I think mine is reasonable, if not optimal – we should put off, until the official price is equal to or greater than the market price, the decision whether to require the treasury again to buy gold from and sell gold to all comers at a fixed price and to settle international claims by gold transfers. Historically, in the United States, convertibility was used not to restore stability in a monetary crisis but to preserve the value of the dollar after monetary stability had been restored.

My plan also calls for immediate coinage of gold by the Treasury Department. Gold coins would be sold to all comers at market prices plus a small fee to cover coinage costs. Gold coinage would be integrated with the gold certificate reserve plan before the official price of gold rises to the market price by adjusting the official price of gold for changes in the ratio of gold coins to currency in the same way that it will be adjusted for changes in the ratios of deposits to currency and nonbank traveler's checks to currency.

To make the coinage provision meaningful, we of course have to make sure, as Richard W. Rahn has pointed out, that increases in the dollar price of gold coins are not subject to capital gains taxes and do not qualify for capital losses deductible.[3] The same exemption should hold for state sales taxes and other taxes or impediments.

In summary, my proposal is to reinstate immediately two of the three elements that constituted the gold standard as it was implemented in the United States until 1933: (1) the use of gold as money and (2) the fractional backing of the currency component of the exchange media money supply with officially valued gold certificates. In addition, my plan will lay the foundation for later review

---

3. Richard W. Rahn, "A Way Out of the Gold Commission's Dilemma," *Wall Street Journal*, 22 October 1981.

and consideration of the third element of the gold standard: convertibility at a fixed dollar price.

BENEFITS OF THE PLAN

If adopted, the certificate reserve requirement plan would provide our monetary system with the anchor that it needs to promote price level and economic stability. Under this plan, currency and exchange media growth would be reduced to noninflationary levels and kept there. The importance of doing this is painfully clear. Over the years, as the growth of our exchange media—M1—has speeded up, inflation has accelerated. From 1956 to 1967, yearly M1 growth averaged 2.4 percent and yearly GNP inflation averaged 2.2 percent. From 1968 to 1980, both averaged 6.4 percent. From 1977 to 1980, yearly M1 growth averaged 7.5 percent and yearly GNP inflation averaged 7.7 percent. As a general rule, the rate of inflation in a given year tracks the rate of monetary growth two years earlier.

Now, some will quarrel with focusing on M1. They will say that until 1980 we did not measure M1 the way we are measuring it now. We did not include negotiable order of withdrawal accounts. We did not include automated transfer service accounts. We did not include credit union share drafts. We did not include "super" negotiable order of withdrawal accounts, which have been authorized only since January 1983. All of this is true. But it signifies only that it is important to define the check deposits component of M1 generically as fully checkable accounts in depository institutions, as my proposal would do, rather than try to provide a list now for all time.

Critics also will argue that the relationship between M1 growth and current dollar GNP growth is slippery and has changed in recent years because of a shift in money demand, or the invention and innovation of new money instruments and new near-money instruments, and new banking techniques. But it would be premature to conclude that the relationship has changed.

Measured from one three-year period to the next since the Korean War, yearly percentage changes in GNP and M1 have been very closely related. Quixotic concerns with complicated econometric forms and with quarter-to-quarter changes should not blind us to the stability and closeness of the relationship between M1 growth and current dollar GNP growth. Given enough time for the economy to adjust, which is no longer than three years, that relationship is indeed close and stable.

The relationship between percentage changes in M1 and percentage changes in nominal GNP is captured in Figure 9–1. The figure plots yearly average percentage changes in M1 on the horizontal axis and yearly average percentage increases in nominal or current dollar GNP on the vertical axis. The data are grouped in three-year non-overlapping periods from 1953 to 1983, but the results would look much the same if I had started with 1954 or 1955. The figure shows that the relationship between the two series is close and stable. This in turn means that despite all the new financial instruments and innovations in recent years—despite repurchase agreements (RP's), overnight Eurodollars, money market mutual funds, a variety of new deposit accounts, zero- and minimum-balance banking, street banking, credit cards, and so forth—the average yearly rate of rise in M1's velocity remains what it was when Dwight Eisenhower was president of the United States. Indeed, it hasn't changed since World War II, except in the period immediately following the outbreak of the Korean War. The behavior of M1 velocity growth is best described as a random walk with drift. The drift or average rate of rise is 3.0 percent a year. In the future, as in the past, velocity's growth is likely to differ substantially from the average in the short run, but we cannot know in advance or even on a current basis whether it will be more than the average or less, or by how much it will differ. In long run periods, by which I mean three years and longer, I am confident that it will approach 3.0 percent a year. As a result, it has been, and it continues to be, a very good bet that in any three-year period, current dollar GNP will increase by 3.0 percent plus the percentage increase in M1.

Moreover, nothing whatever is gained by increasing M1 growth. Accelerating M1 growth ultimately increases only the inflation component of gross national product. It does not increase real growth one-tenth of one percent. In fact, with inflation there is a rise in deadweight production in the form of disseminating information about price changes, hedging operations, and so on.

The fact that Federal Reserve officials refuse to recognize the stability and closeness of the relationship between M1 growth and current dollar GNP growth is precisely why it is important to legislate lids on currency and M1 growth and to allow gold coinage. Indeed, gold coinage would provide interesting and helpful signals and added

Figure 9-1. Annual Percentage Change of M1 and Current Dollar GNP for Three-Year Nonoverlapping Periods, 1953-1982.

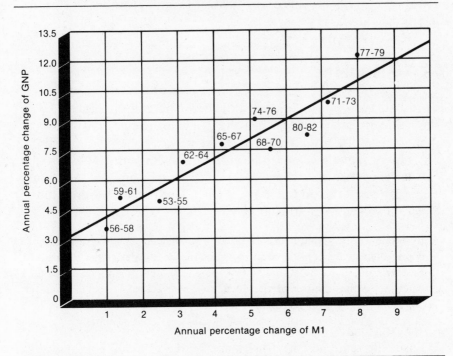

Notes:

1. Percentage change of current dollar GNP = 3.28 + 0.96 * Percentage change of M1
(0.65) (0.13)

Adjusted R^2 = 0.86.

2. The equation shows that a one percentage point rise in the rate of growth of M1 tended to generate a 0.96 percentage point rise in the growth rate of nominal gross national product, which tends to rise 3.28 percent per year in the absence of money growth. The numbers in parentheses below the coefficients 3.28 and 0.96 are standard errors and indicate that the coefficients, themselves, are statistically significant values, that is, values that would not arise by chance. the adjusted R^2 value indicates that 86 percent of the variance in nominal gross national product growth from triennium to triennium can be explained by changes in M1 growth. The Durbin-Watson (DW) statistic indicates that the data are *not* autocorrelated. The standard error of the equation (SEE) statistic indicates that the value of nominal gross national product growth in any triennium can be expected to be between 3.28 percent plus 0.96 times M1 growth plus or minus 1.88 percent with 95 percent confidence.

discipline. No one right now, including those in the board room at the Federal Reserve, can be sure what the Fed will do next year, next month, or in the next three years or even what it will focus on in any future period. So until we provide a lid on monetary growth, financial markets will be unnecessarily volatile, and investors will be unnecessarily hesitant.

SUMMARY

Gold coinage will provide a useful discipline and a useful signal to the monetary authorities. When the demand for gold coins rises, the authorities will know that they should at least think about restraining money growth below the legislative lid. Requiring gold backing for currency also disciplines the money supply process. As former Federal Reserve Board Chairman William McChesney Martin told the Senate Banking Committee in 1965:

> By retaining the traditional gold backing for federal reserve notes, the proposal [then under consideration to repeal the certificate reserve for Federal Reserve bank deposits] would be reassuring to those who, in their continuing concern for the stability of the dollar, see in a gold cover requirement an important element of strength. The value of any currency is so much a product of confidence that one should not disregard this advantage.[4]

Later in the same hearing, Chairman Martin, responding to questions from Senator Douglas, stressed, "The gold cover requirement has some valuable disciplinary effects."[5] (During my testimony before the Gold Commission, I was reminded by Joint Economic Committee Chairman Henry Reuss that Martin was against this same requirement in 1968. He apparently changed his mind, and Reuss asked me what I thought of that. I said that Martin was flatly wrong in 1968; he was right in 1965.)

Finally, I should note that my proposal leaves the Federal Reserve with ample discretion to counteract a perverse change in velocity. If the trend rate of rise of M1's velocity jumps well above the 3.0 percent average of the past thirty years, inflation would rise unless offsetting action were taken. Such a jump in velocity could occur in a

4. U.S. Congress, Senate Committee on Banking and Currency, *Hearings on Gold Reserve Requirements*, 2 February 1965, p. 48.

5. Ibid., p. 58.

war or war-scare emergency. It did so at the start of the Korean War, but it hasn't done so since. However, the rate of rise of velocity could jump if future banking innovations and new near-money instruments allowed proportionately greater economizing on holding exchange media than such innovations and instruments have done in the past. For whatever reason, if a jump occurs, the appropriate response is to keep currency and M1 growth well below the legislated lids. And that can be done just as easily under my proposal as now. The Federal Reserve will be free to operate under the legislated currency and money growth lids. There is no requirement that it operate at the maximum.

What about the opposite case, however—the case in which M1 growth might have to be increased because the change in velocity growth is less than 3 percent a year, or even negative? I would make no provision for this case as long as velocity growth was positive. But an upward revision of the lid on M1 growth would be warranted if velocity should exhibit *negative* growth for a fair period of time—not just for a quarter or even for a year but for, say, two or three years. It would be easy enough to provide for revision if this case came to pass. Indeed, the legislation can provide for automatic review every four or five years by the Congress to determine whether higher lids are warranted. Regardless, it would be unwise not to legislate safeguards now against the recurring nightmare that we have been living with—the nightmare of persistent excesses of currency and money growth—just because there is a chance that in some future time we might want to relax these safeguards. Laws are not made to stop us from ever doing what now appears to be dangerous; they're made to make us deliberate beforehand. In this regard, the Federal Reserve itself should welcome the legislation that I propose. It will increase, not diminish, the Federal Reserve's independence by providing a buffer against strong, sudden, ephemeral, or perverse political winds. Recent history shows that such a buffer is indeed needed.

Chapter 10

GOLD AND ECONOMIC BOOM
Five Case Studies, 1792–1926

Alan Reynolds

The third American experiment with managed money began twelve to sixteen years ago, which is about as long a period as has usually been tolerated in the past. In at least one respect—namely, the successive peaks of record-breaking interest rates—the recent experience has been among the worse. Whenever this occurred before, government officials have turned to monetary reform, if only to alleviate the government's financial dilemma. The results have never been subtle or gradual, but have consisted of a sudden leap to a much higher and more stable growth path.

The reason for linking the dollar to commodities is not simply to stop inflation. A 1932-style credit crunch can do that—for a while. The stronger political incentive for restoring sound money is that it invariably unleashes an economic boom.

THE HAMILTON DOLLAR OF 1792

America's only hyperinflation occurred during the Revolutionary War. By April 1779, George Washington complained that "a wagon load of money will scarcely purchase a wagon load of provisions." Despite oppressive price controls, one index of wholesale prices (1800–59 = 100) rose from 78 in 1775 to 10,554 in 1780, then fell just as abruptly. The phrase "not worth a Continental" survives as a reminder.[1]

In 1781, Alexander Hamilton wrote that "the only cure to our public disorders is to fix the value of the currency we now have ... to a proper standard, in a species that will have the requisite stability."[2] At Hamilton's urging, the Mint Act of April 2, 1792, finally fixed the value of the dollar to gold and silver. Gold was $19.39 an ounce until 1834–37, when it was gradually changed to $20.67.

"The years 1793–1808," writes the historian Douglass North, "were years of unparalleled prosperity."[3] It was, adds Louis Hacker, "a period of unexampled business expansion, one of the greatest, in fact, the United States has had. . . . The exports of the country mounted from $19 millions in 1791 to $93 millions in 1801. . . . During the 1780s, only 33 chartered companies had been set up by the states; during the 1790s, the number of such new companies was 295."[4]

The fiscal consequences of this hard-money prosperity were dramatic. The federal budget deficit amounted to 28 percent of the expenditures in 1792, 21 percent in 1794–95. Aside from small receipts from the sale of land, federal revenues were mainly from a 5 percent tariff and excises on items like liquor and snuff. Although these particular taxes were abolished in 1801, customs duties tripled from 1792 to 1801, internal revenue quintupled, and the surplus by 1802 was almost as large as total spending.

Another benefit of the 1792 monetary reform was lower interest rates on the national debt, which had risen as high as 6 percent. "When the credit of a country is in any degree questionable," wrote Hamilton, "it never fails to give an extravagant premium . . . upon whatever is to be bought on terms of future payment." A modern historian, Stuart Bruchey, confirms that "the resurgence of public credit, by lowering the interest rates on government debt, led in turn to a reduction in the market rate of interest and thus cheapened the capital costs of investment." This easing of interest rates did *not* occur by restricting the supply of money. Available estimates of the

---

1. Alan Reynolds, "Inflation and Controls in 1776," *First Chicago World Report* (First National Bank of Chicago, July 1976), p. 6.

2. Richard Morris, ed., *The Basic Ideas of Alexander Hamilton* (New York: Pocket Library, 1956), pp. 237, 268.

3. Douglass C. North, *The Economic Growth of the United States* (New York: W.W. Norton, 1966), p. 53.

4. Louis M. Hacker, *American Capitalism* (New York: Anvil, 1957), p. 39.

money supply show a very rapid increase from 1799 to 1859, while wholesale commodity prices declined by less than 1 percent a year.[5]

The rough price estimates available for the early United States appear to show some inflation from 1793 to 1796, and again in 1801 and 1805. But these price swings (as well as swings in output and exports) were mainly in farm products, particularly the volatile domestic supply and foreign demand for cotton. The prices of such traded goods have to be considered in the international context.

France and England were experiencing extreme monetary instability at this time, while the gold standard was suspended from 1789 to 1803 in France and from 1797 to 1821 in England. The United States was a relatively tiny participant in that world market. Like one of today's Third World countries, the U.S. economy then relied heavily on a single export commodity (cotton), borrowed heavily from foreigners to finance development, and occasionally defaulted on those foreign loans. It simply was not possible for the United States under any monetary system to completely insulate itself from the wars and monetary vandalism going on in Europe. President Jefferson's trade embargo from December 1807 through March 1809 was a devastating blow to the U.S. economy: U.S. exports fell 80 percent in 1808.[6] Other crippling events were the War of 1812 and the imposition of high U.S. tariffs in 1816 and 1828. Clearly, these problems were not a fault of the monetary system.

In the colorful language of the time, there were also "panics" and "crashes" about every twenty years, though always while the gold standard was suspended. John Kenneth Galbraith complains that "in the years of panic and ensuing depression economic growth certainly slowed and perhaps, on occasion, came to a halt."[7] During the *worst* years, in other words, growth was zero or very slow. Farm prices certainly fell in the 1839–43 "depression," for example, but real GNP rose by 16 percent.[8]

---

5. Stuart Bruchey, *The Roots of American Economic Growth, 1607-1861* (New York: Harper & Row, 1968), pp. 111, 149. See George F. Warren and Frank A. Pearson, *Gold and Prices* (New York: Wiley, 1935), and Roy W. Jastram, *The Golden Constant* (New York: Wiley, 1977), p. 140.

6. To enforce the embargo. "Jefferson conducted a fifteen-month reign of oppression and repression that was unprecedented in American history," according to Forrest McDonald, *The Presidency of Thomas Jefferson* (Lawrence, KS: Kansas University Press, 1976), ch. 7.

7. John Kenneth Galbraith, *Money* (Boston: Houghton Mifflin, 1975), p. 107.

8. Peter Temin, *The Jacksonian Economy* (W. W. Norton, 1969), p. 155.

Anna Schwartz's economic history for the U.S. Gold Commission also implies great instability in the 25 years from 1834 to 1859, but her data show only three years in which real output fell at a 1 percent rate and one (1854) in which output fell by 4 percent. During the other twenty-one years, real growth averaged 5.5 percent per year, despite such growing pains as wildcat banking. Most monetary disturbances in the nineteenth century were, as the Gold Commission agreed, "attributable to the U.S. banking structure rather than the gold standard system."[9]

ENGLAND IN 1821

After 75 years of financial and industrial revolution under the gold standard, Great Britain abandoned the standard during the Napoleonic Wars, beginning on February 27, 1797. According to Asa Briggs, "The re-establishment of metallic currency in Paris and finally, after paper credit experiments, a run on the English country banks, led to a drain of gold from Britain and a serious fall in reserves which led Pitt first to suspend cash payments by Bank of England, and second, to attempt substantially to increase taxation."[10] Succeeding issues of Willard Thorp's classic *Business Annals* record the results of that mix of fiscal and monetary policy: 1798: "Pitt presents income tax"; 1798–1801: "Depression"; 1802: "Income tax repealed.... Prosperity"; 1803: "Income tax re-established"; 1804: "Mild depression."[11]

Commodity prices doubled by 1815, then fell sharply. Britain leaped into protectionism with the infamous Corn Law of 1815, setting quotas on wheat imports to protect the landed aristocracy. Wheat prices had tripled from 1792 to 1812, and, as other prices and wages were falling, the Corn Law pushed wheat prices back up again in 1816 and 1817. "By 1816," notes Roy Jastram, "England was in a deep depression. There was stagnation of industry and trade generally; the iron and coal industries were paralyzed.... Riots occurred spasmodically from May through December."[12]

9. *Report to the Congress of the Commission on the Role of Gold in the Domestic and International Monetary Systems* (Washington, D.C.: Government Printing Office, March 1982), pp. 55–63.

10. Asa Briggs, *The Age of Improvement* (New York: McKay, 1966), p. 169.

11. Quoted in Roy W. Jastram, *Silver: The Restless Metal* (New York: Wiley, 1981), pp. 42–49.

12. Jastram, *The Golden Constant*, p. 113.

Another cause of riots, aside from the Corn Law, was tax revolt. "The most unpopular tax of all was the income tax," writes John Perry "and here the government was forced to give way to public opinion, abolishing the income tax in 1816."[13] The economy then revived in 1817-18, but collapsed in bloody riots the next year. At that point, the government finally turned to monetary reform, partly for the pragmatic (Hamiltonian) reason that by 1815 "interest on the national debt accounted for more than half of the total government expenditure."[14] The interest rate on consols (government bonds) rose above 5 percent in 1816, despite falling prices. This was a frightening interest rate, since the rate on consols averaged 3.6 percent from 1729 to 1931.

"In 1810 the government had ignored the advice of a Select Committee of the Commons that a return to the gold standard was necessary," Derry reports, "but once the war was over it was increasingly difficult to reject similar demands."[15] Pressured by circumstances, as well as by the "Radicals" (including economist David Ricardo), Peel's Committee of Inquiry in 1819 again recommended a gradual return to the gold standard. On May 21, 1821, the Bank of England resumed convertibility of its notes into gold.

What happened next is critical, since many economists share the opinion of a leading monetarist, Allan Meltzer, that "the decision to go back on the gold standard in the 1820s at the price that had prevailed in [1737-1796] . . . was followed by a difficult, hard adjustment."[16]

T. S. Ashton, London's finest historian of the Industrial Revolution, offers a quite different assessment: "In the early 'twenties many circumstances combined to produce high prosperity. The currency was established on a foundation of gold. . . . Huskinson and his colleagues were active in pulling down tariffs, lowering excise duties, and removing restrictions from industry and trade. . . . A substantial part of the National Debt was converted from 5 to 4 or 3½ percent: in 1820 the yield on Consols had been 4.4, by 1824 it was 3.3 . . . and in the early months of 1825 short-term loans were being placed

13. John Derry, *A Short History of 19th Century England* (New York: Mentor, 1963), p. 59.

14. Briggs, *The Age of Improvement*, p. 170.

15. Derry, *A Short History of 19th Century England*, p. 60.

16. *Toward a Stable Monetary Policy: A Debate Between Allan Meltzer and Alan Reynolds* (Washington, D.C.: Heritage Foundation and Institute for Research in the Economics of Taxation, 1982), p. 2.

at a little more than 2½ percent." John Derry likewise notes that "in 1820 prices were already rising and a year later prosperity had already been achieved."[17]

"The years between 1821 and 1825" adds Briggs, "justified promise and prediction. . . . The culminating point was reached in the years 1824–25, which some economic historians have considered as *the first truly modern cyclical* boom in British economic history. Certainly there was a stock market boom as well as a peak of industrial activity, and . . . the volume of domestic building broke all previous records."[18] [Emphasis added.]

ENDING THE GREENBACK ERA

The United States suspended the gold standard in December 1861, at the outbreak of the Civil War. The price of gold rose 158 percent— from $20.67 to $53.35 by July 1864—and wholesale prices rose 153 percent over that period.

From 1865 to 1874, the United States attempted to regulate the value of money by controlling its quantity. This inspired a tax in 1866 on state bank notes, a planned withdrawal of greenbacks until 1868 (followed by increases), and endless debates on how to define and control money. Even then, regulating the quantity of money was not a new idea. As William Graham Sumner wrote: "Nearly every nation which has ever used paper money has fixed its amount, and set limits which it has solemnly promised again and again not to pass, but such promises are in vain. A man might as well jump off a precipice intending to stop half way down. . . . In its more general effects, the paper currency with a fixed limit produces a steady advance in the rate of interest, and also a reduction in prices. . . . If we had a currency of specie value, we should get just as much as we need, and then we should know how much that is, but then, too, we should no longer care."[19]

The National Bureau identified three postwar recessions from 1865 to 1878, with the economy falling during 68 percent of those

17. Philip A.M. Taylor, ed., *The Industrial Revolution in Britain* (Lexington, Mass.: D.C. Heath, 1958), p. 53; Derry, *A Short History of 19th Century England*, p. 81.

18. Briggs, *The Age of Improvement*, p. 211.

19. William Graham Sumner, *A History of American Currency* (New York: Holt, 1884), pp. 214–27.

months. Those recessions, like several others, were probably exaggerated by the practice of confusing lower wholesale prices with lower production. Yet most of the economic growth in this period— curiously emphasized by Milton Friedman and Anna Schwartz—did not occur until after an 1875 law announced the resumption of a gold dollar on January 1, 1879. Manufacturing output, for example, rose by a total of only 12 percent in the six years from 1869 to 1876, but rose 20 percent in the following three years.[20] By any criteria, the nation's second experiment with managed money had to be judged a failure. The United States was eventually compelled to again link the word "dollar" to something tangible.

As in Hamilton's time, a major incentive for returning to gold was to lower the interest rates on the national debt. Interest on a debt of $2.2 million was swallowing 35 percent of the budget in 1875. By 1882, the debt was still high at $1.9 million, but the interest rate on it had dropped by a third, lowering the interest expense to 22 percent of a smaller budget.

Bonds yields had remained historically high through 1873 (above 6 percent) despite falling prices and payment of interest in gold. Interest rates on daily "call money" averaged 10 percent in 1869 and 14 percent in 1873. After the government announced its intent to redeem dollars in gold, bond yield dropped steadily, with Treasury bonds remaining at between 3.2 percent and 4.2 percent from 1879 to 1914. Common stock prices doubled from 1877 to 1881.

The Return of the Gold Standard

The gold standard was restored, without difficulty, in January 1879. An incredible economic expansion began within two months. The next four years, according to Friedman and Schwartz, were "characterized by an unusually rapid rise in the stock of money and in net national product. . . . The stock of money rose over 50 percent . . . and net national product in constant prices nearly 25 percent."[21]

Growth of real income averaged *8.4 percent a year* from 1878 through 1882. Growth of the money supply topped 20 percent in

20. U.S. Bureau of the Census, *Historical Statistics of the United States*, vol. 2 (1975), p. 667.

21. Milton Friedman and Anna Schwartz, *A Monetary History of the United States* (Princeton, N.J.: Princeton University Press, 1963), pp. 96, 243.

two years and averaged 12.6 percent. (Those who regard the gold standard as an austerity program, designed to restrict the money supply, clearly miss the point.) Inflation stood at about 1–3 percent by some measures, but this appears to have been mainly a cyclical recovery in commodity prices. The consumer price index did not rise at all. By 1882, raw steel production was 137 percent higher than it had been in 1878.

The fiscal results were again dramatic, even aside from the reduced interest rates on the debt. Federal tax receipts rose by 47 percent from 1879 to 1882, with no increase in tax rates or tariffs, and the budget surplus rose from $7 million to $146 million—over half of the total budget.

What this gold standard era achieved as a whole can best be visualized by a sample of specific facts, mostly gathered from the *Historical Statistics.*

- Industrial production rose by 534 percent from 1878 to 1913.

- Manufacturing employment increased 51 percent from 1879 to 1889, and 142 percent by 1914.

- Real wage rates rose 28 percent from 1879 to 1889; real wage rates in manufacturing rose by more than 30 percent from 1890 to 1914.

- The U.S. share of world manufacturing output swelled from 23 percent in 1870 to over 35 percent in 1906–10.

- Annual plant and equipment spending doubled in real terms from 1879 to 1884, doubled again by 1890, and rose ten-fold from 1879 to 1910.

- Consumer durables doubled from 1879 to 1892.

- The annual number of patented inventions was virtually unchanged from 1867 to 1878, then surged from 12,903 in 1880 to 25,313 in 1890 and to 39,892 in 1914.

- Copyrights were also flat from 1873 to 1878, then rose from 15,798 to 42,794 by 1890.

- Production of rail freight cars was stepped up from 9,000 in 1878 to 275,000 in 1907.

- Manufacture of fuel and lighting materials increased by 382 percent from 1879 to 1914.

- Production of coal rose 210% from 1893 to 1913; crude steel rose 715%.

- Cotton used in textiles expanded 260% from 1879 to 1909.

- Paper and paperboard output tripled from 1900 to 1915.

- Furniture production rose 263% from 1879 to 1913.

- Electric power increased 18.4% per year from 1882 to 1914.

From March 1882 to May 1885, real growth slowed to about 1 percent a year. Britain had doubled the discount rate to 6 percent in early 1882, cutting into imports from America, and there were strikes in the U.S. telegraph and railroad industries during this period. There was another brief showdown in late 1890, when tariffs were raised and new legislation required the increased purchase of silver with new currency. Although historians often emphasize the setbacks, the period from 1882 to 1892 is nonetheless categorized by Friedman and Schwartz as one of only four segments since the Civil War "displaying a relatively high degree of economic stability." After rising by 8.4 percent a year from 1878 to 1882, real growth slowed to a still respectable 5.3 percent a year from 1882 through 1892.[22]

The Impact of Deflation

The U.S. economy then contracted sharply until mid-1894 and dropped again in 1896. This depression is commonly attributed to the gold standard, as is the unusually low level of farm prices in 1895–96. To the extent that monetary forces were to blame, however, the gold standard again proved to be the solution rather than the problem.

Most of the apparent deflation in 1894–96 was actually a relative decline in farm prices, which then accounted for over half of the wholesale price index. From 1892 to 1894, cotton production rose 36 percent, and cotton prices fell 45 percent. In 1895, the supply of oats expanded 23 percent, barley 41 percent, potatoes 53 percent. Prices fell. From 1894 to 1896, the production of corn increased by a whopping 65 percent, and the price fell 53 percent. Rapid tech-

---

22. Ibid., p. 677, and Victor Zarnowitz, "Business Cycles and Growth," National Bureau of Economic Research Working Paper 665 (1981), table 1.

nological progress also pushed down the prices of manufactured goods.

In July 1896, the Democrats nominated William Jennings Bryan for President, mainly on the theory that inflation could solve the farm glut. Ironically, each such success of those who attacked the gold standard actually contributed to the problem they were trying to solve. Indeed, the Bryan campaign was the main *cause* of the 1896 relapse.

The stock market began to tumble in mid-August and reached the lowest point in more than seventeen years. Hoarding of gold was "only one symptom of a general malady that pervades all circles," wrote *The Commercial and Financial Chronicle*, namely that "the business of the country is still being carried on in some measure almost everywhere under the weight of the free silver populistic scare."

Shortly before the election, "in New York alone more than $1,000,000 of the government's gold was withdrawn in exchange for legal tenders. . . . A single brokerage house is reported to have sold over the counter $3,000,000 in gold in a single day. Interest rates on call money, which had ranged upward to 15 percent throughout the month, rose to 127%. . . . Long lines of men and women stood at the doors of the sub-treasury as well; before the day was over they had withdrawn more than $1,300,000 in gold."[23]

Attempts to blame the farm price decline of 1894–96 on a shortage of gold are incorrect in fact as well as in theory. Annual world gold production increased every year from 1887 to 1899 by a total of 190 percent. Nations are not driven off the gold standard by a loss of gold; they lose gold when they threaten to abandon the gold standard.

The Turning Point

"The defeat of Bryan," note Friedman and Schwartz, "is a convenient and dramatic date to mark the turning point." In a very real sense, Bryan's defeat marked another return to the gold standard, later formalized in the Gold Standard Act of 1900. "Stock market indexes show a rise of close to 70 percent from August 1896 to Au-

23. James A. Barnes, "Myths of the Bryan Campaign," in A. E. Eisenstadt, ed., *American History* (New York: Crowell, 1962), bk. 2, ch. 2.

gust 1899. . . . The stock of money . . . bounded upward at an extra-ordinary rate; by 15 percent from 1897 to 1898, 17 percent from 1898 to 1899, 6 percent from 1899 to 1900, 15 percent from 1900 to 1901 and 9 percent from 1901 to 1902. . . . From 1896 to 1902, net national product in constant prices rose by 45 percent or at a rate in excess of 6 percent per year."[24] The federal budget, which had been deeply in deficit, quickly moved into surplus with the economic expansion.

The cyclical Federal budget deficit from 1894–99 provoked destructive fiscal policies. Tariffs were raised in 1890 and 1894, slowing export growth from 16 percent to 3 percent in 1891 and reducing exports by over 9 percent in 1895. An income tax was briefly enacted during the 1894 slump, and Teddy Roosevelt proposed to Congress during the Panic of 1907 that income and estate taxes be adopted to equalize fortunes. If these fiscal shocks did not initiate the simultaneous downturns, they were at the very least ill-timed.

The electorate returned the Democrats to office in 1913. Tariffs were eased a bit, in line with the party's free trade traditions, but the income tax and Federal Reserve System were also created during a two-year recession that began in January of that year. The unemployment rate doubled, and the 1915 deficit amounted to 8.4 percent of the budget. Before the United States entered the war, wholesale prices rose much more rapidly than the M2 money supply—at an 18 percent annual rate. The rapid prewar inflation appears to reflect a sharp drop in the willingness to hold dollars (a rise in velocity) that coincided with the birth of the Fed.[25]

ENGLAND AFTER 1925

In April 1925, Winston Churchill (then Chancellor of the Exchequer) returned England to a limited gold standard at the traditional prewar rate, the same rate as was defined by Sir Isaac Newton in 1717. Under this rate, a pound would be worth $4.86 in gold dollars. Even today, many economists accept the verdict of Keynes that this was massively deflationary and accounted for the high unemployment from that point on. Actually, most of the deflation occurred from

---

24. Friedman and Schwartz, *A Monetary History*, pp. 138–43.
25. Ibid., p. 206.

1920 to 1923, when wholesale prices fell by 48 percent. The prices of iron and steel (war materials) fell 65 percent from 1920 to 1925, but less than 8 percent from 1926 to 1929. Coal actually *rose* 26 percent in 1926, with a coal-led general strike, but that was obviously unsustainable. Wholesale food prices were fairly stable, down only 1.4 percent from 1923 to 1928. Cotton and wool prices peaked in 1924, then rose again in 1927 and 1928.[26]

British wage rates stopped declining after 1924, and real income rose throughout the rest of the decade at a rate of nearly 4 percent per year. Real net national income per capita had fallen by 1.3 percent in 1915–24, compared with the previous decade, but rose 14.5 percent in 1925–34.[27] Still, this was not the sort of vigorous boom that has accompanied every other return to a commodity standard. Unemployment dropped from 17 percent in 1921 to 9.7 percent in 1927, but continued to hover around 10 percent through 1929. Chronic unemployment was explained at the time by Jacques Rueff and Edwin Cannan, but the explanation was forgotten until it was recently revived by Daniel Benjamin and Levis Kochin of the University of Washington.[28]

Their argument is that unemployment remained high in Britain, and recovery therefore weak, because of what Keynes called "the grave abuses of the dole."[29] In 1920, unemployment benefits for a family of four had been 15 percent of average wages. After that, *nominal* benefits were increased several times while prices fell, and eligibility requirements were eased. Unemployment benefits rose to 48 percent of average wages in 1925, 54 percent in 1931. Almost anyone over the age of sixteen could receive dole money after a few days' wait if they had ever paid payroll taxes for a minimum of thirty weeks. There was no limit at all on how long those benefits could be drawn. Even those who quit were eligible if they waited six weeks. These benefits were soon heavily subsidized out of general

26. Jastram, *The Golden Constant*, p. 202.

27. Gerald Meyer and Robert Baldwin, *Economic Development* (New York: Wiley, 1962), p. 249. For comparative purposes, it is worth noting that the rise in British per capita income was 17 percent for the decade between 1880 and 1889 and 25 percent for the decade between 1890 and 1899.

28. Daniel K. Benjamin and Levis A. Kochin, "Searching for an Explanation of Unemployment in Interwar Britain," *Journal of Political Economy* (June 1979): 441–78.

29. John Maynard Keyes, *Essays in Persuasion* (New York: Norton, 1963), p. 277.

revenues, and the British tax load was quite possibly "the world's heaviest."[30]

Professors Benjamin and Kochin estimate that the liberalization of the dole added only 2.5 to 4 percent to British unemployment in 1921–25, but raised unemployment by 5 to 8 percent in the gold standard years of 1926–31. If not for that huge subsidy to leisure, and the related tax on productive effort, the 1925 restoration of the gold standard would have been as successful as every other example.

On September 19, 1931, Great Britain casually let the pound float (sink) against gold, raising the discount rate from 4.5 percent to 6 percent only after the event.[31] As Keynes's biographer, Sir Roy Harrod observed in 1971, "The British suspension of 1931 was followed by a decade of great disorder in the international monetary system."[32]

Something else happened at the same time, however, that briefly improved Britain's *relative* performance within a collapsing world. In September, the dole was reduced by 10 percent, eligibility requirements tightened, and the duration of benefits limited to twenty-six weeks. If abandoning gold was of any help, it was only because an accelerating inflation after 1935 probably reduced real unemployment benefits until 1938. As usual, the retreat from hard money was soon accompanied by protectionism, with general tariffs imposed in January 1932 for the first time in nearly a century.

It is commonly believed that the British economy recovered about six months sooner than the U.S. economy because, as two monetarist economists recently proposed, "the U.K., abandoning gold in 1931, was able to avoid the further monetary contraction that took place in America."[33] In short, abandoning gold supposedly made it easier for Britain to "reflate."

In actuality, the pound remained convertible into gold, albeit at a variable price; meanwhile the United States suspended convertibility from March 1933 until February 1934. From the U.S. election of November 1932 until a year later, the British pound appreciated by

30. Melchior Palyi, *The Twilight of Gold, 1914–1936* (Chicago: Regnery, 1972), p. 98.

31. Palyi, *The Twilight of Gold*, pp. 268–76.

32. Sir Roy Harrod in "Dollar Crisis: What the Experts Think," *London Telegraph*, 22 August 1971.

33. Wallace Huffman and James Lothian, "U.S.-U.K. Business Cycle Linkages Under the Gold Standard" (Paper for N.B.E.R. conference, "A Retrospective on the Classical Gold Standard," Hilton Head, S.C., March 1982).

57 percent against the pre–Roosevelt dollar (gold at $20.67), and the British economy began to recover at the end of 1932. During the period of U.S. convertibility suspension, the Sauerbeck index of basic commodity prices rose 6.7 percent in Britain, while similar prices went up by 41 percent in the United States. The broader wholesale price index rose 30 percent in the United States from April 1933 to September 1934, while British wholesale prices were up by only about 3 percent in 1934.[34] The United States discovered that inflation is quite possible with high unemployment; Britain discovered that an early recovery is consistent with a stronger currency.

The American recovery was aided by deposit insurance, while the British recovery owed much to lower real unemployment benefits. Ending the U.S.-led deflation was necessary for recovery, but, as we can see from the facts above, the deflation was not caused by the gold standard.

Before the Federal Reserve was established, the only serious deflations occurred during periods when a country was *not* on a commodity standard, such as the United States in 1781–91 or 1865–78. This was because, under a commodity standard, the public could easily increase its liquid assets as needed by converting gold or silver into cash.

The severe deflations beginning in 1920 and during 1929–31, however, illustrated the Fed's power to deliberately counteract this balancing force. The rise in the discount rate to a record 7 percent in June 1920 "was a deliberate act of policy involving a reaction stronger than needed since a gold inflow had already begun," note Friedman and Schwartz. In 1931, "The U.S. gold stock rose during the first two years of contraction. . . . The United States did not follow gold-standard rules. We not only sterilized it, we went much further. . . . Foreign commentors were particularly critical of the monetary policy of the United States."[35]

The Fed, in short, more than neutralized the curative powers of convertibility in 1920–21 and 1929–31. Even as the world attempted to acquire more dollars by offering gold, the government body thwarted that effort by tightening convertibility in the face of falling commodity prices. The Fed, in other words, bought gold

34. See Warren and Pearson, *Gold and Prices*, pp. 87, 157-59, 177-91; Jastram, *The Golden Constant*, p. 202.

35. Friedman and Schwartz, *A Monetary History*, pp. 360-61.

and sold bonds. Its loans and securities were reduced by 24 percent from 1928 to 1930 to offset $455 million in gold imports (which reached over $600 million by 1931).

FRANCE IN 1926

Among major countries, the one least affected by the depression and the trade war was also the last to leave the gold standard in 1936 — namely, France. From 1919 to 1926, France operated under a quantity rule for money, with legal limits on printing currency and monetizing government debt. Yet inflation continually increased more rapidly than the money supply because the demand for money fell. After Britain returned to gold, the French franc lost half its value against gold-convertible currencies in the year ending July 1926, and wholesale prices rose 50 percent.[36]

Poincaré formed a new government on July 25, 1926, and instituted a series of tax and monetary reforms by August 7. New currency had to be backed by added gold or gold-convertible foreign exchange. The top income-tax rates were cut in half, and taxes on inheritances and securities were also reduced, though some specific excise taxes were later adjusted for the previous inflation. Tax revenues were not increased in real terms, but were 15 percent lower in 1926 than they were in 1922.

The fundamental problem was monetary, but it had fiscal consequences. Although the budget deficit had shrunk by 68 percent from 1923 to 1925, the monetary collapse made it necessary to finance the debt with short maturities at escalating interest rates. Long-term interest rates had averaged about 3.2 percent under the prewar gold standard, but exceeded 10 percent by mid-1926. Within three months of the Poincaré reform, however, the government was able to sell 40-year bonds at 7 percent to retire short-term debt. From August 1926 to August 1927, the commercial bill rate fell from 5.8 percent to 2 percent.

36. This section on France is extracted from my paper "The Poincaré Miracle" for the Committee for Monetary Research and Education (Arden House, N.Y., Oct. 30, 1981). The best primary sources are James H. Rogers, *The Process of Inflation in France* (New York: Columbia University Press, 1929) and Robert M. Haig, *The Public Finances of Postwar France* (New York: Columbia University Press, 1929).

Looking back on the French reform, in 1929 Columbia University Professor James Rogers reminds us that "an almost entirely negligible reduction in the total [French] debt has so far been accomplished. Mostly what has happened is that the extremely large and ever threatening current debt burden has been partially transferred to the future." That is, the stronger currency made it possible to sell long bonds, reducing the interest expense on the national debt.

The gold cover on currency (a form of quantity rule) proved too restrictive, and the economy slipped into recession in October 1926. In order to arrest the sudden decline in prices, the franc was pegged to the dollar in December, effectively putting France back on the gold standard. The French stock market rose immediately by 164 percent through February 1929—twice as fast as in the United States—and stocks remained higher even in 1933 than they had been in early 1926.

Real output *per capita* rose by 5.9 percent in 1928 and 9.5 percent in 1929, remaining above the 1927 level as late as 1934.[37] The M2 money supply increased by 10.7 percent in 1927, 16.3 percent in 1928, and 6.7 percent a year through 1929-31. Wholesale prices dropped slightly in early 1927 and were essentially unchanged in 1928-29.[38]

THE RELEVANCE OF HISTORY

Other examples of the restoration of commodity standards are generally less relevant to the current world situation, because they occurred during extreme inflations. A brief review of what happened to Germany before and after World War I, however, highlights some similarities with more temperate monetary crises.

Germany had adopted a gold standard from 1876 to 1914 and experienced only one true recession (1891) during the entire period.[39] After World War I, of course, Germany experienced the most famous hyperinflation on record—averaging 322 percent a month from August 1922 to November 1923. Thomas Sargent points out that the

37. U.S. Department of Commerce, *Long-Term Economic Growth, 1860-1970* (Washington, D.C.: 1973), p. 283.

38. Palyi, *The Twilight of Gold*, p. 312; Warren and Pearson, *Gold and Prices*, p. 22.

39. Paul McGouldrick, "Operation of the Reichsbank Under the Gold Standard" (Paper for N.B.E.R. Conference, March 1982).

runaway inflation in Germany, as well as in Austria, Hungary, and Poland, "were each ended by restoring convertibility to the dollar or equivalently to gold." Inflation was immediately ended despite a "rapid rise in the 'high powered' money supply in the months and years after the rapid inflation had ended." In Germany, for example, wholesale prices increased by only 3.8 percent from December 1923 to December 1924, though M1 rose 261 percent in that period. Per capita production rose 67 percent from 1923 to 1925, and the related gains in real tax revenues balanced the budget.[40]

In the other episodes examined earlier, however, the events leading up to monetary reform can be more easily compared to the current situation. These are some of the features these past periods had in common:

- They were all initiated during the deflationary aftermath of a relatively moderate inflation.

- Government budgets were an acute concern, usually with a combination of deficits, growing interest expense, and tax resistance.

- There had already been many years of experience in trying to regulate or limit the quantity of money.

- Interest rates were always historically high, *particularly in real terms.*

The results of monetary reform were also similar:

- Real output always expanded very rapidly for at least four years.
- The money supply grew even more rapidly.
- There was no sustained inflation or deflation.
- Interest rates were always reduced, and long-term rates almost never exceeded 5 to 6 percent.

The most recent return to a partially gold-based monetary system was the Bretton Woods accord. Convertibility between the dollar and gold was restricted to central banks, but that did not necessarily make gold a purely superfluous constraint. Any excess supply of dollar-denominated liquid assets would tend to spill over into a balance of payments deficit through U.S. purchases of foreign goods

40. Thomas Sargent, "The Ends of Four Big Hyperinflations" (Federal Reserve Bank of Minneapolis, 1981).

and assets. Foreign exporters, for example, would then convert surplus dollar balances into domestic currencies, and their central banks would end up holding more dollars than they wanted. By converting excess dollar balances into gold, central banks thus acted as agents for the public. A gold-convertible dollar became an objective standard to which other countries could peg their exchange rates, achieving efficiencies of sharing a common currency. Stabilizing the dollar value of international gold reserves also helped to prevent synchronized waves of global inflation and deflation.

"Dollars came to be accepted as international money," wrote James Tobin, "partly because of the U.S. commitment to foreign central banks to convert their dollars into gold on demand."[41] The "diluted" postwar gold standard, added Milton Friedman, "has unquestionably served to inhibit 'tinkering' with the currency."[42]

"As long as the reserve centre is concerned to maintain convertibility," explained John Williamson, "the fact that its currency is serving as a reserve currency does not avoid the need to maintain a satisfactory payments position: failure to do so results in a loss of confidence which is liable to provoke requests for conversion of its currency into gold."[43] "There is no intrinsic reason," adds Jurg Niehans, "why a gold-dollar system should not be viable indefinitely. . . . The willingness of central bankers to regard gold and dollars as perfect substitutes, however, depends on their confidence in convertibility." By 1971, however, it became obvious that the U.S. had an extremely weak commitment to convertibility, and would not undertake even a modest monetary tightening in order to stem an accelerating outflow of capital and gold. Bretton Woods did not "break down"—it was deliberately destroyed by U.S. politicians and their economists.[44]

During the first U.S. recovery under this regime, beginning in 1950, real GNP in the United States grew at a 13.5 percent annual rate for four quarters. The Bretton Woods system was reinforced from November 1961 to March 1968 by the London gold pool,

41. James Tobin, *National Economic Policy* (New Haven, Conn.: Yale University Press, 1966), p. 177.

42. Milton Friedman, *Essays in Positive Economics* (Chicago: University of Chicago Press, 1953), p. 140.

43. John Williamson, *The Failure of World Monetary Reform, 1971–1974* (New York: New York University, 1977), p. 30.

44. Jurg Niehans, *The Theory of Money* (Baltimore, Md.: Johns Hopkins University Press, 1978), pp. 163–64.

which kept the price of gold firmly anchored at $35. Before that, real growth had averaged only 2.3 percent in the United States from 1956 to 1960. In the fourth quarter of 1961, however, when the gold pool began, real GNP jumped at a 10.6 percent rate and averaged 5.7 percent through the first quarter of 1966. Again, this was accompanied by rapid growth of liquid assets, 4 to 5 percent bond yields, and little inflation. Annual growth of M2 averaged 8.1 percent from 1962 to 1965 – not significantly different from the 8.5 percent rate of 1972–75, or the 8.6 percent rate from 1977 to 1980. Something else obviously changed in the latter years to account for the huge increase in price volatility and the equally dramatic slowdown of world output and trade.

Between March 1968 and August 1971, the United States severed any predictable links between the key reserve currency and the real world. The value of a dollar became a matter of continual guesswork. The results were exactly the same as in each of the historical episodes discussed before:

- Waves of inflation followed by liquidation, bankruptcies, and falling commodity prices.

- Long-term interest rates usually rising, even during the periods of falling prices.

- Longer, more frequent economic crises simultaneous with a trend of slowing or falling production.

- A shrinking tax base and rising government interest expense, producing government budget strains and tax resistance.

These same symptoms invariably arose during previous attempts to regulate the quantity of money, and the first reaction was usually to raise taxes or tariffs. It was only after the fiscal approach backfired that governments reluctantly turned to monetary reform. Circumstances, not theories, compelled the change, but only after at least a dozen years of growing discomfort.

The third American experiment with managed money began twelve to sixteen years ago, which is about as long as has usually been tolerated in the past. In at least on respect – namely, the successive peaks of record-breaking interest rates – the recent experience has been among the worst. Whenever this occurred before, government officials always turned to monetary reform, if only to alleviate the government's financial dilemma. When that happened, the results were never subtle or gradual, but a sudden leap to a much higher and more stable growth path.

The reason for linking the dollar to commodities is not simply to stop inflation. A 1932-style credit crunch can do that—for a while. The stronger political incentive for restoring sound money is that it invariably unleashes an economic boom.

Chapter 11

FREE BANKING AS AN ALTERNATIVE MONETARY SYSTEM

Lawrence H. White

Our current stagflationary malaise has reactivated the interest of American and European economists and policy analysts in the topic of alternative monetary institutions. Many economists and other observers perceive—and perceive rightly—that the institutions of their national monetary authorities are responsible for monetary disorder. The stress on *institutions* reflects the recognition—again correct— that monetary trends can neither be explained by reference to the personalities in positions of monetary authority nor be corrected by mere substitution of one set of faces for another. Nor can improvement be made by offering the existing authorities yet more good advice. In order to understand present conditions and to reform them, one must instead look to the incentive structure and the effective constraints surrounding the suppliers of money and credit.

This paper aims to contribute to the debate over alternative monetary institutions by discussing the features of a particular alternative system—free banking—that has not yet received professional or public attention commensurate with its attractiveness and importance. The central part of the paper will explore the properties of a free

The central theoretical section of this paper draws on Chapter 1 of the author's doctoral dissertation, *Free Banking in Britain* (Cambridge: Cambridge University Press, 1984). Axel Leijonhufvud and Robert E. Hall made constructive criticisms of an earlier draft of this paper. Jack High and Jennifer Roback offered useful comments on its theoretical section. The author alone should be held responsible for the views expressed.

banking system in a theoretical manner. By "free banking" we refer generally to the unrestricted competitive issue of currency and deposit money by private banks on a convertible basis. We do not refer specifically to the so-called free banking systems adopted by a number of American state governments between the late 1830s and the Civil War. For the sake of easy conceptualization, we will focus on specie (full-bodied gold or silver coin) as the base money for which bank money is redeemable. What we say below is nonetheless applicable, with suitable modification, to any system with a commodity or other base money whose quantity is not subject to manipulation by a government monetary authority (for example, a paper-based system in which the stock of irredeemable paper currency is permanently frozen).

THE RELEVANCE OF FREE BANKING

It may be helpful as a preface to our discussion to locate free banking within the framework of the debates over monetary institutions. In decades past, the issue of alternative monetary frameworks was treated primarily as a question of the desirability of "rules" or "discretion" for a monetary authority, the rationale for whose existence was not questioned.

Today it is widely recognized that allowing a monetary authority to pursue discretionary monetary policy carries two dangers that are not mutually exclusive. The first danger, one which has long been stressed by Milton Friedman and other monetarists,[1] is that the activist pursuit of policy objectives by use of monetary "tools" is almost certain to do more harm than good. Fine tuning is impossible because of the inherently insufficient predictability of the impact of policy actions. The Federal Reserve Board's discretionary actions have proven historically to be a major cause of instability in the American economy. Stop-go monetary policy, because it makes business conditions unpredictable, inhibits long-term investment. The Fed has also proven susceptible to political pressure for cheaper credit.

1. Milton Friedman, "The Case for a Monetary Rule," in *An Economist's Protest* (Glen Ridge, N.J.: Thomas Horton, 1972), pp. 65–67.

This line of thought has been given new emphasis by writers adopting the rational expectations perspective.[2] Only unanticipated policy has a systematic impact on real variables, and its impact is typically to *dis*coordinate an otherwise self-righting economy by misleading agents who are trying to read price signals. An activist policy only adds noise to the signals.

The second danger of discretionary policy, one which has recently been stressed by public choice theorists, is that a government unconstrained in its power over the creation of base money can be expected systematically to abuse that power.[3] Inflationary creation of base money serves to enlarge the government's command over real resources in a way hidden from the populace. The wealth-redistributive character of monetary injections makes them suitable for use as a vote-buying tool.

These groups of economists who recognize the dangers of discretionary monetary policy typically propose as an alternative that the monetary authority be bound to obey a fixed rule of conduct, sometimes called a "monetary constitution." The particular rule commonly suggested by monetarists in the United States is that the Fed be duty-bound to manipulate the monetary base so that some particular monetary aggregate conforms to a fixed growth rate of k percent, where k is a predetermined magnitude chosen for its consistency with price stability or some other goal. The dangers of this sort of rule, and of fixed monetary rules in general, have not been much emphasized in recent years. It therefore seems appropriate to review them at some length. One may wholeheartedly agree with the monetarist, rational expectations, and public choice arguments against discretionary policy, and even agree that almost any constraint that made the behavior of the monetary authority steadier and less inflationary would be an improvement, and yet be alive to the hazards of fixed rules and to the existence of other alternatives.

2. Robert E. Lucas, "An Equilibrium Model of the Business Cycle," *Journal of Political Economy* 83 (1975): 1139; Bennett T. McCallum, "Price-Level Stickiness and the Feasibility of Monetary Stabilization Policy with Rational Expectations," *Journal of Political Economy* 85 (1977): 631–32.

3. H. Geoffrey Brennan and James M. Buchanan, *Monopoly in Money and Inflation* (London: Institute of Economic Affairs, 1981); Richard E. Wagner, "Boom and Bust: The Political Economy of Economic Disorder," *Journal of Libertarian Studies* 4 (1980): 1–37. For a guide through the policy-relevant aspects of the rational expectations and political business cycle literatures, see Gerald P. O'Driscoll, Jr., "Rational Expectations, Politics, and Stagflation," in M.J. Rizzo, ed., *Time, Uncertainty, and Disequilibrium* (Lexington, Mass.: D.C. Heath, 1979), ch. 7, pp. 153–76.

The primary hazard of putting the monetary authority on automatic pilot is that the economic system lacks an unchanging magnetic north pole. An inflexible rule of conduct will have consequences unintended by its designer should the orientation points of monetary environment move in ways unanticipated at the time of design. Allowing that the rule may be modified when conditions dictate is equivalent to having no fixed rule at all.

For the sake of specificity, let us focus on the monetarist suggestion that the growth path of some monetary aggregate be dictated in advance. In practice, a particular monetary aggregate—the monetary base, M_1, M_2, M_3, or something larger—must be singled out. The limits of permissible deviation must be specified, either for the aggregate's growth rate over any period of a particular length or for its magnitude at particular dates stretching indefinitely into the future.[4] It is considered desirable to peg the growth of a monetary aggregate not because this is an end in itself, of course, but because the growth rates of prices and nominal income are believed to be geared to the growth rate of the monetary aggregate in a fairly constant ratio. The ratio is, however, unlikely to stay constant for any particular monetary aggregate. It is subject both to short-term volatility and to long-term structural change. Monetarists used to speak of pegging the growth rate of M_1. The recent meiosis of M_1 into M_{1A} and M_{1B}—and its even more recent reversal—should at least alert them to the fact that any particular monetary aggregate is a statistical artifact, liable to lapse eventually into irrelevance with further steps in the ongoing evolution of the payments mechanism and financial markets. The likelihood of such developments is enhanced by steps toward the deregulation of the banking and financial industries. It hardly need be added that the ultimate effect of electronic funds transfer systems on the income velocity of M_1, for example, can hardly be predicted with the confidence necessary for the drafting of a lasting monetary constitution.

To choose one of today's broader monetary aggregates as the permanent pivot upon which the entire monetary system is to swing hereafter must surely be an act of alarming boldness in the light of recent evidence of the mutability of commercial monetary institutions. The more perceptive monetarists have begun to acknowledge

---

4. The former method of specification projects an ever widening cone of permissible magnitudes into the future, the latter only a band, around the desired trend.

the danger. Leland B. Yeager has recently noted "the institutional developments that seem to be blurring distinctions between banks and other financial institutions and between the medium of exchange and near-moneys and even blurring the very concepts of money and its quantity." He recognizes that "if control over the quantity of money *does* become impractical and even conceptually elusive, some substitute must be found." We might add that those who wish to elevate the k percent rule to the status of a constitutional amendment must be willing to turn a blind eye to such possibilities. Yeager goes on correctly to point out that some nominal magnitude must be set exogenously to the banking system in order to render the purchasing power of money determinate. He concludes with this confession:

> The method whose possible obsolescence has been worrying us is control of the number of units of medium of exchange in existence. Another is specification of the money price of some commodity or composite of commodities, with that price being kept meaningful by unrestricted two-way convertibility. Belatedly I must admit that the arguments for the gold standard or a composite-commodity standard are more intellectually respectable than I used to think and teach.[5]

Convertibility into gold or silver coin pins down nominal prices without reliance on an obsolescent quantity rule. Indeed, it carries no presumption that a monetary authority even exists.

Quite apart from the unpredictability that technical change imposes on the relationship between any particular monetary aggregate and other nominal variables, we should note another source of unpredictability. The introduction of this element is, ironically, quite in the spirit of rational expectations.[6] It is this: The estimated coefficients of the relationships between monetary aggregates and other nominal variables are, strictly regarded, relevant only to the past monetary regime under which they were observed. They are liable to change under the impact of such a policy innovation as the adoption of a k percent M_i growth rule. The choice of particular values of k and i can hardly be based with confidence upon such estimates.

5. Leland B. Yeager, "What are Banks?" *Atlantic Economic Journal* 4 (December 1978): 13.

6. Robert E. Lucas, "Econometric Policy Evaluation: A Critique," in K. Brunner and A. H. Meltzer, eds., *The Phillips Curve and Labor Makrets* (New York: North-Holland, 1976), pp. 19–46.

This objection was raised to the monetarist proposal by Jacob Viner twenty years ago:

> Even if we accept an empirical constancy of relations discovered in the past as demonstrating a logical relation in that period, the introduction into the economic universe of a specific rule of behavior for the money supply would constitute an alteration of potential significance in the nature of that universe, and . . . we must not take for granted that the relation of the price level to the supply of money will be even approximately the same after such a rule is adopted and effectively enforced as it was before. The transformation of a hitherto unpredictable economic variable to one which everyone can predict with certainty is almost certain to have some effect, though one unpredictable in advance, on the pattern of its relations to other economic variables.[7]

In addition to these questions of unforeseeable change in the long-term trend of the velocity of any particular monetary aggregate, there is the distinct question of the short-run variability of the money multiplier, the relationship between a monetary target variable and the monetary base that the authority can directly manipulate. The M–1 money multiplier as measured by the Federal Reserve Bank of St. Louis has looked fairly stable even since the introduction of money-market deposit accounts in December 1982 and "super NOW" accounts in January 1983. But this appearance is misleading: it is primarily due to the fact that shifts in bank reserve ratios, properly counted as shifts in the money multiplier, are incorporated into the St. Louis Fed's measure of the "adjusted" monetary base through a component called the "reserve adjustment magnitude." Hence recent shifts in funds from high-reserve to low-reserve accounts have shown up as changes in the adjusted monetary base rather than as shifts in the money multiplier.[8]

It is generally said that although variations in money multipliers prevent the Federal Reserve from accurately hitting monetary targets on a short-term (month-to-month or quarter-to-quarter) basis, it can on a sufficiently long-term basis hit its targets with reasonable

---

7. Jacob Viner, "The Necessary and the Desirable Range of Discretion to be Allowed to a Monetary Authority," in L. B. Yeager, ed., *In Search of a Monetary Constitution* (Cambridge: Harvard University Press, 1962), p. 255.

8. Federal Reserve Bank of St. Louis, *U.S. Financial Data* (29 April 1983), pp. 1, 5. It should be noted, however, that the ratio of currency to total checkable deposits, another component of the multiplier, thus far seems genuinely to have been little affected by the new accounts. See Federal Reserve Bank of St. Louis, *U.S. Financial Data* (6 May 1983), p. 1.

accuracy. The very vagueness of this formulation should alert us to the question of whether the permissible band around the Fed's target can be drawn tightly enough to neutralize the disruptive swings in monetary growth rates that have characterized Fed policy in the past. If a past quarter's deviation of M_1 from target were treated entirely as a bygone, in practice there would be no rule constraining the path of M_1. The rule must dictate correction of errors to get M_1 back within the permissible band or cone. It must also dictate the speed of correction. The framers of a monetary growth rule must recognize an unfortunate trade-off between short-term money-market instability caused by veering back to path more sharply and medium-term general instability caused by correcting course more slowly. F. A. Hayek has pointed out the extreme danger of erring in the first direction:

> As regards Professor Friedman's proposal of a legal limit on the rate at which a monopolistic issuer of money was to be allowed to increase the quantity in circulation, I can only say that I would not like to see what would happen if under such a provision it ever became known that the amount of cash in circulation was approaching the upper limit and that therefore a need for increased liquidity could not be met.[9]

Public knowledge of the approach to the limit would create an alarm that would temporarily raise desired cash balances and so exacerbate the liquidity crunch.

There is a simple way to enhance the predictability of velocity and the money multiplier, of course: tighten the rein of banking regulation in order to block out financial innovations and all other sources of variation. The reserve requirements of Federal Reserve System member banks were sometimes defended on this basis. The onerousness of these requirements prompted an exodous of banks from the system. The Fed's predictably bureaucratic response was to demand an end to the banks' freedom to leave the system on the grounds that a loss of member banks was weakening its control over the money supply. Those provisions of the Monetary Control Act of 1980 that extended reserve requirements to all banks were then a step in the direction of tighter regulation for the sake of firmer control.[10] So

9. F. A. Hayek, *Denationalisation of Money*, 2d ed. (London: Institute of Economic Affairs, 1978), p. 77.

10. For a thorough account of the act, see Jeffrey Rogers Hummel, "The Deregulation and Monetary Control Act of 1980," *Policy Report* 2 (December 1980): 1–11.

were recent extensions of reserve requirements to new forms of bank-issued interest-bearing certificates. Whether these controls achieve their ostensible end or not—it is likely that frequent regulatory changes *decrease* the predictability of the monetary system—they hamper domestic banks in their competition with other financial institutions and with foreign banks, and they harm the interests of the consumers of banking services.

The unfortunate fact is that achievement of a workable, rigid, specific monetary rule may be inconsistent with deregulation of the banking industry.[11] The likelihood that this is indeed the case should give pause to those who, like Milton Friedman, support the fixed monetary rule as a device for enhancing economic liberty.[12] It would certainly be a perversion of policy, from the viewpoint of one sympathetic to the free working of markets, to restrict the banking industry's ability to serve consumers so that those administering monetary policy might have an easier time of it.

Free banking offers an escape from this policy box. The rules-discretion conundrum presupposes the existence of a monetary authority whose behavior must be either dangerously inflexible or dangerously flexible. An evident means of resolving this dilemma is to cultivate a monetary system not under the rule of a central authority. The most readily conceived system of this sort is that of free banking. A leading virtue of a free banking system is that it steers clear of both the hazards of discretionary monetary policy and the hazards of rigid monetary policy by freeing the monetary system entirely from bureaucratic control. Free banking is at the same time consistent with both determinateness of the purchasing power of the monetary unit and deregulation of the banking industry.

Some might object to this way of framing the alternatives that convertibility of currency—into gold or silver coin, for example—constitutes the imposition of a "rule." Several recent advocates of various forms of the gold standard have fostered this view by referring to convertibility as a "price rule" in contrast to the monetarist quantity rule. This way of speaking ceases to be helpful once we move beyond designing devices for channeling the behavior of a monetary authority. It obliterates an important distinction between

11. On deregulation and technical change in the banking industry, see Joe Cobb, "Deregulation of Banking: How Far, How Fast?" *Journal of Retail Banking* (September 1981).

12. See Milton Friedman, "Should There Be an Independent Monetary Authority?" in Yeager, ed., *Monetary Constitution*, p. 243.

designed order and spontaneous order.[13] Within a free banking system, where there are many issuing banks but no government-sponsored central bank, convertibility prevails naturally without any legislature imposing it. Convertibility arises simply from the contractual agreement made by each issuer on the face of each note to redeem that note on demand for a specific quantity of specie.

We may briefly note the relevance of free banking to more recent discussions of alternative monetary frameworks. Two alternatives have particularly attracted attention in the United States: the gold standard and the system of competing private currencies proposed by Hayek. Roy W. Jastram has pertinently remarked on the new-found respectability of the gold standard among professional economists.[14] Readers of the *Wall Street Journal* in recent years have confronted a spate of columns and opinion pieces on the gold standard, pro and con. The question of gold gained widespread attention with the creation of the United States Gold Commission by the federal government.[15]

The boomlet of interest in the possibilities of private provision of currency has taken place mostly within academia. Professor Hayek deserves our recognition for opening this field to policy discussion, though earlier work of a less polemical sort had been done by others.[16] Free banking should be of interest to students both of the gold standard and of free currency competition. The system of competitive currencies under a specie standard has received scant notice in the recent literature, though it lies in an area of intersection between the gold standard and free currency competition.

We need not dwell here on the historical record of free banking, impressive though it is. I have elsewhere undertaken to examine the

13. For an extended discussion of this distinction, see F. A. Hayek, *Rules and Order*, vol. 1 of *Law, Legislation and Liberty* (Chicago: University of Chicago Press, 1973), ch. 2.

14. Jastram's remarks are quoted by Lindley H. Clark, Jr., "Creating an Adequate Scarcity of Dollars," *Wall Street Journal*, 28 July 1981, 27.

15. The Commission's findings, primarily authored by economist Anna J. Schwartz, appear in *The Report to the Congress of The Commission on the Role of Gold in International Monetary Systems* (Washington, D.C.: Government Printing Office, 1982), 2 vols. The "minority report" submitted by the Commission's two pro-gold members has also been published under separate covers: Ron Paul and Lewis Lehrman, *The Case for Gold* (Washington: Cato Institute, 1982).

16. See particularly Benjamin Klein, "The Competitive Supply of Money," *Journal of Money, Credit and Banking* 6 (1974): 423–53. For surveys of the literature on competing currencies, see Pamela J. Brown, "Constitution or Competition? Alternative Views on Monetary Reform," *Literature of Liberty* 5 (1982): 7–52, and James Rolph Edwards, "Monopoly and Competition in Money," *Journal of Libertarian Studies* 4 (1980): 107–17.

most clear-cut case of free banking on record, that of Scotland from 1716 to 1844.[17] During its free banking era, Scotland experienced remarkable economic growth with relatively little macroeconomic instability. The banking system enjoyed complete immunity from panics and runs. The American free banking era is not a clear-cut case because of the tangle of regulations and entry requirements variously placed on banks of issue from state to state and because of the prohibition on interstate branch banking (which survives in large part even today). Vera Smith has aptly characterized the American system during this era as "decentralization without freedom."[18]

THE THEORY OF A FREE BANKING SYSTEM

We now turn to the task of explaining in theory the operation of a free banking system. Several authors have claimed that freedom of banknote issue, even when issuers are bound to redeem notes for specie, implies either (1) an unlimited supply of banknotes and a correspondingly unlimited depreciation of the currency or (2) a perpetual and undampened oscillation in the quantity and value of the currency.[19] The most thorough way to evaluate these claims is to examine generally the operation of a free banking system, seeking to discover whether the self-interested actions of individual agents in that system give rise to equilibrating or disequilibrating processes.

In what follows, we first consider the equilibrium of an individual bank of issue within a free banking system. The bank issuing gold-convertible bank notes may be thought of as a profit-maximizing firm. For simplicity, we may assume that the firm holds only specie (gold and silver coin) and interest-earning commercial bills as assets and that it issues only bank notes and deposits as liabilities. The bank maximizes its profits subject to the accounting constraint that assets equal liabilities plus equity.

---

17. See Lawrence H. White, *Free Banking in Britain* (Cambridge: Cambridge University Press, 1984), ch. 2. For another short summary of the Scottish experience, see Rondo Cameron, *Banking in the Early Stages of Industrialization* (New York: Oxford University Press, 1967), ch. 3.

18. Vera C. Smith, *The Rationale of Central Banking* (London: P. S. King, 1936), ch. 4. See also Hugh Rockoff, "The Free Banking Era: A Reexamination," *Journal of Money, Credit and Banking* 6 (1974): 141–67.

19. For a recent example of the second claim, see Brennan and Buchanan, *Monopoly in Money,* pp. 17–18.

The upshot of this exercise is that the desired note circulation of the bank, considered as a choice variable for the bank, is limited by cost considerations. The rising marginal costs of maintaining notes in circulation set a limit to the bank's ability to expand permanently its holdings of bills and specie through issue of its notes. It may be nearly costless to print up additional notes and to *initiate* their circulation through bill purchases, but it is quite another matter to *maintain* their circulation in a competitive environment under convertibility. We discuss the various investments that a bank must undertake to make its notes relatively attractive for the public to hold.

We next consider the equilibrium of a free banking system as a whole. We assume that it operates within a small, open economy on an international specie standard. In this case, the domestic purchasing power of money is determined by the world purchasing power of specie. The demand for real currency balances by the domestic public then determines the desired nominal currency stock. The total stock of specie in the economy is determined by the conjunction of (1) this desired currency stock with (2) the public's desired ratio of coin to notes, (3) the desired specie-to-note reserve ratios of the various issuing banks, and (4) the shares of the circulation supplied by those banks. Changes in these four variables will change the domestic stock of specie in predictable directions, with the adjustment taking place through international specie flows.

We then examine the market mechanisms that move the banks within a free banking system toward equilibrium and so restrain them from overissuing. Having seen that the public's desired quantity of a particular bank's notes is a determinate magnitude, given that bank's optimizing expenditures, we consider the process by which the actual quantity is adjusted to the desired quantity. We show that the over-issuing bank will find excess notes returning to it for redemption as note holders shed their excess notes. Reflux occurs either (1) through direct customer redemption or, more commonly, (2) through redemption demands from other banks that have accepted the excess notes as deposits. The second route involves the note exchange system, an interbank clearing mechanism that we discuss.

However the excess notes return, the overexpansive bank will find its specie reserve dwindling. It must end its expansion and contract to protect itself from running out of reserves. The process by which the notes return may involve temporary changes in domestic prices and self-reversing international specie flows. These will be of greater magnitude the greater the relative size of the expansive bank (or group of banks acting in concert), suggesting the preferability of free banking to central banking under a specie standard.

Finally, we explain why independent issuing banks left to their own devices in a free banking system will be led, as if by an invisible hand, to participate in a note exchange system.

The Individual Bank of Issue

Considered as an economic agent, a business firm is conventionally depicted in economic theory as pursuing self-interest in the specific sense of profit maximization. A recent literature has sought to model the banking firm in this manner, drawing on the familiar optimization techniques of the neoclassical theory of the firm. The object of the literature has been to derive the formal conditions for the bank's optimal size and balance sheet composition.[20] We shall here adapt this approach to the situation of a note-issuing bank, treating the volume of its notes in circulation and the volume of its deposits as choice variables. With the aid of our model, we shall demonstrate that a profit-maximizing bank under the constraints of a free banking system does not attempt to push its notes into circulation *ad infinitum*. Rather, the issuing bank seeks to maintain a definitely limited circulation. In this section, we pursue the argument verbally. The mathematics of the optimization problem may be found in the chapter Appendix.

Consider a simplified version of the balance sheet of the issuing bank (Table 11–1), listing just two assets: specie and bills. The specie (precious metal in coined form) of the bank is its vault cash. Bills are its interest-earning assets. Purchase of commercial bills, or equivalently the granting of loans, is the usual means by which our bank issues its notes. The balance sheet lists three liabilities: notes, deposits, and equity capital. The outstanding notes of the bank constitute non-interest-bearing sight claims against its specie. Its deposits (which may be thought of either as demand deposits or as time deposits) are interest-bearing claims against its specie. Its capital is

---

20. For a survey of economic literature on the profit maximization model of bank behavior, see Ernst Baltensperger, "Alternative Approaches to the Theory of the Banking Firm," *Journal of Monetary Economics* 6 (1980): 1–37.

Table 11–1. Balance Sheet of the Issuing Bank.

Assets		*Liabilities + Equity*	
(Specie)	*S*	*N*	(Notes)
(Bills)	*B*	*D*	(Deposits)
		K	(Equity capital)

the fund originally contributed to the bank by its shareholders plus its accumulated earnings.

Double-entry bookkeeping imposes the balance sheet constraint that assets equal the sum of liabilities plus equity: $S + B = N + D + K$. Taking equity as given, this implies that the bank cannot make additional loans (acquire more bills) without also either attracting additional depositors and note holders or losing specie. Although a greater volume of interest-earning assets taken by itself means a greater gross income for the bank, the bank must weigh this against the negative income factors (typically called "costs")[21] that necessarily accompany it. Conceptually, we may distinguish three sorts of costs that the bank faces: simple operating costs, liquidity costs, and interest payments to liability holders. All three costs naturally increase with the volume of the bank's assets and liabilities. Beyond some point, their sum increases faster than revenue, and so expansion beyond that point is unprofitable.

We may offer a more concrete interpretation to the various operating costs that the bank faces. The operating costs associated with discounting and holding commercial bills of exchange are costs of information, transaction, and self-insurance. They are expenses incurred in ascertaining the credit-worthiness of bill issuers, in enforcing the repayment obligation upon maturation of the bills, and in absorbing some percentage of bad debts. These costs presumably rise at the margin, since as the bank expands its discounting, it must resort to borrowers whose credit-worthiness it knows less well. The bank must either incur greater unit costs to screen these borrowers or suffer a great percentage of defaulters among them. The operating costs of holding specie are costs of storage and security.

It is important to understand the costs associated with maintaining notes in circulation, if only because in the past century the oppo-

---

21. Strictly speaking, these are not always costs in the opportunity-cost sense.

nents of free banking so often built their case on the implicit assumption that a bank of issue could extend its circulation gratuitously. It is one thing to print up notes and to *initiate* their circulation; it is quite another to *maintain* their circulation in a competitive environment. Where the plurality of competing issuers gives the public a choice among brands of bank notes, each issuer must expend resources in giving its brand the qualities most attractive to at least some members of the public. Notes beyond the quantity wanted by the public will not remain in circulation but will return to the issuer upon whom they are claims, as we shall see below. We should expect the rivalry among note issuers to be in many ways similar to the present-day rivalry among issuers of checking accounts.

Perhaps the most elementary quality dimension on which the public may be expected to distinguish among bank note brands, as it does now among checking account brands, is ease of redemption. To attract a greater clientele requires, therefore, such expenses as longer operating hours, a greater number of tellers, additional local branch offices, and more extensive advertising of the availability of these conveniences. A second area of quality competition, one that Benjamin Klein has stressed with regard to inconvertible currencies, is public confidence in the reliability of an issuer's notes.[22] Individuals will be less disposed to hold the notes of a less trustworthy issuer, and so issuers must compete to convince the public of their superior reliability. Under a system of private bank notes convertible at par into specie, the primary aspect of reliability is the assurance that convertibility will not be delayed or denied on account of the bankruptcy, illiquidity, or fraud of the issuing bank. Confidence-bolstering expenditures would include the construction and maintenance of an impressive bank edifice, publicity of the bank's sound financial health, "image" advertising, and whatever else might reassure note holders that theirs are not the notes of a fly-by-night outfit. A secondary aspect of reliability is the ease with which the authenticity of individual notes may be ascertained. Enhancing public confidence in their genuine character might call for greater expenditures on designing, engraving, watermarking, and signing of notes, or for a more gen-

22. Klein, "Competitive Supply of Money"; idem, "Money, Wealth, and Seignorage," in K. E. Boulding and T. F. Wilson, eds., *Redistribution Through the Financial System* (New York: Praeger, 1978), ch. 1; idem, "Competing Monies, European Monetary Union, and the Dollar," in M. Fratianni and T. Peeters, eds., *One Money for Europe* (London: Macmillan, 1978), ch. 4.

erous (costly) policy toward counterfeit notes tendered by innocent parties.

A potential third area of circulation-promoting expense is the payment of an explicit interest yield to note holders.[23] For competition to compel an issuer to make such payments in practice, the payment must more than compensate the note holder for the trouble of collecting the payment, and the operating cost of making the payment could not render interest-bearing notes unprofitable for the issuer. A characteristic feature of hand-to-hand currency, however—a feature that helps sustain the demand to hold it even where interest-bearing checking accounts are available—is the comparative ease associated with using it in small transactions. To collect interest for the holding of a bank note would require going through a bothersome procedure such as having the date of original issue stamped upon it and having the accumulated interest calculated with each paying over of the note. Since the bother involved is the same for any denomination of note, whereas the interest yield rises with the magnitude of the denomination and the length of time between transfers, we would be more likely to observe interest payments on notes of large denominations and notes that circulate more slowly (these are likely to coincide) than on notes of smaller denominations and notes that circulate more rapidly. The use of large bank notes in a modern economy, however, is itself likely to be less convenient than the use of checking deposits. Competitive free banking is therefore not inconsistent with an absence of interest-bearing currency. Notice that traveller's checks today, even though they are paid over only once and are issued competitively, do not bear interest.

The operating costs associated with deposits are similar to those associated with notes. Depositors, like note holders, must be assured of the trustworthiness of the bank whose liabilities they hold. Deposit and withdrawal flows, like demands to change notes for specie and vice versa, must be serviced.

We call "liquidity costs" the expenses that the bank must bear in the event of an impending exhaustion of specie. These costs may be thought of concretely as the transactions and shipping costs of arranging to purchase (or to borrow) specie and have it delivered on short notice. Should a temporary deficiency not result in an immediate declaration of bankruptcy, these costs may also include what-

23. Klein raises this possibility: "Competitive Supply of Money," p. 441.

ever expense is necessary to compensate inconvenienced customers. Expected liquidity costs increase with an increase in the volume of notes or deposits (for a given volume of specie reserves) and decrease with an increase in specie reserves (for a given volume of notes and deposits).

Profit-maximizing equilibrium requires that the bank meet a number of equimarginal conditions. Its marginal net revenue from holding bills (yield minus the marginal operating costs of bill holding) must be equated to its marginal net benefit from holding specie (reduction in expected liquidity cost minus the marginal operating coss of specie holding). The bank must be indifferent between holding extra bills and holding extra specie of the same market value, since it can trade one for the other in the market. The marginal net revenue from holding bills must also be equated to the sum of the marginal operating cost and the marginal expected liquidity cost of maintaining notes in circulation. The rising marginal costs associated with a growing volume of bank notes outstanding set a limit to the extent of the bank's discounting operations (i.e., its purchases of bills with its notes). The marginal net revenue from holding bills must also be equated to the sum of the interest payments, operating costs, and expected liquidity costs associated with a marginal addition to the stock of deposits. The rising marginal costs of attracting and servicing deposits set a limit to the extent of the bank's purchases of bills with funds from that source.

Profit maximization similarly implies that the marginal net benefit from holding specie is equated to the total marginal cost of maintaining notes in circulation. The rising marginal costs of maintaining a note circulation set a limit to the bank's ability profitabily to effect permanent purchases of specie with its notes, just as they set a limit to its purchases of bills. The marginal net benefit from holding specie must also be equated to the total marginal cost of acquiring it by attracting and maintaining an increased stock of deposits. The rising marginal costs of expanding the bank's deposit business set a limit to the bank's ability profitably to acquire specie from depositors. Finally, the marginal cost of enlarging the bank's assets by an expansion of its note circulation is equated to the marginal cost of enlargement by expansion of deposits. At the margin, the two sources of funds are equally costly.

Beyond the point defined by these conditions, the bank's marginal costs of expansion will rise, although its marginal revenue from bill holding will not. The profit-maximizing bank under the constraints of a competitive free banking system will therefore seek to issue definitely limited quantities of notes and deposits. It cannot expand the volume of its notes or deposits gratuitously.

The System as a Whole

Having considered the equilibrium position of an individual bank of issue, we now consider the equilibrium position of the system as a whole. We may illuminate certain properties of a free banking system by analyzing the relationship between the quantity of money (the nonbank public's holdings of specie plus bank notes plus checking deposits) and the total stock of specie held by banks and the public. The specie stock is in some respects the analogue of what in the present system is called the monetary base or the stock of high-powered money. A free banking system differs from the present American banking system in having its reserve ratios determined entirely by bankers' prudence rather than by a monetary authority's requirements or by a combination of required reserve ratios plus some prudential margin. This difference makes the system no less determinate.

The free banking model differs more fundamentally in being a small open economy with fixed exchange rates and hence having a nominal money stock determined "outside" the banking system by the conjunction of the public's desired real money balances and the purchasing power of specie, both regarded as data for the system. This difference means that the banking system does not determine the domestic quantity of money given the monetary base, as today, but instead determines the quantity of specie. The nominal quantity of bank reserves plus basic currency is not determined by a monetary authority, as in a fiat money–central banking system. Hence, no central authority has the power to create monetary disturbances by altering the quantity of high-powered money.

Under present-day conditions of flexible exchange rates, the size of the monetary base is determined by the monetary authority. Changes in the domestic monetary base, given the fractional reserve ratios of the banks, lead to even larger changes in the nominal stock of currency and bank deposits held by the public. Prices rise until the expanded stock of money is willingly held. It is more natural for a free banking system, however, to operate within a small, open economy with fixed exchange rates, as Scotland did during its free banking period. We accordingly assume that the basic money of our free banking system, gold and silver coin, is money throughout the world economy. Precious metals may be freely imported and exported, with a negligible impact on the worldwide purchasing power of the metals. Interregional specie flows bring the actual specie stock of the region into adjustment with its equilibrium stock in accordance with David Hume's specie flow mechanism.[24] In this case, with the purchasing power of money given to our economy by the world market, the public's desired stock of real money balances determines the desired nominal money stock.[25] Exogenous changes in desired real money balances lead, *ceteris paribus*, to changes in the desired stock of specie, both directly and by their effect on desired bank specie reserves. The new desires will be met by interregional specie flows.

The relationship of the money stock to the quantity of specie depends, for a given desired stock of money, upon the relative quantities of specie, notes, and checking deposits desired by members of the public and upon the various quantities of specie reserves relative to notes in circulation and checking deposits desired by the issuing banks, weighted by their respective shares of total note circulation and total checking deposits. The *actual* quantity of specie relative to notes and checking deposits tends toward the public's specific *desired* quantity. Should the actual quantity be below the desired quantity, the public will convert notes and deposits with the issuing banks. We may similarly assume that each bank adjusts its actual quantity of vault specie relative to outstanding note circulation and checking deposits in accordance with the specific relationships it desires to maintain and that members of the public adjust their note

24. David Hume, "Of the Balance of Trade," in E. Rotwein, ed., *Writings on Economics* (Madison: University of Wisconsin Press, 1955). Or, if one prefers, in accordance with that version of the monetary approach to the balance of payments wherein purchasing power parity holds even in the immediate run. For that approach, see Donald N. McCloskey and J. Richard Zecher, "How the Gold Standard Worked, 1880–1913," in J. A. Frenkel and H. G. Johnson, eds., *The Monetary Approach to the Balance of Payments* (London: Allen & Unwin, 1976).

25. Adam Smith had this in mind in postulating his so-called law of reflux, that is, the long-run invariance of the total nominal currency stock to changes in the volume of bank notes; see *The Wealth of Nations*, ed. Edward Cannan, 2 vols., (Chicago: University of Chicago Press, 1976), 1: 318–20.

holdings so that the various issuing banks' shares of the total circulation tend toward the specific shares desired in the aggregate by the public. We examine below the mechanisms of adjustment in this last case.

When the public desires to hold a greater share of its money in the form of specie rather than in notes or deposits, and when particular banks desire to hold a greater quantity of specie reserves relative to notes and deposits in circulation, a short-run equilibrating tendency will arise for specie to flow in from outside the region. As a particular bank's percentage share of the total note circulation increases, a tendency for specie to flow in will arise if and only if the consequent addition to the bank's desired specie reserves is greater than the consequent reduction in desired reserves of the banks whose market shares decline. The converse propositions also hold.

Mechanisms Regulating the Currency Stock

We are now in a position to examine generally the working of a note exchange mechanism and other processes regulating the issue of bank notes. We saw above that the solution of the issuing bank's optimization problem determined, under reasonable assumptions concerning cost functions, a unique profit-maximizing magnitude for the stock of its notes in circulation. For issuer i, we denote this value N^{i*}. Because we have treated the "selling" costs of promoting the demand to hold its notes as simple production costs, which indeed they are from the banking firm's point of view, N^{i*} represents the public's desired quantity of bank i notes given that bank's optimizing expenditures. (We need not bother to distinguish in this section between nominal and real quantities of notes, given the context of convertibility of notes into a medium whose purchasing power is determined on a global basis.)

A general consideration of the possibilities for quality competition among bank note issuers, then, is sufficient to demonstrate that the desired stock of any particular bank's notes is a determinate magnitude under free banking. We do not have to resort to a special assumption that each issuer enjoys a geographic monopoly or that for some other reason each member of the public holds the notes only of a single bank. We do not have to suppose that within a region of many issuers some individuals refuse to accept the notes of some banks in payments,[26] so long as individuals do refuse to *hold* various brands of notes indefinitely in any but particular desired quantities.

Let us now consider the process by which the actual stock of notes issued by an individual bank — call it bank A — is adjusted to the public's desired stock. We consider the case in which the actual stock exceeds the desired stock, $N^A > N^{A*}$. This situation of an excess stock of notes may arise either because bank A has expanded its issue of notes without warrant or because the demand to hold them has fallen. Perhaps the most readily conceived scenario is one in which bank A, beginning from an initial optimum, expands its loans and discounts of bills, placing additional notes into the hands of its loan customers and the persons to whom they in turn spend away their loan proceeds, but does nothing to increase N^{A*}. We assume that bank A is one of many issuing banks within a region, all accepting one another's notes and participating in a regular note exchange. The region is defined as the geographic area of circulation of the participating banks' notes. We begin from an equilibrium situation in which neither specie nor any other banks' notes are in excess supply. We make the *ceteris paribus* assumption that underlying money-holding preferences do not shift.

There are three ways in which individual agents may in the immediate run respond to an excess holding of bank A notes: (1) They may redeem the notes for specie at the counter of the issuing bank; (2) they may place the notes into a deposit account, possibly interest-bearing, at their preferred banks; (3) they may hold the notes as buffer stock with the intention of spending the notes away to other agents within the region. This last action spreads the impact of the overissue over time. In general, agents will choose a combination of these courses of action in the light of their preferences and perceived situations.

Under the first course of action, direct redemption for specie, the reflux of the excess notes is immediate. The issuing bank immediately experiences a loss of specie reserves as they are paid across the counter. In actual experience, we may expect this path of reflux to be of minor importance. In the typical case, individual agents would probably find it more convenient to deal with their regular banks

26 Ludwig von Mises operates on this assumption; see *Human Action*, 3d rev. ed. (Chicago: Henry Regnery, 1966), p. 437. Our account parallels his in other respects. Mises notes (p. 438) that the assumption can be relaxed to allow for the case where excess notes return via innerbank settlements, but he does not develop this case.

(assuming that their banks accept the notes of bank A), depositing the notes and withdrawing coin from their deposit accounts if desired.

The second course of action, deposit of the notes, brings the note exchange mechanism into play, supposing that the bank receiving the deposit is not the bank of issue in question. The note exchange is simply the periodic settlement among participating banks of the claims represented by their notes. These claims are collected by the banks when they accept deposits and loan repayments in one another's notes. (We examine below why issuing banks may be expected to agree to mutual acceptance and to join in a note exchange system.) The deposit of an unusually large volume of bank A notes in other banks will result in an adverse clearings balance against bank A at the note exchange. The balance must be settled by the transfer of an agreed-upon medium—we may assume it to be specie—from bank A to the other banks. Thus the reflux of excess notes placed on deposit at other banks is delayed only until the date of the next note clearing. At that time, the expansive bank A suffers a loss of reserves, whereas the more conservative banks enjoy a corresponding gain of reserves.

Note that neither of these courses necessarily brings the individual agents to final portfolio equilibrium: They may hold an excess stock of specie or deposits. But we have traced the process far enough to show that bank A has begun to feel a loss of reserves.

Excess notes redeposited with bank A do not immediately subject it to a loss of reserves. Thus, the immediate check on overissue is attenuated according to the share of the holders of the excess notes who do their deposit banking with bank A. But redeposited notes do subject bank A to greater expenses in interest payments without bringing the added reserves that deposits of specie or another banks' notes bring.

Notes held or spent within the region by agents following the third course of action do not immediately return to the issuer. Instead, they remain in circulation for the time being, where their holders, in spending them, exert upward pressure on prices. In due course, these excess notes will be returned to the issuing bank through the first and second routes, redemption and deposit, as note holders reassert their preferences. But we must trace out the intervening sequence.

To some extent, the excess stock of notes will bring about an increased spending on goods imported from outside the region we have been considering. This spending will result directly as agents draw down excess currency balances and may also result indirectly as they respond to the rise in local prices brought about by increased spending on local goods. Increased spending on imports will in turn give rise to a balance of payments deficit for the region. Because local notes are not acceptable outside the region, the balance must be settled in specie. Local banks will temporarily lose specie to the rest of the world during the adjustment process. The loss will not be permanent under the *ceteris paribus* assumption that there are no underlying shifts in money-holding preferences. The regional efflux of specie will instead be self-reversing.[27]

The expansive bank A will bear the brunt of the specie lost through the direct spending response, since by hypothesis the excess currency balances consist exclusively of its notes. Since these notes do not circulate outside the region, they must be redeemed for specie first, either directly (course 1) or indirectly via deposits in other banks (course 2). The shift in spending in response to higher local prices will impinge upon the reserves of other banks in the region, since holders of all note brands within the region face higher prices. Recall, however, that these banks simultaneously enjoy positive clearings from the reflux of notes through the deposit route.

We thus conclude that the overexpansive bank in a free banking system will sooner or later be disciplined by a loss of its reserves. The process will run its course sooner, to the extent that excess notes are immediately vented in the first two ways, or later, to the extent that they are initially vented in the third way (which must eventually result in their being returned to the issuer in the first two ways). Having started from an initial profit-maximizing equilibrium position, bank A, with smaller reserves, is now placed in a suboptimal position. Its reduced specie holding subjects it to an unacceptably high risk of exhausting its liquid reserve and consequently defaulting on its note obligations. In terms of our model, the net benefit from holding additional specie now exceeds the marginal net revenue from

27. This statement is made in the spirit of the monetary approach to the balance of payments. See Ludwig von Mises, *The Theory of Money and Credit*, trans. H. E. Batson, new enl. ed. (Irvington-on-Hudson, N.Y.: Foundation for Economic Education, 1971), pp. 184–85, for the argument that interregional gold flows must be self-reversing when arising from shocks not accompanied by shifts in relative demands to hold money.

holding bills. An increase in specie reserves and a decrease in bill holdings is called for.

In order to reestablish its initial equilibrium position following a period of overissue, the expansive bank must reverse course. It must pursue a relatively restrictive policy for a period. During this period of "underissue," it will enjoy positive clearings against the other banks and so may replenish its own reserves. At the same time the region as a whole will experience an influx of specie to restore the holdings of its inhabitants and banks to their equilibrium levels.

We have thus far confined ourselves to the case of an overissuing bank acting alone. The same process, leading back to equilibrium through disciplinary reserve losses from an initial overissue, will also operate in the case of overissue by a group of many or all banks within a region acting in concert. There is, however, a potentially important difference of degree involved: the larger the share of total circulation and deposits supplied by the expanding banks, the greater the role of the relatively disruptive process of external drain in bringing the expansion to an end.

That reflux through the note exchange will not check a joint expansion should be clear. Supposing the group of banks to expand by a common factor, no consequent adverse clearings will arise among members of the group. Adverse clearings will not arise among a group of banks in consequence of whatever degree of expansion is common to all. Each member of the group will meet the increased volume of notes returned upon it by way of deposit in other member banks with an equally increased volume of notes of those other banks deposited with it. There will of course be a loss of reserves from members of the group to any nonexpansive banks. Should the expanding group comprise all the banks in a region, the system as a whole must eventually be checked by loss of reserves to the world beyond the region and to the specie holdings of its customers (who will desire additional specie holdings as prices rise in the short run). If the region comprises the world, only the last check — internal drain to meet the public's desired real specie holdings — operates on bank reserves.

The Genesis of the Note Exchange

Our discussion in the previous section presupposed the existence of an effectively functioning note exchange system embracing a number of independent banks of issue. Here we attempt to explain why the independent issuing banks in a free banking system will be led, as if by an invisible hand, to promote the institution of a general note exchange system. Our method of explanation follows that of Carl Menger, who set out to explain in invisible-hand fashion the emergence of the institution of money.[28] This method of explanation of the origins of social institutions, and of course the phrase "invisible hand," may be traced to Adam Smith and earlier writers of the Scottish enlightenment. An invisible-hand explanation shows how the decentralized actions of purely self-interested agents may, without their intending it, give rise to a cohesive order.[29]

Consider an initial situation in which several banks in a region issue convertible bank notes, yet none accepts any other's notes for deposit or loan repayment. Holders of bank i notes must instead go through a costly intermediate step, either of returning the notes to bank i for redemption in specie or of engaging the services of an agent who does so for a fee (a local money changer) should they wish to pay them into a different bank. The salability of bank i notes is limited in comparison with specie: Specie can, but the notes cannot, buy deposits in other banks. This limitation has both a minor direct and a major indirect effect on N^{i*}, since N^{i*} is presumably a function of the salability of bank i notes. The indirect effect is that sellers who regularly deposit their currency receipts in bank j will likely refuse to exchange their merchandise for bank i notes at par. The salability of bank i notes is thus further impeded and N^{i*} further reduced.

If other banks accepted bank i notes, those notes would enjoy increased salability and consequently a greater demand to hold them in preference to specie. In this situation, a pair of issuers — call them banks F and G — would find that each improves its position by both agreeing to accept the other's notes at par. Mutual acceptance increases both N^{F*} and N^{G*}. At the same time, banks F and G would both find it profitable to enter into a regular note exchange arrangement. Neither bank would wish to accumulate the other's notes *ad*

28. Carl Menger, *Principles of Economics*, trans. James Dingwall and Bert F. Hozelitz (New York: New York University Press, 1981), ch. 8.

29. Smith, *Wealth of Nations*, 1: 477. For a brief philosophical discussion of the attractiveness of invisible-hand explanations, together with a list of examples, see Robert Nozick, *Anarchy, State, and Utopia* (New York: Basic Books, 1974), pp. 18–22. See also the essays by Hayek cited there.

infinitum or to reissue them in place of its own. If the banks demanded redemption from one another without arranging a note exchange—for example, if bank F presented its bank G notes for redemption without allowing bank G to offset its liability by relinquishing its accumulated bank F notes—both banks would incur greater expected liquidity costs from the increased variance of net specie outflow, not to mention greater transportation costs of bringing the specie back home, than they would if they arranged a note exchange. Bank F's claims on bank G's specie are then offset by bank G's reciprocal claims. Each bank would want to set the regularity or frequency of the exchange in order to equate the marginal reduction in expected liquidity costs from more frequent exchange to the marginal increase in operating costs from more frequent exchange.[30]

The availability of further gains in bank note salability will make it mutually profitable for other banks to join the note exchange arrangement. They may join singly, or they may enter into other note exchange arrangements that later merge with the first pair. Eventually, a single note exchange will include all profit-seeking banks within a region.[31] No bank aims to establish a systemwide note exchange—bank C would benefit as much and possibly more if banks D, E, and F did not exchange among themselves—yet their profit-seeking actions have that unintentional result.

The arrangements among the banks need not be symmetric. Bilateral dealings of this sort exhibit an indeterminacy in distributing the gains from trade.[32] All banks voluntarily joining a note exchange presumably gain from its existence, however. The mutual acceptance arrangement improves the negotiability of every participant's notes. There is room for every bank to enjoy an increase in the demand to

30. Since this trade-off may not be the same for both banks, no particular frequency may satisfy the equimarginal condition for both banks. There may, therefore, be room for implicit or explicit side payments to reach a joint optimum.

31. The region will extend to the perimeter beyond which banks find that the augmentation of note demand from participation is too slight to offset the operating costs of participation. These operating costs include losses from accepting forged notes of other banks, losses that likely will increase at the geographic margin as the region expands.

32. We may cite historical examples: Although the Scottish note exchange system seems to have been completely symmetrical, the Suffolk Bank note exchange system in Boston was asymmetrical and may be viewed as involving a transfer to the Suffolk Bank of some portion of the other banks' gains from the arrangement. On the Suffolk system, see George Trivoli, *The Suffolk Bank* (Leesburg, Va.: Adam Smith Institute, 1979).

hold its notes, since the public substitutes holdings of notes for hold-ings of specie at the margin.[33]

In a bilateral note exchange, the clearing balance is computed sim-ply between the two participants. Where third and further banks enter the arrangement, it is likely to be cheaper to conduct the ex-change multilaterally than as a series of bilateral exchanges. A single clearing balance is computed for each bank against all other banks, and settlements are paid into and out of a central pool. We assumed above that adverse clearing balances at the note exchange were set-tled in specie. Certainly, a bank with a positive balance could insist upon specie, given the legal commitments of other issuers to con-vertibility of their notes into specie. But the costs of settlement can likely be economized by agreeing to substitute for specie shipments the transfer of some other agreed-upon medium. All banks might, for example, hold specie reserves on deposit with a single institution, which clears note exchange balances by transferring the deposits on its books. Or they might transfer holdings of an especially liquid interest-earning asset issued outside the banking system.[34] In either case the disciplinary power of the note exchange against overissues by an individual bank would not be attenuated. A bank could still not permit an outflow of reserves to persist. Unanticipated reserve losses would still place the bank in a suboptimal position and signal it to contract its issues.

THE RATIONALE OF FREE BANKING

Having developed an account of the self-regulating manner in which a free banking system operates, we may in this final section attempt briefly to answer likely criticisms and misinterpretations of the case for free banking. In doing so, we will suggest what we consider the compelling advantages of free banking as a monetary system.

We do not claim on behalf of free banking that it uniquely or most effectively serves any particular macroeconomic policy goal such as price level stability, price level predictability, interest rate stability,

---

33. We therefore strongly question the suggestion that the Suffolk system imposed a net loss on the rural banks and that the city banks constituted a cartel formed for the purpose of extracting a transfer from the rural banks; see, for example, Gerald Gunderson, *A New Economic History of America* (New York: McGraw-Hill, 1976), p. 195.

34. The Suffolk system operated in the former way, the Scottish system in the latter.

or reduced opportunity costs of holding currency (though it is consistent with improvements in each of these directions). On the contrary, its special virtue is that it frees money from use as a tool by those of constructivist bent who would impose tidy designs upon the economy. A free banking system is subservient only to the forces of competition among the producers of monetary services attempting to meet consumers' demands profitabily. For that reason, it will not be popular with the economist who believes that a monetary system ought to be designed, that is, ought by rational construction to promote the ends this economist finds desirable. It is no doubt possible to design a monetary system that would—so long as the real world conforms to the *ceteris paribus* conditions of the designer's model and so long as the monetary authorities behave virtuously—outperform a free banking system in respect to achieveing a specific target.[35] One designer's target, however, may be inconsistent with another's target, and both may be inconsistent with the preferences of the consumers of monetary services.

It is commonly argued by proponents of managed fiat money that it is "inefficient" to allow a commodity stock to serve as the monetary base. Efficiency or inefficiency, however, is a property of alternative means considered in relation to the same end. A designed government-run monetary system may be more efficient than free banking in serving the narrow goals of the designer, of the monetary authority created, or of the government that adopts the design. This in no way bears on the question of whether the system is efficient in the usual economic sense, where the satisfaction of given consumer preferences is taken as the relevant goal. An example should illustrate this point. David Ricardo, one of the earliest monetary constructivists, denounced as wastefully inefficient the use of gold coins of large denominations as currency when paper currency could be made to serve in their stead. He admitted, however, that consumers offered a choice preferred to hold the coins.[36] A forced substitution of paper for those coins in such a circumstance would not have been efficient in serving the ends of monetary consumers.

35. If that target involves the magnitude of an index number, such as the consumer price index used as a proxy for the purchasing power of money, the government's index compilers must also behave virtuously. For a critique of Irving Fisher's plan to stabilize the price index see Mises, *Money and Credit*, pp. 401–6.

36. David Ricardo, *Pamphlets and Papers 1815–1823*, vol. 4 of *The Works and Correspondence of David Ricardo*, ed. Pierro Sraffa (Cambridge: Cambridge University Press, 1951), pp. 65–66.

Benjamin Klein has emphasized the important point that, where consumers have a choice, their willingness to hold a particular brand of currency depends on the confidence they have that its issuer will not cheat them. An issuer of inconvertible currency must be trusted not to inflate its supply unexpectedly.[37] An issuer of convertible currency must correspondingly be trusted not to refuse redemption. An issuer of specie must be trusted not to debase its metallic content. The metal itself must be trusted not to fall in relative value. Put another way, trustworthiness is an important quality of the economic good we call money.

Klein pertinently applies this idea to the question of the efficiency of substituting bank notes for specie. Bank note producers did not gain a foothold in the currency industry until they could produce trustworthy currency cheaply enough in competition with specie. He then comments: "A forced movement from commodity to pure fiduciary money, for example, in the nineteenth century, would have implied a negative social saving."[38]

We may take this argument a step further. The forced substitution of fiat for convertible currency, like the Ricardian forced substitution of convertible currency for coin, is by no means efficient when it contravenes consumer preference for what is considered a more trustworthy currency. Lowering production costs does not constitute efficiency when the resulting product is one of lower quality in consumers' eyes. The actual forced movement in the twentieth century from a gold-convertible dollar to an inconvertible dollar must have represented a "negative social saving," to use Klein's phrase, if currency users would have preferred to continue using gold and gold-convertible currency. The federal government's resort to confiscation of gold and prohibition of gold clause contracts in 1933 indicated its awareness of such a preference.

---

37. That is, inflate its supply to a degree not compensated by the nominal interest yield of the currency. An anticipated 5 percent drop in purchasing power per unit is of no concern provided that the money yields an offsetting 5 percent in explicit interest. On confidence, see Klein, "Competitive Supply of Money," pp. 432–38.

38. Klein, "Money, Wealth, and Seignorage," p. 10. Virtually an identical statement appears in Klein, "Competing Monies," p. 77. We have interpreted Klein's use of the phrases "fiduciary money" and "credit money" as references to convertible bank notes. We interpret the above-quoted phrase "pure fiduciary money" as a reference to inconvertible or fiat money. It is important not to blur the distinction between the sort of confidence involved in convertible currency and that involved in fiat currency.

A comparison of the subsequent behavior of the purchasing power of the dollar to its previous behavior suggests that the public's trust in gold-convertible currency rather than in fiat currency was not misplaced.[39] George Bernard Shaw gave a succinct statement of the rationale for trusting gold over paper:

> To sum up, the most important thing about money is to maintain its stability.... With paper money this stability has to be maintained by the Government. With a gold currency it tends to maintain itself.... You have to choose (as a voter) between trusting to the natural stability of gold and the natural stability of the honesty and intelligence of the members of the Government. And, with due respect for these gentlemen, I advise you, as long as the Capitalist system lasts, to vote for gold.[40]

It might be argued that today the shoe is on the other foot—that specie-convertible currency must bear the burden of proving itself to be the currency most efficient at meeting consumer wants in a free market. This argument has some force. It applies especially to novel alternative monetary systems such as F. A. Hayek's private inconvertible currencies and Robert E. Hall's composite commodity standard, to name two recent proposals.[41] Only the market can adjudicate among competing claimants to the status of most desirable currency. It cannot be said, however, that the continued dominance of the Federal Reserve note represents a free market verdict.

Market competition among currencies remains closed in the United States today, despite the relegalization of gold ownership and gold clause contracts. Unrestricted competition among currencies would require at least the following reforms: (1) an end to any forced tender laws that compel acceptance of government currency in discharge of debt and thereby prevent private contracts in other media of exchange from being legally enforced; (2) an end to any legal restrictions on entry into banking and finance that prevent private entrepreneurs from offering, for example, specie-convertible notes and deposits; and (3) changes in any tax laws that restrict accounting or

39. Michael David Bordo, "The Classical Gold Standard: Some Lessons for Today," *Federal Reserve Bank of St. Louis Review* 63 (May 1981): 2–17. See also Table 7–2 in Richard M. Timberlake's contribution to this volume.

40. George Bernard Shaw, *The Intelligent Woman's Guide to Socialism and Capitalism* (New York: Brentano's, 1928), p. 263.

41. See Hayek, *Denationalisation of Money*; Robert E. Hall, "Explorations in the Gold Standard and Related Policies for Stabilizing the Dollar," in Hall, ed., *Inflation: Causes and Effects* (Chicago: University of Chicago Press for National Bureau of Economic Research, 1982).

transactions using alternative currency units. As concrete evidence of legal barriers to entry, we note that an experiment with privately issued indexed currency and deposits in Exeter, New Hampshire, from June 1972 to January 1974 was ended under legal pressure from the Securities and Exchange Commission.[42]

It should not be argued that a single producer of currency is efficient for natural monopoly reasons. Such reasons would provide no rationale for legal barriers to entry. But more importantly, behind such claims lies an intellectual confusion. Consideration of free banking on a commodity-convertible basis allows us to recognize that the question of a natural monopoly in the production of money is distinct from the question of an inherent market tendency toward convergence on a single monetary standard. The latter exists for the reasons Carl Menger spelled out: every transactor promotes his self-interest by using the single most salable commodity in the economy as a medium of exchange.[43] Roland Vaubel finds natural monopoly characteristics in the production of currency because he fails to make this distinction.[44] He confines his attention to competing inconvertible currencies, each currency constituting its own standard. Benjamin Klein, although he takes note of free banking as a case of "multiple monies convertible into a single dominant money," unfortunately persists in asserting that "the money industry is essentially a natural monopoly," as though this were the same as asserting the existence of a tendency toward a single dominant money.[45]

Where the single dominant money is a commodity like gold or silver coin, there is no reason to suppose that a natural monopoly — in the standard sense of continually falling average costs — exists at any level: mining of the metal, coinage, issue of convertible bank notes, or issue of higher order deposit monies. There is no reason to suppose that a single producer could capture the entire market for ore, coins, bank notes, or deposits. That all coins are manufactured of like metals in like weights, and that all notes and deposits are redeemable for standard coin, no more indicates a natural monopoly

42. "Paying with Constants Instead of Dollars," *Business Week*, 4 May 1974, 29.

43. Menger, *Principles of Economics*, ch. 8. For a modern version of Menger's theory, see Robert A. Jones, "The Origin and Development of Media of Exchange," *Journal of Political Economy* 4 (1976): 757–75.

44. See Roland Vaubel, "Free Currency Competition," *Weltwirtschaftliches Archiv* 113 (1977): 437.

45. Klein, "Competitive Supply of Money," pp. 439–42; idem, "Competing Monies," pp. 78–79.

in money production than the standardization of brick composition and size indicates a natural monopoly in brick production.

Nor should it be argued that the recent volatility of gold and silver prices indicates that precious metals are no longer suitable for use as a monetary base.[46] That price volatility has resulted largely from speculation concerning the profitability of holding metals relative to that of holding dollar-denominated assets. If the dollar were redefined as so many grams of silver, say, or if silver supplanted the Federal Reserve note as the dominant money, this motive for speculation in silver would cease. There would no longer be any scope for buying or selling silver in hopes that its dollar price might rise or fall. The silver market would become one with the market in U.S. currency. There might still be speculation in silver against other currencies, but only for the motives that spur dollar speculation in currency markets today. There is no reason to believe that the market for a specie-convertible money would be more subject to price volatility than the market for a fiat money. In fact, there is good reason to believe the reverse. As is well known, the relative price elasticity of both the supply and the nonmonetary (industrial and consumer) demand for the precious metal would add elements tending to stabilize the metal's purchasing power in the face of shifts in the demand to hold specie and specie-convertible money.

Our theoretical discussion in the central part of this paper assumed that the monetary base consisted of coins minted of a metal used worldwide as currency. For the first area to move from a fiat money system to a free banking system, this would not be the case. Our small, open economy model would have to be modified to recognize that the purchasing power of the monetary unit would be determined jointly with the equilibrium nominal domestic monetary base. The determinateness of the system would by no means be impaired. The free banking area would continue to have floating exchange rates against other currency areas and so would continue to be insulated against monetary shocks emitted by foreign fiat currency suppliers. Undeniably, it would experience a new susceptibility to shifts in the supply curve for the monetary metal, but, as argued above, this is surely less worrisome than the present susceptibility of the system to

46. Hall, "Explorations in the Gold Standard," pp. 7–8; although he concedes that "a U.S. gold standard might have stabilized the gold market" in recent times, he claims groundlessly that "large changes in the price level would certainly have occurred" anyway had the U.S. currency been gold based.

shifts in the behavior of the monetary authority. Were other areas to adopt the specie standard of the original free banking area, money holders in the original area would profit from an appreciation in the value of their money on world markets.

The rationale for implementing the reforms necessary for free currency competition, apart from their other obvious microeconomic benefits, is simply this: If government fiat money really does suit consumers best, there is no rationale for impediments to its potential competitors. It may be that the inherent market tendency to converge upon a single standard money or monetary base would allow the government fiat currency unit to retain its monetary role even if all such impediments were removed.[47] The central part of this paper supports the position that we have no basis in doubts about its stability to resist the emergence of a free banking system on a specie standard. Further argument would be necessary to establish the case that the dollar ought to be made redeemable for gold or silver coin or bullion in order to facilitate the emergence of free banking on a specie standard. That argument would have to appeal to redemption of outstanding currency as the best way to make the transition to a monetary system built upon a base money freely chosen by the market. If one believes that the particular brand of inconvertible currency issued by the present government monetary authority ought not to be excluded from the competition among base monies, there is no reason that any gold the government holds — in the United States it is held primarily at Fort Knox — should not at least be distributed to the public, as Richard H. Timberlake has suggested.[48]

Unlike other forms of denationalized money, free banking has a history. It developed naturally, where permitted, out of a pure specie monetary system, which had developed naturally out of barter. There is no question that free banking on a specie standard can function in real world markets. Were it not for the legislative creation of central banks, primarily to meet the demands of central governments for inflationary finance, free banking would indeed be with us today.

47. For the author's suspicion that this might be the case, see Lawrence H. White, "Gold, Dollars, and Private Currencies," *Policy Report* 3 (June 1981): 9. In this case, a free banking system might build upon a permanently frozen stock of paper currency previously issued by government.

48. Richard H. Timberlake, Jr., "Government Gold," *Bankers Magazine* 163 (March–April 1980): 22–23.

APPENDIX
MATHEMATICS OF THE OPTIMIZATION PROBLEM

Double-entry bookkeeping imposes the balance sheet constraint

$$S + B = N + D + \overline{K}$$

The bank's expected profit function is:

$$\pi = r_b B - r_d D - C - L$$

where

π = expected profit

$r_b \equiv$ the yield rate earned on bills held

$r_d \equiv$ the yield rate paid on deposits

$C \equiv$ total operating costs

$L \equiv$ expected liquidity costs.

The yield rates r_b and r_d are treated as exogenously given to the bank, that is, as invariant with respect to the quantity of bills in purchases and deposits it attracts. This price-taking assumption could easily be modified to allow for price-searching behavior. Operating costs are assumed to be a twice-differentiable function of the balance sheet entries:

$$C = f(S, B, N, D) \quad .$$

We may assume the expected liquidity cost function $L = g(S, N, D)$ to take a somewhat specific form:

$$L = \int_S^\infty p(X - S)\, \phi\,(X|N, D)\, dX$$

where

$p \equiv$ percentage adjustment cost for impending specie deficiency, for simplicity assumed constant, so that realized cost $p(X - S)$ is linear in the size of the deficiency, X - S

$X \equiv$ net specie outflow during the period

$\phi\,(X|N, D) \equiv$ the probability density function over X, conditional on N and D.

The practical import of this equation is that expected liquidity costs decrease with an increase in S (N and D held constant). It is natural to assume in addition that ϕ ($X|N, D$) behaves in such a way that expected liquidity costs increase with an increase in N or D (S held constant). Letting a subscript denote partial differentiation with respect to the subscripted variable, we may therefore write:

$$L_S < 0, L_N > 0, L_D > 0 \ .$$

The implications of profit maximization for the bank may be derived most clearly by setting out its choice problem as a Lagrangean constrained maximization problem:

$$\pi\,(S, B, N, D, \overline{K}) = r_b B - r_a D - C - L + \lambda\,(\overline{K} - S - B + N + D)$$

$$\pi_s \ = \ -C_s - L_s - \lambda \ = \ 0$$

$$\pi_B \ = \ r_b - C_B - \lambda \ = \ 0$$

$$\pi_N \ = \ -C_N - L_N + \lambda \ = \ 0$$

$$\pi_D \ = \ -r_d - C_D - L_D + \lambda \ = \ 0$$

$$\pi_\lambda \ = \ \overline{K} - S - B + N + D \ = \ 0$$

$$\therefore \ r_b - C_B \ = \ -C_s - L_s \ = \ C_N + L_N \ = \ r_d + C_D + L_D \ \ .$$

Chapter 12

A FREE-MARKET POLICY TO STABILIZE THE PURCHASING POWER OF THE DOLLAR

Robert E. Hall

Nothing better illustrates the need for wholesale monetary reform than the sorry history of rising prices and unstable interest rates over the past two decades. Successive episodes of extreme monetary restriction and sky-high interest rates have failed to halt the downward slide in the purchasing power of the dollar. But the picture is brighter for the microeconomic aspects of monetary policy. A commendable move toward deregulation of financial markets began recently. The monopoly power of banks has been moderated by extending the right to offer checking accounts to savings banks and others. Burdensome regulation of interest rates is gradually being lifted. All of this is to the good. Deregulation of banks and their competitors is desirable for the same reasons that deregulation of airlines is desirable — more people get more services at lower prices.

Much remains to be done by way of financial deregulation. Barriers to entry in financial services will remain even after the process already set in motion is complete. For example, Sears Roebuck ought to be free to provide checking accounts and other services whenever and wherever its customers want, but it cannot today and will not be able to in the future under existing legislation. Sears should be free to sell interest-bearing notes in small denominations as well, as they have proposed several times. Every time, they have been thwarted by federal regulators.

Both past experience and forthcoming deregulation make clear the futility of a monetary policy founded on the principle of stable growth of some measure of the money stock. Past measures of the money stock were artifacts of federal regulations. As the regulations disappear, these measures become meaningless. Some monetarist adherents of money growth rules have gone so far as to suggest arresting or even reversing financial deregulation solely for the purpose of retaining a meaningful money stock. They elevate the arbitrary principle of constant money growth above the basic microeconomic principle of efficient free markets.

Even in an economy where regulation makes a money growth rule meaningful and feasible, it is bad policy. Stable growth of money does not bring the desired stability of prices and interest rates. Ever since the government began collecting data, the relation between the money stock and total economic activity (as measured, say, by the dollar volume of GNP) has shifted unexpectedly from month to month and year to year.[1] With a fixed money stock, every time the public wants to hold a little more money, interest rates shoot up and real activity declines.

The Federal Reserve was created precisely with the idea that it would accommodate shifts in money demand. The panic of 1907, which occurred in a system of partly fixed money, convinced Congress of the need for a more elastic money. They created the Fed and gave it the power to issue more money as required by the economy. Unfortunately, the Fed was not told how to decide when the economy really needed more money and when the injection would instead bring higher prices. An unhappy sequence of errors followed. In the Great Depression, the Fed watched inactively as the financial system collapsed instead of fulfilling its creators' intention of pumping in reserves when they were needed. Many less serious episodes of financial stress followed in the postwar years. The pattern of credit crunch and ensuing recession (or near-recession) became familiar from the repeated experiences of 1966–67, 1969–71, 1973–75, 1980, and 1981–82. On the other side, the Fed created excess money, with corresponding inflation, more or less continuously after 1964, except in the crunches.

---

1. John P. Gould and Charles R. Nelson, "The Stochastic Structure of the Velocity of Money," *American Economic Review* 64 (1974): 405.

The Federal Reserve has not been in the hands of fools in the past two decades. It was hardly unaware that monetary constriction brings recession and monetary expansion ultimately brings inflation. The Fed lacked any firm guidance on how to balance the two goals of stable real activity and stable prices. During most of the years of the transition to high inflation over the past two decades, the Fed has erred on the side of too low interest rates and excess stimulus. During crunches, it has made the opposite mistake. Though this diagnosis is widely accepted in retrospect, policy remains destabilizing because the Fed has not been given the appropriate operating rule to avoid problems in the future.

The only consistent advice on the principles underlying monetary policy has come from the monetarists, who tell the Fed to ignore everything that is happening in the economy and simply stick to a predetermined path for the money stock. Whatever monetary crisis this policy brings is just the cost of meeting the Fed's highest obligation, the sound dollar. The principle of blinding itself to interest rates and real activity has been elevated to an ideology recently by a school of hard-line monetarists advocating a thorough financial shakedown with sharply reduced real activity as the sure cure for inflation. The advice was followed at considerable cost in Britain in the late 1970s and early 1980s.

Is there a sensible free-market alternative to monetarism? Can we offer a simple operating rule to the Federal Reserve that meets the three goals of a stable price level, stable interest rates, and full financial deregulation? Or should we follow the monetarists in subordinating stable interest and deregulation in the hope that stable money growth will bring stable prices? I will argue in the rest of this paper that a well-designed free-market policy involving an adaptive setting of interest rates can bring more stable prices and much more stable interest than the monetarist prescription of steady money growth. As a free-market policy, it supports and encourages complete financial deregulation, a development that has brought confusion to monetarism. I will also argue in some detail that the adaptive interest rate policy is superior to the gold standard or other commodity standards as the basis of the monetary system.

THE GOVERNMENT'S POWER TO DEFINE
THE DOLLAR

The government has the power to set forth a legal definition of the monetary unit. Though an economy can function reasonably well without a government-sponsored unit, history suggests that an economy gains from such a unit. Uniformity in quoting prices, maintaining accounts, and stating forward contracts has the same virtues as uniform standards for switching and transmitting telephone calls.[2] A government definition of a monetary unit need not involve any compulsion to use the unit. Further, private enterprise can provide all monetary assets and transaction services; the government need not intervene in asset markets or regulate transaction services. To create a monetary unit, the government must clearly state to the courts what action legally settles a debt stated in the unit. In today's economy, currency issued by the Federal Reserve is legal tender. Once a debtor conveys legal tender to a creditor in the prescribed quantity, the courts consider the debt settled. Nothing in the system requires that legal tender actually change hands. Rather, the creditor's right to demand legal tender establishes precisely how much purchasing power the debtor must convey to settle the debt.

Over the two centuries of U.S. independence, the government has exercised its power to define the dollar in two main ways.[3] Starting in 1792, the dollar was defined in terms of quantities of gold or silver. In the late nineteenth century, the dollar was literally 0.0484 of an ounce of gold, though paper instruments of the government—namely, greenbacks—were also legal tender. With the establishment of the Federal Reserve in 1914, the dollar became defined in terms of paper instruments of the Fed. Conveying gold to settle a debt was actually made illegal in 1933, and the definition of the dollar lost all meaningful contact with anything but paper at that point.

In addition to the metallic and paper definitions of the dollar adopted by the United States at various points in its history, a third type of definition is available: One country can define its monetary

2. For an elaboration of this point, see Robert E. Hall, "The Government and the Monetary Unit" (Stanford University, 1981). (Processed.)

3. An excellent source on U.S. monetary institutions is James Willard Hurst, *A Legal History of Money in the United States, 1774-1970* (Lincoln: University of Nebraska Press, 1973).

unit in terms of the currency of a second country. The third technique is most appropriate for a small country. Until the destabilization of the pound sterling in the early 1970s, for example, Hong Kong simply defined its own dollar as a fixed fraction of a pound.[4] Only very small, highly dependent nations have chosen to do this in the past decades, for it requires a complete abdication of national monetary policy. Canada, for example, might profitably declare the U.S. dollar as legal tender. Then it could dismantle its entire inefficient apparatus for regulating Canadian financial institutions and abolish the Bank of Canada. Canadian banks could create currency and checking accounts without limit, payable in dollars, but these dollars would be convertible on demand into U.S. dollars, which would unambiguously determine their purchasing power. The Canadian price level and interest rates would be determined in Washington, not Ottawa. Though Canada is highly unlikely to move in this direction, it is interesting that two nations with disastrous records in maintaining the purchasing power of their own monetary units— Israel and Uruguay—have permitted the development of extensive unregulated financial institutions based on the U.S. dollar. And dollar-denominated financial instruments other than currency and checking accounts are in widespread use throughout the world.

As the proprietor of the dominant monetary unit in the world today, the United States does not really have the option of defining the dollar in terms of other units. Were we to define the dollar as, say, two Swiss francs, with the hope of taking advantage of the extraordinary stability of that unit, we would probably destabilize the Swiss economy rather than improve our own. The world economy would best be served by stabilizing the dollar through some other method and then encouraging other nations to define their monetary units in terms of the dollar. A return to the Bretton Woods system makes good sense, provided the United States adopts the right technique for stabilizing the purchasing power of the dollar and limiting swings in dollar interest rates. The goal of stable interest rates is particularly important for international stability; recent research is unanimous in associating unstable exchange markets with unstable interest rates in the short run and unstable purchasing power only in the long run. The tremendous appreciation of the dollar in 1981 far

---

4. A concise history of the novel monetary institutions of Hong Kong appears in the *Asian Monetary Monitor* (July–August 1981).

outstripped anything justified by the meager progress against inflation made by U.S. policy; instead, it was the response to extraordinary U.S. interest rates.

A return to a gold definition of the dollar is under active discussion today. Though gold advocates favor a more roundabout way to establish a gold definition, the simplest approach would be a straightforward announcement that the dollar is one grain of gold. Then the dollar price of gold would be fixed at $480 per ounce. But fixing the dollar price of gold has a fatal defect that I will elaborate on shortly: It stabilizes the purchasing power of the dollar in terms of gold, not in terms of the cost of living. Any type of gold standard invites wild fluctuations in the dollar cost of living.

The third option facing reformers of the U.S. monetary system is based, like the present system, on defining the dollar in terms of paper instruments of the federal government. My own review of the alternatives suggests that this is the way for free-market economists to turn for vast improvements in monetary policy. Bad management of paper money, not the idea itself, accounts for the sorry record of monetary policy in the past two decades. Further, paper money with stable purchasing power is fully consistent with complete deregulation of financial markets, including the abolition of reserve requirements and the lifting of restrictions on private currency. The value of government money need not rest on the monopoly power of the government.

MONETARY STABILITY WITH PAPER MONEY

The most basic problem in monetary policy is holding the price level approximately constant. A secondary problem is making the transition from positive rates of inflation to zero inflation. Though the transition issue is hardly unimportant today, I want to defer the issue until I have shown how we could maintain a constant price level once systematic inflation was squeezed out. At the most concrete level, the problem is the following. Every month, the Bureau of Labor Statistics gathers data and calculates the cost-of-living index. Suppose its value this month is arbitrarily set at 100. Next month, almost all the product prices in the index will change a little, and the index will be a bit above or a bit below 100. Monetary policy needs to move in the direction that pushes the price down if it exceeds 100 and raises it if it falls short. Occasionally, when a sharp movement in the price level comes from oil, agriculture, or elsewhere, the corrective action may need to be more than a nudge. In short, we need to set up a monetary policy giving us a policy lever that can be pushed in one direction to lower prices and the other to raise prices. When the policy is in place, we will spend half the time trying to lower prices and the other half trying to raise them.

Now I will describe a set of monetary institutions containing precisely such a policy lever, namely, the interest rate on short-term government debt. The upshot of the analysis will be a suggestion that the Fed raise the interest rate whenever prices are too high and lower the rate when prices are too low.

The first essential feature of the new monetary institutions is to retain the paper money of the Federal Reserve as the unique legal tender along with its equivalent, reserve deposits at the Fed. I will refer to legal tender as the U.S. dollar, to distinguish it from dollar-denominated instruments issued by private businesses. Second, all restrictions on the issuance of dollar instruments are to be lifted. Existing banks can provide checking accounts, currency, and small-denomination interest-bearing notes in any volume they choose, and so can any other business, including Sears Roebuck. Transaction services and financial intermediation are to be opened up to competitition for exactly the same reason that the airline industry was opened up. One restriction applies to everybody, a restriction that is in force already: Anyone promising to pay in dollars can be required to pay in U.S. dollars on the demand of the creditor. Demand instruments—currency and checking accounts—must be paid off immediately in U.S. dollars whenever the owner or depositor requests. Term instruments—anything promising payment on a prescribed date—must be paid off on that date in U.S. dollars if the creditor requires it. The requirement for payment in U.S. dollars exists today; I am only emphasizing the importance of retaining the requirement when any business has the theoretical right to issue its own dollars. American Express might well succeed in placing its own dollar bills in circulation, but nobody would be required to accept them as payment for debts. Only American Express's continuous, effective promise to redeem them for U.S. dollars would make them acceptable to the general public.

The new monetary system involves no required reserves. Reserve requirements in the current system are nothing more than taxes on financial institutions and have no microeconomic justification. However, the requirement for payment in U.S. dollars will create a reserve demand for those dollars. Much of the demand will arise, as it does today, from banks and other institutions offering demand instruments like checking accounts. They must always be prepared for a significant bulge in requests for payment in U.S. dollars. Consequently, they will hold small positive stocks of U.S. dollars, just as banks hold a certain amount of vault cash and excess reserves in today's system. But most reserves will be held, again as they are today, in the form of very short term, interest-bearing instruments that offer easy conversion into U.S. dollars. Chief among these is the U.S. treasury bill. There can never be any doubt about the U.S. government's promise to deliver U.S. dollars when a treasury bill matures. Consequently, a portfolio of treasury bills offers an effective way to stand ready to pay off account holders in U.S. dollars without holding a significant stock of idle funds in actual dollars.

The reserve demand for treasury bills is substantial. It accounts for a treasury bill yield below the highest quality private short-term instruments of 0.5 to 2 percentage points. Commercial banks own about a fifth of all marketable federal debt outside the government; this is more than one dollar in treasury instruments for each three dollars in checking accounts.[5] Reserve demand is not limited to banks. Treasury bills are held by businesses, brokers, and wealthy individuals in anticipation of the need to make payments in U.S. dollars. The recent development of mutual funds owning nothing but short-term treasury instruments is another sure sign of the importance of the reserve demand for these instruments and of claims on them.

The interest rate on treasury bills is under the direct control of monetary policy. Indeed, from the onset of World War II until 1951, monetary policy was conducted by pegging the bill rate at levels around 1 percent. Unlike the money growth targets prescribed by monetarists, interest rate targets are easily achieved and easily verified. There are no conceptual ambiguities in measuring bill rates and no conundrums created by deregulation. But as monetarists and virtually all other economists have noted, pegging interest rates can be terribly unstable and inflationary if the peg is badly chosen. Con-

5. See the *Economic Report of the President* (Washington, D.C.: Government Printing Office, 1981), table B-59.

ducting monetary policy by stabilizing the treasury bill rate requires a careful choice of the rule for choosing the target rate. A well-chosen rule will give close to an ideal monetary policy, satisfying all three criteria of stable prices, moderate fluctuations in interest rates, and full financial deregulation. The wrong rule invites a repetition of the experience of the 1940s.

Monetary policy controls the treasury bill rate through open-market operations. Whenever the Fed issues new U.S. dollars and buys treasury bills, the bill rate falls, and vice versa. There is simply no doubt about the Fed's ability to control the bill rate to within a small fraction of a percentage point. This remains true through sharp inflation or deflation, recession or boom, as the experience of the 1940s amply revealed. Unlike the monetarists, who face an uphill battle convincing the Fed that it has the power to control the money supply, and yet other economists who want the Fed to stabilize a measure of total credit or even total dollar output of the entire economy, advocates of interest-based policies are on firm ground in suggesting to the Fed that it do something that comes naturally. Moreover, the Fed will retain the power to set the treasury bill rate through any conceivable deregulation. Its power rests on the unique characteristics of the U.S. dollar and the treasury bill. As long as the Fed is the sole government agency capable of issuing U.S. dollars, it will have complete control over the treasury bill interest rate.

Control over the treasury bill rate confers control over the price level. This proposition is no more than an application of the very general principle of monetary economics, enunciated by Don Patinkin and James Tobin, that the price level can be fixed by controlling the dollar volume of monetary assets and the interest rate paid by those assets.[6] Monetarism applies the principle by asking the Fed to fix the quantity of a narrow concept of monetary assets that pay an interest rate of zero. Though monetarism is a consistent application of the principle, it is not the best.

The best application takes a broad concept of monetary assets — namely, the total short-term debt of the federal government — and fixes its interest rate not far below the earnings of private investments. Further, it deliberately varies the interest rate to offset de-

6. Don Patinkin, "Financial Intermediaries and the Logical Structure of Monetary Theory," *American Economic Review* 51 (March 1961): 95–116; and James Tobin, "A General Equilibrium Approach to Monetary Theory," *Journal of Money, Credit, and Banking* 1 (1969): 15.

partures of the price level from the target level. In the long run, the Fed's choice of interest rate influences the price level inversely: High interest rates mean low prices and vice versa. For the moment, I will assume that the government deficit is held at low levels so that the total dollar volume of government debt grows only as fast as the total real output of the economy. If so, the rate of inflation will always be roughly zero, and the Fed chooses alternative price levels as it chooses alternative levels of the treasury bill rate.

If the Fed chooses a low interest rate — that is, a rate well below the rate paid by private investments — treasury bills will be financially unattractive as a way of holding reserves. Banks and other reserve holders will conserve on treasury bills as a form of reserves, holding relatively few bills per dollar of total assets or per dollar of total income in the economy. To accommodate the low real demand for bills, the real stock of bills will fall. Because the stock of bills is fixed in dollar terms, the fall in the real stock is accomplished by an increase in the price level, that is, a decline in the purchasing power of the stock of bills. In short, low interest rates mean high prices.

On the other hand, if the Fed chooses a high interest rate, close to the earnings of private investments, treasury bills will become an attractive way to hold wealth even apart from the reserve motive. There is no effective upper limit to the demand for bills; if they pay enough, they can compete with any of the several trillion dollars in total U.S. wealth. High demand for bills in real terms is accommodated with a fixed dollar volume of bills by a low price level, which expands the purchasing power of that fixed volume.

In the long run, control over the treasury bill rate gives the Fed control over the price level. Whenever the price level is a little too high, the Fed should raise interest rates, and whenever too low, it should lower them. In the short run, of course, prices do not respond immediately to the interest rate signal sent by the Fed. Instead, the interest rate set by the Fed for treasury bills strongly influences interest rates on all investments in the short run. A violent increase in interest rates wreaks havoc in many parts of the economy, notably in homebuilding, the auto industry, and investment in business plant and equipment. A gentle nudge from a moderate increase in interest rates has the same effect, in moderation. In the short run, a cautious increase in the treasury bill rate will limit demand for goods and services in many parts of the economy, introduce a little more slack, and take pressure off prices. As prices decline, real activity is gradually restored to its earlier level. By this mechanism, the economy will eventually reach the point of long-run equilibrium with a higher treasury bill rate, a lower price level, and full employment.

Now, I can be very specific about how the Fed should proceed. In the middle of every month, the Bureau of Labor Statistics reports the cost-of-living index. The Fed's target is to keep the index at 100. Each month, it should determine the treasury bill rate in the following way: For each percentage point by which prices are above 100, it should raise the bill rate over its level of the last month by a tenth of a percentage point. Similarly, for each percentage point by which the price level is below target, it should lower the bill rate by a tenth of a percentage point. If prices stay persistently above target from month to month (as they generally will after some inflationary impulse), this policy will gradually intensify the anti-inflationary pressure of higher interest rates. Eventually, the pressure will begin to work, prices will subside to 100, and interest rates will stabilize.

Everyone should understand that this policy controls prices in the long run but not precisely in the short run. Because it is cautious in using the influence of interest rates on the price level, it tolerates periods of a year or two when the price level is a few points above or below 100. The Fed is like the captain of a supertanker who makes cautious adjustments to the ship's course, knowing that the important thing is to make port, not to stay exactly on course. Wild swings of the rudder are pointless for a ship with a great deal of momentum and relatively little initial response to the rudder.

The major source of difficulty for monetary policy in the past decade has been inflationary shocks from primary materials—food and energy. In 1974, when the economy was just recovering from the agricultural debacle of 1972–73 and just beginning to absorb the impact of much higher oil prices, the Fed held the line on money growth and tolerated a tremendous increase in interest rates. Real activity collapsed at the end of 1974, and the economy entered its most serious postwar recession. Had an interest-based policy been in effect, the Fed would have reacted to the increase in demand for U.S. dollars in 1974 by accommodation in the first few months. The price level would have reached perhaps 3 to 4 percent above target by late 1974, but without serious recession. At this point, the Fed would have been raising the treasury bill rate by 30 to 40 basis points each month. As the restrictive effects of higher interest rates began to take hold, real activity would have declined gradually and prices would have begun to return to their normal level of 100. Many of the more destructive events of 1974-75, including financial failures and the collapse of the stock market, would probably have been avoided. The period would probably still be remembered as a recession, but not as one so sharp and deep.

One of the many desirable features of the adaptive interest rate policy is its ability to find the appropriate level for interest rates in the long run. We do not know what level of interest rates would stabilize the dollar at its current purchasing power with the current volume of government debt, but we do know that the adaptive policy will find it. The policy is like the thermostat in a house. When the furnace is installed, the builder has only a vague idea how much fuel it will take to keep the house warm. But as long as the thermostat turns the furnace on when the house is a little too cool and off when a little too warm, the house will stay at the right temperature.

The monetarist opponents of adaptive policy take the position that monetary policy ought not to react to what is happening in the economy. By analogy, they would also recommend that home owners preset the amount of fuel burned in their furnaces and so boil on hot days and freeze on cold days. But hundreds of millions of very simple thermostats function perfectly in the U.S. every day, and the same principle could easily be applied to the management of the U.S. economy.

There remain two problems requiring further discussion. First, the total dollar volume of government debt is controlled by the spending and taxing policies of the federal government, not by the Fed. Government deficits bring inflation, in the sense that a higher level of debt brings higher prices unless interest rates are raised. However, monetary policy does not need to build in any special response to federal deficits. As a deficit raises prices slightly, the Fed will automatically respond under the simple adaptive rule to raise the treasury bill rate appropriately. Deficits are no threat to price stability. But the public should be made to understand that deficits bring higher interest rates.

Second, there is a substantial problem of the transition to stable prices. It would be irresponsible to put the adaptive interest policy into effect immediately to try to stabilize prices at today's level. The adaptive policy cannot overcome the substantial momentum of inflation any more than the captain of the supertanker can reduce the huge mass and lack of maneuverability of the ship. Rather, the captain formulates orders with the ship's characteristics in mind. In the same way, good monetary policy recognizes the facts of life. During the transition, we should adopt a target path of prices that phases out inflation at about 1 percent per year. Starting from, say, 8 percent inflation, the Fed should publish a trajectory for prices that does not reach price stability until eight years from the onset of the policy. This will give a monthly target level for prices, and the adjustment of the treasury bill rate should take place in relation to the monthly target.

So far, I have presented the justification for the adaptive interest rate policy on solid economic grounds. The basic principle that higher interest rates bring lower prices is sound monetary economics and is not disputed by any serious economist. The core of the argument in favor of the adaptive policy is this simple principle. But it is worth noting as a subsidiary element of the case that there is now a substantial body of scientific evidence giving another reason for stabilizing interest rates. Long-term asset markets appear to be far more sensitive to short-term interest rates than they should be according to received economic doctrine. The stock market falls much further under tight money and high interest rates than it should if stock prices are really the present discounted value of future corporate earnings.[7] The same thing is true of long-term bond markets.[8] The notion that these markets function according to expectations about the future has been rejected by a number of serious investigators. When President Reagan's economic advisers told him that the sign that his program was working would be high short-term interest rates but low long-term rates and a strong stock market, they were living in a dream world. Tight money regularly devastates the stock and bond markets, and recent experience is no exception. Weak stock and bond markets very seriously undermine incentives to invest and expand business operations. For this reason, the anti-inflationary tool of high interest rates needs to be used with caution.

Is government control over the interest rate on treasury bills truly a free-market policy? It should be clear that any application of the Patinkin-Tobin principle of controlling one nominal magnitude and

---

7. Robert J. Shiller, "Do Stock Prices Move Too Much to be Justified by Subsequent Changes in Dividends?" *American Economic Review* 71 (1981): 421.

8. Kenneth J. Singleton, "Expectations Models of the Term Structure and Implied Variance Bounds," *Journal of Political Economy* 88 (1980): 1159.

one nominal interest rate represents a government intervention. It is a particularly benign intervention compared with the monetarist principle of strict control on the business activities of banks. It is even benign compared with the establishment of a metallic definition of the dollar, because the definition stimulates a reserve demand for a real resource. An interest rate policy with full financial decontrol may not be exactly a free-market policy, but it is closer than any alternative in which the government retains its responsibility for maintaining and stabilizing a common monetary unit.

THE GOLD STANDARD AND ITS RELATIVES

Disappointments with conventional tight money have produced an upsurge of interest in returning to a gold or other commodity definition of the dollar. Here I will appraise commodity-based monetary systems according to the three criteria established earlier: stability of the purchasing power of the dollar, stability of interest rates, and consistency with unregulated financial markets.

Let me start with the indirect gold standard proposed by Arthur Laffer and a number of other so-called supply-side economists.[9] Under their proposal, the government would modify its policy in two ways. First, the U.S. dollar would be backed by a fixed amount of gold, perhaps 0.4 grains per dollar. Second, the government would stand ready to buy and sell gold at a fixed price, say, $1 per grain ($480 per ounce). The combination of the two moves would give the gold market control over the U.S. money supply—precisely what its advocates see as its advantage and its opponents as its danger. Discretion over the quantity of money would be eliminated. Under a threat of inflation and diminished dollar value, the public would trade in some of its dollars for gold and the money supply would shrink. In the short run, rising interest rates would halt the process. In the long run, inflation would ease, and the original threat would disappear.

The first defect of the indirect gold standard is its failure to come to grips with the microeconomic issues of monetary policy. It would retain the inefficient features of the current system, including reserve requirements and prohibition of many forms of competition with

9. Ron Paul and Lewis Lehrman, *The Case for Gold* (Washington, D.C.: Cato Institute, 1982).

banks. Further, as with the current system, every move toward deregulation would increase the price level. Good free-market principles would be unjustly tarnished by their association with inflation. For example, the elimination of reserve requirements would considerably reduce the demand for U.S. dollars. As the stock declined, gold would flow into the market. The purchasing power of gold would decline, and, with a fixed link between the dollar and gold, the purchasing power of the dollar would decline by the same amount. Because the U.S. monetary gold stock would be a substantial fraction of the gold available in the world market, this problem would present a serious restriction on the move to deregulate. Like their monetarist colleagues, advocates of the indirect gold standard would find themselves opposing the application of free-market principles to money markets.

A free-market variant of the gold standard is available; in fact, it is not too different from the system of the nineteenth century. Under this direct gold standard, the dollar would simply be defined as a certain quantity of gold, perhaps one grain. Anyone owed dollars could require payment in grains of gold. The right to be paid in gold would rarely be exercised. Instead, creditors would actually take payment in checks or other convenient forms of payment. The purpose of the gold payment requirement is to guarantee the purchasing power of the dollar in terms of gold. The market value of financial instruments payable in dollars could not drop below one grain of gold to the dollar, or their owners would immediately cash them in for their gold value. A promise to pay dollars is a promise to pay gold or to convey something else of equal purchasing power. Under this system, the purchasing power of the dollar becomes the same thing as the purchasing power of gold.

The other major flaw in the gold standard, direct or indirect, is fatal: The purchasing power of gold is so unstable that linking the dollar to gold would bring far worse instability of prices than anything ever seen in U.S. history.[10] Even the nineteenth-century gold standard brought deflation and then inflation in amounts that cumulated to unpleasant changes in the purchasing power of the dollar. The gold standard dramatically limited inflation relative to experi-

10. See Robert E. Hall, "Explorations in the Gold Standard and Related Policies for Stabilizing the Dollar," in R. Hall, ed., *Inflation* (Chicago: University of Chicago Press, 1983).

ence during the Civil War or during the 1970s, but it did not completely stabilize the price level by any means. Over the period from 1880 to 1910, annual rates of inflation measured over five-year intervals varied from – 1.3 percent per year in 1890–95 to 2.1 percent per year in 1905–10. There was continual, mild inflation around 2 percent per year from 1895 to 1910 because of shifts in the world supply of gold. Though annual rates of inflation never reached troublesome levels, the compounding of inflation year after year meant that the gold standard was quite ineffective in stabilizing the long-run purchasing power of the dollar. Between 1895 and 1912, the cost of living rose 40 percent. Forward economic arrangements made in 1895 were seriously dislocated by the surprising decline in the real value of the dollar over the ensuing two decades.

Recent turbulence in gold markets casts even more serious doubt on the wisdom of a dollar defined in terms of a fixed quantity of gold. Between 1968 and 1970, the purchasing power of an ounce of gold fell by 18 percent. Then its purchasing power rose by 350 percent to a peak in 1974, declined by 32 percent over the next two years, and then rose by 600 percent to another peak in 1980. Had the United States been on the gold standard over this period, there would have been considerable inflationary pressure in 1968–70, 1974–76, and 1981 and crushing deflation in 1970–74 and 1976–80. Because a U.S. gold standard might have stabilized the gold market over this period had we been on the gold standard, it is not accurate to say that the changes in the U.S. price level would have been as large as the actual changes in the purchasing power of gold, but large changes in the price level would certainly have occurred. The fixed gold standard is not the answer for price stability.

Proponents of the indirect gold standard have conceded the instability of the purchasing power of gold and have included vague exceptions to the operating rules so that the dollar price of gold could be raised or the gold backing of the dollar reduced when OPEC or other major influences drive up the world price of gold. But it is not at all clear that they have solved this central problem of the gold standard.

Two remedies are known for the instability of the purchasing power of gold: systematic adjustment of the gold content of the dollar to offset the instabilities and the use of a commodity or basket of commodities with more stable purchasing power than gold. Even better, the two remedies can be combined in an adjustable nongold commodity standard.

Elsewhere, I have described an example of an up-to-date commodity standard.[11] It defines the dollar in terms of a package of four commodities—ammonium nitrate, copper, aluminum, and plywood—whose combined purchasing power has been stable over the past thirty years. These are homogeneous, standardized commodities already traded in organized markets. A unit called the ANCAP would contain fixed physical quantities of the four commodities. Then the dollar would be defined as x ANCAPS; monetary policy would consist in choosing an x that would stabilize the purchasing power of the dollar. If strong demand for one of the commodities in the ANCAP threatened to raise the purchasing power of the ANCAP, monetary policy would reduce the ANCAP content of the dollar to head off the resulting deflation. If ammonium nitrate, copper, aluminum, or plywood became plentiful, inflation in dollar prices would follow unless the ANCAP content of the dollar were raised.

Though it might be satisfactory to tell the monetary authorities that it was their job to adjust the ANCAP definition of the dollar in order to keep the cost-of-living index as close as possible to 100, an alternative is to prescribe the operating policy along the lines suggested by Irving Fisher.[12] Each month, the number of ANCAPs making up a dollar would be raised by 0.1 percent for each percent by which the cost of living exceeds 100 or lowered by 0.1 percent for each percent by which it falls short. Here again, monetary policy is to act as a thermostat, keeping the cost of living at 100 by manipulating a policy instrument—the ANCAP content of the dollar—in the direction indicated by the most recent value of the cost of living.

In one respect, a commodity definition of the dollar is a free-market economist's dream. Monetary policy can be conducted by one person, who receives the cost-of-living index from the Bureau of Labor Statistics and then announces next month's definition of the dollar. All of the existing apparatus of the Federal Reserve could be dismantled. Regulation of financial institutions would be eliminated. Government intervention in money would be at its irreducible minimum.

Though a commodity definition of the dollar has substantial microeconomic advantages over the current system of monetary control, it does have an intrinsic flaw: When the dollar is defined in terms of commodities, people will accumulate stocks of those com-

11. Ibid.
12. Irving Fisher, *Stabilizing the Dollar* (New York: Macmillan, 1920).

modities purely because of their monetary role. The historical operation of gold standards has made this plain. When banks and other institutions are required to redeem their financial instruments in gold on demand, they will hold precautionary balances of gold. From time to time, the public will decide to move into gold and will find it easy to do so by redeeming demand instruments. Two major runs on gold occurred around the turn of the century in the United States. Not only does the possibility of a run make a bank hold substantial amounts of gold, but a run creates political pressure to suspend the gold definition of the dollar in the short run (which happened in both episodes) and to abandon the gold standard in the long run. Even when a commodity standard is functioning smoothly, the stocks of commodities held for monetary reasons are economically inefficient. These stocks tie up real resources in a function that could be served equally well by paper reserves.

According to microeconomic logic, each function in the economy ought to be provided in the least expensive way. But given political reality, politicians feel the need to do something whenever an economic crisis occurs, and the obvious solution to a run on commodity reserves is to suspend or repeal the commodity payment requirement. These two influences converge to make a commodity standard difficult to sustain. It would be far better, then, to start with a well-run fiduciary monetary system, where these problems cannot arise.

CONCLUDING REMARKS

The two major intellectual forces in the design of monetary policy—monetarism and the indirect gold standard—are on a collision course with basic microeconomic principles. Both rely on deep government intervention in financial markets in order to create a well-defined stock of money, which is then made to grow smoothly or is regulated by its relation to the gold stock. Though a free-market version of the gold standard could be created, it—along with any commodity standard—creates an inefficient demand for monetary reserves held in the form of commodities.

There is no free-market version of monetarism. Not only does monetarism rest fundamentally on government regulation of money and money substitutes, but monetarist policy in practice creates periodic crises of high interest rates followed by recession. Because the stock market and long-term debt markets weaken dramatically during these crises, incentives for creating and expanding businesses are seriously eroded. Monetarist attempts to erase inflation over too brief a period threaten to undermine the significant progress made recently in restoring incentives through tax reform.

The best hope for the consistent application of free-market principles is the creation of a sound U.S. dollar through manipulation of the interest rates on short-term government debt. Higher interest rates inevitably bring lower prices. We can keep the price level at 100 simply by raising interest rates gently whenever prices are above 100 and lowering them when prices are below 100. No inefficient regulation of banks or their nonbank competitors is needed to give the Federal Reserve the power to set the interest rate on treasury bills. All it has to do is buy and sell bills in the open market. Stabilizing interest rates rather than monetary aggregates avoids interest-rate crises and their attendant destructive effects on the real economy. By the three criteria set forth at the outset of this paper—stable prices, stable interest rates, and complete financial deregulation—the adaptive interest rate policy best meets our needs for monetary policy.

Chapter 13

THE FUTURE MONETARY UNIT OF VALUE

Friedrich A. Hayek

Very few people will remember, or will have noticed, a footnote that appeared in *The Constitution of Liberty*, which I wrote twenty-one years ago. At that time, I said:

> Though I am convinced that modern credit banking as it has developed requires some public institutions such as central banks, I am doubtful whether it is necessary or desirable that they (or the government) should have a monopoly of the issue of any kind of money. The state has, of course, the right to protect the name of the unit of money which it (or anybody else) issues, and if it issues "dollars," to prevent anybody else from issuing tokens with the same name. As it is its task to enforce contracts, it must also be able to determine what is "legal tender" for the discharge of any obligations contracted. But there seems to be no reason at all why the state should ever prohibit the use of other kinds of media of exchange, be it some commodity or money issued by another agency, domestic or foreign. One of the most effective measures for protecting the freedom of the individual might indeed be to have constitutions prohibiting all peacetime restrictions on transactions in any kind of money or precious metals.[1]

This idea seemed to have been developing quietly in my mind, and sixteen years later, in growing despair about the continuing deterioration of the monetary situation, I threw out, almost as a bitter joke, the suggestion that, as things were developing, our only hope of ever

1. F. A. Hayek, *The Constitution of Liberty* (Chicago: University of Chicago Press, 1960), pp. 520–21.

again having good money probably required that we take from government the monopoly of issuing money and hand this task over to private enterprise. Once seriously examined, this proved to be a more and more attractive idea and it finally appeared to me as the only definite solution to the increasingly hopeless position we were encountering with monetary conditions everywhere. I then systematically expounded the concept in *The Denationalization of Money*, a second, expanded version of which was published in 1978.[2]

My proposal would entitle private concerns to define and create new monetary units of their own choosing and to issue liabilities denominated in these units. The public would be allowed to hold such moneys in whatever amounts they chose and to make contracts for payment in terms of whatever moneys they chose. I now intend to consider how such a system could be brought about.

DESIGNING A NEW MONETARY ORDER

In endeavoring to design a better monetary order, we at once encounter the difficulty of not really knowing what we want. What would be a really good money? Not the least harm the immemorial and nearly universal government monopoly of the issue of money has done is to deprive us of the chance to find out experimentally what kind of money would really serve us best. To the present day, money is that part of the market order that government has most suppressed. It is also the part of the market order that silly rulers and economists have most tinkered with. Yet neither economists nor politicians invented the market, though some have come to understand it a little, and it will not be present knowledge but discoveries by free experimentation that can show us the best solutions. Those who needed money chiefly as an indispensable tool of trade, and who first discovered it as a means for making most trade possible, were soon forced to use what government gave them. And government jealously guarded its monopoly, for purposes quite different from those for which money had been introduced.

Since ancient times, governments have claimed an exclusive right over coinage. The very word "seigniorage," used to denote the fee

2. F. A. Hayek, *The Denationalisation of Money*, 2d ed. (London: Institute of Economic Affairs, 1978).

governments have charged for minting coin, signifies that coinage was considered an exclusive right of the sovereign. And even in England it was an open question whether the monarch had a legal right openly to debase the coinage in order to raise revenue.[3]

Today money is chiefly not an effective medium of exchange but a tool of government for fleecing us and for "managing" the economy. As a result, we are obliged to admit that we have little empirical evidence of how the various conceivable methods of supplying money would operate and almost none about what kind of money the public would select if it had an opportunity to choose freely between several different and clearly distinguishable kinds of money. For this we must rely largely on our theoretical imagination and try to apply to a special problem that understanding of the functioning of competition that we have gained in other fields.

In justification of its monopoly, government could, of course, argue that a single uniform kind of money used in all transactions constitutes such an advantage that it is worth sacrificing potential improvements. A single unit of account in which all prices are quoted and in which all units of currency and all financial assets are denominated is undoubtedly a great advantage. Yet it is questionable whether this excuse can still be accepted once we recognize how much avoidable harm is done by the kind of money we now have. And certainly a major reason for not having better money is that there has not been enough experimentation to lead to agreement about what kind would be desirable. Selective evolution was cut off by authority before we had a chance to explore adequately the different possible solutions of the problem. That, surely, was too high a price to pay for what may have been a temporary convenience.

The basic contention on which the validity of my further argument rests is that if people were wholly free to choose which moneys they wished to use in their daily transactions, those would do best who preferred a money with a stable purchasing power. Such a money would, therefore, be most likely to emerge from monetary experimentation and evolution. Sixty years ago I began my work on monetary theory by questioning the belief, then universally accepted, that the purchasing power of money should be kept stable. I then suggested that it was more desirable for the purchasing power of

3. F. W. Maitland, *The Constitutional History of England* (Cambridge: Cambridge University Press, 1908), p. 260.

money over consumer goods to increase over time.[4] But I have since become convinced that a money of stable value is really the best we can hope for. If the value of money were stable, then the price of any commodity about which we have no special information would be as likely to rise as to fall; on balance the unforeseen price changes would just offset each other. If the level of average prices were stable, then a rise (or fall) of the money price of any commodity would also indicate a rise (or fall) in price relative to most other commodities. A rise in price could not occur, as it often does today, if the commodity had actually become relatively cheaper than most other goods whose prices had increased more. This advantage of a stable money over all unstable ones would be particularly significant for the calculations of enterprise but hardly less so for the holders of employment contracts and for savers. A stable measure of value would eliminate much of the uncertainty that everyone holding a contract stipulating future payments is now compelled to bear. And the important consequences of an availability of different currencies would be not only that people would prefer to make contracts in terms of a currency they could trust, but even more that, though they might be ready to accept any currency for payment for their goods, they would not wish to hold, and indeed would rapidly exchange, any currency they did not trust into one they did. This would very quickly either wholly drive out any currency whose issuers did not keep its purchasing power constant, or at least force its issuers at once to alter their policy as soon as even a slight discount of their currency's value showed itself in the market.

This may at first appear to be in conflict with the so-called Law of Gresham, which says that "bad money drives out the good" (a concept known to the ancient Greeks more than two thousand years ago). But it is a misunderstanding of Gresham's Law to believe that the tendency for bad money to drive out good money makes a government monopoly necessary, even though the distinguished economist W. S. Jevons stated the law in the form that better money cannot drive out worse precisely to prove this. What Jevons and so many others seem to have overlooked is that Gresham's Law applies only to different kinds of money between which a fixed exchange rate is enforced by law. If the law makes two kinds of money perfect sub-

---

4. F. A. Hayek, *Monetary Theory and the Trade Cycle* (London: Jonathan Cape, 1933), pp. 114ff.

stitutes for the payment of debts, and forces creditors to accept a coin of a smaller content of gold in the place of one with a larger content, debtors will, of course, pay only in the former and find a more profitable use for the substance of the latter. With variable exchange rates, however, the inferior quality money would be valued at a lower rate, and people would try to get rid of it as quickly as possible, particularly if it threatened to fall further in value. The selection process would go on toward whatever they regarded as the best sort of money among those issued by the various agencies, and it would rapidly drive out money found inconvenient or worthless.

Indeed, whenever inflation has become really rapid, all sorts of objects of a more stable value, from potatoes to cigarettes and bottles of brandy to eggs and foreign currencies like dollar bills, have come to be increasingly used as money; so that at the end of the great German inflation, some contended that Gresham's Law was false and the opposite true. It is not false, but it applies only if a fixed rate of exchange between different forms of money is enforced.[5]

I have not space here to consider the reasons why, almost since coins were first introduced more than two and a half thousand years ago, governments have invariably abused their monopoly shamelessly,[6] to the grave damage of people at large. Nor have I space to explain in detail why the international gold standard, which for a short period in the past provided us with better money than we ever had before or have had since, can in fact not be restored in an effective form.[7] Thus, completely depriving governments of their power over money has by now probably become easier than attempting to prevent them from abusing that power.

If governments were deprived of their power over money, private firms would quickly begin to define new monetary units and to issue liabilities denominated in terms of these units. Competition among issuers would compel them to seek to define their units in ways most useful to the public and to make them available to the public at the most attractive feasible terms.

---

5. Hayek, *Denationalisation of Money.*

6. With the exception only of the short periods during which they divested themselves of discretion by making a fixed quantity of one of the precious metals the legal unit.

7. To restore the gold standard would, in brief, require a return to beliefs that have been destroyed, and to do so would probably cause such fluctuations in the value of gold that the standard would break down before long.

DEVELOPING AN INTERNATIONAL
MONETARY UNIT

A primary objective of any monetary system must be to keep the world economy functioning efficiently. Since to do so we clearly need some international standard, and since we can obtain current information about the international price system only from the wholesale prices of the more widely traded standardized raw materials, the closest approach to a general stability of the purchasing power of a monetary unit would probably be the stabilization of an index number of the prices of these raw materials. Competing issuers would no doubt offer a number of competing monetary units, defined in terms of alternative collections of commodities, whose values they would pledge to stabilize. The public would thus have the opportunity to select the most useful monetary standard as well as the most efficient and reliable issuers of money. The issuer of a new monetary unit could make the money unit redeemable in such amounts of other currencies as would be required at any time to buy the whole collection of different raw materials defining the standard unit. Such a commitment would effectively stabilize the value of the issuer's money unit in terms of the particular collection of raw materials defining the standard unit. Any difference in value between the monetary unit and the standard unit would create opportunities of arbitrage that would at once restore equality between their values.

Of course, neither the composition nor the weights attached to each of the different commodities could be kept constant indefinitely. The issuer would have to have the option of changing the list of different commodities and the weights attached to each as their importance in trade changed. The issuer would have to assure the holders of the units—in order to protect them against concealed changes in value—that at the moment of any change, the aggregate value of the new basket of commodities, at current market prices, would be the same as that of the old basket (and, probably, that for a limited period, holders of the units would have the choice of demanding redemption in terms of the new basket or the old).

Any such new international unit provided by a particular issuer would, of course, have to have a distinct name, and for the purposes of this discussion I will call it a "Solid." The success of such an experiment might well depend on the persuasiveness and suitability of the name chosen. I must confess that I have thought of a much more attractive name, indeed one that would probably be worth millions. But since I have had legal advice that a protective trademark (or copyright protection) can be obtained under current law only by persons or firms actively dealing in the article in question, I have no choice but to keep it secret for the time being. So, as second best, I will use the name "Solid" in describing my scheme for a privately issued monetary unit that, I believe, might (in spite of the inevitable resistance of government) well be introduced—though at first not as circulating tokens but as transferable deposits redeemable in the current kind of hand-to-hand money or tokens that for the time being governments will probably not allow private agencies to issue.

Though the different credit units of this kind would of course all have to bear different names and might at first represent different collections of commodities, after a period of competitive experimentation, most or all that survived would probably keep constant value relations to each other, even if the units were of different magnitude. Once the advantages of such units with stable buying power were generally recognized, and once some suppliers had demonstrated their ability to maintain the value of their units and had thus established a flourishing business depending wholly on maintaining this trust, such a system would be preserved because any supplier of such stable credits who failed to maintain their value would be rapidly driven out by a mass flight from the unstable money.

OFFERING CREDIT ACCOUNTS IN A STABLE UNIT

I had originally visualized that, from the beginning, the suppliers of private moneys would provide them not only in the form of book credits but also in the form of corresponding notes or tokens for fractional values. But although years of further reflection on the problem have only confirmed my belief that this ought to be the final solution of our money problems—and is the only way we will ever again get back to honest money while at the same time ridding ourselves of the evils of crisis, depressions, unemployment, and general disorganization of the market—I cannot close my eyes to the fact that any hope for a voluntary abdication by governments of their present monopolies of the issues of circulating currency is utopian. Governments have become dependent on their power to create money for financing their own activities, since it allows them to spend in excess of the revenue they can obtain from honest taxation. They also regard their control over money as so essential a weapon of their economic policy that they will probably defend to the last not merely all the explicit powers the law has conferred upon them, but also any others they can obtain. Though it may be doubtful whether many governments actually possess a constitutional right to prohibit the private issue of an alternative circulating money, there can be little doubt that they could, through the manipulation of such rules as those of legal tender, prevent any attempt in this direction from being successful.

But under present conditions, this applies only to currency or hand-to-hand money, that is, to pieces of paper or tokens passing physically from person to person as a general medium of exchange. We are still used to regarding this as the basic money, through which most of today's trade—dependent on expression as a multiple of some such units of hand-to-hand money—is transacted. This is, however, a misleading impression. The exclusive right to issue the tokens that serve as legal tender for the discharge of obligations contracted in terms of them does not preclude the use of credit accounts in other units as a general means of exchange. Transactions could easily take place by the transfer of funds from the account of one individual to the account of another just as they occur today in the vast number of cases. The difference would be that the accounts would be denominated in terms of monetary units over which governments had no control and which, therefore, would be likely to maintain a constant value. At least where no foreign exchange restrictions are in force—and even these presumably restrict only transactions in specified amounts of named national currencies—general laws do not seem to prohibit the keeping of accounts entitling creditors to receive on demand such amounts of other moneys as at the time would enable them to buy at current market rates a corresponding part (or multiple) of the basket of raw materials defining the unit in which the account is kept.

I am now coming to the crucial problem: Would it be possible and profitable for a banking institution to offer such accounts, denominated in Solids, Ducats, Stables, or whatever the name might be, which it would undertake to redeem on demand with such amounts of the various other currencies as would be required to buy on the established commodity exchanges the stated collection of the various raw materials whose aggregate value defined the unit in question? The difficulties of the task derive from the circumstance that in order to maintain any particular value of the unit, the bank must stand ready to buy or sell at the stated rates *any* amount of such units that might be offered to or demanded from it.

The only control the bank could exercise would be through lending and borrowing (i.e., creating and extinguishing such deposits) at different terms, that is, by altering the rates of interest it charged its borrowers or paid its depositors or by altering the service fee it charged for running these accounts. Providers of such accounts would, of course, have to be constantly aware that they had no control over the total amount of such liquid assets available to the members of the community or to the inhabitants of any clearly delimitable region. The total amount of such assets available to the public would depend on the ability of competing financial institutions to provide such assets in the amounts demanded by the public. The aim of any single institution would be to offer, in competition with other institutions, a clearly distinguishable asset desired by the public as a liquid reserve because it was trusted to preserve its value. This assurance could be offered only by standing ready, at all times, to redeem these deposits by the "cash" actually needed to buy the designated collection of raw materials. Yet, if a number of separate institutions succeeded in supplying their clientele with differently named but equivalent amounts of fully liquid units of media of exchange at market prices, then in terms of any one of these units, the general price level of commodities would remain stable.

Could any individual bank control the volume of its on-demand commitments so that it would at all times be able to deliver instantly the amounts of other currencies sufficient to buy at market prices the stated collection of commodities? The chief difficulty would arise from the fact that if it were to prevent the value of its unit from rising *above* the announced level, it would have to be prepared to accept any amount on deposit that might be offered to it at the announced terms. In other words, the public might well find the new unit so attractive that—unless its supply could be rapidly expanded to meet the public's demand to hold the unit—its value might appreciate above the value of the standard unit in terms of which it was defined. Such a premium would reflect the public's confidence that the purchasing power of the new unit was more likely to be maintained than the purchasing power of other currencies. To control the volume of its on-demand commitments in order to ensure a stable value for its unit, the individual bank would have to be prepared to accept any amount on deposit that was offered to it at the announced terms—that is, at the buying and selling prices of its own unit in terms of other currencies and the interest it paid or the service charge it imposed for maintaining such deposits. Accepting any amount on deposit that was offered might at times create the difficult problem of finding sufficient opportunities for investing these amounts in assets that were themselves likely to preserve their value. For controlling such fluctuations in the demand for its deposits, the bank would in effect have only two instruments. First, it could vary the difference between the buying and selling prices of its own unit in terms of other kinds of money. For example, if it took $2 to buy the standard unit that defined one Solid, and the bank maintained the same buying and selling prices of Solids in terms of dollars, the bank would create Solid accounts at the rate of 0.5 Solids for every dollar deposited and would pay out dollars from such accounts at the rate of 0.5 Solids per dollar as long as the purchasing power of the dollar in terms of the standard unit did not change. But if the bank found that the demand for Solid accounts was greater than it could supply, it could reduce the demand for Solid accounts to its capacity of providing them by raising the selling price of Solids; for example, while creating Solid accounts at the rate of 0.5 Solids per dollar, the bank would only convert the Solids back into dollars at the rate of 0.55 Solids to the dollar. The second instrument the bank could use would simply be to reduce the interest it paid on deposits or to increase the service charge it imposed for maintaining them.

It is clear that banks will have much to learn before they can be certain that they know how to deal successfully with these tasks. To be able to provide millions with their liquidity reserves, and to earn the interest they would have to earn in order to pay interest on the funds thus deposited with them, could well prove the greatest banking success ever for those who first solve these problems. I would gladly wish the highest gains to those who succeed in conferring on the world the inestimable benefit of at last providing a medium of exchange through which markets could function as well as they should be able to function. And if such a stable money were established—though it would exist under many different denominations and trademarks, with each kind issued under the name of, and with the responsibility assumed by, a different institution—the successful suppliers could probably not for any length of time be denied the right to issue corresponding tokens representing fractional units. At least locally, because of their fixed relation to the basic credit unit, such fractional units would soon displace the traditional "official" cash. And before long, governments would probably learn to insist that their taxes be paid in the new stable units—an event that would constitute the final victory of the system.

The second point is that, once credit accounts in a stable unit are provided by some institutions, governments could hardly prevent the development of *credit cards* that, with the consent of both parties, instantly converted the amount due in a local currency into its equivalent, at the current rate, of a stable unit. Debtor and creditor would know that a certain amount of purchasing power would be due by or to them within a fixed period. Although governments would probably long resist the use within their territory of any hand-to-hand money other than their own, they could hardly long prevent such a use of credit cards. I have little doubt that as soon as such stable private units were available, the issuers of credit cards would be well advised to use them. Indeed, I believe that it will be through the credit card rather than through any kind of circulating token money that the government monopoly of the issue of money will ultimately be broken. It is a money governments cannot confiscate when it is carried across frontiers and scarcely even when claims in terms of it are held by the recipient. The permissibility of the use of such credit cards for payments in terms of a stable unit would probably soon become the passport for access of a country not only to international tourism but also to international trade. Few countries would long wish to exclude their citizens from the profitable business of offering credits in stable units.

It is a different question whether it would be advisable for the issuers of credit cards themselves to enter into the business of offering such stable credit accounts. This might make it more difficult, if not even impossible, for them to control the total volume of such deposits effectively enough to secure the constant value of their units. This question will have to be carefully studied by people who understand the mechanism of the credit card business better than I do.

ASSURING STABILITY OVER TIME

Of the many other consequences, some of which I deal with more fully elsewhere, I will here consider at greater length one that I had initially not even perceived but that now appears to be the most important. It seems to me that the emergence of a new stable international unit of value not dependent on the arbitrary will of anybody would have hidden far-reaching effects. If throughout the world there were a large number of nominally different monetary units, all maintaining themselves in circulation only so long as they preserved the same value as most others, the collapse of any one of them as a result of malfeasance or mistaken policies would not do as much harm as the collapse of any currency does today. The holders of balances of a currency that lost part or all of its value would, of course, lose all that, just as they do today. But the greatest losses caused today by the devaluation of a currency are not those to the individuals actually holding amounts of that money but to those who have contractual claims expressed in terms of it. As I have explained:

> With the availability of at least some stable currencies, the present absurd practice of making 'legal tender' a mere token which may become valueless but still remain effective for the discharge of debts contracted in what has been an object of a certain value, is bound to disappear. It was solely the power of governments to force upon people what they had not meant in their contracts that had produced this absurdity. With the abolition of the government monopoly of issuing money, the courts would soon learn to understand, and I trust also statute law soon provide, that justice requires all debts to be paid in terms of units of value which the contracting parties intended, and not in what government decrees made a substitute for them. After the development of a widely accepted common standard of values, the courts would have in most cases no difficulty in determining the approximate magnitude of the abstract value intended by the parties to a contract by the value of such and such an amount of a widely accepted currency. If a currency in terms of which a contract had been made depreciated seriously beyond a reasonable range, a court would not allow the parties to gain or lose from the malpractice of a third party that issued the currency. They would be able without difficulty to determine the amount of some other currency in which the debtor was entitled and obliged to discharge his obligation.

> As a result, even the complete collapse of one currency would not have the disastrous consequences which a similar event has today. Though the holders of cash of a particular currency either in the form of notes or of demand

deposits might lose the whole value, this would be a relatively minor disturbance compared with the general shrinkage or wiping out of all claims to third persons expressed in that currency. The whole structure of long-term contracts would remain unaffected, and people would preserve their investments in bonds, mortgages and similar forms of claims, even though they might lose all their cash if they were unfortunate enough to have used the currency of the institution that failed. There could never occur such a complete disappearance of any common standard of debts, or such wiping out of all monetary obligations, as has been the final effect of all major inflations in the past. Long before this could happen, everybody would have deserted the depreciating unit, and no old obligation could be discharged in it.[8]

Above all, however, such a semiautomatic regulation of the supplies of the main kinds of money, assuring the stability of their purchasing power, would eliminate the causes of the alternation of inflationary booms and periods of depression and unemployment that have plagued societies ever since deliberate attempts at a central control of the quantity of money were made.

To sum up, the money we now have is not a fully fledged product of the process of cultural evolution, but a kind of deformed child that has suffered from being forced to pass through unduly restricted channels and has thus been kept from realizing its potential. It has been made to serve purposes to which it is not adapted. People will still have to discover that money is neither a suitable tool of economic policy nor an instrument that government can honestly use to secure greater means than the people are prepared to grant it. Money is an imperfect link in the self-steering mechanism of the market. We must learn how to make that link more effective.

8. Hayek, *Denationalisation of Money*, pp. 124–25.

SELECTED BIBLIOGRAPHY

Anderson, Benjamin. *Economics and the Public Welfare: Financial and Economic History of the United States, 1914-1946.* New York: Van Nostrand, 1949.

_____. *The Great Depression.* New York: Macmillan, 1934.

_____. *The Value of Money.* New York: Macmillan, 1926.

Baxter, W.T. "The Accountant's Contribution to the Trade Cycle." *Economica* (May 1955): 99-112.

Bresciani-Turroni, Costantino. *The Economics of Inflation: A Study of Currency Depreciation in Post-War Germany.* New York: Kelley, 1976.

Brough, William. *Open Mints and Free Banking.* New York: Putnam, 1894.

Brunner, Karl, ed. *The Great Depression Revisited.* Boston: Matinus Nijhoff, 1981.

Buchanan, James M., Richard E. Wagner, and John Burton. *The Consequences of Mr. Keynes.* London: Institute of Economic Affairs, 1978.

Cairnes, John E. *Essays on Political Economy: Theoretical and Applied.* 1873. Reprint. New York: Augustus M. Kelley, 1965.

Cantillon, Richard. *Essai sur la nature du commerce en general.* Edited by Henry Higgs, 1931. 1755. Reprint. New York: Kelley, 1964.

Carroll, Charles H. *The Organization of Debt into Currency, and Other Essays.* Princeton, N.J.: Van Nostrand, 1962.

Commission on the Role of Gold in the Domestic and International Monetary Systems. *Report to Congress.* 2 vols. 1982.

De Roover, Raymond. *Business, Banking, and Economic Thought in Late Medieval and Early Modern Europe.* Chicago: University of Chicago Press, 1974.

Dewey, Davis R. *Financial History of the United States.* New York: Kelley, 1969.

Dorn, James A., ed. "The Search for Stable Money." *Cato Journal* 3 (Spring 1981).

Farrer, Thomas H. *Studies in Currency, 1898.* New York: Kelley, 1968.

Federal Reserve Bank of Boston. *After the Phillips Curve: Persistence of High Inflation and High Unemployment.* Proceedings of a conference held at Edgartown, Massachusetts, June 1978. Boston: Federal Reserve Bank of Boston.

Federal Reserve Bank of St. Louis and Center for the Study of American Business. *Stabilization Policies: Lessons from the 1970s and Implications for the 1980s.* St. Louis: Center for the Study of American Business, Washington University, April 1980.

Fetter, Frank A. "Some Neglected Aspects of Gresham's Law." *Quarterly Journal of Economics* 46 (1931-32): 480-95.

Fisher, Irving. *The Purchasing Power of Money.* New York: Kelley, 1963.

Friedman, Milton. "A Monetary and Fiscal Framework for Economic Stability." *American Economic Review* 38 (June 1948).

_____. *Essays in Positive Economics.* Chicago: University of Chicago Press, 1953.

_____. *The Optimum Quantity of Money and Other Essays.* Chicago: Aldine, 1969.

_____, and Anna J. Schwartz. *A Monetary History of the United States, 1867-1960.* Princeton: Princeton University Press, 1963.

Gouge, William M. *A Short History of Paper Money and Banking in the United States.* New York: Kelley, 1968.

Groseclose, Elgin. *Fifty Years of Managed Money: The Story of the Federal Reserve.* New York: Books, Inc., 1966.

_____. *Money and Man: A Survey of Monetary Experience.* Norman: University of Oklahoma Press, 1976.

Guttman, Nathan, and Patricia Meehan. *The Great Inflation: Germany, 1919-1923.* New York: Saxon House, 1975.

Haberler, Gottfried. *Prosperity and Depression: A Theoretical Analysis of Cyclical Movements.* 4th ed., pp. 5-84. Cambridge, Mass.: Harvard University Press, 1958.

_____; F.A. Hayek; M.N. Rothbard; and L. von Mises. *Austrian Theory of the Trade Cycle, and Other Essays.* Washington, D.C.: Ludwig von Mises Institute for Austrian Economics, 1983.

Hawtrey, Ralph G. *The Art of Central Banking.* Clifton, N.J.: Kelley, 1965.

_____. *A Century of Bank Rate.* Clifton, N.J.: Kelley, 1965.

Hayek, Friedrich A. "Capital and Industrial Fluctuations." *Economica* 4 (1934).

_____. *Choice in Currency: A Way to Stop Inflation.* London: Institute of Economic Affairs, 1977.

_____. *The Constitution of Liberty.* Chicago: University of Chicago Press, 1960.

_____. *The Denationalisation of Money.* London: Institute of Economic Affairs, 1976.

_____. *Monetary Nationalism and International Stability.* New York: Kelley, 1971.

_____. *Monetary Theory and the Trade Cycle.* New York: Kelley, 1975.

_____. *New Studies in Philosophy, Politics, Economics, and the History of Ideas.* Chicago: University of Chicago Press, 1978, pp. 165-78, 191-231.

_____. *Prices and Production.* 1935. Reprint. New York: Kelley, 1967.

_____. *Profits, Interest and Investment, and Other Essays on the Theory of Industrial Fluctuations.* New York: Kelley, 1975.

_____. *The Pure Theory of Capital.* 1941. Reprint. Chicago: Midway Reprint, University Press, 1975.

_____. "Three Elucidations of the Ricardo Effect." *Journal of Political Economy* 77 (March/April 1977).

_____. *A Tiger by the Tail: The Keynesian Legacy of Inflation.* San Francisco: Cato Institute, 1979.

_____. *Unemployment and Monetary Policy.* Cato Paper No. 3. San Francisco: Cato Institute, 1979.

Hazlitt, Henry. *The Failure of the "New Economics."* New Rochelle, N.Y.: Arlington House, 1959.

_____. *What You Should Know About Inflation.* New York: Funk & Wagnalls, 1968.

_____, ed. *The Critics of Keynesian Economics.* New Rochelle, N.Y.: Arlington House, 1977.

Hutt, William H. *The Theory of Idle Resources.* Indianapolis: Liberty Press, 1977.

Jevons, William S. *Money and the Mechanism of Exchange.* London: Kegan Paul, 1905.

Kirzner, Israel M. *The Economic Point of View: An Essay in the History of Economic Thought,* Kansas City: Sheed & Ward, 1976, pp. 91-107.

_____. *Perception, Opportunity, and Profit.* Chicago: University of Chicago Press, 1979.

Lachman, Ludwig M. *Macroeconomic Thinking and the Market Economy.* Menlo Park, Calif.: Institute for Humane Studies, 1978.

_____. "A Reconsideration of the Austrian Theory of Industrial Fluctuations." *Economica* 7 (May 1940).

Law, John. *Money and Trade Considered.* Clifton, N.J.: Kelley, 1966.

Lindahl, Erik R. *Studies in the Theory of Money and Capital.* New York: Kelley, 1970.

Lombra, Raymond E. "Policy Advice and Policy Making: Economic, Political, and Social Issues." In Michael P. Dooley et al., eds., *The Political Economy of Policy Making.* Beverly Hills and London: Sage Publications, 1979.

Lombra, Raymond, and Michael Moran. "Policy Advice and Policy Making at the Federal Reserve." *Carnegie-Rochester Conference Series* 13 (Autumn 1980).

Lucas, Robert. *Studies in Business-Cycle Theory.* Cambridge, Mass.: MIT Press, 1980.

Machlup, Fritz. *The Stock Market, Credit and Capital Formation.* New York: Macmillan, 1940.

MacManus, T.; R. Nelson; and C. Phillips. *Banking and the Business Cycle.* New York: Macmillan, 1937.

Maisel, Sherman J. *Managing the Dollar.* New York: Norton, 1973.

McGrane, Reginald C. *Foreign Bondholders and American State Debts.* New York: Macmillan, 1935.

Miller, Harry E. *Banking Theories in the United States Before 1860.* New York: Kelley, 1972.

Mises, Ludwig von. *Human Action: A Treatise on Economics.* Chicago: Regnery, 1966, pp. 398-478, 538-86, 780-803.

_____. *On the Manipulation of Money and Credit.* Dobbs Ferry, N.Y.: Free Market Books, 1978.

_____. *Planning for Freedom and Other Essays and Addresses.* South Holland, Ill.: Libertarian Press, 1962.

_____. *Socialism: An Economic and Sociological Analysis.* Translated by J. Kahane. New Haven, Conn.: Yale University Press, 1951. This edition is translated from the second German edition (1932) of Mises's *Die Gemeinwirtschaft* (1922).

_____. *The Theory of Money and Credit.* Irvington-on-Hudson, N.Y.: Foundation for Economic Education, 1971.

Niehans, Jurg. *The Theory of Money.* Baltimore: Johns Hopkins University Press, 1978.

O'Driscoll, Gerald P., Jr. *Economics as a Coordination Problem: The Contributions of Friedrich A. Hayek.* Kansas City: Sheed Andrews & McMeel, 1977.

_____, and Sudha R. Shenoy. "Inflation, Recession, and Stagflation." In *The Foundations of Modern Austrian Economics*, edited by Edwin G. Dolan, pp. 185-211. Kansas City: Sheed & Ward, 1976.

Palyi, Melchior. *The Inflation Primer.* Chicago: Regnery, 1972.

_____. *The Twilight of Gold, 1914-1936: Myths and Realities.* Chicago: Regnery, 1972.

Patinkin, Don. *Studies in Monetary Economics.* New York: Harper & Row, 1972.

Raguet, Condy. *A Treatise on Currency and Banking.* New York: Kelley, 1967.

Rickenbacker, William F. *Death of the Dollar.* New York: Dell, 1970.

Ringer, Fritz. *The German Inflation of 1923.* New York: Oxford University Press, 1969.

Rist, Charles. *The Triumph of Gold.* Westport, Conn.: Greenwood, 1961.

_____ . *History of Monetary and Credit Theory.* New York: Kelley, 1966.

Robbins, Lionel. *The Great Depression.* Plainview, N.Y.: Books for Libraries, 1934.

Rothbard, Murray N. *America's Great Depression.* Kansas City: Sheed & Ward, 1975.

_____ . "Austrian Definitions of the Supply of Money." In Louis M. Spadaro, ed., *New Directions in Austrian Economics*, pp. 143–56. Kansas City: Sheed Andrews & McMeel, 1978.

_____ . "The Austrian Theory of Money." In Edwin G. Dolan, ed., *The Foundations of Modern Austrian Economics*, pp. 160–84. Kansas City: Sheed & Ward, 1976.

_____ . *The Case for a 100% Gold Dollar.* Alexandria, Va.: Libertarian Review Press, 1974.

_____ . *Man, Economy, and State: A Treatise on Economic Principles.* Los Angeles: Nash, 1970, pp. 160–271, 661–759.

_____ . *The Panic of 1819: Reaction and Policies.* New York: Columbia University Press, 1962.

_____ . *What Has Government Done to Our Money?* Novato, Calif.: Libertarian Publishers, 1978.

Rueff, Jacques. *The Age of Inflation.* Chicago: Regnery, 1964.

_____ . *Monetary Sin of the West.* New York: Macmillan, 1972.

Select Committee on the High Price of Gold, House of Commons. *The Paper Pound of 1797–1921* ed. Edwin Cannan, 1979. New York: Kelley, 1969.

Sennholz, Hans, ed. *Gold Is Money.* Westport, Conn.: Greenwood, 1975.

Simmons, Henry C. "Rules versus Authorities in Monetary Policy." *Journal of Political Economy* 44 (February 1936).

Smith, Vera C. *The Rationale of Central Banking.* London: King, 1936.

Stein, Herbert. *The Fiscal Revolution in America.* Chicago: University of Chicago Press, 1969.

Thornton, Henry. *An Inquiry into the Nature and Effects of the Paper Credit of Great Britain.* New York: Kelley, 1965.

Wainhouse, Charles Edward. "Hayek's Theory of the Trade Cycle: The Evidence from the Time Series." Ph.D. dissertation, New York University, 1982.

Walker, Amasa. *The Science of Wealth.* Boston: Little, Brown, 1867.

Warburton, Clark. *Depression, Inflation, and Monetary Policy: Selected Papers, 1945–1953.* Baltimore: Johns Hopkins University Press, 1966.

White, Lawrence. *Free Banking in Britain.* Cambridge: Cambridge University Press, 1983.

Wicker, Elmus R. *Federal Reserve Monetary Policy, 1917–1933.* New York: Random House, 1966.

Wicksell, G. Knut. *Interest and Prices: A Study of the Causes Regulating the Value of Money.* Clifton, N.J.: Kelley, 1965.

_____. *Lectures on Political Economy.* Vol. 2. Clifton, N.J.: Kelley, 1968.

Wiegand, G. Carl, ed. *The Menace of Inflation: Its Causes and Consequences.* Old Greenwich, Conn.: Devin-Adair, 1976.

Yeager, Leland B. "Essential Properties of the Medium of Exchange." *Kyklos*, 1968.

_____, ed. *In Search of a Monetary Constitution.* Cambridge, Mass.: Harvard University Press, 1962.

INDEX

ABOUT THE EDITOR

Barry N. Siegel, Professor of Economics at the University of Oregon, received his Ph.D. in economics from the University of California, Berkeley. He has been Assistant Professor of Economics at the University of Utah (1957–1961); Associate Professor at the University of Oregon (1961–1966); Smith-Mundt Visiting Lecturer of Economics, University of Nuevo Leon in Monterrey, Mexico (1960); Fulbright Lecturer in Monetary Theory, Yugoslavian Institute of Economic Research in Belgrade (1967–1968); and Von Mises Visiting Professor, Hillsdale College (Fall 1981).

Dr. Siegel's academic interests span the fields of macroeconomics, monetary theory and policy, public finance, and the economics of education. He is the author of *Aggregate Economics and Public Policy; Inflation and Economic Development: The Mexican Experience; Money, Banking, and the Economy: A Monetarist View*; and *Thoughts on the Tax Revolt*, and a contributor to *Cooperation Financiera en America Latina, The Federal Reserve Portfolio, Latin American Economic Integration*, and *Public Finance and Welfare*. His articles have appeared in such publications as *American Economic Review, Challenge, El Trimestro Economico, Lectures in Public Finance, Oregon Business Review*, and the *Western Economic Journal*.

ABOUT THE AUTHORS

Michael David Bordo, a native of Canada, received his B.A. from McGill University in Montreal, his M.Sc. from the London School of Economics, and his Ph.D. from the University of Chicago. Currently Professor of Economics at the University of South Carolina, he has been Assistant Professor (1969–76) and Associate Professor (1976–81) at Carleton University in Ottawa; consultant to the Bank of Canada (1971); Visiting Associate Professor, Lund University in Sweden (Summer 1977); Visiting Associate Professor, University of California, Los Angeles (1980); consultant to the Executive Director of the Congressional Gold Commission (1981); and Visiting Scholar, Federal Reserve Bank of St. Louis (1981).

Dr. Bordo's publications include co-editorship of *A Retrospective on the Classical Gold Standard, 1821–1931*, contributions to the books *The Choice of an Exchange Rate System; The Long-Run Behavior of Velocity, 1870–1975; Recent Developments in the Study of Business and Economic History*; and *Theories of Economic Institutions*; and articles in the *Canadian Journal of Economics; Economic Inquiry; Explorations in Economic History; Federal Reserve Bank of St. Louis Review; History of Political Economy; Journal of Economic History; Journal of Economic Literature; Journal of Monetary Economics; Journal of Money, Credit, and Banking; Journal of Political Economy; Research in Economic History; Scandinavian Journal of Economics*; and other journals.

Stephen J. DeCanio, Professor of Economics at the University of California, Santa Barbara, received his B. A. in mathematics from the University of California, Berkeley, and his Ph. D. in economics from Massachusetts Institute of Technology. He taught economics at Simmons College (1969), was a Teaching Assistant at MIT (1969-70), and has been Assistant Professor at Tufts University (1970-72) and Assistant Professor (1972-76) and Associate Professor (1976-78) at Yale University.

Dr. DeCanio's academic interests span the fields of economic history, the application of price theory to industrial organization and antitrust, econometrics and statistics, agricultural history, and the economics of racial discrimination. The author of *Agriculture in the Postbellum South: The Economics of Production and Supply*, he has written many articles and reviews that have appeared in such scholarly journals as *Economic History Review; Explorations in Economic History; Journal of Economic History; Journal of Political Economy; National Tax Journal; Quarterly Journal of Economics; Review of Economics and Statistics;* and *Reviews in American History*.

Robert E. Hall, co-author of *Low Tax, Simple Tax, Flat Tax*, is Professor of Economics at Stanford University and Senior Research Fellow at Hoover Institution. He received his B. A. in economics from the University of California at Berkeley and his Ph. D. from Massachusetts Institute of Technology. A Phi Beta Kappa (1963) and the recipient of a Woodrow Wilson fellowship, a National Science Foundation fellowship, and several Ford Foundation fellowships, Dr. Hall has been Assistant Professor at the University of California, Berkeley (1967-70); Associate Editor, *Journal of the American Statistical Association* (1968-70); Associate Professor, MIT (1970-74); Associate Editor, *Econometrica* (1970-77); Professor, MIT (1974-78); Fellow, Center for Advanced Study in the Behavioral Sciences, Stanford University (1977-78), Professor, Stanford University (1978-present), and Senior Fellow, Hoover Institution, Stanford University (1978-present).

Dr. Hall contributed to the volumes *The Effect of Tax Incentives on Investment, Income Maintenance and Labor Supply; The Phillips Curve and Labor Markets; Price Indexes and Quality Change*; and *Work Incentives and Income Guarantees*, and his articles have been widely published in such journals as *American Economic Review; Annals of Economic and Social Measurement; Brookings Papers on*

Economic Activity; Economica; Journal of Political Economy; and *Review of Economic Studies.*

Friedrich A. Hayek, the 1974 Nobel Laureate in Economic Science, is Professor Emeritus of Economics at the University of Freiburg and Professor Emeritus of the Committee on Social Thought at the University of Chicago. Educated at the University of Vienna, he has been Director of the Austrian Institute for Economic Research (1927–31); Lecturer in Economics, University of Vienna (1929–31); Tooke Professor of Economic Science and Statistics at the University of London (1931–50); Professor of Social and Moral Science, University of Chicago (1950–62); and Professor of Economics, University of Freiburg (1962–1968).

Widely regarded as one of the foremost economists and social theorists of modern times, Professor Hayek has authored or edited over 20 volumes and written more than 140 scholarly articles for journals around the world. His books include *Choice in Currency; The Constitution of Liberty; The Counterrevolution of Science; The Denationalisation of Money; Individualism and Economic Order; John Stuart Mill and Harriet Taylor; Law, Legislation and Liberty; Monetary Nationalism and International Stability; Monetary Theory and the Trade Cycle; New Studies in Philosophy, Politics, Economics and the History of Ideas; The Political Ideal of the Rule of Law; Prices and Production; Profits, Interest, and Investment; The Pure Theory of Capital; The Road to Serfdom; The Sensory Order; A Tiger by the Tail*; and others.

Jonathan R. T. Hughes received his B.S. in economics from Utah State University and his D. Phil. in social studies from Oxford University. He has been a Visiting Fellow at Nuffield College (1962–63) and All Souls College (1971–72). Currently Professor of Economics at Northwestern University, he has been Research Economist, Federal Reserve Bank of New York (1955–56); Assistant Professor, Purdue University (1956–57); Visiting Assistant Professor, Columbia University (1957–58); Associate Professor, Purdue University (1961–66); Member, Council of Research in Economic History (1968–present); President, Economic History Association (1980–81); and Ford Foundation Visiting Research Professor and Visiting Professor of Economics, University of California at Berkeley (1981).

Dr. Hughes's books include *American Economic History* (with L. E. Davis and D. McDougall); *Fluctuations in Trade, Industry, and Finance; The Governmental Habit; Industrialization and Economic History; Social Control in the Colonial Economy; The Vital Few*; and a recent text, *American Economic History*; and his articles have been published in numerous scholarly journals.

Axel Leijonhufvud, who completed his undergraduate studies at the University of Lund, received his M.A. in economics from the University of Pittsburgh and his Ph.D. in economics from Northwestern University. Currently Professor of Economics at the University of California, Los Angeles, he has been a Visiting Professor at the Stockholm School of Economics and Commerce (1969); at the Institute for Advanced Studies in Vienna, Austria (June 1976); at the Institute for Advanced Studies in Jerusalem, Israel (1978); at Nihon University in Tokyo, Japan (January 1980); at the Université Louis Pasteur in Strasbourg, France (1980); and at the University of Konstanz, West Germany (June–July, 1982, 1983, and 1984). He was an Overseas Fellow of Churchill College and Marshall Lecturer of Cambridge University (1974) and Member, Institute for Advanced Study, Princeton (1983–84). In addition, he has lectured at over a hundred universities and institutes in the United States and a number of foreign countries.

Dr. Leijonhufvud is the author of *On Keynesian Economics and the Economics of Keynes* (1968); *Keynes and the Classics* (1969); and *Information and Coordination: Essays in Macroeconomics* (1981). His articles and reviews have appeared in numerous journals and conference proceedings.

Alan Reynolds, Vice President and Chief Economist of Polyconomics, Inc., was Vice President and Economist with the First National Bank of Chicago and Editor of the bank's *First Chicago World Report* (1976–81). Previously he was Senior Economist at Argus Research in New York and Economics Editor for *National Review*. He remains on the editorial staff of *National Review* as well as those of *Reason* and *American Spectator*.

A graduate of the University of California, Los Angeles, Mr. Reynolds has served as an advisor to numerous groups, among them the Lehrman Institute, U.S. Chamber of Commerce, the U.S. Industrial Council, the American Productivity Center, and the Manhattan Institute. Over the past decade his work on economic issues has appeared in a variety of journals and popular publications, including *Cato Journal, Fortune, Harvard Business Review, Policy Review*, and *Wall Street Journal*. Mr. Reynolds has also contributed to several recent anthologies: *Champions of Freedom, Democratic Capitalism, Energy Coverage—Media Panic, Instead of Regulation*, and *Supply-Side Economics in the 1980s*.

Murray N. Rothbard, Professor of Economics at Polytechnic Institute of New York, received his Ph.D. in economics from Columbia University. He has been Instructor at City College of New York (1948–49); Senior Analyst for the William Volker Fund (1961–62); Associate of the University Seminar in the History of Legal and Political Thought at Columbia University (1964–present); and a consultant to the U.S. Commission on Gold. He is S.J. Hall Distinguished Visiting Professor of Economics, University of Nevada, Las Vegas (1984–85).

Editor of the *Journal of Libertarian Studies* and the *Journal of Austrian Economics*, Dr. Rothbard has contributed to more than twenty-five volumes and has written more than fifty articles and reviews for scholarly journals. He is the author or editor of *America's Great Depression; Capital, Interest and Rent; The Case for a 100% Gold Dollar; Conceived in Liberty; Education: Free and Compulsory; Egalitarianism as a Revolt Against Nature and Other Essays; The Ethics of Liberty; For a New Liberty; Foundations of Modern Austrian Economics; Herbert Hoover and the Crisis of American Capitalism; Man, Economy, and State; The Mystery of Banking; A New History of Leviathan* (with R. Radosh); *The Panic of 1819; Power and Market; Toward a Reconstruction of Utility and Welfare Economics; What Has Government Done to Our Money?*, and many other books. His numerous articles have been published in both scholarly and popular publications.

Richard H. Timberlake received his B.A. from Kenyon College in Ohio, his M.A. from Columbia University, and his Ph.D. from the University of Chicago. He is currently Professor of Banking and Finance at the University of Georgia. His research interests include the history of central banking and an evaluation of the scope of private enterprise money in the United States.

Dr. Timberlake has taught economics at Muhlenberg College (1948–51), Norwich University (1953–55), Rensselaer Polytechnic Institute (1955–58), Florida State University (1958–63), and the

University of Georgia (1964–present), and has served as Research Consultant to the Federal Reserve Bank of Richmond (1970–71). He is the author of *Money, Banking and Central Banking; Origins of Central Banking in the United States*; and *Money and Banking* (with E. Selby), plus articles and reviews in *American Economic Review; Banker's Magazine; Banking; International Review of Banking History; Journal of Economic History; Journal of Finance; Journal of Monetary Economics; Journal of Money, Credit, and Banking; Journal of Political Economy; Kredit and Kapital; National Review; Quarterly Review of Economics and Business; Southern Economic Journal; Western Economic Journal*; and other journals.

Charles E. Wainhouse, Senior Economist at Citibank in New York, is Adjunct Assistant Professor of Economics at New York University. He received his B.A. in economics from Long Island University, his M.Sc. from the London School of Economics and Political Science, and his Ph.D. from New York University.

Dr. Wainhouse is the author of *Hayek's Theory of the Trade Cycle.* He has pioneered in the application of engineering modeling techniques (state space) to economic time series, and has used these techniques to develop interest rate and exchange rate forecasts. He has participated in the development and design of a macroeconomic model used to forecast GNP, NIA series, and economic indicators.

Robert E. Weintraub was serving as Senior Economist, U.S. Congress Joint Economic Committee, at the time of his death on September 12, 1983. He received his B.A. in economics from Williams College and his M.A. and Ph.D. in economics from the University of Chicago. Previously he was Research Economist, National Bureau of Economic Research (1954–55); Research Economist, Brookings Institution (1955–56); Assistant Professor, Northwestern University (1955–56); Associate Professor, City College of New York (1956–65); Professor, University of California, Santa Barbara (1965–73); Senior Economist, Subcommittee on Domestic Finance, Committee on Banking and Currency, U.S. House of Representatives (1963–65, 1968, 1972, 1973–74); Senior Economist, Committee on Banking, U.S. Senate (1975); and Director, Office of Capital Markets Policy, U.S. Treasury (1976).

In addition to his book *Monetary Economics* and his contributions to *Crisis in Economic Theory; The Political Economy of Policymak-*

ing; Readings in Economics; and *Targets and Indicators of Monetary Policy*; Dr. Weintraub authored a number of monographs, including *Deficits; The Federal Reserve System After Fifty Years; The Impact of the Federal Reserve System's Monetary Policies on the Nation's Economy*; and *A Study of Selected Banking Services by Bank Size, Structure, and Location.*

Lawrence H. White received his A. B. from Harvard University and his M. A. and Ph. D. from the University of California, Los Angeles. He is currently Assistant Professor of Economics, New York University. Awarded several foundation and institutional fellowships, he has focused his research interests on monetary theory, monetary history, and the history of economic thought.

Dr. White is the author of *Free Banking in Britain* and a contributor to *Currency Competition and European Monetary Union* and *Method, Process, and Austrian Economics*. His work on competitive monetary institutions includes articles in *American Economic Review* and other journals.

J. Stuart Wood received his Ph. D. in finance and economics from New York University and is currently Associate Professor of Finance and Economics at Loyola University School of Business. His research interests focus on the subjects of business cycle theory; economic analysis and forecasting; energy economics; financial theory in capital markets, security returns, security market processes, security analysis, and portfolio analysis; monetary theory; and theory of entrepreneurship.

Dr. Wood is the author of *Entrepreneurship and the Coordination of Expectations in the Stock Market.* He has taught at Tulane University, the University of Connecticut and Pace University, and he has been an Alpha Kappa Psi Fellow and Senior Investment Analyst Consultant to the Common Stock Department of Prudential Insurance Company. In addition to an MBA from New York University, he holds an M. S. in Aerospace Engineering from Princeton University.